Yanmar

YANMAR MARINE DIESEL ENGINES 3JH3(B)(C)E(A), 4JH3(B)(C)E, 4JH3CE1

Service Manual

Yanmar

YANMAR MARINE DIESEL ENGINES 3JH3(B)(C)E(A), 4JH3(B)(C)E, 4JH3CE1

Service Manual

ISBN/EAN: 9783954273430
Erscheinungsjahr: 2013
Erscheinungsort: Bremen, Deutschland

© maritimepress in Europäischer Hochschulverlag GmbH & Co. KG, Fahrenheitstr. 1, 28359 Bremen. Alle Rechte beim Verlag und bei den jeweiligen Lizenzgebern.

www.maritimepress.de | office@maritimepress.de

Bei diesem Titel handelt es sich um den Nachdruck eines historischen, lange vergriffenen Buches. Da elektronische Druckvorlagen für diese Titel nicht existieren, musste auf alte Vorlagen zurückgegriffen werden. Hieraus zwangsläufig resultierende Qualitätsverluste bitten wir zu entschuldigen.

MARINE DIESEL ENGINE

MODEL

3JH3(B)(C)E(A), 4JH3(B)(C)E
4JH3CE1

FOREWORD

This service manual has been complied for engineers engaged in sales, service, inspection and maintenance. Accordingly, descriptions of the construction and functions of the engine are emphasized in this manual while items which should already be common knowledge are omitted.

One characteristic of a marine diesel engine is that its performance in a vessel is governed by the applicability of the vessel's hull construction and its steering system.

Engine installation, fitting out and propeller selection have a substantial effect on the performance of the engine and the vessel. Moreover, when the engine runs unevenly or when trouble occurs, it is essential to check a wide range of operating conditions — such as installation to the hull and suitability of the ship's piping and propeller — and not just the engine itself. To get maximum performance from this engine, you should completely understand its functions, construction and capabilities, as well as proper use and servicing.

Use this manual as a handy reference in daily inspection and maintenance, and as a text for engineering guidance.

Model 4JH3E has been used for the illustrations in this service manual, but they apply to models 3JH3E, 3JH3BE, 3JH3CE, 4JH3BE, and 4JH3CE as well.

METRIC
ALL DIMENSIONS IN MILLIMETERS
UNLESS OTHERWISE SPECIFIED

The EPA (U.S. Federal) and Air Resources Board (ARB, California) Off-road Compression Ignition engines regulations

The engines for EPA regulations will be used in the States, and the engines for ARB regulations will only be used in the State of California.

1. Engine identification (3JH3E series)

With the regulations on engine emission worldwide, it has become necessary to identify engines in a manner to determine which regulations they comply with, hence

a) Emission control label as shown below which will contain:

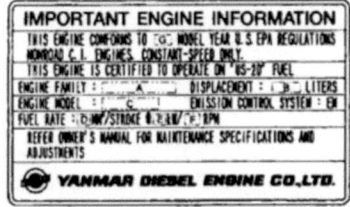
(EPA label)

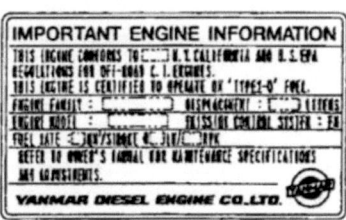
(EPA and ARB label)

*Emission Control is accomplished through Engine Modification (EM-Design)

- EPA certified 3JH3E series engines : E/# A01158 and after.
- ARB(EPA)certified 3JH3E series engines : installed the tamper resistance device to prevent illegal change of fuel injection volume and high idling speed. (Fuel injection volume : cap type, High idling speed : wire and lead seal)

● Engine family name as assigned by EPA/ARB identifying engine family group

YYDXM1.50D3N and this identifies

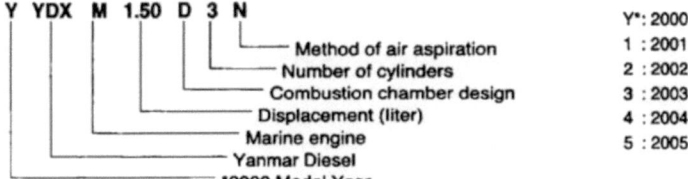

Y*: 2000	
1 : 2001	
2 : 2002	
3 : 2003	
4 : 2004	
5 : 2005	

- Method of air aspiration
- Number of cylinders
- Combustion chamber design
- Displacement (liter)
- Marine engine
- Yanmar Diesel
- *2000 Model Year

b) Label location:

Emission control label (engine top)

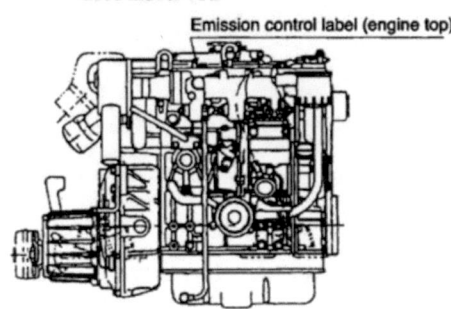

2. Exhaust Gas Regulations

This engine conforms to the EPA exhaust gas regulations (19kW and under 37kW) for a low emission engine.

The ARB standard is the same as the EPA's

Exhaust emission		EPA Standard (Tier 1) (Max.) Variable speed (EPA E3 Mode)	Condition
NOx+NMHC	g/kWh	9.5	· EPA recommended fuel is used.
CO		5.5	
PM		0.8	
Transit smoke ACC/LUG/PEAK	%	—	

(Middle column for NOx+NMHC / CO / PM shows "19kW and under 37kW")

3. Guarantee Conditions for Emission Standard

The following guarantee conditions are set down in the operation manual. In addition to making sure that these conditions are met, check for any deterioration that may occur before the required periodic maintenance times.

● Requirement on engine installation condition

(1) Air intake depression   kPa (mmH₂O)

Permissible
≤ −0.49 (−50)

(2) Exhaust gas back pressure   kPa (mmH₂O)

Permissible
≤7.84 (800)

● Fuel oil and lubricating oil

(1) Fuel : The diesel fuel oil [ISO 8217 DMA, BS 2869 A1 or A2 (Cetane No.45 min.)]
(2) Lube oil : API grade, class CD

● Do not remove the seals restricting injection quantity and engine speed.

● Perform maintenance without fail.
   Note: Inspections to be carried out by the user and by the maker are divided and set down in the "List of Periodic Inspections" on the operation manual and should be checked carefully.

EPA allows to apply Maintenance schedule for Emission related parts as follows.

	Check Fuel Injection Nozzle and clean	Adjust, cleaning and repair of Fuel Injection Pump, Fuel Valve Nozzle and Turbocharger
kW ≤ 130	1500 hours of use and at 1500-hour intervals thereafter	3000 hours of use and at 3000-hour intervals thereafter

● Quality guarantee period for exhaust emission related parts
   For exhaust emission related parts, follow the inspections outlined in the "List of Periodic Inspections", on the operation manual, and use the table below to carry out inspections based on operation hours or time in years. Whichever comes first is the guarantee period.

19 ≤ Range < 37	3000 hours or 5 years

The specific emissions-related parts are   (1) Fuel injection nozzle   (2) Fuel injection pump
                                           (3) Turbocharger.(if installed)

The EPA (U.S. Federal) and Air Resources Board (ARB, California) Off-road Compression Ignition engines regulations

The engines for EPA regulations will be used in the States, and the engines for ARB regulations will only be used in the State of California.

1. Engine identification (3JH3E series)

With the regulations on engine emission worldwide, it has become necessary to identify engines in a manner to determine which regulations they comply with, hence

a) Emission control label as shown below which will contain:

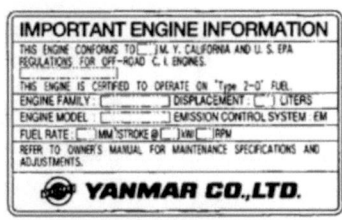

(EPA and ARB label)

*Emission Control is accomplished through Engine Modification (EM-Design)

- ARB(EPA)certified 3JH3E series engines : installed the tamper resistance device to prevent illegal change of fuel injection volume and high idling speed.
  (Fuel injection volume : cap type, High idling speed : wire and lead seal)
- The emission standard is the same as the EPA's

● **Engine family name as assigned by EPA/ARB identifying engine family group**

IYDXM1.50D3N and this identifies

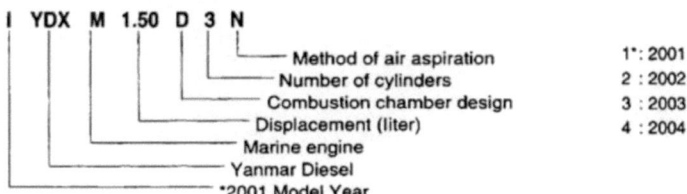

```
I YDX M 1.50 D 3 N
                  └─── Method of air aspiration      1*: 2001
              └─────── Number of cylinders           2 : 2002
          └─────────── Combustion chamber design     3 : 2003
      └─────────────── Displacement (liter)          4 : 2004
    └───────────────── Marine engine
  └─────────────────── Yanmar Diesel
└─────────────────────*2001 Model Year
```

b) Label location:

Emission control label (engine top)

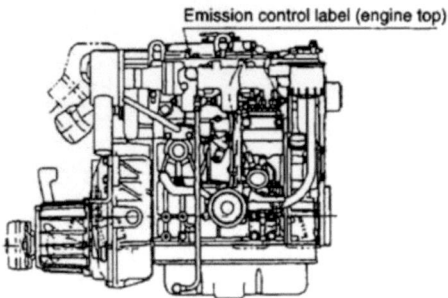

MODELS
3JH3(B)(C)E(A), 4JH3(B)(C)E
4JH3CE1

Chapter 0 FOR SAFETY
1. For Safe Servicing ··0-1
2. Precaution for Safe Servicing ································0-2

Chapter 1 GENERAL
1. Exterior Views ··1-1
2. Specifications ···1-3
3. Engine Outline ···1-6
4. Piping Diagrams ···1-10

Chapter 2 INSPECTION AND SERVICING OF BASIC ENGINE PARTS
1. Cylinder Block ···2-1
2. Cylinder Head ···2-4
3. Piston and Piston Pins ··2-11
4. Connecting Rod ···2-15
5. Crankshaft and Main Bearing ·····························2-18
6. Camshaft and Tappets ·······································2-21
7. Timing Gear ···2-24
8. Flywheel and Housing ··2-26

Chapter 3 FUEL INJECTION EQUIPMENT
1. Fuel injection Pump Service Data ························3-1
2. Governor ···3-4
3. Disassembly, Reassembly and Inspection of Fuel injection pump ···3-14
4. Adjustment of Fuel Injection Pump and Governor 3-24
5. Fuel Feed Pump ··3-30
6. Fuel injection Nozzle ···3-32
7. Troubleshooting ···3-36
8. Tools ··3-38
9. Fuel Filter ··3-40
10. Fuel Tank ···3-41
11. Troubleshooting ···3-42
12. Fuel inspection timing adjustment for EPA/ARB certified engine (3JH3E series) ········3-45

Chapter 4 INTAKE AND EXHAUST SYSTEM
1. Intank System ··4-1
2. Exhaust System ··4-2

Chapter 5 LUBRICATION SYSTEM
1. Lubrication System ···5-1
2. Lube Oil Pump ··5-2
3. Lube Oil Filter ···5-6
4. Lube Oil Cooler ···5-8
5. Rotary Waste Oil Pump (Optional) ·······················5-9

Chapter 6 COOLING WATER SYSTEM
1. Cooling Water System ··6-1
2. Sea Water Pump ···6-3
3. Fresh Water Pump ···6-5
4. Heat Exchanrger ··6-8
5. Pressure Cap and Sub Tank ·······························6-10
6. Thermostat ··6-12
7. Bilge pump and Bilge Strainer (Optional) ···········6-14

Chapter 7 REDUCTION AND REVERSING GEAR
Marine Gear Models [KM3A],[KM35A]
1. Construction ··7-1
2. Shifting Device ··7-7
3. Inspection and Servicing ····································7-12
4. Disassembly ··7-20
5. Reassembly ··7-25

Marine Gear Models [KM3P],[KM35P]
1. Construction ··7-29
2. Shifting Device ··7-35
3. Inspection and Servicing ····································7-40
4. Disassembly ··7-48
5. Reassembly ··7-53

Chapter 8 REMOTE CONTROL (OPTIONAL)
1. Remote Control System ·······································8-1
2. Remote Control Installation ·································8-2
3. Remote Control Inspection ··································8-4
4. Remoto Control Adjustment ·································8-5

Chapter 9 ELECTRICAL SYSTEM
1. Electrical System ··9-1
2. Battery ···9-5
3. Starter Motor ···9-8
4. Alternator   Standard, 12V/55A ·························9-22
5. Alternator   12V/80A (OPTIONAL) ····················9-30
6. Instrument Panel ···9-40
7. Warning Devices ···9-42
8. Air Heater (Optional) ···9-45
9. Electric type Engine Stopping Device (Optional) ······9-46
10. Tachometer ···9-48

Chapter 10 DISASSEMBLY AND REASSEMBLY
1. Disassembly and Reassembly Precautions ········10-1
2. Disassembly and Reassembly Tools ··················10-2
3. Disassembly and Reassembly ··························10-14
4. Table of Standard Measurements for Maintenance 10-35
5. Tightening torque ···10-40
6. Test Running ···10-41

Chapter 11 TROUBLESHOOTING
1. Troubleshooting ··11-1

CHAPTER 0
FOR SAFETY

1. For Safe Servicing ···0-1
2. Precaution for Safe Servicing ·····························0-2

1. For Safe Servicing

- Most accidents are caused by failing to observe basic safety rules and precautions. To prevent accidents, it is important to recognize the signs of approaching problems, and eliminate the problems in the early stage before they can cause accidents.
  Please read this manual carefully before starting repairs or maintenance to fully understand safety precautions and appropriate inspection and maintenance procedures. Attempting a repair or maintenance job without sufficient knowledge may cause an unexpected accident.

- It is impossible to cover every possible danger in repair or maintenance in the manual. Sufficient consideration for safety is required in addition to the matters marked ⚠ CAUTION. Especially for safety precautions in a repair or maintenance job not described in this manual, receive instructions from a knowledgeable leader.

- Safety marks used in this manual and their meanings are as follows:

DANGER indicates an imminently hazardous situation which, if not avoided, will result in death or serious injury.

WARNING indicates a potentially hazardous situation which, if not avoided, could result in death or serious injury.

CAUTION indicates a potentially hazardous situation which, if not avoided, may result in minor or moderate injury.

- Any matter marked [NOTICE] in this manual is especially important in servicing. If not observed, the product performance and quality may not be guaranteed.

2. Precaution for Safe Servicing

(A) Service Shop (place)

⚠ WARNING • **Place allowing sufficient ventilation**

Jobs such as engine running, part welding and polishing the paint with sandpaper should be done in a well-ventilated place.
[Failure to Observe]
Very dangerous for human body due to the possibility of inhaling poisonous gas or dust.

⚠ CAUTION • **Sufficiently wide and flat place**

The floor space of the service shop for inspection and maintenance should be sufficiently wide and flat without any holes.
[Failure to Observe]
An accident such as a violent fall may be caused.

⚠ CAUTION • **Clean, orderly arranged place**

No dust, mud, oil or parts should be left on the floor surface.
[Failure to Observe]
An unexpected accident may be caused.

⚠ CAUTION • **Bright, safety illuminated place**

The working place should be illuminated sufficiently and safely.
For a job in a dark place where it is difficult to see, use a portable safety lamp.
The bulb should be covered with a wire cage for protection.
[Failure to Observe]
The bulb may be broken accidentally causing ignition of leaking oil.

⚠ CAUTION • **Place equipped with a fire extinguisher**

Keep a first aid kit and fire extinguisher close at hand in preparation for fire emergencies.

(B) Working Wear

⚠ CAUTION ● **Wears for safe operation**

Wear a helmet, working clothes, safety shoes and other safety protectors suited to the job. It is especially important to wear well-fitting work clothes.
[Failure to Observe]
A serious accident such as trapping by a machine may occur.

(C) Tools to be Used

⚠ WARNING ● **Appropriate holding and lifting**

Never operate when the engine is supported with blocks or wooden pieces or only with a jack.
To lift and hold the engine, always use a crane with a sufficient allowance in limit load or a rigid jack.
[Failure to Observe]
A serious accident may occur.

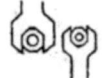

⚠ WARNING ● **Use of appropriate tools**

Use tools appropriate for the jobs to be done. Use a correctly sized tool for loosening or tightening a machine part.
[Failure to Observe]
A serious injury or engine damage may occur.

(D) Use of Genuine Parts, Oil and Grease

⚠ CAUTION ● **Always use genuine parts.**

[Failure to Observe]
Shortening of engine libe or an unex pected accicdent may arise.

(E) Bolt and Nut Tightening Torque

⚠ WARNING ● **Always tighten to the specified torque if designated in the manual.**

[Failure to Observe]
Loosening or falling may cause parts damage or injury.

(F) Electrical Parts

⚠ WARNING ● **Harness short-circuit**

Disconnect the battery negative ⊖ terminal before starting the service job.
[Failure to Observe]
Short-circuiting of a harness may occur to start a fire.

⚠ WARNING ● **Battery charging**

Since flammable gas is generated during battery charging, keep anything which could cause a fire away from the battery.
[Failure to Observe]
Explosions may occur.

⚠ WARNING ● **Battery electrolyte**

Since the electrolyte is diluted sulfuric acid, do not let it be splashed onto the clothes or skin.
[Failure to Observe]
The clothes or skin may be burnt.

(G) Waste Treatment

⚠ CAUTION Observe the following instructions with regard to waste disposal. Negligence of each instruction will cause environmental pollution.

- Waste fluids such as engine oil and cooling water shall be discharged into a container without spillage onto the ground.
- Do not let waste fluids be discharged into the sewerage, a river or the sea.
- Harmful wastes such as oil, fuel, solvents, filter elements and battery shall be treated according to the respective laws and regulations. Ask a qualified collecting company for example.

(H) Handling the Product

● **Supplying the Fuel**
When supplying the fuel, always keep any fire source like a cigarette or match away.

[Failure to Observe]
A fire or explosion may arise.

● **Pay attention to hot portions.**
Do not touch the engine during running or immediately after it is stopped.

[Failure to Observe]
Scalding may be caused by a high temperature.

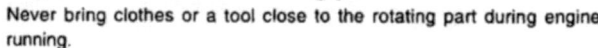

● **Pay attention to the rotating part.**
Never bring clothes or a tool close to the rotating part during engine running.

[Failure to Observe]
Injury may be caused by entrapping.

● **Safety Label Check**
Pay attention to the product safety label.
A safety label (caution plate) is affixed on the product for calling special attention to safety.
If it is missing or illegible, always affix a new one.

California Proposition 65 Warning

Diesel engine exhaust and some of its constitutions are known to the State of California to cause cancer, birth defects, and other reproductive harm.

California Proposition 65 Warning

Battery posts, terminals, and related accessories contain lead and lead compounds, chemicals known to the State of California to cause cancer and reproductive harm.

CHAPTER 1

GENERAL

1. Exterior Views ··1-1
   - 1-1 3JH3E ··1-1
   - 1-2 4JH3E ··1-2
2. Specifications ··1-3
   - 2-1 3JH3E, 3JH3BE, 3JH3CE ··························1-3
   - 2-2 4JH3E, 4JH3BE, 4JH3CE ··························1-4
   - 2-3 3JH3E A, 3JH3BE A, 3JH3CE A ···············1-4- i
   - 2-4 4JH3E(KM35P), 4JH3BE(KM35A), 4JH3CE1 ······1-4- ii
   - 2-5 Sales condition, Marine gear ····················1-5
3. Engine Outline ··1-6
   - 3-1 3JH3E (with KM3P Marine gear) ···············1-6
   - 3-2 3JH3BE (with KM3A Marine gear) ············1-7
   - 3-3 4JH3E (with KM3P Marine gear) ···············1-8
   - 3-4 4JH3BE(with KM3A Marine gear) ·············1-9
   - 3-5 3JH3E A (with KM35P Marine gear) ········1-9- i
   - 3-6 3JH3BE A (with KM35A Marine gear) ·····1-9- ii
   - 3-7 4JH3E (with KM35P Marine gear) ··········1-9-iii
   - 3-8 4JH3BE(with KM35A Marine gear) ········1-9-iv
4. Piping diagrams ··1-10
   - 4-1 3,4JH3(B)(C)E ··································1-10

Chapter 1 General
1. Exterior Views

1. Exterior Views

1-1 3JH3E

● Operation Side

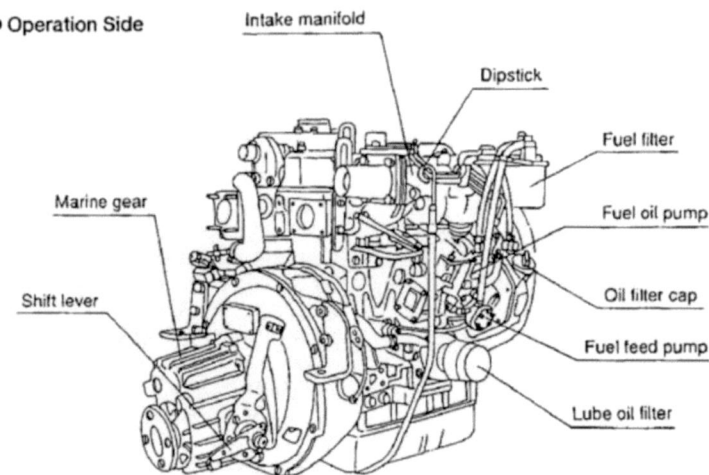

● Non Operation Side

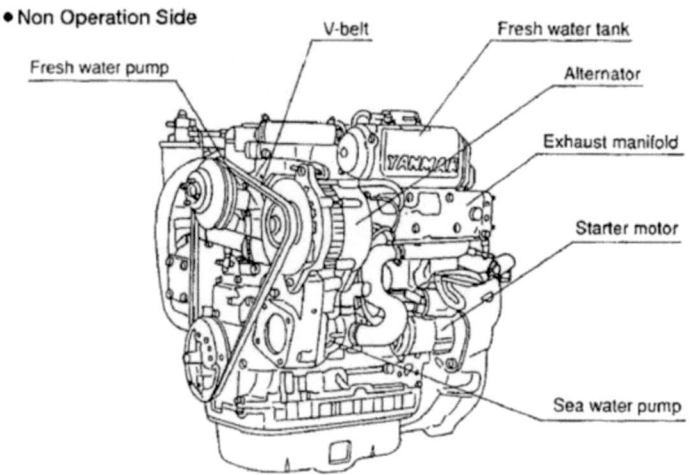

〈Note〉 This illustration shows Yanmar marine gear (Model : KM3P) when it has been attached.

1-2 4JH3E

- Operation Side

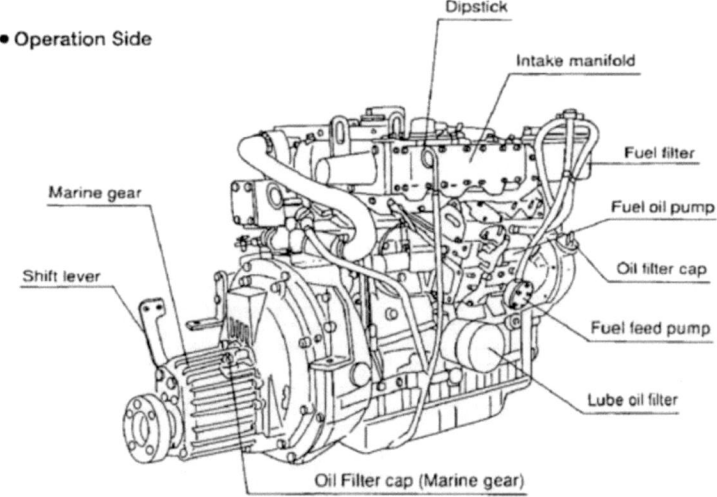

- Non Operation Side

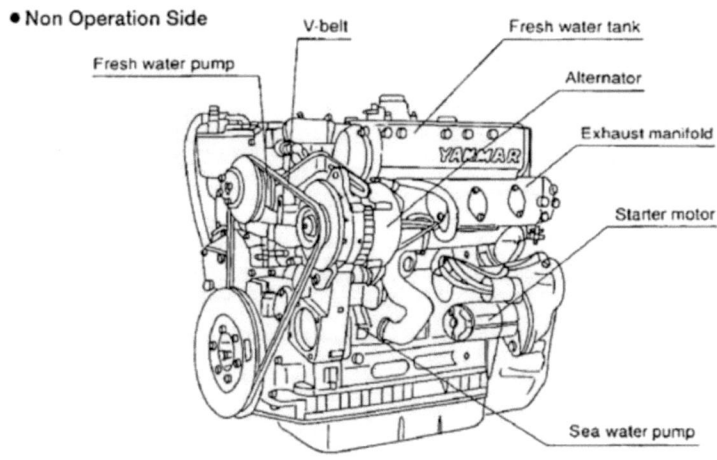

⟨Note⟩ This illustration shows Yanmar marine gear (Model : KM3P) when it has been attached.

Chapter 1 General
2. Specifications
3,4JH3(B)(C)E

2. Specifications

2-1 3JH3E, 3JH3BE, 3JH3CE

Model				3JH3E	3JH3BE	3JH3CE
Type				\multicolumn{3}{l|}{Vertical 4-cycle water cooled diesel engine}		
Combustion system				\multicolumn{3}{l|}{Direct injection}		
Aspiration				\multicolumn{3}{l|}{Normal aspiration}		
Number of cylinders				\multicolumn{3}{l|}{3}		
Bore × stroke			mm	\multicolumn{3}{l|}{84 × 90}		
Displacement			ℓ	\multicolumn{3}{l|}{1,496}		
One hour rating output (flywheel output)	Output/crankshaft speed		kW/rpm (HP/rpm)	\multicolumn{3}{l|}{26.5/3650 (36/3650)}		
	Brake mean effective pressure		kgf/cm²	\multicolumn{3}{l|}{5.93}		
	Piston speed		m/sec.	\multicolumn{3}{l|}{10.95}		
Continuous rating output (DIN6270A) flywheel output	Output/crankshaft speed		kW/rpm (HP/rpm)	\multicolumn{3}{l|}{29.4/3800 (40/3800)}		
	Brake mean effective pressure		kgf/cm²	\multicolumn{3}{l|}{0.621 (6.33)}		
	Piston speed		m/sec.	\multicolumn{3}{l|}{11.4}		
Compression ratio				\multicolumn{3}{l|}{17.7}		
Fire order				\multicolumn{3}{l|}{240° 240° 240° 1 — 3 — 2 — 1}		
Fuel injection pump				\multicolumn{3}{l|}{YPES-CL (with Timer)}		
Fuel injection timing (b.T.D.C.)			degree	\multicolumn{3}{l|}{FID 12° [For EPA certified FIC :15±1, (FID:14±1)]}		
Fuel injection pressure			kgf/cm²	\multicolumn{3}{l|}{200±5}		
Fuel injection nozzle				\multicolumn{3}{l|}{Hole type}		
Direction of rotation	(Crankshaft)			\multicolumn{3}{l|}{Counter-clock wise viewed from stern}		
Power take off				\multicolumn{3}{l|}{At Flywheel side}		
Cooling system				\multicolumn{3}{l|}{Constant high temperature fresh water cooling Fresh water : Centrifugal pump Sea water :Rubber impeller pump}		
Lubrication system				\multicolumn{3}{l|}{Forced lubrication with trochoid pump}		
Starting system	Starting motor			\multicolumn{3}{l|}{DC 12V,1.2kW}		
	AC generato			\multicolumn{3}{l|}{12V,55A (12V80A : Option)}		
Marine Gear	Model			KM3P	KM3A	(Sail Drive SD-31 can be used directly on location.)
	Type			Mechanical cone clutch	Mechanical cone clutch (torque limiter no angle)	
	Reduction rate (ahead/astern)		i/i	2.36/3.16 2.61/3.16 3.20/3.16	2.33/3.04 2.64/3.04	—
	Propeller speed (ahead/astern)		rpm	1610/1203 1457/1203 1188/1203	1629/1249 1441/1249	—
	Standard propeller (Dia. ×pitch×number)		mm		—	
	Propeller shaft dia. × Countershaft dia.		mm		—	
	Lubrication system			\multicolumn{2}{l	}{Splash}	
	Lube oil pan	Total capacity	ℓ	0.35	0.45	—
		Effective capacity	ℓ	0.05	0.05	—
	Cooling system			—	—	—
	Weight		[kg]	[13]	[13]	—
Dimensions	Overall length		mm	755.6	752.8	545.8
	Overall width		mm	\multicolumn{2}{l	}{520.6}	520.6
	Overall height		mm	\multicolumn{2}{l	}{628.6}	628.6
Engine weight without marine gear (dry)			kg	\multicolumn{2}{l	}{186}	173
Lubricating oil capacity Effect/max.			ℓ	4.4/1.8	4.9/2.1	4.9/2.1

(Note) Rating condition : ISO — 3046/1, 1HP ≒ 0.7355 kW

Printed in Japan
HINSHI-H8009

Chapter 1 General
2. Specifications

3,4JH3(B)(C)E

2-2 4JH3E, 4JH3BE, 4JH3CE

Engine Model				4JH3E	4JH3BE	4JH3CE
Type				\multicolumn{3}{c}{Vertical 4-cycle water cooled diesel engine}		
Combustion system				\multicolumn{3}{c}{Direct injection}		
Aspiration				\multicolumn{3}{c}{Normal aspiration}		
Number of cylinders				\multicolumn{3}{c}{4}		
Bore × stroke			mm	\multicolumn{3}{c}{84 × 90}		
Displacement			ℓ	\multicolumn{3}{c}{1.995}		
One hour rating output (flywheel output)	Output/crankshaft speed		kW/rpm (HP/rpm)	36.8/3650 (50/3650)		34.6/3650 (47/3650)
	Brake mean effective pressure		kgf/cm²	6.18		5.81
	Piston speed		m/sec.	\multicolumn{3}{c}{10.95}		
Continuous rating output (DIN6270A) flywheel output	Output/crankshaft speed		kW/rpm (HP/rpm)	41.2/3800 (56/3800)		38.2/3800 (52/3800)
	Brake mean effective pressure		kgf/cm²	\multicolumn{3}{c}{6.65}		
	Piston speed		m/sec.	\multicolumn{3}{c}{11.4}		
Compression ratio				\multicolumn{3}{c}{17.7}		
Fire order				\multicolumn{3}{c}{1 —180°— 3 —180°— 4 —180°— 2 —180°— 1}		
Fuel injection pump				\multicolumn{3}{c}{In-line type YPES-CL (with Timer)}		
Fuel injection timing (b.T.D.C.)			degree	\multicolumn{3}{c}{(b.T.D.C.) 12°}		
Fuel injection pressure			kg/cm²	\multicolumn{3}{c}{220±5}		
Fuel injection nozzle				\multicolumn{3}{c}{Hole type}		
Direction of rotation	(Crankshaft)			\multicolumn{3}{c}{Counter-clock wise viewed from stern}		
Power take off				\multicolumn{3}{c}{At Flywheel side}		
Cooling system				\multicolumn{3}{c}{Constant high temperature fresh water cooling / Fresh water : Centrifugal pump / Sea water : Rubber impeller pump}		
Lubrication system				\multicolumn{3}{c}{Forced lubrication with trochoid pump}		
Starting system	Starting motor			\multicolumn{3}{c}{DC 12V,1.2kW}		
	AC generato			\multicolumn{3}{c}{12V,55A (12V, 80A : option)}		
Marine Gear	Model			KM3P	KM3A	(Sail Drive SD-31 can be used directly on location.)
	Type			Mechanical cone clutch	Mechanical cone clutch (torque limiter no cradle)	
	Reduction rate (ahead/astern)		i/i	2.36/3.16 2.61/3.16	2.33/3.04 2.64/3.04	—
	Propeller speed (ahead/astern)		rpm	1610/1203 1457/1203	1629/1249 1441/1229	—
	Standard propeller (Dia. × pitch × number)		mm		—	
	Propeller shaft dia. × Countershaft dia.		mm		—	
	Lubrication system			\multicolumn{3}{c}{Splash}		
	Lube oil pan	Total capacity	ℓ	0.35	0.45	—
		Effective capacity	ℓ	0.05	0.05	—
	Cooling system			—	—	—
	Weight		[kg]	[13]	[13]	—
Dimensions	Overall length		mm	\multicolumn{2}{c}{849.6}	639.8
	Overall width		mm	\multicolumn{2}{c}{563.1}	563.6
	Overall height		mm	\multicolumn{2}{c}{623.6}	623.6
Engine weight without marine gear (dry)			kg	\multicolumn{2}{c}{223}	210
Lubricating oil capacity Effect/max.			ℓ	\multicolumn{3}{c}{5.3/1.1 at engine installation angle 0°}		

(Note) Rating condition : ISO — 3046/1, 1HP ≒ 0.7355 kW

1—4

Chapter 1 General
2. Specifications

_3,4JH3(B)(C)E_

2-3 3JH3E A, 3JH3BE A, 3JH3CE A

(Note) Engine name 3JH3E A, ... designated by engine factory.
Shown as 3JH3E, 3JH3CE in the name plate.

Model				3JH3E A	3JH3BE A	3JH3CE A
Type				\multicolumn{3}{c}{Vertical 4-cycle water cooled diesel engine}		
Combustion system				\multicolumn{3}{c}{Direct injection}		
Aspiration				\multicolumn{3}{c}{Natural aspiration}		
Number of cylinders				\multicolumn{3}{c}{3}		
Bore × stroke			mm	\multicolumn{3}{c}{84 × 90}		
Displacement			L	\multicolumn{3}{c}{1.496}		
Continuous output (flywheel output)	Output/crankshaft speed		kW/min⁻¹ (PS/min⁻¹)	\multicolumn{3}{c}{26.5/3650 (36/3650)}		
	Brake mean effective pressure		MPa (kgf/cm²)	\multicolumn{3}{c}{0.581 (5.93)}		
	Piston speed		m/sec.	\multicolumn{3}{c}{10.95}		
Max. output (flywheel output)	Output/crankshaft speed		kW/min⁻¹ (PS/min⁻¹)	*29.4/3800 (40/3800)	\multicolumn{2}{c}{**28.7/3800 (39.1/3800)}	
	Brake mean effective pressure		MPa (kgf/cm²)	\multicolumn{3}{c}{0.621 (6.33) (at 25℃ fuel oil temp)}		
	Piston speed		m/sec.	\multicolumn{3}{c}{11.4}		
Compression ratio				\multicolumn{3}{c}{17.7}		
Fire order				\multicolumn{3}{c}{240° 240° 240° 1 — 3 — 2 — 1}		
Fuel injection pump				\multicolumn{3}{c}{YPES-CL(with timer)}		
Fuel injection timing (b.T.D.C.)			degree	\multicolumn{3}{c}{FID 12 {For EPA certified FIC:15±1,(FID:14±1)}}		
Fuel injection pressure			MPa(kgf/cm²)	\multicolumn{3}{c}{21.6±0.5(220±5)}		
Fuel injection nozzle				\multicolumn{3}{c}{Hole type}		
Direction of rotation	(Crankshaft)			\multicolumn{3}{c}{Counter-clockwise viewed from stern}		
Power take off				\multicolumn{3}{c}{At flywheel side}		
Cooling system				\multicolumn{3}{c}{Constant high temperature fresh water cooling Fresh water : Centrifugal pump Sea water : Rubber impeller pump}		
Lubrication system				\multicolumn{3}{c}{Forced lubrication with trochoid pump}		
Starting system	Starting motor			\multicolumn{3}{c}{DC 12V, 1.2kW}		
	AC generato			\multicolumn{3}{c}{12V,55A (12V, 80A : option)}		
Marine Gear	Model			KM35P	KM35A	
	Type			Mechanical cone clutch	Mechanical cone clutch	{Sail Drive SD-40 can be used directly on location.}
	Reduction rate(ahead/astern)			2.36/3.16 2.61/3.16	2.33/3.04 2.64/3.04	——
	Propeller speed (ahead/astern)		min⁻¹	1610/1203 1457/1203	1629/1249 1441/1249	——
	Lubrication system			\multicolumn{3}{c}{Splash}		
	Lube oil pan	Total capacity	L	0.5	0.65	——
		Effective capacity	L	0.05	0.15	——
	Cooling system			——	——	——
	Mass		kg	12	13	——
Dimensions	Overall length		mm	762.1	760.7	545.8
	Overall width		mm	\multicolumn{2}{c}{520.6}	520.6	
	Overall height		mm	\multicolumn{2}{c}{624.9}	624.9	
Engine mass without marine gear (dry)			kg	185	186	173
Lubricating oil capacity max/effect. (oilpan)			L	4.5/1.1(rake 8°)	5.0/1.2(rake 0°)	5.0/1.2(rake 0°)

(Note) 1.Rating condition : ISO 3046-1,8665 2. IPS=0.7355kW   *: 25℃ at the fuel injection pump inlet.
       3. Fuel oil condition : Density at 15℃=0.860, Fuel oil temp.   **: 40℃ at the fuel injection pump inlet.

Printed in Japan
HINSHI-H8009

Chapter 1 General
2. Specifications

3.4JH3(B)(C)E

2-4 4JH3E(KM35P), 4JH3BE(KM35P), 4JH3CE1

(Note) Engine name 4JH3BE designated by engine factory. Shown as 4JH3E in the name plate.

Engine Model			4JH3E(KM35A)	4JH3BE(KM35A)	4JH3CE1
Type			Vertical 4-cycle water cooled diesel engine		
Combustion system			Direct injection		
Aspiration			Natural aspiration		
Number of cylinders			4		
Bore × stroke		mm	84 × 90		
Displacement		L	1.995		
Continuous output (flywheel output)	Output/crankshaft speed	kW/min^{-1} (PS/min^{-1})	36.8/3650 (50/3650)		
	Brake mean effective pressure	MPa (kgf/cm^2)	0.606 (6.18)		
	Piston speed	m/sec.	10.95		
Max. output (flywheel output)	Output/crankshaft speed	kW/min^{-1} (PS/min^{-1})	*41.2/3800 (56/3800)	**40.3/3800 (54.7/3800)	
	Brake mean effective pressure	MPa (kgf/cm^2)	0.652 (6.65) (at 25℃ fuel oil temp)		
	Piston speed	m/sec.	11.4		
Compression ratio			17.7		
Fire order			180° 180° 180° 180° 1 — 3 — 4 — 2 — 1		
Fuel injection pump			In-line type YPES-CL(with timer)		
Fuel injection timing (b.T.D.C.)		degree	FID 12		
Fuel injection pressure		MPa(kgf/cm^2)	21.6±0.5(220±5)		
Fuel injection nozzle			Hole type		
Direction of rotation	(Crankshaft)		Counter-clockwise viewed from stern		
Power take off			At flywheel side		
Cooling system			Constant high temperature fresh water cooling Fresh water : Centrifugal pump Sea water : Rubber impeller pump		
Lubrication system			Forced lubrication with trochoid pump		
Starting system	Starting motor		DC 12V, 1.2kW		
	AC generato		12V,55A (12V, 80A : option)		
Marine Gear	Model		KM35P	KM35A	Sail Drive SD-40 can be used directly on location.
	Type		Mechanical cone clutch	Mechanical cone clutch	
	Reduction rate(ahead/astern)		2.36/3.16 2.61/3.16	2.33/3.04 2.64/3.04	———
	Propeller speed (ahead/astern)	min^{-1}	1610/1203 1457/1203	1629/1249 1441/1249	———
	Lubrication system		Splash		
	Lube oil pan	Total capacity	L	0.5	0.65	———
		Effective capacity	L	0.05	0.15	———
	Cooling system		———	———	———
	Mass		kg	12	13	———
Dimensions	Overall length	mm	856.1	854.7	639.8
	Overall width	mm	563.1		563.1
	Overall height	mm	619.9		619.9
Engine mass without marine gear (dry)		kg	223		210
Lubricating oil capacity max/effect. (oilpan)		L	4.5/1.2(rake 8°)	5.0/1.4(rake 0°)	

(Note) 1.Rating condition : ISO 3046-1,8665 2. IPS=0.7355kW
3. Fuel oil condition : Density at 15℃=0.860, Fuel oil temp.
*: 25℃ at the fuel injection pump inlet.
**: 40℃ at the fuel injection pump inlet.

Printed in Japan
HINSHI-H8009

Chapter 1 General
2. Specifications

3.4JH3(B)(C)E

2-5 Sales condition, Marine gear

Reduction ratio (Marine gear model)	No. of blades	Outer diameter of propeller	Moment of propeller inertia $N \cdot m^2 (kgf \cdot m^2 = GD^2)$	Propeller materials	Engine application
3.20 (KM3P)	3	≦ 490	≦ 2.25(0.23)	Bronze	3JH3(B)E
	4	≦ 460			
2.61 (KM3P) (KM35P)	3	≦ 470	≦ 1.86(0.19)		3JH3(B)E(A)
2.64 (KM3A) (KM35A)	4	≦ 440			
2.36 (KM3P) (KM35P)	3	≦ 450	≦ 1.47(0.15)		4JH3(B)E
2.33 (KM3A) (KM35A)	4	≦ 425			

3. Engine Outline

3-1 3JH3E (with KM3P Marine gear)

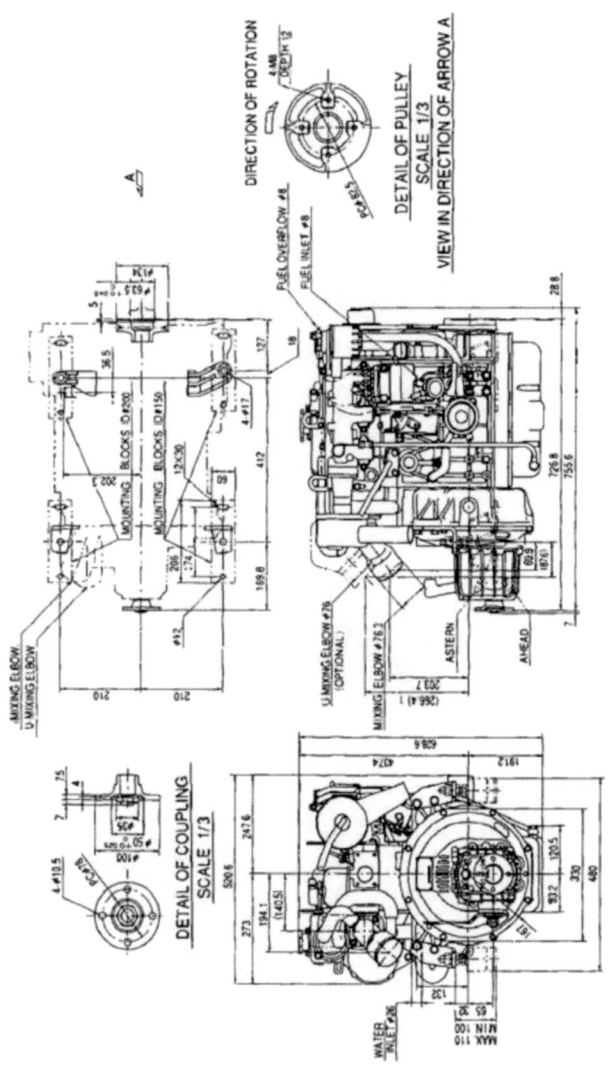

Chapter 1 General
3. Engine Outline _____ 3,4JH3(B)(C)E

3-2 3JH3BE (with KM3A Marine gear)

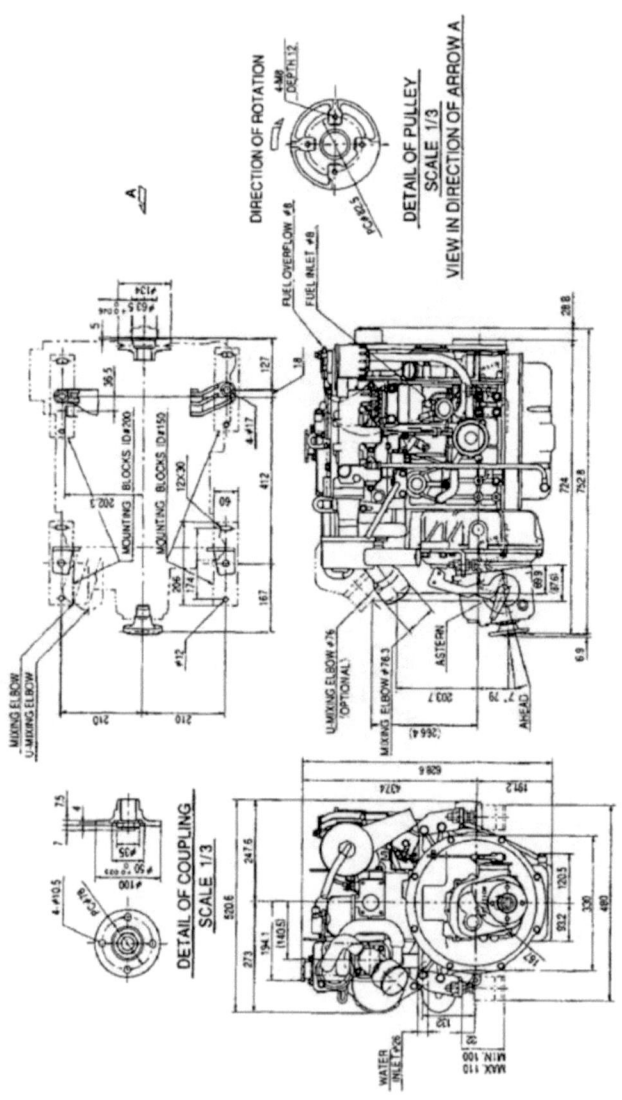

Chapter 1 General
3. Engine Outline

3-3 4JH3E (with KM3P Marine gear)

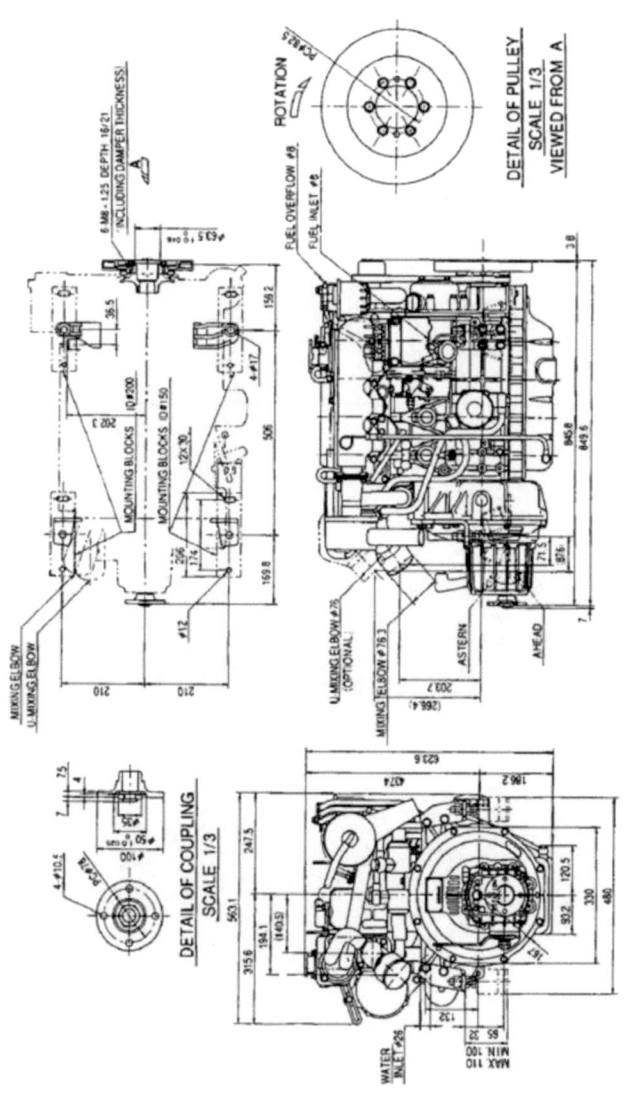

Chapter 1 General
3. Engine Outline

3-4 4JH3BE (with KM3A Marine gear)

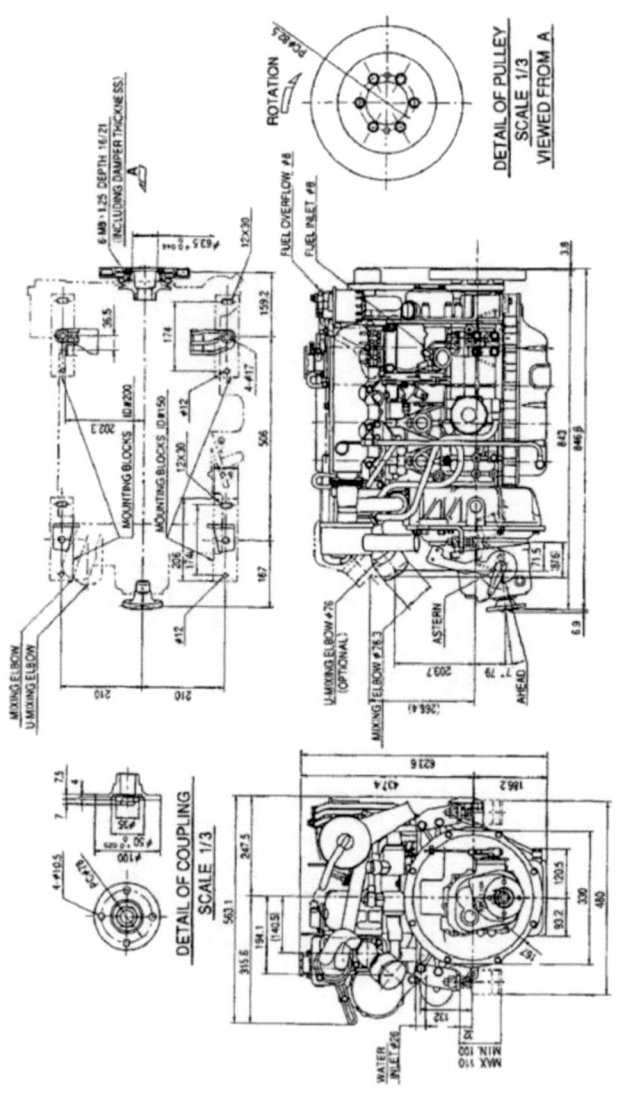

Chapter 1 General
3. Engine Outline

3-5 3JH3E A (with KM35P Marine gear)

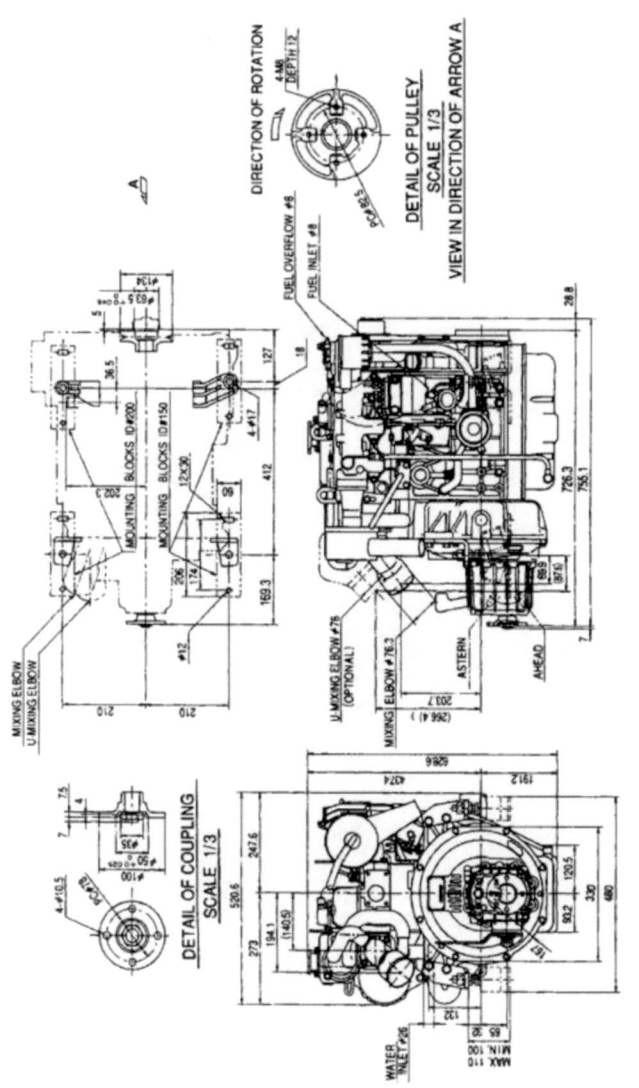

Chapter 1 General
3. Engine Outline

3-6 3JH3BE A (with KM35A Marine gear)

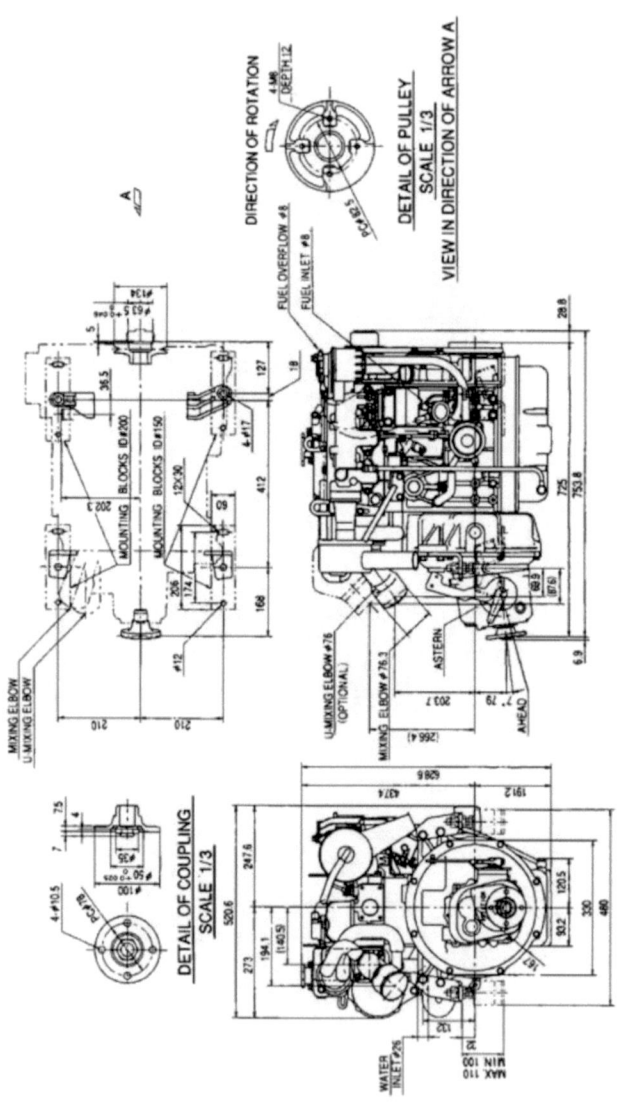

Chapter 1 General
3. Engine Outline

3,4JH3(B)(C)E

3-7 4JH3E (with KM35P Marine gear)

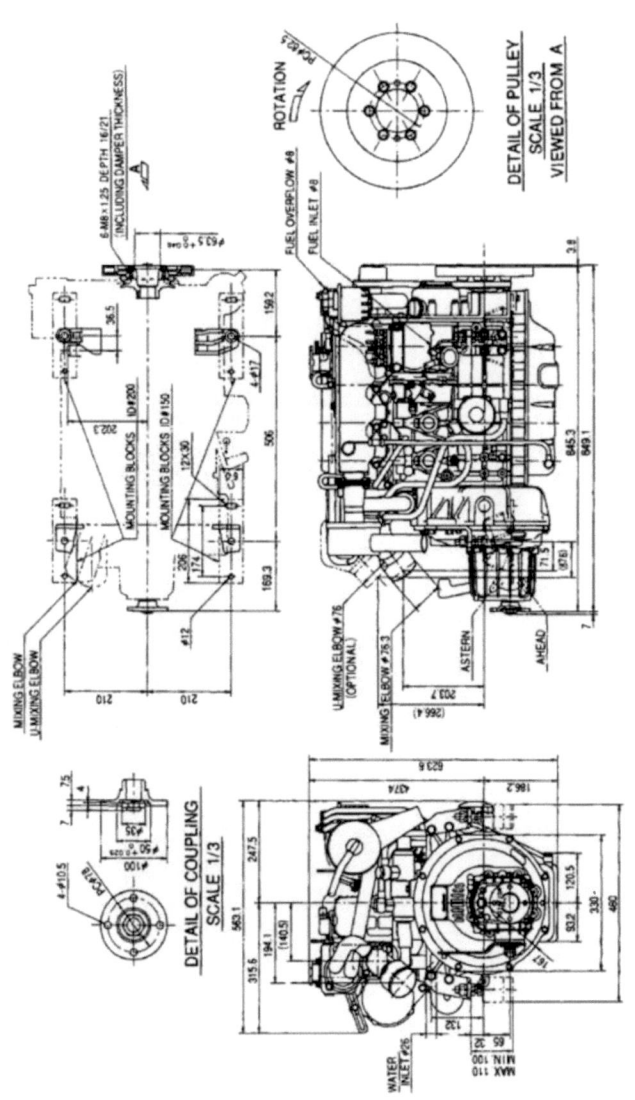

3. Engine Outline

3-8 4JH3BE (with KM35A Marine gear)

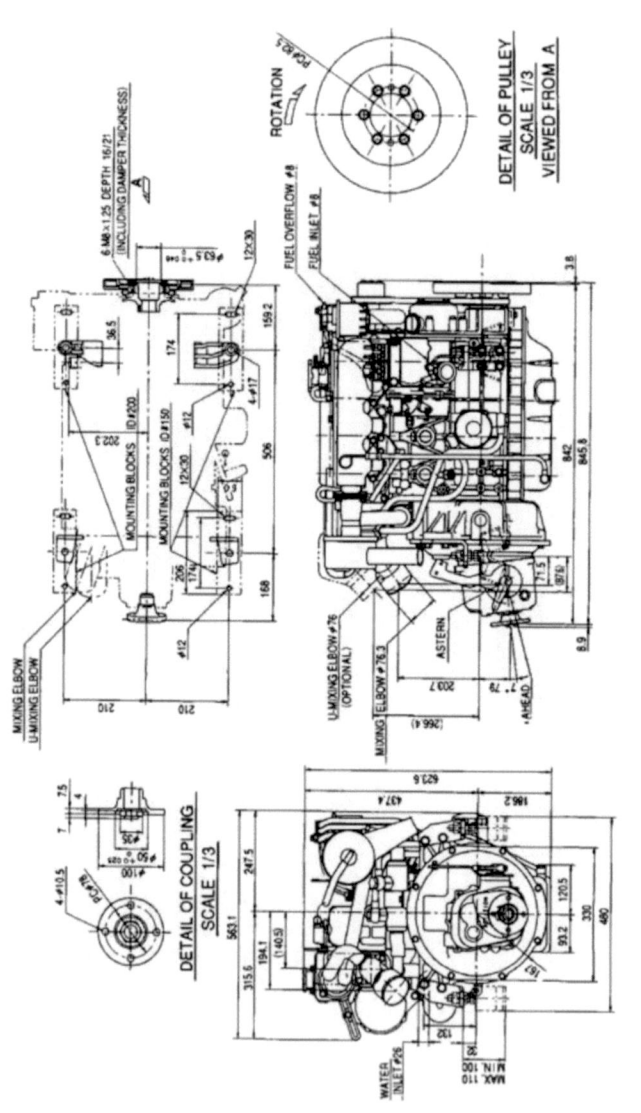

Chapter 1 General
4. Piping Diagrams _____ 3,4JH3(B)(C)E

4. Piping Diagrams

4-1 3,4JH3(B)(C)E

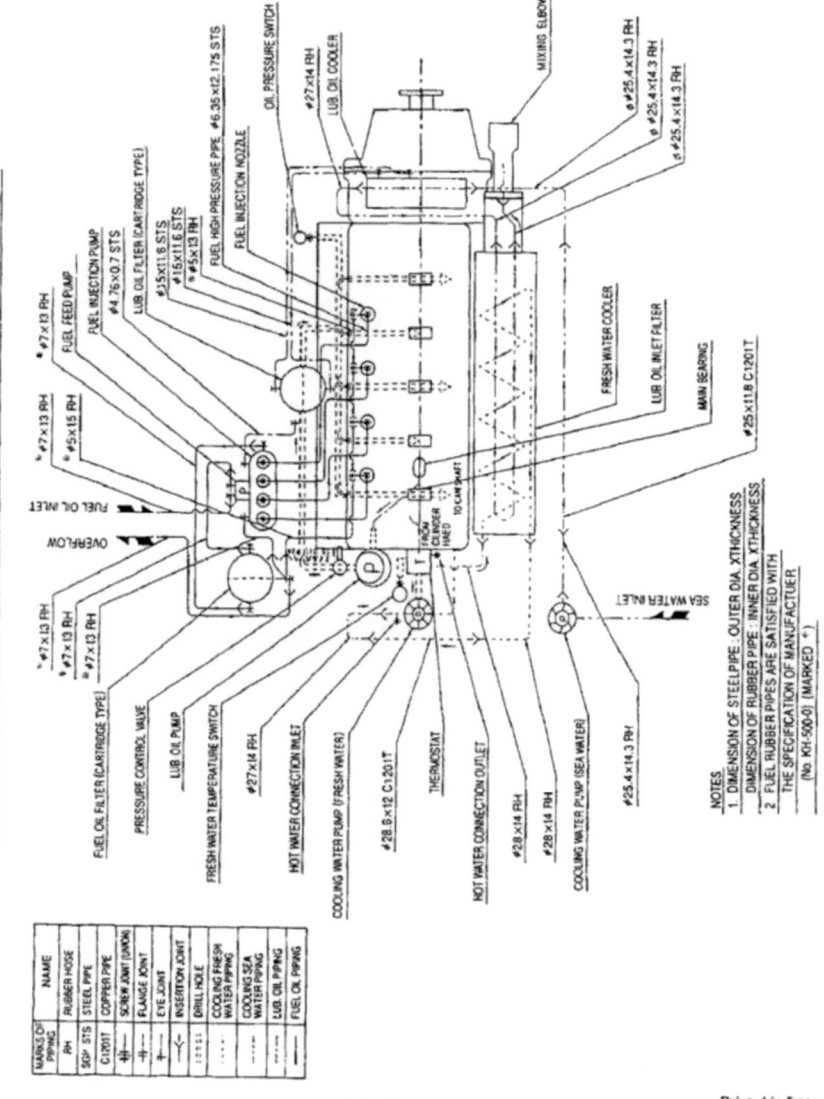

CHAPTER 2

INSPECTION AND SERVICING OF BASIC ENGINE PARTS

1. Cylinder Block ··2-1
    1-1 Inspection of parts ··2-1
    1-2 Cleaning of oil holes ···2-1
    1-3 Color check procedure ··2-1
    1-4 Replacement of cup plugs ···2-2
    1-5 Cylinder bore measurement ···2-3
2. Cylinder Head ··2-4
    2-1 Inspecting the cylinder head ··2-5
    2-2 Valve seat correction procedure ···2-6
    2-3 Intake/exhaust valves, valve guides ····································2-6
    2-4 Valve springs ···2-8
    2-5 Assembling the cylinder head ··2-9
    2-6 Measuring top clearance ···2-9
    2-7 Intake and exhaust valve arms ···2-9
    2-8 Adjustment of valve head clearance ···································2-10
3. Piston and Piston Pins ··2-11
    3-1 Piston ···2-12
    3-2 Piston pin ··2-12
    3-3 Piston rings ···2-13
4. Connecting Rod ···2-15
    4-1 Inspecting the connection rod ··2-15
    4-2 Crank pin bushing ··2-16
    4-3 Piston pin bushing ··2-16
    4-4 Assembling piston and connecting rod ································2-17
5. Crankshaft and Main Bearing ··2-18
    5-1 Crankshaft ··2-18
    5-2 Main bearing ···2-20
6. Camshaft and Tappets ··2-21
    6-1 Camshaft ··2-21
    6-2 Tappets ··2-22
7. Timing gear ···2-24
    7-1 Inspecting the gears ···2-24
    7-2 Gear timing marks ···2-25
8. Flywheel and Housing ···2-26
    8-1 Specifications of flywheel ··2-26
    8-2 Dimensions of flywheel and mounting flange ·······················2-27
    8-3 Ring gear ··2-28
    8-4 Position of top dead center and fuel injection timing ············2-28
    8-5 Damper disc and cooling fan ···2-29

Printed in Japan
HINSHI-H8011

1. Cylinder Block

The cylinder block is a thin-skinned, (low-weight), short skirt type with rationally placed ribs. The side walls are wave shaped to maximize ridigity for strength and low noise.

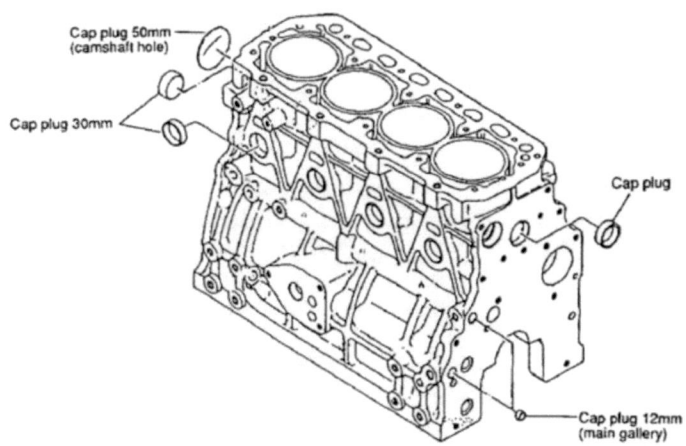

1-1 Inspection of parts

Make a visual inspection to check for cracks on engines that have frozen up, overturned or otherwise been subjected to undue stress. Perform a color check on any portions that appear to be cracked, and replace the cylinder block if the crack is not repairable.

1-2 Cleaning of oil holes

Clean all oil holes, making sure that none are clogged up and the blind plugs do not come off.

Color check kit

	Quantity
Penetrant	1
Developer	2
Cleaner	3

1-3 Color check procedure

(1) Clean the area to be inspected.
(2) Color check kit
    The color check test kit consists of an aerosol cleaner, penetrant and developer.
(3) Clean the area to be inspected with the cleaner.
    Either spray the cleaner on directly and wipe, or wipe the area with a cloth moistened with cleaner.
(4) Spray on red penetrant
    After cleaning, spray on the red penetrant and allow 5 ~10 minutes for penetration. Spray on more red penetrant if it dries before it has been able to penetrate.
(5) Spray on developer
    Remove any residual penetrant on the surface after the penetrant has penetrated, and spray on the developer.
    If there are any cracks in the surface, red dots or a red line will appear several minutes after the developer dries.
    Hold the developer 300~400mm away from the area being inspected when spraying, making sure to coat the surface uniformly.
(6) Clean the surface with the cleaner.

NOTE : *Without fail, read the instructions for the color check kit before use.*

Chapter 2 Basic Engine
1. Cylinder Block   3.4JH3(B)(C)E

1-4 Replacement of cup plugs

Step No.	Description	Procedure	Tool or material used
1	Clean and remove grease from the hole into which the cup plug is to be driven. (Remove scale and sealing material previously applied.)	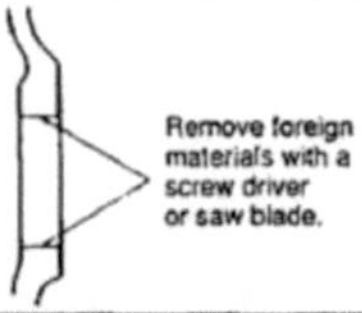 Remove foreign materials with a screw driver or saw blade.	• Screw driver or saw blade • Thinner
2	Remove grease from the cup plug.	Visually check the nick around the plug.	• Thinner
3	Apply Threebond No. 4 to the seat surface where the plug is to be driven in.	Apply over the whole outside of the plug.	• Threebond No. 4
4	Insert the plug into the hole.	Insert the plug so that it sits conectly.	
5	Place a driving tool on the cup plug and drive it in using a hammer. 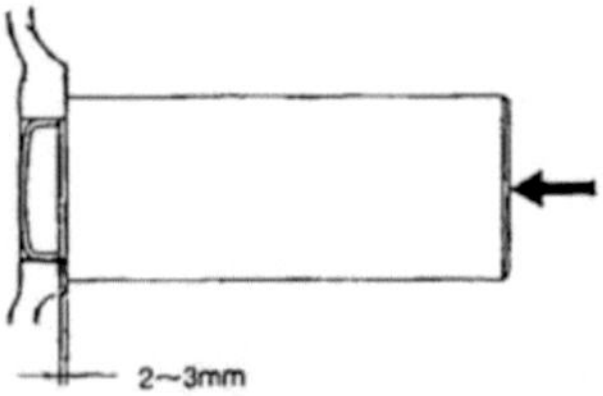	Drive in the plug parallel to the seating surface. 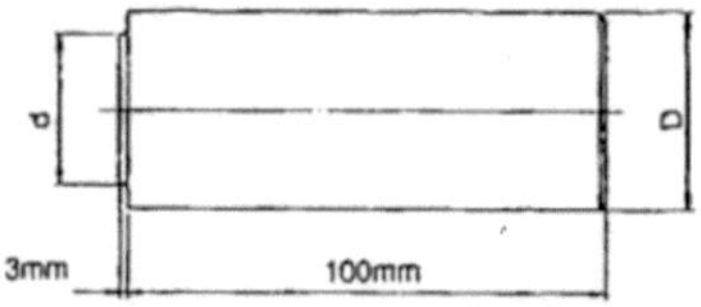	• Driving tool • Hammer

2~3mm

3mm   100mm

*Using the special tool, drive the cup plug so that the edge of the plug is 2mm (0.0787in.) below the cylinder surface.

mm

Plug dia.	d	D
⌀12	⌀11.9~12.0	⌀20
⌀30	⌀29.9~30.0	⌀40

1. Cylinder Block

3,4JH3(B)(C)E

1-5 Cylinder bore measurement

Measure the bore diameter with a cylinder gauge at the positions shown in the figure.
Replace the cylinder bore when the measured value exceeds the wear limit. Measurement must be done at least at 3 positions as shown in the figure, namely, top, middle and bottom positions in both directions along the crankshaft rotation and crankshaft center lines.

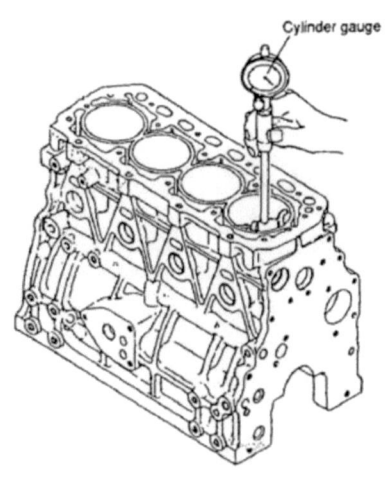

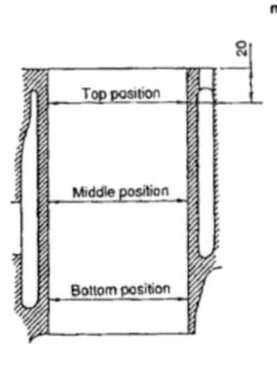

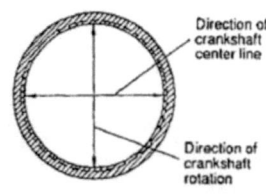

mm

	Standard	Wear limit
Cylinder bore dia.	⌀84.00〜⌀84.03	⌀84.20
Cylinder roundness	0〜0.01	0.03

2. Cylinder Head

The cylinder head is of 4-cylinder integral construction, mounted with 18 bolts. Special alloy stellite with superior resistance to heat and wear is fitted on the seats, and the area between the valves is cooled by a water jet.

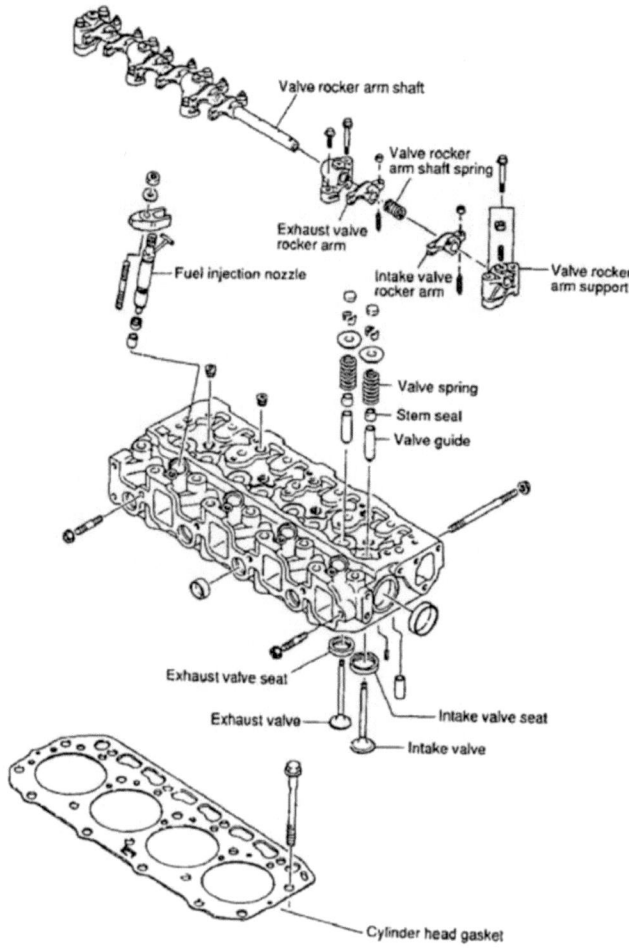

Chapter 2 Basic Engine
2. Cylinder Head

3.4JH3(B)(C)E

2-1 Inspecting the cylinder head

The cylinder head is subjected to very severe operating conditions with repeated high pressure, high temperature and cooling. Thoroughly remove all the carbon and dirt after disassembly and carefully inspect all parts.

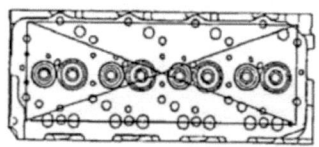

2-1.1 Distortion of the combustion surface

Carefully check for cylinder head distortion as this leads to gasket damage and compression leaks.
(1) Clean the cylinder head surface.
(2) Place a straight-edge along each of the four sides and each diagonal. Measure the clearance between the straight-edge and combustion surface with a feeler gauge.

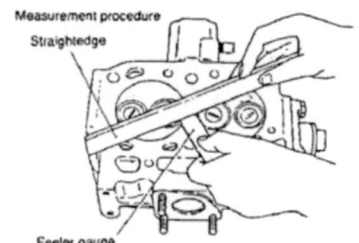

mm

	Standard	Wear limit
Cylinder head distortion	0.05 or less	0.15

2-1.2 Checking for cracks in the combustion surface

Remove the fuel injection nozzle, intake and exhaust valve and clean the combustion surface. Check for discoloration or distortion and conduct a color check test to check for any cracks.

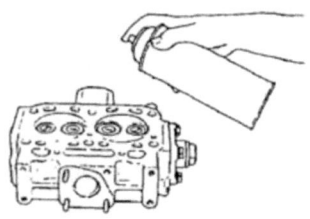

2-1.3 Checking the intake and exhaust valve seats

Check the surface and width of the valve seats.
If they are too wide, or if the surfaces are rough, correct to the following standards:

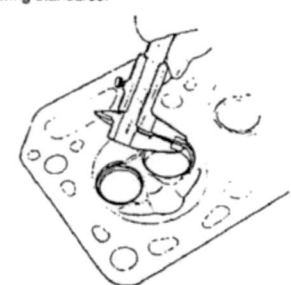

Seat angle	Intake	120°
	Exhaust	90°

Seat width	Standard	Wear limit
Intake	1.07~1.24	1.74
Exhaust	1.24~1.45	1.94

Intake valve seat

Exhaust valve seat

Standard dimension

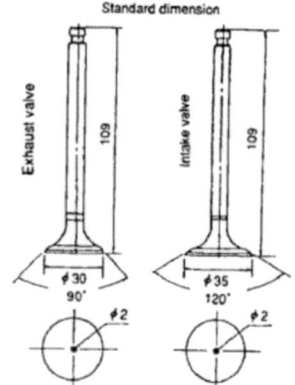

2-2 Valve seat correction procedure

The most common method for correcting unevenness of the seat surface with a seat grinder is as follows:

(1) Use a seat grinder to make the surface even.
   As the valve seat width will be enlarged, first use a 70° grinder, then grind the seat to the standard dimension with a 15° grinder.

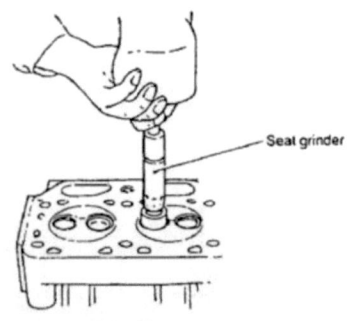

Seat grinder	Intake valve	30°
	Exhaust valve	45°

NOTE : When seat adjustment is necessary, be sure to check the valve and valve guide. If the clearance exceeds the tolerance, replace the valve or the valve guide, and then grind the seat.

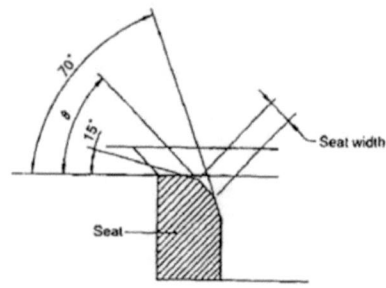

(2) Knead valve compound with oil and finish the valve seat with a lapping tool.
(3) Final finishing should be done with oil only.

Lapping tool
Use a rubber cap type lapping tool for cylinders without a lapping tool groove slit.

NOTE : Clean the valve and cylinder head with light oil or the equivalent after valve seat finishing is completed and make sure that there are no grindings remaining.

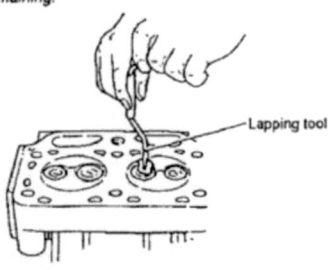

NOTE : 1. Insert adjusting shims between the valve spring and cylinder head when seats have been refinished with a seat grinder.
2. Measure valve distortion after valve seat refinishing has been completed, and replace the valve and valve seat if it exceeds the tolerance.

2-3 Intake/exhaust valves, valve guides

2-3.1 Wearing and corrosion of valve stem

Replace the valve if the valve stem is excessively worn or corroded.

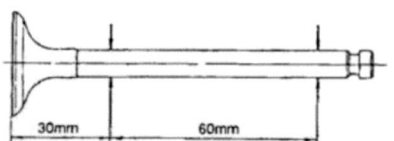

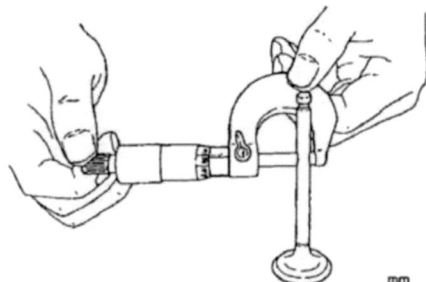

mm

Valve stem outside dia.	Standard	Wear limit
Intake	⌀7.960~⌀7.975	⌀7.900
Exhaust	⌀7.955~⌀7.970	⌀7.900

Chapter 2 Basic Engine
2. Cylinder Head

_3.4JH3(B)(C)E_

2-3.2 Inspection of valve seat wear and contact surface

Inspect for valve seat scratches and excessive wear. Check to make sure the contact surface is normal. The seat angle must be checked and adjusted if the valve seat contact surface is much smaller than the width of the valve seat.

NOTE: Keep in mind the fact that the intake and discharge valve have different diameters.

2-3.3 Valve sinking

Over long periods of use and repeated lappings, combustion efficiency may drop. Measure the sinking distance and replace the valve and valve seat if the valve sink exceeds the tolerance.

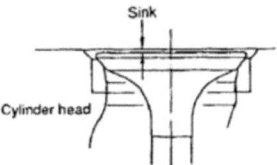

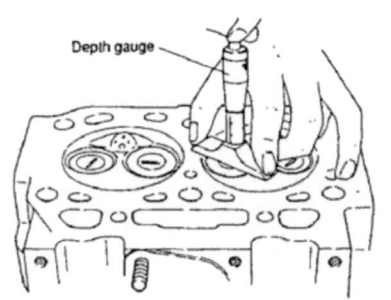

mm

	Standard	Wear limit
Valve sink	0.306~0.506	1.0

2-3.4 Valve guide

(1) Measuring inner diameter of valve guide.
Measure the inner diameter of the valve guide and replace it if it exceeds the wear limit.

mm

		Standard	Wear limit
Valve guide inside dia.	Intake	⌀8.010~⌀8.025	+0.2
	Exhaust	⌀8.015~⌀8.030	+0.2

NOTE: The inner diameter standard dimensions assume a pressure fit.

(2) Replacing the valve guide
Use the insertion tool and tap in the guide with a mallet.

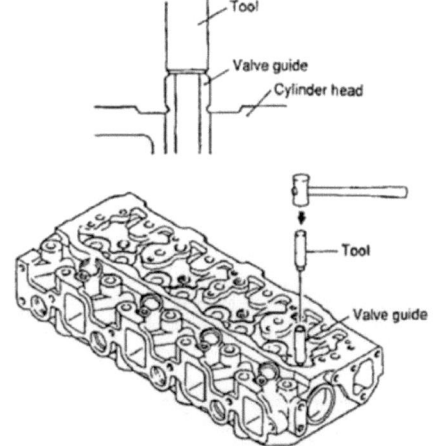

The intake valve guide and exhaust valve guide are of different shapes/dimensions. The one with a groove around it is the exhaust valve guide and the one without is the intake valve guide.

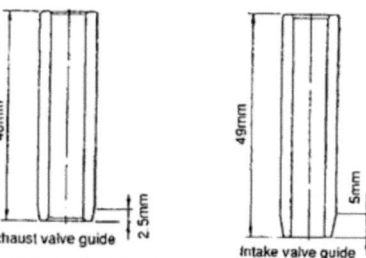

(3) Valve guide projection
The valve guide should project 15mm from the top of the cylinder head.

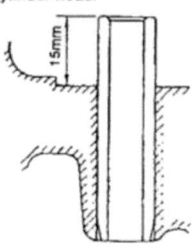

Chapter 2 Basic Engine
2. Cylinder Head

3,4JH3(B)(C)E

(4) Valve stem seals
The valve stem seals in the intake/exhaust valve guides cannot be re-used once they are removed - be sure to replace them.
When assembling the intake/exhaust valves, apply an adequate quantity of engine oil on the valve stem before inserting them.

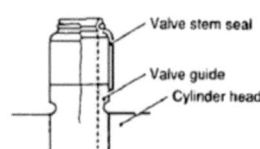

2-4 Valve springs

2-4.1 Checking valve springs
(1) Check the spring for scratches or corrosion.
(2) Measure the free length of the spring.

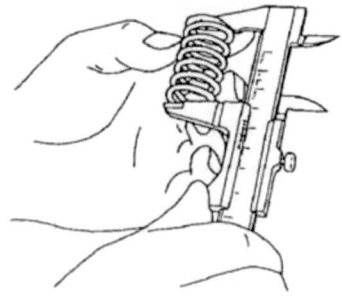

(3) Measure inclination.

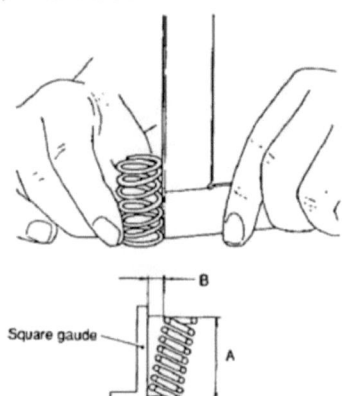

(4) Measure spring tension.

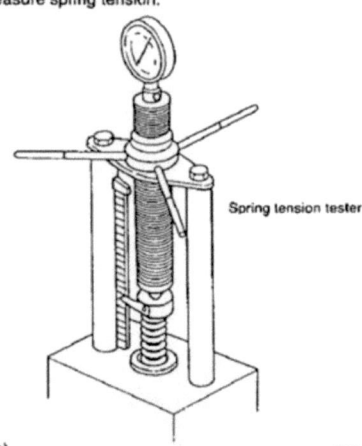

Spring tension tester

(Inside)   mm

Valve spring	Standard	Wear limit
Free length	44.4	43.0
Distortion	—	1.1
Tension (1mm pressure)	2.36/3.101	—

<Remarks> Tension is shown for the smaller pitch.

Assembling valve springs.
The side with the smaller pitch (painted yellow) should face down (cylinder head).

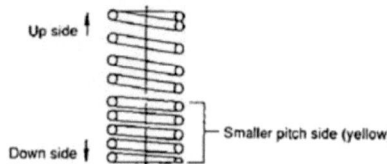

NOTE : The pitch of the valve spring is not even. The side with the smaller pitch (yellow) should face down (cylinder head) when assembled.

(5) Spring retainer and spring cotter
Inspect the inside face of the spring retainer, the outside surface of the spring cotter, the contact area of the spring cotter inside surface and the notch in the head of the valve stem. Replace the spring retainer and spring cotter when the contact area is less than 70%, or when the spring cotter has been recessed because of wear.

2-5 Assembling the cylinder head

Partially tighten the bolts in the specified order and then tighten to the specified torque, being careful that the head does not get distorted.

(1) Clean out the cylinder head bolt holes.
(2) Check for foreign matter on the cylinder head surface where it comes in contact with the block.
(3) Coat the head bolt threads and nut seats with lube oil.
(4) Use the positioning pins to line up the head gasket with the cylinder block.
(5) Match up the cylinder head with the head gasket and mount.

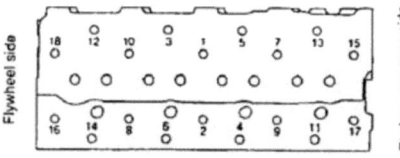

Exhaust manifold side / Intake manifold side / Flywheel side / Timing gear case side

kg-m

	First	Second
Tightening torque	4.5~5.5	8.7~9.3

2-6 Measuring top clearance

(1) Place a high quality fuse (φ1.5mm, 10mm long) in three positions on the flat part of the piston head.
(2) Assemble the cylinder head gasket and the cylinder block and tighten the bolts in the specified order to the specified torque.
(3) Turn the crank, (in the direction of engine revolution), and press the fuse against the piston until it breaks.
(4) Remove the head and take out the broken fuse.
(5) Measure the three positions where each fuse is broken and calculate the average.
(0.71~0.75mm is ideal)

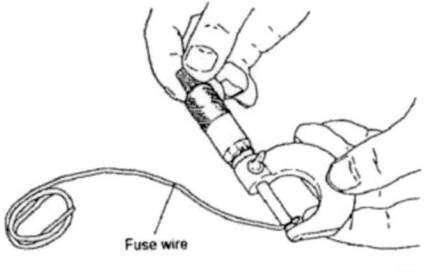

Fuse wire

mm

Top clearance	0.660~0.780

2-7 Intake and exhaust valve arms

Valve arm and valve arm bushing wear may change opening/closing timing of the valve, and may in turn affect engine performance according to the extent of the change.

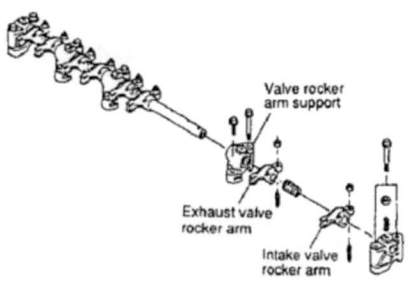

Valve rocker arm support
Exhaust valve rocker arm
Intake valve rocker arm

(1) Valve arm shaft and valve arm bushing
Measure the outer diameter of the shaft and the inner-diameter of the bearing, and replace if wear exceeds the limit.

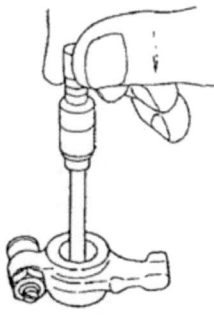

mm

	Standard	Wear limit
Intake and exhaust valve rocker arm A shaft outside dia.	15.966~15.988	15.955
Intake and exhaust valve rocker arm B inside dia.	16.000~16.010	16.090
Valve rocker arm shaft and bushing clearance at assembly	0.016~0.054	0.140

Replace the valve arm shaft bushing if it moves and replace the entire valve arm if there is no tightening clearance.

2. Cylinder Head

(2) Valve spring
Check the valve arm spring and replace it if it is corroded or worn.

(3) Valve arm and valve top retainer wear
Inspect the contact surface of the valve arm and replace it if there is abnormal wear of flaking.

(4) Inspect the contact surface of the valve clearance adjustment screw and push rod and replace if there is abnormal wear or flaking.

2-8 Adjustment of valve head clearance

(1) Make adjustments when the engine is cool.

	mm
Intake and exhaust valve head clearance	0.2

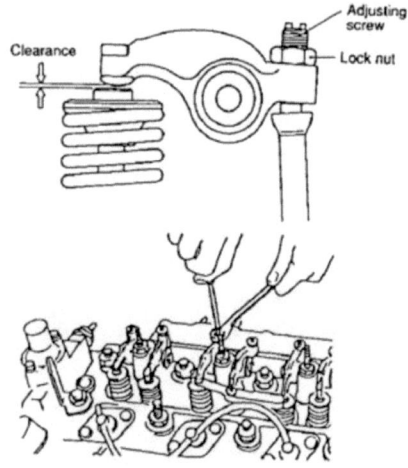

(2) Be sure that the opening and closing angles for both the intake and the exhaust valves are checked when the timing gear is disassembled (The gauge on the flywheel is read when the push rod turns the flywheel).

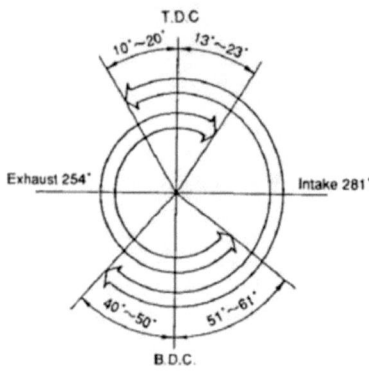

(3JH3E, 3JH3BE, 3JH3CE)

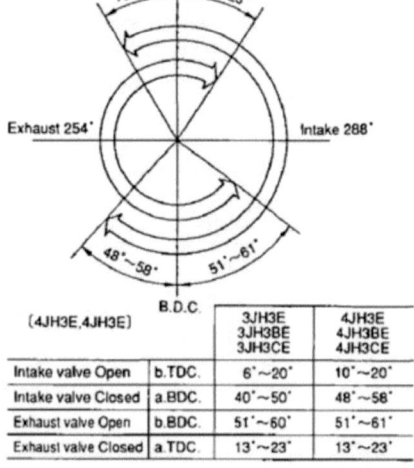

(4JH3E, 4JH3E)		3JH3E 3JH3BE 3JH3CE	4JH3E 4JH3BE 4JH3CE
Intake valve Open	b.TDC.	6°~20°	10°~20°
Intake valve Closed	a.BDC.	40°~50°	48°~58°
Exhaust valve Open	b.BDC.	51°~60°	51°~61°
Exhaust valve Closed	a.TDC.	13°~23°	13°~23°

3. Piston and Piston Pins

Pistons are made of a special light alloy with superior thermal expansion characteristics, and the top of the piston forms a swirl type toroidal combustion chamber. The opposite face of the piston combustion surface is oil-jet cooled.
Piston for engines with superchargers have a valve ress for the intake and exhaust valves.
The clearance between the piston and cylinder liner is kept at the pronper valve by the piston cylinder liner property fit effected during assembly at the Yanmmar factory.

IMPORTANT:
Piston shape differs among engine models. If an incorrect piston is installed, combustion performance will drop. Be sre to check the applicable engine model identification mark (I.D.Mark) on the piston to insure use of the correct part.

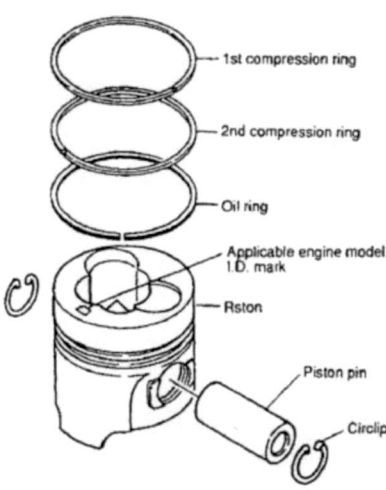

ID Mark for Piston
L
Ml.
Ms
S

Chapter 2 Basic Engine
3. Pistons and Piston Pins

3,4JH3(B)(C)E

3-1 Piston

3-1.1 Piston head and combustion surface
Remove the carbon that has accumulated on the piston head and combustion surface, taking care not to scratch the piston. Check the combustion surface for any damage.

3-1.2 Measurement of piston outside diameter/ inspection
(1) Replace the piston if the outsides of the piston or ring grooves are worn.
(2) Measure the piston 22mm from the bottom at right angles to the piston pin.

3-1.3 Replacing the piston
A floating type piston pin is used in this engine. The piston pin can be pressed into the piston pin hole at room temperature (coat with oil to make it slide in easily).

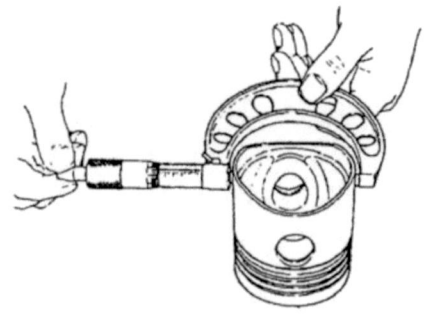

3-2 Piston pin
Measure the outer diameter and replace the pin if it is excessively worn.

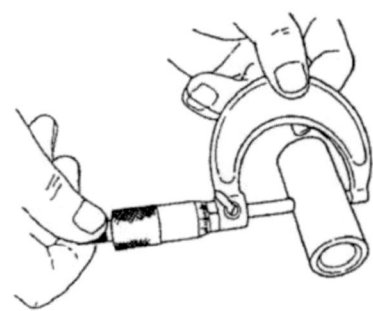

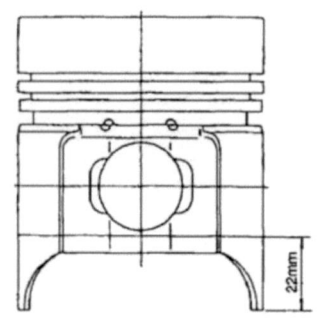

Standard	Wear limit
83.945~83.975	83.90

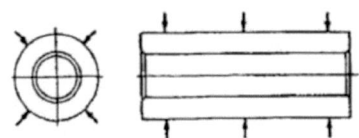

mm

	Standard	Wear limit
Piston pin insert hole dia.	⌀26.000~26.009	⌀26.020
Piston pin outside dia.	⌀25.987~26.000	⌀25.900
Standard clearance	0~0.022	0.12

3-3 Piston rings

There are 2 compression rings and 1 oil ring. The absence of an oil ring on the piston skirt prevents oil from being kept on the thrust surface and in turn provides good lubrication.

		Standard	Wear limit
First piston ring	Groove width	2.065~2.080	—
	Ring width	1.970~1.990	—
	Groove and ring clearance	0.075~0.110	0.2
Second piston ring	Groove width	2.035~2.050	—
	Ring width	1.970~1.990	—
	Groove and ring clearance	0.045~0.080	0.2
Oil ring	Groove width	4.015~4.030	—
	Ring width	3.975~3.990	—
	Groove and ring clearance	0.025~0.060	0.2

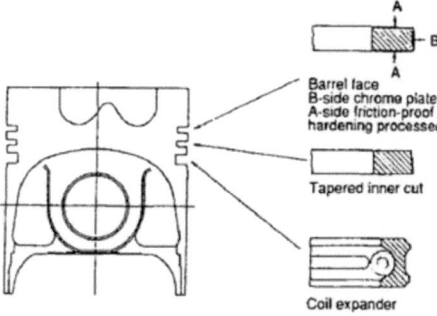

Barrel face
B-side chrome plated,
A-side friction-proof hardening processed

Tapered inner cut

Coil expander

3-3.2 Measuring piston ring gap

Press the piston ring onto a piston liner and measure the piston ring gap with a gauge. Press on the ring about 30mm from the bottom of the liner.

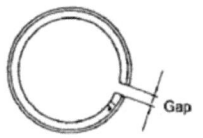

Gap

3-3.1 Measuring the rings.

Measure the thickness and width of the rings, and the ring-to-groove clearance after installation. Replace if wear exceed the limit.

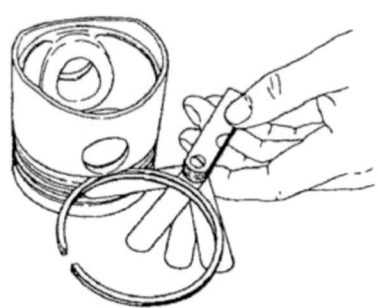

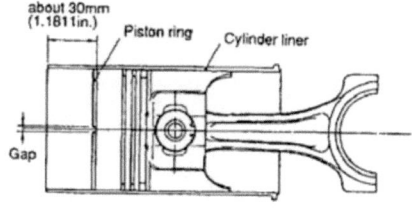

about 30mm (1.1811in.) Piston ring   Cylinder liner

Gap

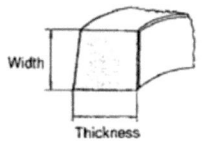

Width

Thickness

	Standard	Wear limit
First piston ring gap	0.20~0.40	1.5
Second piston ring gap	0.20~0.40	1.5
Oil ring gap	0.20~0.40	1.5

3-3.3 Replacing the piston rings

(1) Thoroughly clean the ring grooves when replacing piston rings.
(2) The side with the manufacturer's mark (near piston ring gap) should face up.

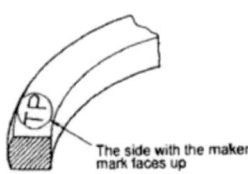
The side with the maker mark faces up

(3) After fitting the piston ring, make sure it moves easily and smoothly.
(4) Stagger the piston rings at 120° intervals, making sure none of them line up with the piston.

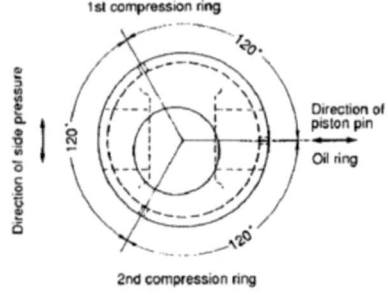

(5) The oil ring is provided with a coil expander. The coil expander joint should be opposite (staggered 180°) the oil ring gap.

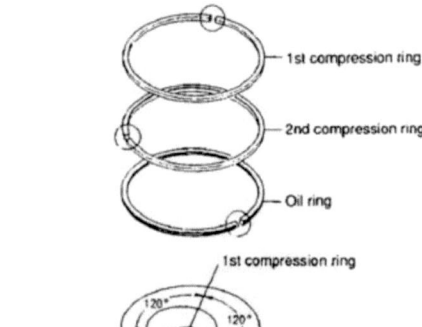

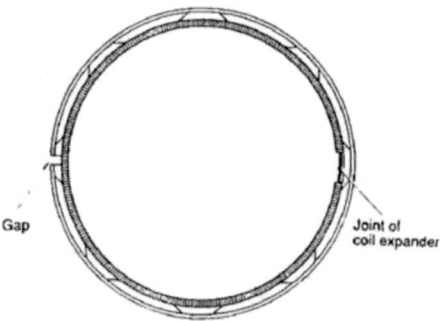

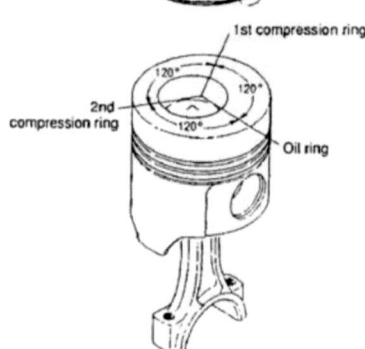

4. Connecting Rod

The connecting rod is made of high-strength forged carbon steel.
The large end with the aluminium metal can be separated into two and the small end has a 2-layer copper alloy coil bushing.

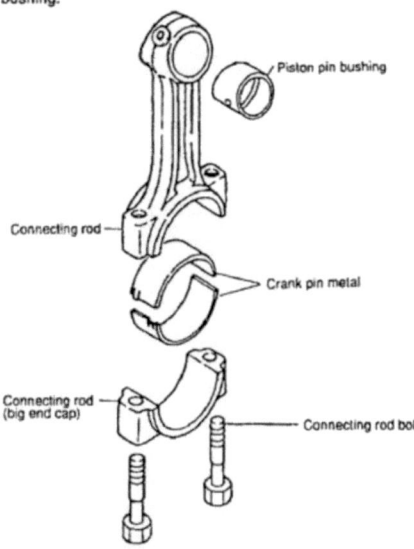

Piston pin bushing
Connecting rod
Crank pin metal
Connecting rod (big end cap)
Connecting rod bolt

4-1 Inspecting the connection rod

4-1.1 Twist and parallelism of the large and small ends

Insert the measuring tool into the large and small ends of the connecting rod. Measure the extent of twist and parallelism and replace if they exceed the tolerance.

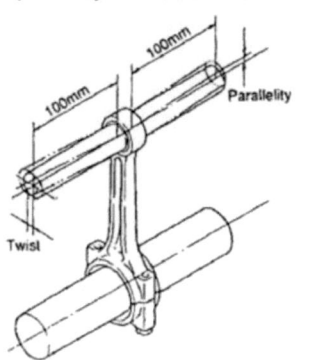

Parallelity
Twist

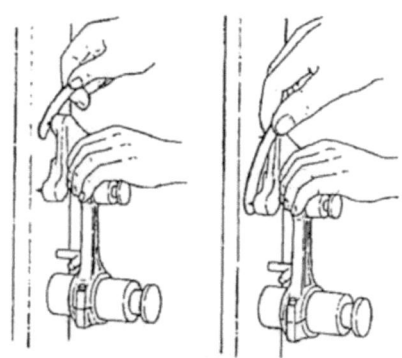

Measuring twist and parallelity

mm

	Standard	Wear limit
Connecting rod twist and parallelity	less than 0.05 (at 100mm)	0.07

4-1.2 Checking thrust clearance

Fit the respective crank pins to the connecting rod and check to make sure that the clearance in the crankshaft direction is correct.

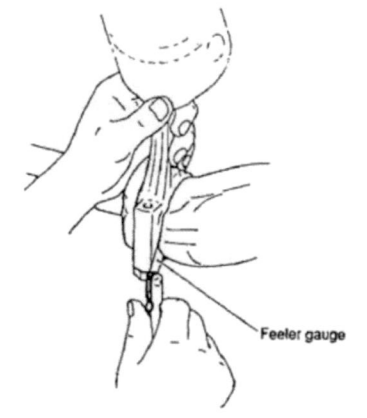

Feeler gauge

mm

	Standard	Wear limit
Connecting rod side clearance	0.20~0.40	0.55

Chapter 2 Basic Engine
4. Connecting Rod

3,4JH3(B)(C)E

4-2 Crank pin bushing

4-2.1 Checking crank pin bushing
Check for flaking, melting or seizure on the contact surface.

4-2.2 Measuring crank pin oil clearance
Use a plastic gauge.

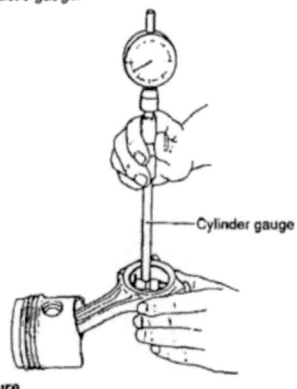
Cylinder gauge

Procedure
(1) Use the press gauge (Plastigage) for measuring oil clearance in the crank pin.
(2) Mount the connecting rod on the crank pin (tighten to specified torque).

Connecting rod tightening torque	4.5~5.5kg-m

(3) Remove the connecting rod and measure the broken plastic gauge with measuring paper.

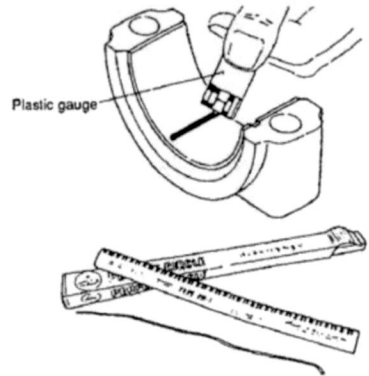
Plastic gauge

4-2.3 Precautions on replacement of crank pin bushing
(1) Wash the crank pin bushing.
(2) Wash the large end cap, mount the crank pin bushing and make sure that it fits tightly on the large end cap.
(3) When assembling the connecting rod, match up the large end and large end cap number. Coat the bolts with engine oil and gradually tighten them alternately to the specified torque.
If a torque wrench is not available, make match marks on the bolt heads and large end cap (to indicate the proper torque position) and retighten the bolts to those positions.

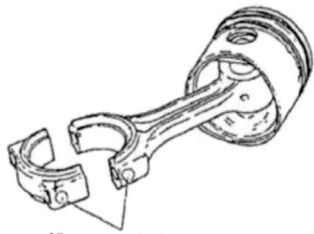
Alignment mark (Punched mark)

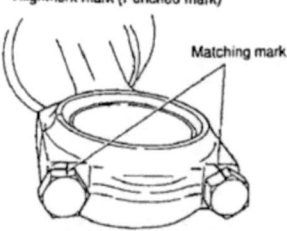
Matching mark

(4) Make sure there is no sand, metal cuttings or other foreign matter in the lube oil, and that the crankshaft is not scratched. Take special care in cleaning the oil holes.

4-3 Piston pin bushing
(1) Measuring piston pin clearance.
Excessive piston pin bushing wear may result in damage to the piston pin or the piston inself.

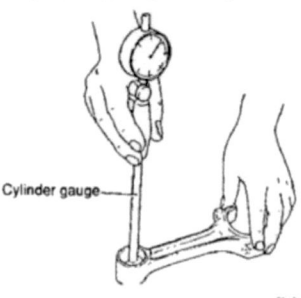
Cylinder gauge

Chapter 2 Inspection and Servicing of Basic Engine Parts
4. Connecting Rod

_3.4JH3(B)(C)E_

	Standard	Wear limit
Pin pin bushing inside dia	26.025~26.038	26.10
Piston pin and bushing oil clearance	0.025~0.051	0.2

mm

Since the small end is tapered, bush insertion is extremely difficult. Any minor mistake will cause abnormalities such as twist and bite. Do not insert the bush on-site.
(No piston pin bush spare part is available. It is included in the con-rod assembly supplied as a spare part.)

4-4 Assembling piston and connecting rod
The piston and connecting rod should be assembled so that the match mark on the connecting rod large end faced the fuel injection pump side and the combustion chamber above the piston is close to the fuel injection pump.

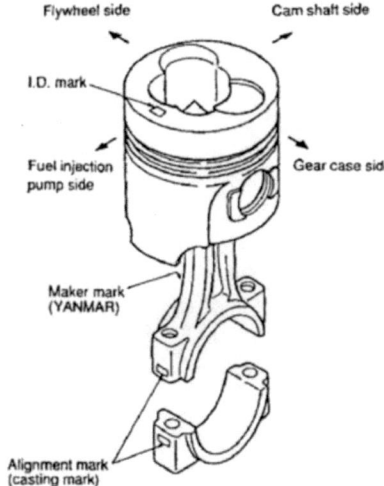

Flywheel side
Cam shaft side
I.D. mark
Fuel injection pump side
Gear case side
Maker mark (YANMAR)
Alignment mark (casting mark)

5. Crankshaft and Main Bearing

The crank pin and crankjournal have been induction hardened for superior durability, and the crankshaft is provided with four balance weights for optional balance. The crankshaft main bearing is of the hanger type. The upper metal (cylinder block side) is provided with an oil groove. There is no oil groove on the lower metal (bearing cap side). The bearing cap (location cap) of the flywheel side has a thrust metal which supports the thrust load.

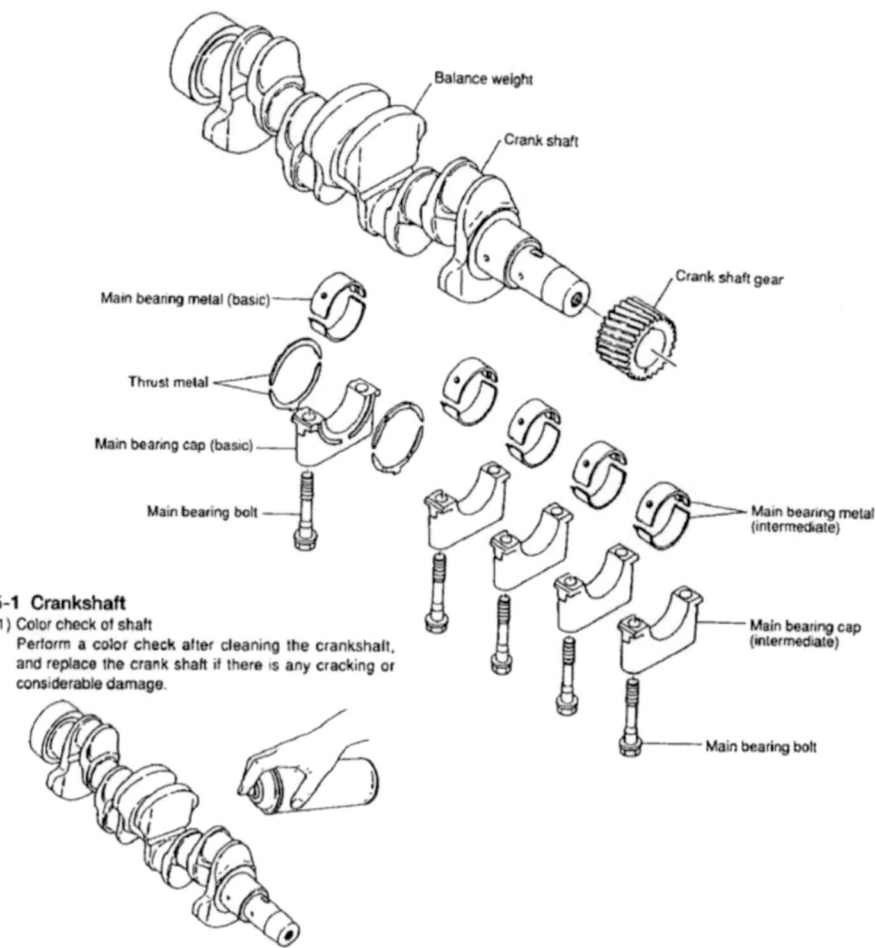

5-1 Crankshaft
(1) Color check of shaft
Perform a color check after cleaning the crankshaft, and replace the crank shaft if there is any cracking or considerable damage.

Chapter 2 Basic Engine
5. Crankshaft and Main Bearing

3,4JH3(B)(C)E

(2) Bending of the crankshaft

Support the crankshaft with V-blocks at both ends of the journals. Measure the deflection of the center journal with a dial gauge while rotating the crankshaft to check the extent of crankshaft bending.

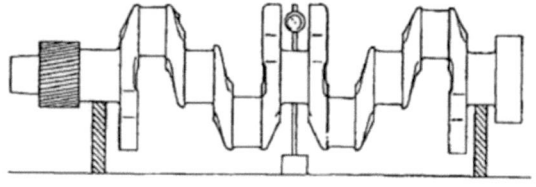
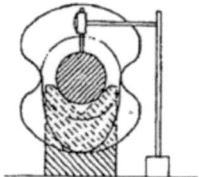

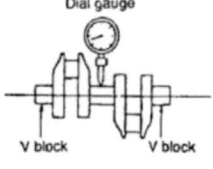
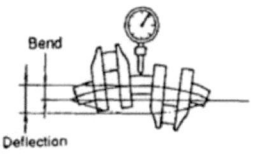

	mm
Crankshaft bend	Less than 0.02 mm

(3) Measuring the crank pin and journal

Measure the extent of journal wear (roundness, taper). Regrind it to the proper shape if it is within the outer diameter limit, and replace if not.

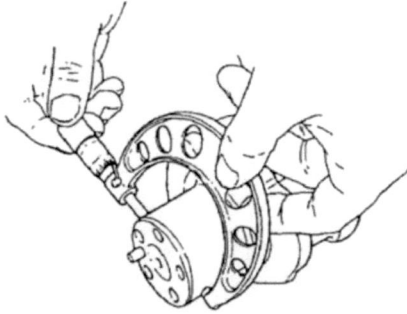
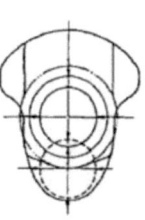
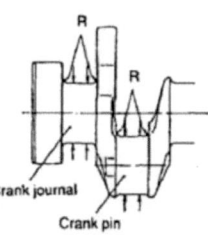

mm

		Standard	Wear limit
Crank pin	Outside dia.	φ47.952~67.962	47.91
	Crank pin and bearing oil clearance	0.038~0.068	0.25
Crank journal	Outside dia.	49.952~49.962	49.75
	Crank journal and bearing oil clearance	0.036~0.068	0.15
Fillet rounding of crank pin and journal		3.500~3.800	—

Chapter 2 Basic Engine
5. Crankshaft and Main Bearing

3,4JH3(B)(C)E

(4) Checking side clearance of the crankshaft

After assembling the crankshaft, tighten the main bearing cap to the specified torque, and move the crankshaft to one side, placing a dial gauge on one end of the shaft to measure thrust clearance.
This measurement can also be effected by inserting the gauge directly into the clearance between the thrust bearing and crankshaft thrust surface.
Replace the thrust bearing if it is worn beyond the limit.

mm

	Standard	Wear limit
Crankshaft side gap	0.14~0.22	0.30

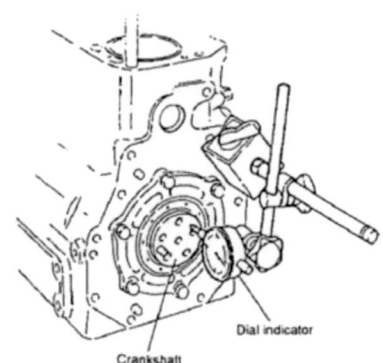

Dial indicator
Crankshaft

5-2 Main bearing

(1) Inspecting the main bearing
Check for flaking, seizure or burning of the contact surface and replace if necessary.

(2) Measuring the inner diameter of metal
Tighten the cap to the specified torque and measure the inner diameter of the metal.

Bearing cap bolt tightening torque	9.8~10.2kgf-m

NOTE : When assembling the bearing cap, keep the following in mind.
1) The lower metal (cap side) has no oil groove.
2) The upper metal (cylinder block side) has an oil groove.
3) Check the cylinder block alignment No.
4) The "FW" on the cap lies on the flywheel side.

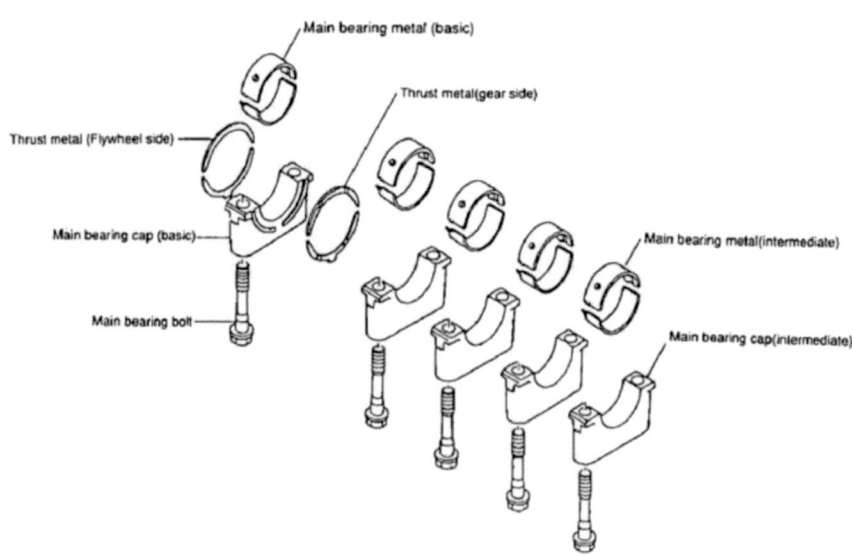

2—20

Printed in Japan
HINSHI-H8009

6. Camshaft and Tappets

6-1 Camshaft

The camshaft is normalized and the cam and bearing surfaces are surface hardened and ground. The cams have a curve that minimized the repeated shocks on the valve seats and maximizes valve seat life.

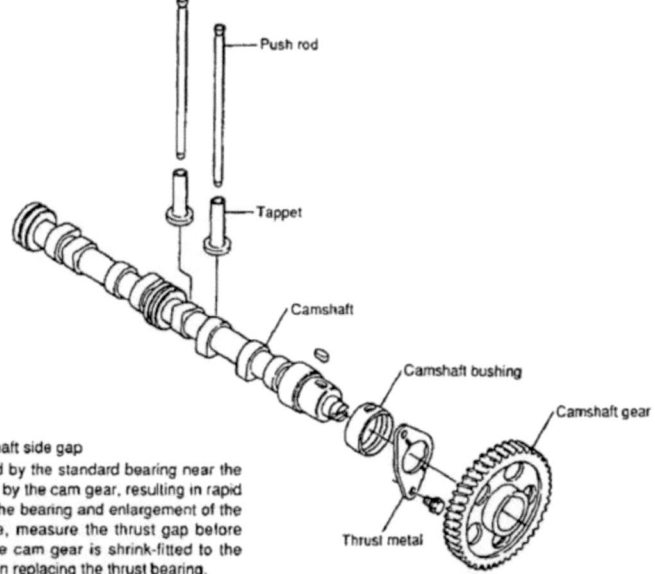

(1) Checking the camshaft side gap

The load is received by the standard bearing near the end of the camshaft by the cam gear, resulting in rapid wear of the end of the bearing and enlargement of the side gap. Therefore, measure the thrust gap before disassembly. As the cam gear is shrink-fitted to the cam, be careful when replacing the thrust bearing.

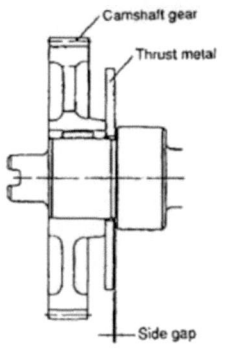

(2) Measure the camshaft height, and replace the cam if it is worn beyond the limit.

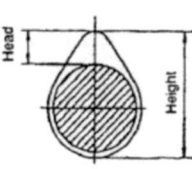

Camshaft height   mm

	Standard	Wear limit
Intake cam	38.635~38.765	38.40
Exhaust cam		

mm

	Standard	Wear limit
Camshaft side gap	0.05~0.25	0.4

Chapter 2 Basic Engine
6. Camshaft and Tappets
_3,4JH3(B)(C)E_

(3) Measure the camshaft outer diameter and the camshaft bearing inner diameter. Replace if they exceed the wear limit or are damaged.

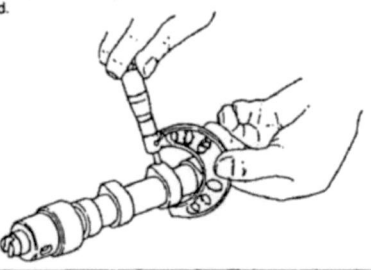

mm

	Standard			Wear limit
	Gear case side	Intermediate	Flywheel side	
Camshaft journal outside dia.	44.925~44.950	44.910~44.935	44.925~44.950	44.8
Camshaft journal bushing inside dia.	44.990~45.050	—	—	—
Cylinder block bearing inside dia.	—	45.000~45.025	45.000~45.025	—
Oil clearance	0.040~0.125	0.065~0.115	0.050~0.100	0.2

(4) Bending of the crankshaft
Support both ends of the crankshaft with V-blocks, place a dial gauge against the central bearing areas and measure bending. Replace if excessive.

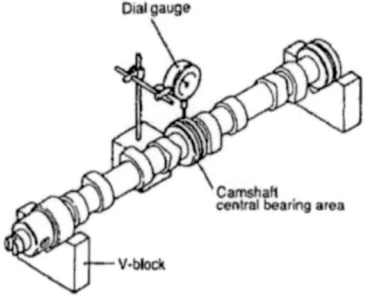

NOTE: The reading on the dial gauge is divided by two to obtain the extent of bending.

mm

	Wear limit
Camshaft deflection	Less than 0.02

6-2 Tappets

(1) The tappets are offset to rotate during operation and thereby prevent uneven wearing. Check the contact of each tappet and replace if excessively or unevenly worn.

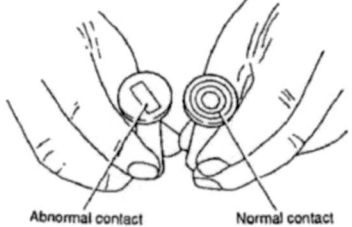

Abnormal contact   Normal contact

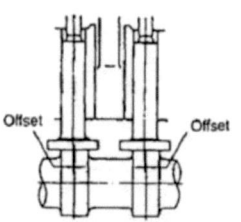

Offset   Offset

NOTE: When removing tappets, be sure to keep them separate for each cylinder and intake/exhaust valve.

Chapter 2 Basic Engine
6. Camshaft and Tappets

3,4JH3(B)(C)E

(2) Measure the outer diameter of the tappet, and replace if worn beyond the limit.

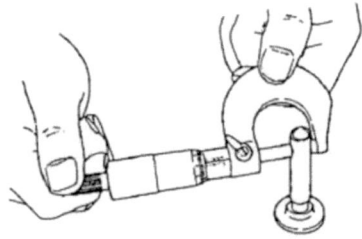

mm

	Standard	Wear limit
Tappet stem outside dia.	11.975~11.990	11.93
Tappet guide hole inside dia. (cylinder block)	12.000~12.018	12.05
Tappet stem and guide hole oil clearance	0.010~0.043	0.10

(3) Measuring push rods.
Measure the length and bending of the push rods.

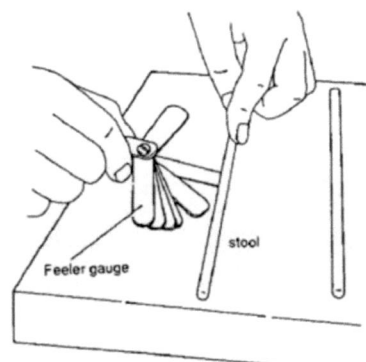

mm

	Standard	Wear limit
Push rod length	178.25~178.75	—
Push rod bend	Less than 0.03	0.3
Push rod dia.	8.5	—

2-23

7. Timing Gear

The timing gear is helical type for minimum noise and specially treated for high durability.

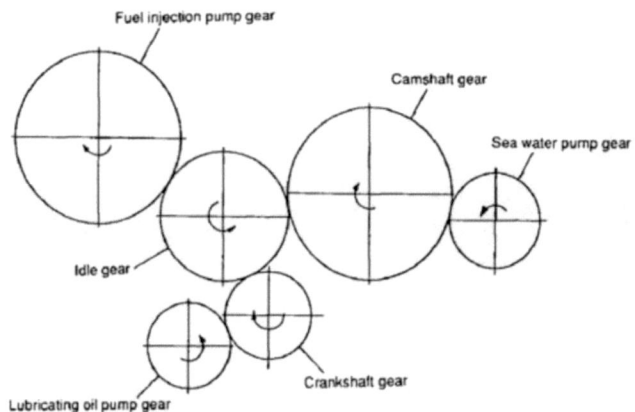

mm

	No. of teeth	Face width	Spiral angle	Center distance	Back lash	Back lash Wear limit
Sea water pump gear	31	12.0	right	92.544~92.592	0.07~0.15	0.2
Camshaft gear	56	18.0	left	105.318~105.380	0.07~0.15	0.2
Idle gear	43	18.0	right	75.525~75.573	0.07~0.15	0.2
Crankshaft gear	28	40.0	left			
Lubricating oil pump gear	29	8.0	right	60.629~60.677	0.11~0.19	0.22
Idle gear	43	18.0	right	105.254~105.316	0.04~0.12	0.2
Fuel injection pump gear	56	10.0	left			

7-1 Inspecting the gears

(1) Inspect the gears and replace if the teeth are damaged or worn.
(2) Measure the backlash of all gears that mesh, and replace the meshing gears as a set if wear exceeds the limit.

NOTE: If backlash is excessive, it will not only result in excessive noise and gear damage, but also lead to bad valve and fuel injection timing and a decrease in engine performance.

(3) Idling gear
The bushing is pressure fitted into the idling gear. Measure the bushing inner diameter and the outer diameter of the shaft, and replace the bushing or idling gear shaft if the oil clearance exceeds the wear limit.
A, B and C are inscribed on the end of the idling gear. When assembling, these marks should align with those on the cylinder block.

Chapter 2 Basic Engine
7. Timing Gear

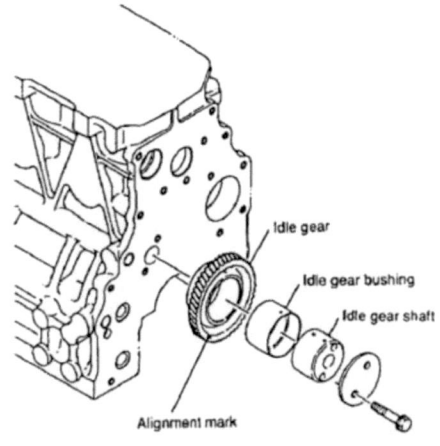

	Standard	Wear limit
Idle shaft dia.	45.950~45.975	45.88
Idle shaft bushing inside dia.	46.000~46.025	—
Idle shaft and bushing oil clearance	0.025~0.075	0.15

mm

7-2 Gear timing marks
Match up the timing marks on each gear when assembling (A, B and C).

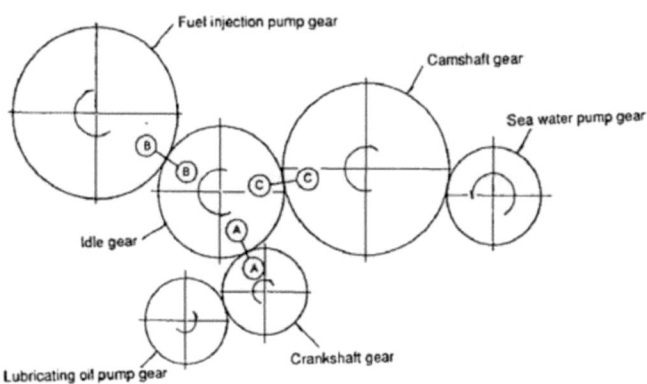

8. Flywheel and Housing

The function of the flywheel is through inertia, to rotate the crankshaft in a uniform and smooth manner by absorbing the turning force created during the combustion stroke of the engine, and by compensating for the decrease in turning force during the other strokes.
The flywheel is mounted and secured by 6 bolts on the crankshaft end at the opposite end to the gear case; it is covered by the mounting flange (flywheel housing) which is bolted to the cylinder block.
the fitting surface for the damper disc is on the crankshaft side of the flywheel. The rotation of the crankshaft is transmitted through this disc to the input shaft of the reduction and reversing gear. The reduction and reversing gear is fitted to the mounting flange.
The flywheel's unbalanced force on the shaft center must be kept below the specified value for the crankshaft as the flywheel rotates with the crankshaft at high speed.
To achieve this, the balance is adjusted by drilling holes in the side of the flywheel, and the unbalanced momentum is adjusted by drilling holes in the circumference.
The ring gear is shrink fitted onto the circumference of the flywheel, and this ring gear serves to start the engine by meshing with the starter motor pinion.
The stamped letter and line which show top dead center of each cylinder are positioned on the flywheel circumference, and by matching these marks with the arrow mark at the hole of the flywheel housing, the rotary position of the crankshaft can be ascertained in order to adjust tappet clearance or fuel injection timing.

8-1 Specifications of flywheel

Engine Model			3JH3(B)(C)E	4JH3(B)(C)E
Outside dia. of flywheel		mm	⌀300	⌀300
Width of flywheel		mm	74	74
Weight of flywheel (including ring gear)		kg	20.4kg	20.4kg
GD^2 value		kg·m²	1.15	1.15
Circumferential speed		m/s	59.7 (at 3800rpm)	59.7 (at 3800rpm)
Speed fluctuation rate		σ	1/128 (at 3800rpm)	1/409 (at 3800rpm)
Allowable amount of unbalance		g·cm	32	32
Fixing part of damper disc	Pitch circle dia. of bolts	mm	170	170
	No. of bolts X bolt dia.		6-M8 thread equally spaced	6-M8 thread equally spaced
Fixing part of crankshaft	Pitch circle dia. of bolts	mm	66	66
	No. of thread holes	mm	6-M10	6-M10
	Fit joint dia.		⌀85.000~85.035	⌀85.000~85.035
Model of reduction and reversing gear			KM3P, KM3A	KM3P, KM3A
Ring gear	Center dia.	mm	322.58	322.58
	No of teeth		127	127

8-2 Dimensions of flywheel and mounting flange

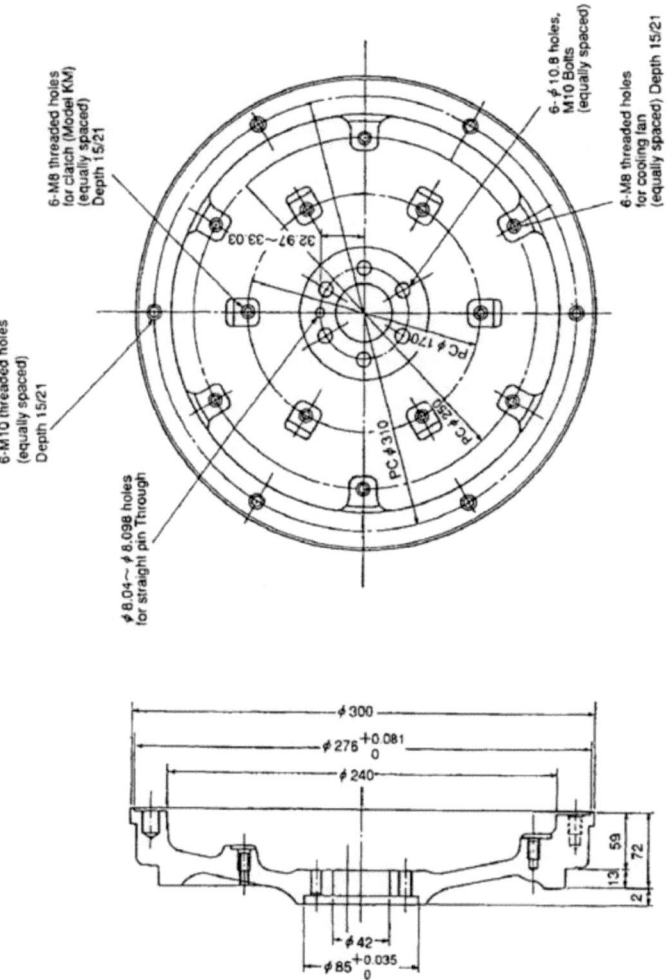

Chapter 2 Basic Engine
8. Flywheel

3,4JH3(B)(C)E

8-3 Ring gear

When replacing the ring gear due to excessive wear or damaged teeth, heat the ring gear evenly at its circumference, and after it has expanded drive it gradually off the flywheel by tapping it with a hammer, a copper bar or something similar around the whole circumference.

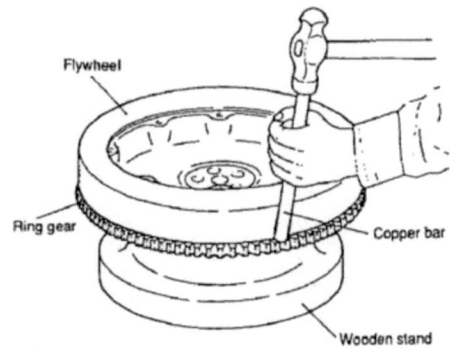

	mm
Interference of ring gear	0.21~0.45

8-4 Position of top dead center and fuel injection timing

(1) Marking

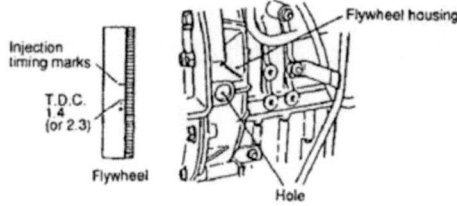

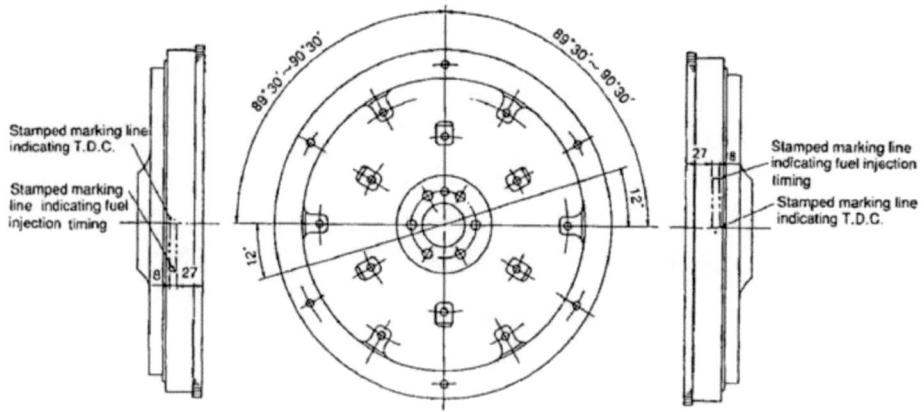

Chapter 2 Basic Engine
8. Flywheel

(2) Matching mark

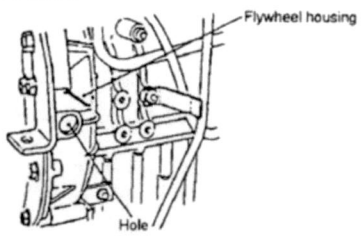
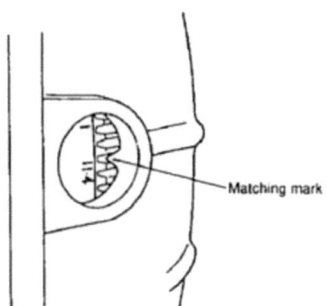

The matching mark is made at the hole of the flywheel housing.

8-5 Damper disc and cooling fan

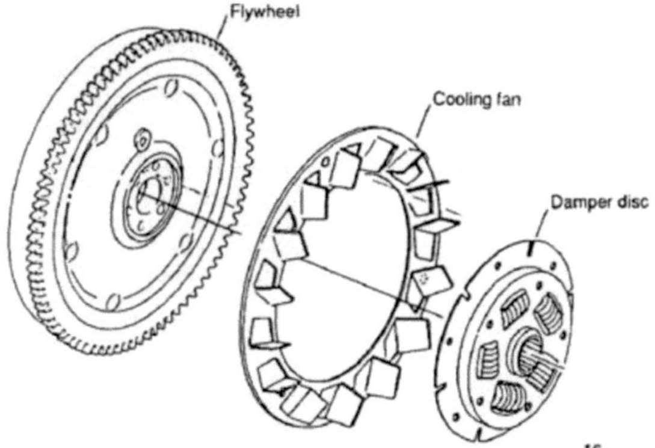

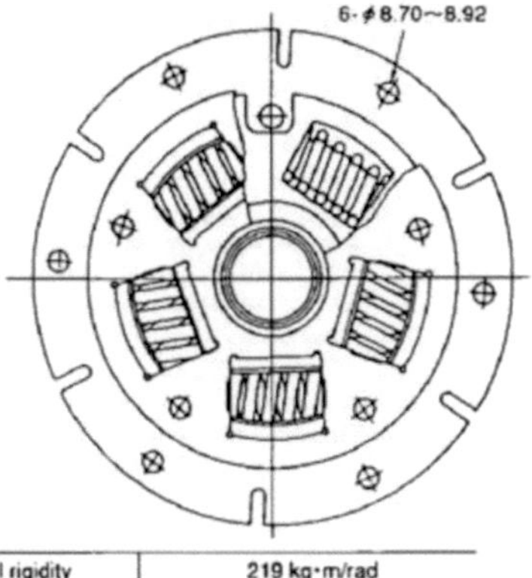

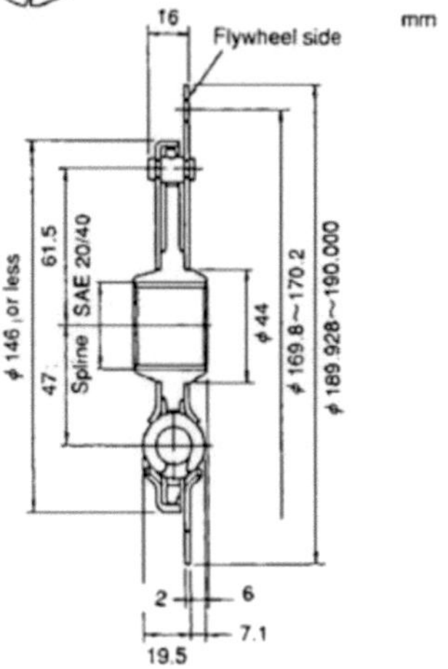

Torsional rigidity	219 kg·m/rad
Max. angle of torsion	7.3×10^{-3} rad
Stopper torque	20.8 kg·m

CHAPTER 3

FUEL INJECTION EQUIPMENT

1. Fuel Injection Pump Service Data ········· 3-1
   - 1-1 3JH3(B)(C)E ········· 3-1
   - 1-2 4JH3(B)(C)E ········· 3-1
2. Governor ········· 3-4
   - 2-1 Cold start knob (For 4JH3(B)(C)E only) ········· 3-4
   - 2-1 Disassembly Reassembly and Inspection of Governor ········· 3-6
   - 2-3 Assembling governor ········· 3-10
3. Disassembly, Reassembly and Inspection of Fuel Injection pump ········· 3-14
   - 3-1 Disassembly of fuel injection pump ········· 3-15
   - 3-2 Inspection of fuel injection pump ········· 3-19
   - 3-3 Reassembly of fuel injection pump ········· 3-20
4. Adjustment of Fuel Injection Pump and Governor ········· 3-24
   - 4-1 Preparations ········· 3-24
   - 4-2 Adjustment of top clearance ········· 4-25
   - 4-3 Adjusting of injection timing ········· 3-26
   - 4-4 Plunger pressure test ········· 3-27
   - 4-5 Delivery valve pressure test ········· 3-27
   - 4-6 Adjusting injection volume (uniformity of each cylinder) ········· 3-27
   - 4-7 Adjustment of governor ········· 3-28
5. Fuel Feed Pump ········· 3-30
   - 5-1 Construction of fuel feed pump ········· 3-30
   - 5-2 Fuel feed pump specifications ········· 3-30
   - 5-3 Disassembly and reassembly of fuel feed pump ········· 3-31
   - 5-4 Plunger pressure test ········· 3-27
6. Fuel Injection Nozzle ········· 3-32
   - 6-2 Functioning of fuel injection nozzle ········· 3-32
   - 6-2 Fuel injection nozzle disassembly ········· 3-33
   - 6-3 Fuel injection nozzle inspection ········· 3-34
   - 6-4 Fuel injection nozzle reassembly ········· 3-34
   - 6-5 Adjusting fuel injection nozzle ········· 3-35
7. Trouble shooting of fuel injection pump ········· 3-36
   - 7-1 Troubleshooting of fuel injection pump ········· 3-36
   - 7-2 Major faults and troubleshooting ········· 3-36
8. Tools ········· 3-39
9. Fuel filter ········· 3-40
   - 9-1 Fuel filter specifications ········· 3-40
   - 9-2 Fuel filter inspection ········· 3-40
10. Fuel Tank ········· 3-41
11. Troubleshooting (Concerning engine fuel injection equipment) ········· 3-42
12. Fuel inspection timing adjustment for EPA / ARB certified engine (3JH3E series) ········· 3-45

1. Fuel Injection Pump Service Data

1-1 3JH3(B)(C)E

Engine model				3JH3(B)(C)E	
Part code (Back No.)				729270-51300(B759)	
Adjustment SPEC				ENG SPEC	SERVICE STD
Item	Fuel valve (Valve pressure)			BJ(220)	(170)
	Nozzle type		ID mark	150P225TCO	DN-12SD12
	Fuel injection pipe		mm	⌀2×360	⌀2×600
Injection Adjustment	Starting	Pump rpm	N_s(rpm)	200	—
		Average injection volume	Q_s(mm³/st)	45±3.5	—
	Rated load	Pump rpm	N_o(rpm)	1900	—
		Injection volume Q_0(mm³/st)	Nonuniformity %	27.5±0.75 ±3	—
	Torque rize	Pump rpm	N_T(rpm)	—	—
		Injection volume Q_T(mm³/st)	Nonuniformity %	—	—
	Hi-idle	Pump rpm	N_H(rpm)	2070$^{+10}_{-0}$	—
		Injection volume	Q_H(mm³/st)	6~7	—
	Idle	Pump rpm	N_i(rpm)	400	—
		Q_i (mm³/st)	Nonuniformity %	9~10 ±10	—
Cam			(mm)	8.0	
Plunger dia.			(mm)	⌀8	
Delivery			(mm)	36 (0.22)	
Pre-stroke			(mm)	3.0	
Top clearance			(mm)	0.5	
Gov spring (K×L)			(mm)	0.431×42	

1-2 4JH3(B)(C)E

Engine model				4JH3(B)(C)E, 4JH3CE1	
Part code (Back No.)				729670-51300(B760)	
Adjustment SPEC				ENG SPEC	SERVICE STD
Item	Fuel valve (Valve pressure)			BJ(220)	(170)
	Nozzle type		ID mark	150P225TCO	DN-12SD12
	Fuel injection pipe		mm	⌀2×400	⌀2×600
Injection Adjustment	Starting	Pump rpm	N_s(rpm)	200	—
		Average injection volume	Q_s(mm³/st)	55~60	—
	Rated load	Pump rpm	N_o(rpm)	1900	—
		Injection volume Q_0(mm³/st)	Nonuniformity %	29±0.75 ±3	—
	Torque rize	Pump rpm	N_T(rpm)	—	—
		Injection volume Q_T(mm³/st)	Nonuniformity %	—	—
	Hi-idle	Pump rpm	N_H(rpm)	2070$^{+10}_{-0}$	—
		Injection volume	Q_H(mm³/st)	6~7	—
	Idle	Pump rpm	N_i(rpm)	400(325)	—
		Q_i(mm³/st)	Nonuniformity %	9~10 ±10	—
Cam			(mm)	8.0	
Plunger dia.			(mm)	⌀8	
Delivery			(mm)	36 (0.22)	
Pre-stroke			(mm)	3.0	
Top clearance			(mm)	0.5	
Gov spring (K×L)			(mm)	0.431×42	

Chapter 3 Fuel Injection Equipment
1. Fuel Injection Pump Service Data

● 3JH3(B)(C)E

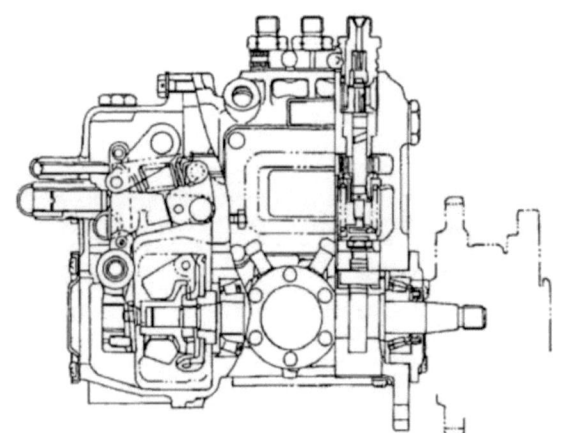

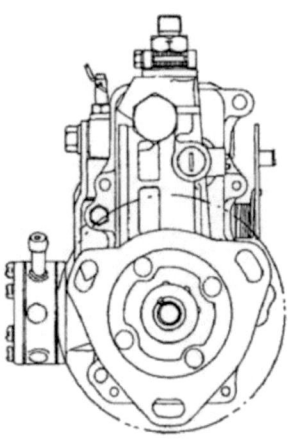

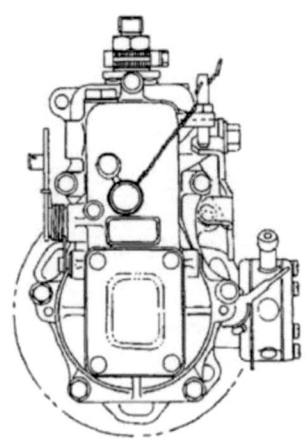

Chapter 3 Fuel Injection Equipment
1. Fuel Injection Pump Service Data

● 4JH3(B)(C)E

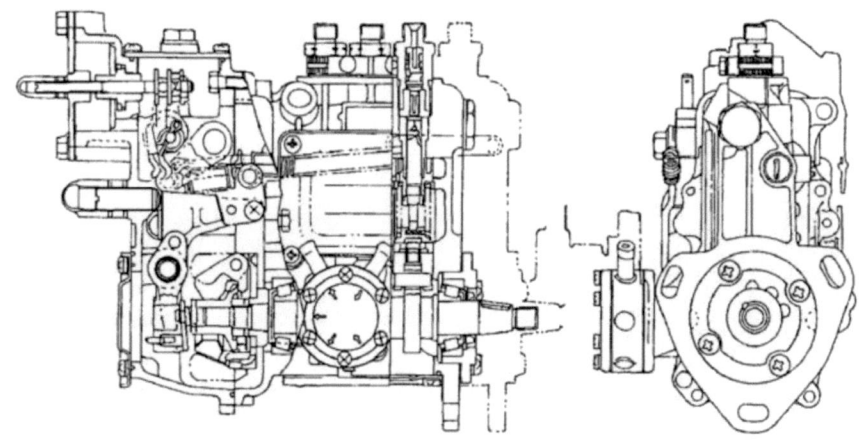

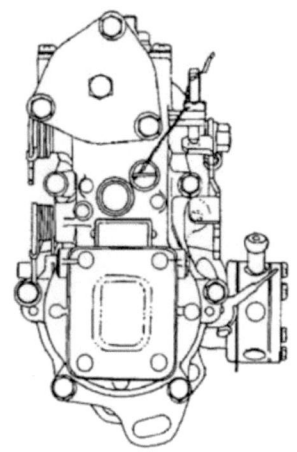

2. Governor

2-1 Cold start knob (For 4JH3(B)(C)E only)

(1) When the engine is difficult to start due to low temperatures, pull out the Cold start knob to facilitate the starting operation.

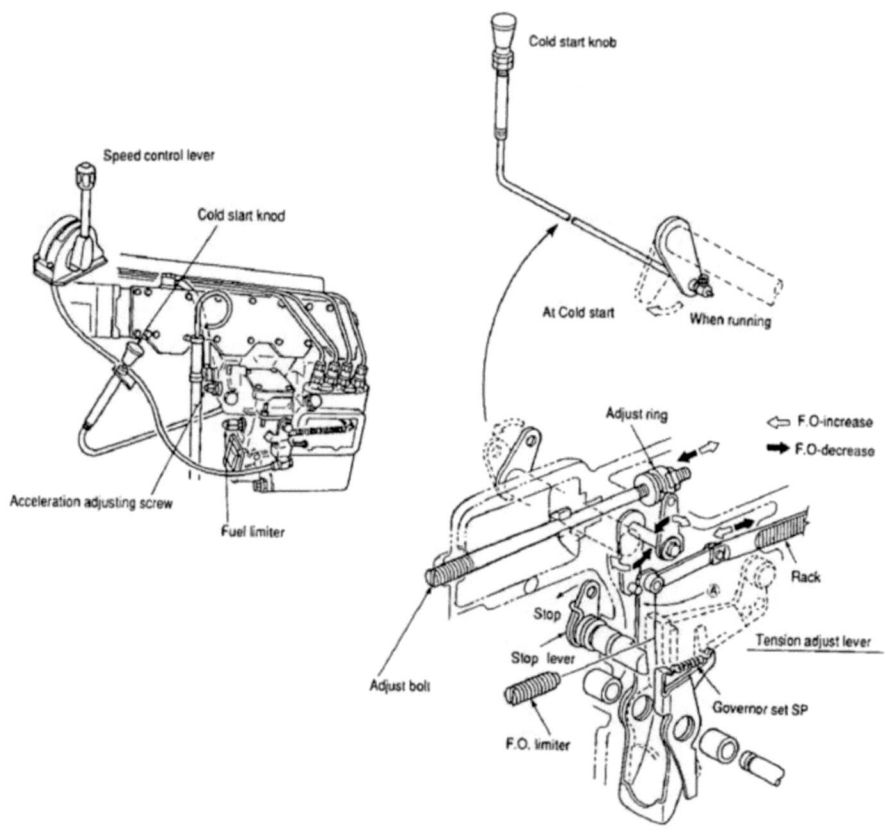

Chapter 3 Fuel Injection Equipment
2. Governor

(3) Operation of cancel knob
1. Since this device is the device that limits the fuel injection amount for starting the engine in cold temperatures (below −5℃), it is necessary to increase the fuel injection amount.
2. If the engine is hard to start in cold temperatures, start the engine by pulling the cold start knob.
3. Once the engine is started, push the knob back into resume the function of the boost compensator.

(4) Adjustment of cold start knob
The initial rack of this device has been adjusted properly at the time of shipment. However, the acceleration can be increased at the request of the customer. Watch the color of the exhaust while making the adjustment.

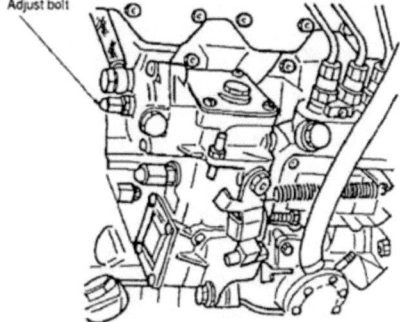

Adjust bolt

(Procedure)
Remove the cap nut of adjust bolt, loosen the lock nut and adjust the bolt with the blade-type screw driver.

Right turn	Large effect	• Higher acceleration • More black exhaust
Left turn	Small effect	• Lower acceleration • Less black exhaust

Chapter 3 Fuel Injection Equipment
2. Governor

2-2. Disassembly Reassembly and Inspection of Governor

This illustration shows the fuel injection pump for model 4JH3(B)(C)E. Model 3JH3(B)(C)E differs only in the number of cylinders. However, only the fuel injection pump for model 4JH(B)(C)E has a boost compensator.

2-2-1 Governor disassembly
(1) Remove the governor case.

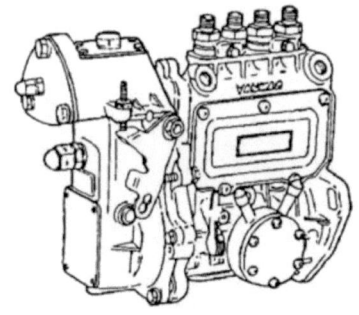

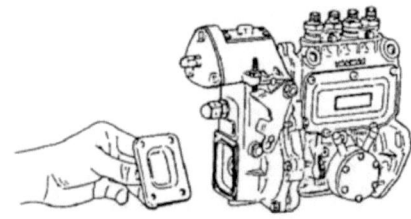

NOTE: Loosen the hex bolt on models with an angleich spring.

(2) Remove the control lever hex nut, and pull out the control lever from the control lever shaft.

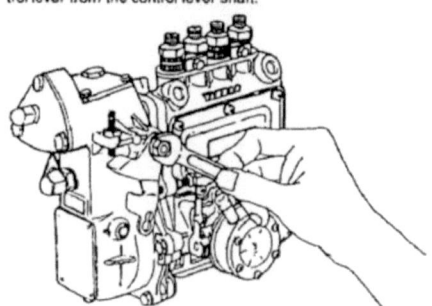

(3) Remove the governor case bolt. Remove the governor case (parallel pin) from the fuel pump until while lightly tapping the governor case with a wooden hammer. Create a gap between the governor case and fuel pump by moving parts of the governor lever.

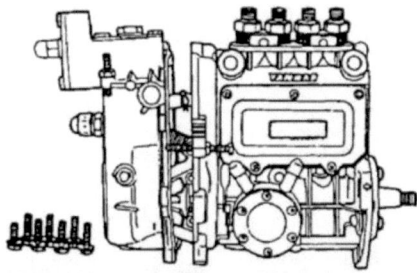

(4) Pull out the governor link snap pin by inserting needle nosed pliers between the fuel pump and governor case.

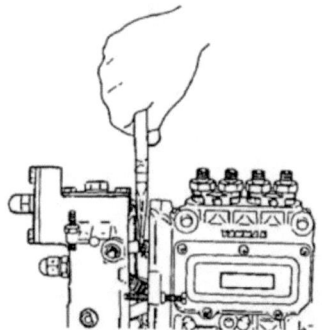

(5) The governor and fuel pump come apart by sliding the governor case and fuel pump apart and pulling out the link pin of the fuel control rack.

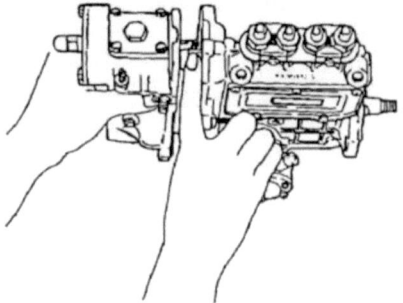

Chapter 3 Fuel Injection Equipment
2. Governor

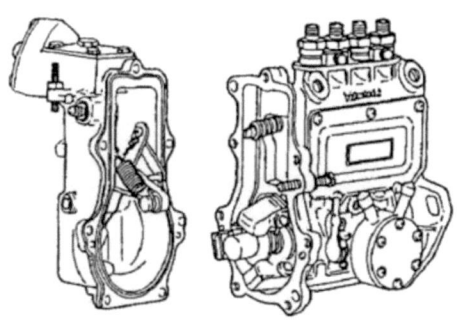

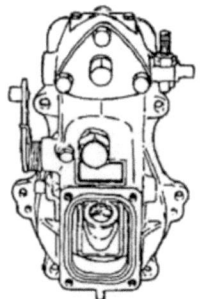

(8) Remove the snap-rings on both ends of the governor lever shaft.

(6) Remove the stop lever return spring from the governor lever shaft.

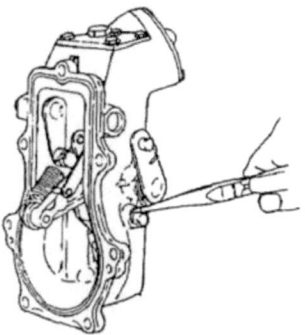

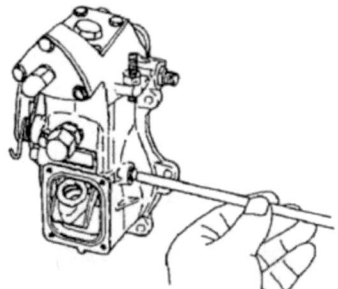

(9) Put a rod 8 mm in dia. or less in one end of the governor lever shaft, and tap the governor shaft until the O-ring comes out the other side of the governor case.

(7) Use needle nose pliers to unhook the governor spring from the tension lever and control lever shaft.

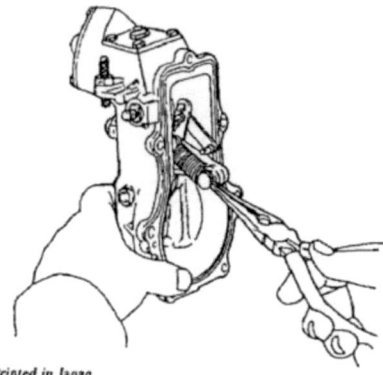

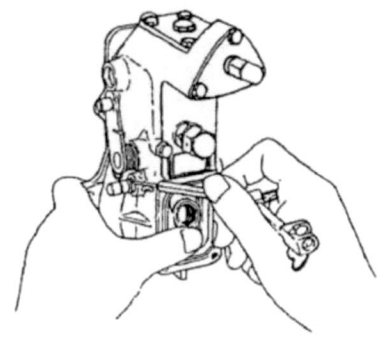

(10) After removing the O-ring, lightly tap the end of the shaft that you removed the O-ring from, and remove the governor lever shaft. Then remove the governor shaft assembly and washer.

Chapter 3 Fuel Injection Equipment
2. Governor
_3,4JH3(B)(C)E_

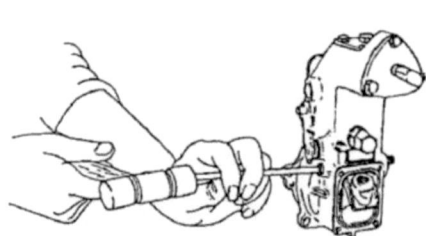

NOTE : The governor assembly consists of the governor lever, tension bar, bushing, throttle spring and shifter, and is normally not disassembled.
The spring pin is removed when you replace the shifter or throttle spring.

(12) When you need to pull out the stop lever, remove the stop lever shaft stop pin, and lightly tap the inside of the governor case.

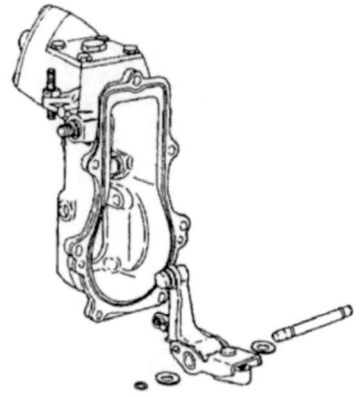

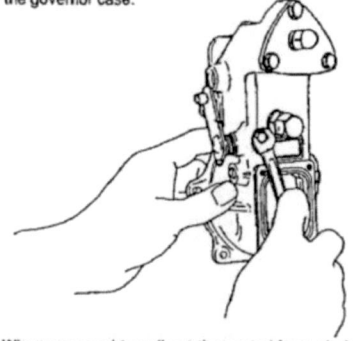

(11) Remove the governor link from the governor lever.

(13) When you need to pull out the control lever shaft, tap the end of the shaft with a wood hammer.

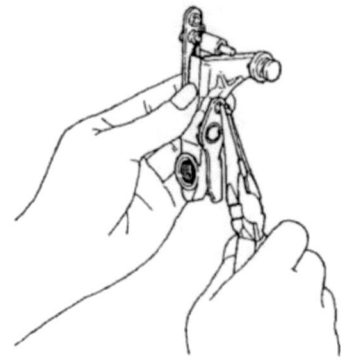

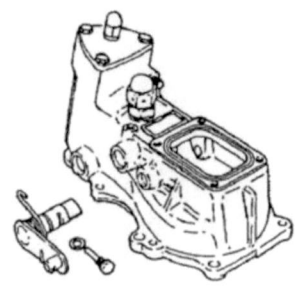

NOTE : 1. Do not remove the fuel limit nut from the governor case unless necessary.

Chapter 3 Fuel Injection Equipment
2. Governor
3,4JH3(B)(C)E

(14) Pull out the governor sleeve on the end of the fuel camshaft by hand.

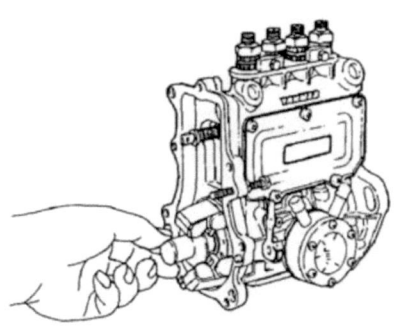

(15) Turn the governor weight with a box spanner two or three times to loosen it, stopping it with the hole in the fuel coupling ring or holding the coupling with a vise.

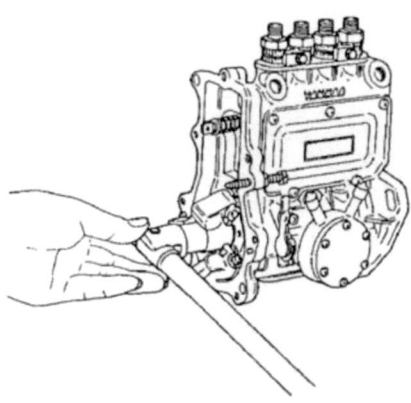

(16) Remove the governor weight assembly from the fuel pump cam using the governor weight pulling tools.

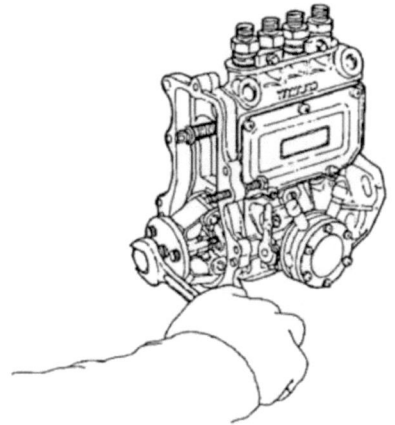

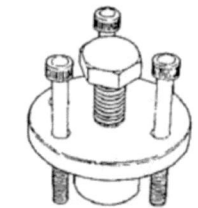

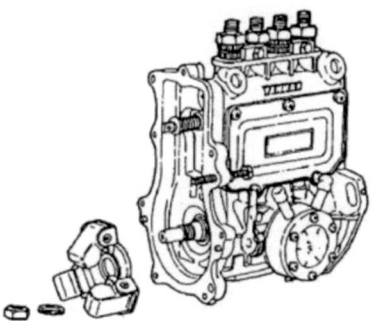

NOTE : When the taper fit comes apart after you have removed the nut, the governor weight may fly out - Be Careful.

NOTE : The governor weight assembly is made up of the governor weight, support and pin. Do not disassemble.

Chapter 3 Fuel Injection Equipment
2. Governor

2-2-2 Inspection of governor

Inspection of governor weight assembly
(1) Replace the governor weight if it does not open and close smoothly.

(2) Replace the governor weight if the contact surface with governor sleeve is extremely worn.
(3) Replace if there is governor weight support/pin wear or the caulking is loose.
(4) Replace if the governor weight support stopper is excessively worn.

Inspection of governor sleeve

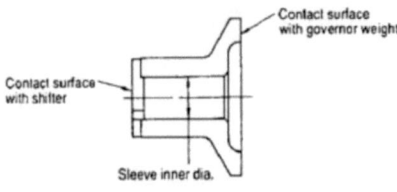

(1) Replace the governor sleeve if the contact surface with governor weight is worn or there is pitching.
(2) Replace the governor sleeve if the contact surface with shifter is considerably worn or there is pitching.
(3) If the governor sleeve does not move smoothly above the cam shaft due to governor sleeve inner dia. wear or other reasons, replace.

Inspection of governor shaft assembly
(1) Measure the clearance between the governor shaft and bushing, and replace if it exceeds the limit.

mm

Standard Clearance	Limit
0.065~0.124	0.5

(2) Inspect the shifter contact surface, and replace the shifter (always by removing the pin to disassemble) if it is worn or scorched.
(3) Disassemble and replace throttle springs that are settled, broken or corroded by pulling the spring pin.
(4) Check link parts for bends or kinks that will cause malfunctioning, and replace any parts as necessary.

NOTE : 1. Side gap on top of governor lever shaft.

mm

Standard side gap	0.4

2. Replace the governor lever, tension bar, bushing, shifter and throttle spring as an assembly.

(5) Inspection of springs
1) Check the governor spring and other springs and replace if they are broken, settled or corroded.
2) Measure the free length of the governor spring, and replace if it exceeds the limit.
   See service data sheet for free length of governor spring.

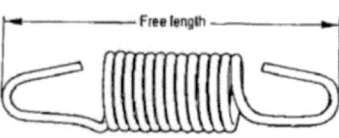

Governor spring spec. table

Spring constant	kg/mm	0.32
Free length	mm	12

2-3 Assembling governor

Inspect all parts after disassembly and replace any parts as necessary. Before starting reassembly, clean new parts and parts to be reused, and put them in order.
Make sure to readjust the unit after reassembly to obtain the specified performance.

(1) Insert the governor weight assembly in the taper portion at the end of the fuel pump camshaft, stopping it with the hole in the fuel coupling ring or holding the coupling with a vise, mount the rest, and tighten the governor weight nut.

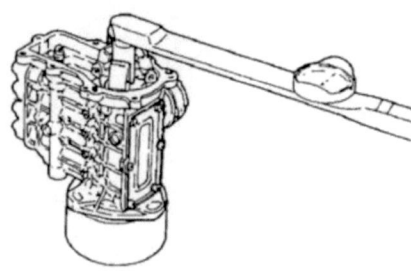

kg-m

Governor weight nut tightening torque	4.5~5.0

Chapter 3 Fuel Injection Equipment
2. Governor
3,4JH3(B)(C)E

(2) Open the governor (weight to the outside, and insert the sleeve in the end of the fuel pump camshaft.

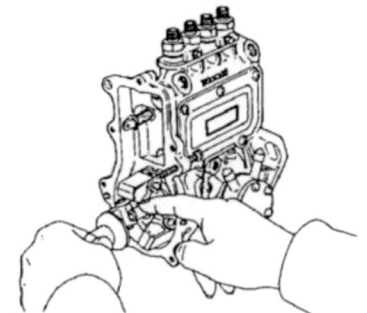

NOTE : Make sure that the sleeve moves smoothly after inserting it.

(3) When the stop lever has been disassembled, mount the stop lever return spring on the stop lever, tap the stop lever lightly with a wooden hammer to insert it, and tighten the stop lever stop pin.

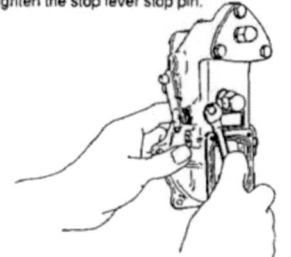

(4) When the control lever shaft has been removed, lightly tap the control lever shaft and washer from inside the governor case, using an appropriate plate.
(5) If the governor has been disassembled, tap in the spring pin.

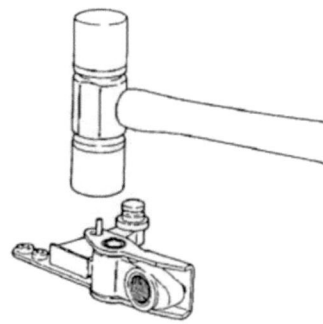

(6) Mount the governor lever assembly to the governor link.

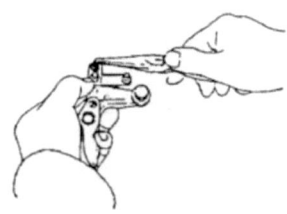

NOTE : 1. Make sure that the correct governor link mounting holes are used, and that it is mounted in the correct direction.
2. Make sure that the governor link moves smoothly.

(7) Put the governor lever shaft assembly in the governor case, insert the governor lever shaft, and tap it in until the O-ring groove comes out the opposite side of the governor case.

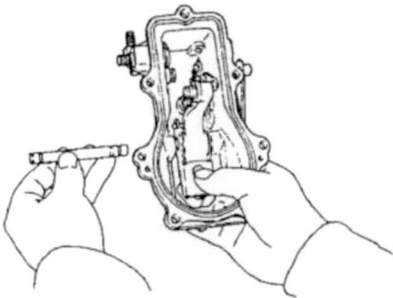

NOTE : 1. Fit the O-ring to the side you have tapped in.

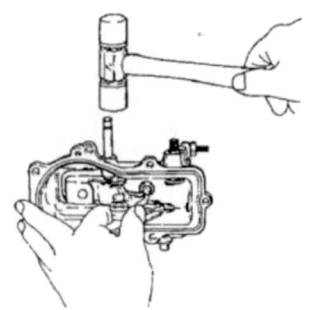

2. Be sore to insert the governor lever shaft in the correct direction.

Chapter 3 Fuel Injection Equipment
2. Governor
3.4JH3(B)(C)E

3. Don't forget to mount the washers to both sides of the governor lever.

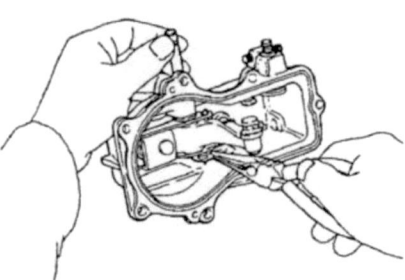

(8) After you have mounted the O-ring, tape the governor lever in the opposite direction, and mount the E-shaped stop rings on the grooves at both ends.

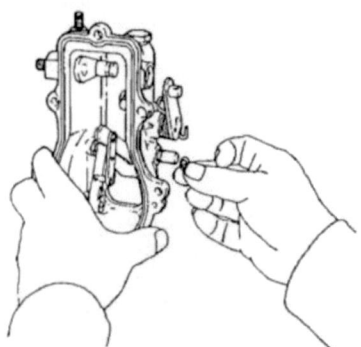

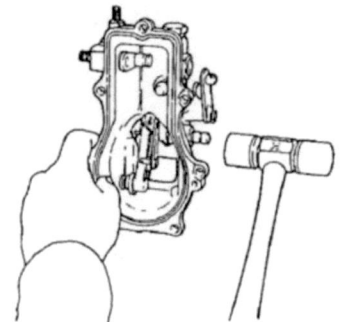

NOTE : After mounting the governor lever assembly, make sure the governor lever assembly moves smoothly.

(9) Fit the stop lever return spring to the end of the governor lever shaft.

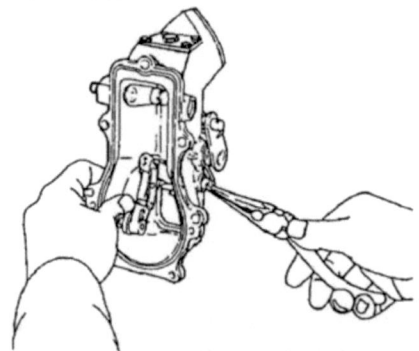

(10) Hook the governor spring on the control lever shaft and tension lever hook with radio pliers.

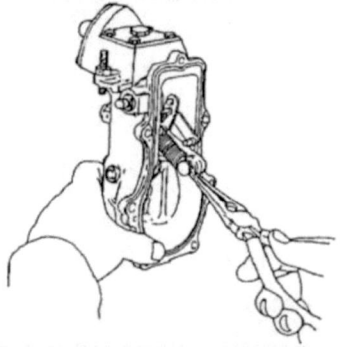

(11) Pull the governor link as far as possible towards the governor case mounting surface, insert the governor link pin in the fuel control rack pin hole and fit the snap pin on it.

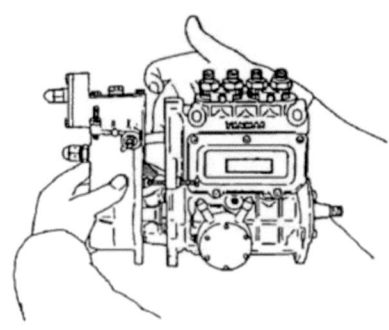

Chapter 3 Fuel Injection Equipment
2. Governor

(12) Mount the governor case to the fuel pump unit while lightly tapping it with a wooden hammer, and tighten the bolts.
(13) Place the adjusting spring and adjusting rod on the governor case cover adjusting bolt, and mount the governor case cover.

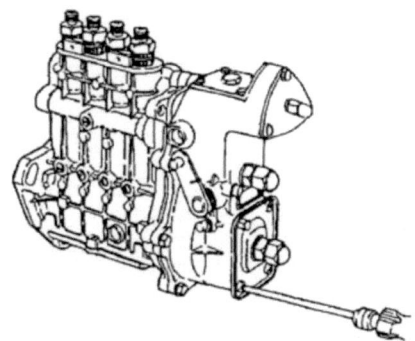

(14) Insert the control lever in the control lever shaft, and tighten the nut.

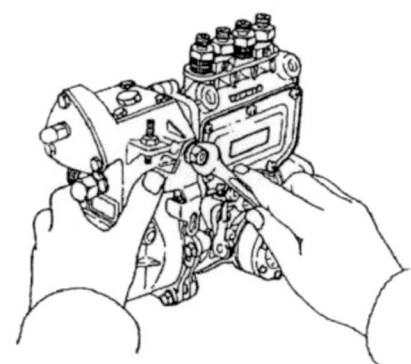

NOTE : Move the control lever back and forth to make sure that the entire link moves smoothly.

3. Disassembly, Reassembly and Inspection of Fuel Injection Pump

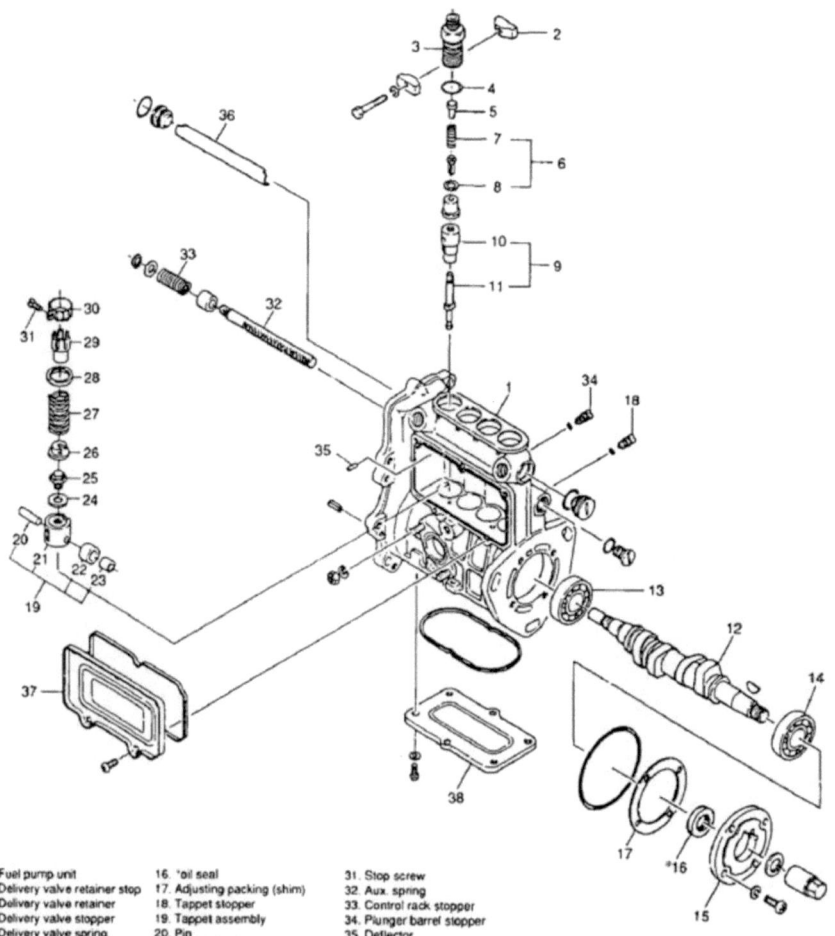

1. Fuel pump unit
2. Delivery valve retainer stop
3. Delivery valve retainer
4. Delivery valve stopper
5. Delivery valve spring
6. Delivery valve assembly
7. Delivery valve
8. Delivery valve seat
9. Plunger assembly
10. Plunger barrel
11. Plunger
12. Fuel pump camshaft
13. Bearing
14. Bearing
15. Bearing holder
16. *oil seal
17. Adjusting packing (shim)
18. Tappet stopper
19. Tappet assembly
20. Pin
21. Roller guide
22. Roller (outer)
23. Roller (inner)
24. Adjusting shim
25. Adjusting bolt
26. Plunger spring rest B
27. Plunger spring
28. Plunger spring rest A
29. Control sleeve (reduction ring)
30. Control pinion B
31. Stop screw
32. Aux. spring
33. Control rack stopper
34. Plunger barrel stopper
35. Deflector
36. Pump side cover
37. Pump bottom cover

NOTE : 1. Some models are equipped with ball bearings and some with taper roller bearings.

2. *Oil seal : Some models are equipped with oil seals and some are not. The shape of the bearing holder differs for models with and without oil seals.

Chapter 3 Fuel Injection Equipment
3. Disassembly, Reassembly and Inspection of Fuel Injection Pump

3.4JH3(B)(C)E

3-1 Disassembly of fuel injection pump

When disassembling the fuel pump, separate the parts for each cylinder and be careful not to get them mixed up. Be especially careful to keep the plunger/plunger barrel, delivery valve/delivery valve seat and other assemblies separate for each cylinder (the parts of each assembly must be kept with that assembly and put back in the same cylinder).

Preparation
1. Wash off the dirt and grease on the outside of the pump with cleaning oil (kerosene or diesel oil) before disassembly.
2. Perform work in a clean area.
3. Take off the fuel pump bottom cover and remove lubricant oil.
4. Turn the fuel pump upside down to drain fuel oil.

(2) Remove the fuel feed pump.

NOTE : Do not disassemble the fuel feed pump. See instructions for fuel feed pump for details.

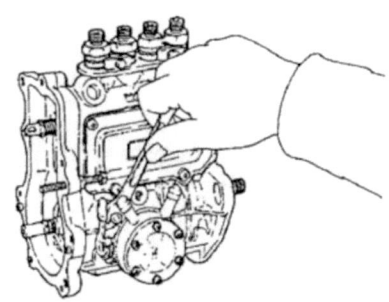

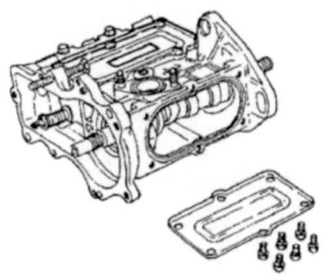

(1) Loosen the nut with a box spanner and take it off, holding it with the hole in the fuel coupling ring or holding the coupling with a vise and take out the governor weight assembly.

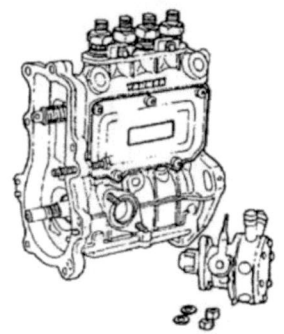

(3) Remove the fuel pump side cover.

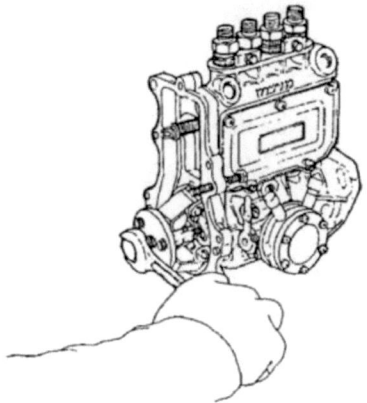

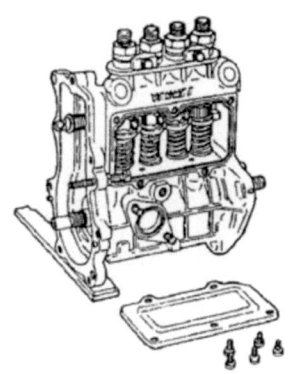

Chapter 3 Fuel Injection Equipment
3. Disassembly, Reassembly and Inspection of Fuel Injection Pump

3.4JH3(B)(C)E

(4) Turn the camshaft until the roller guide is at the maximum head, and insert the plunger spring support plate in between the plunger spring washer B (lower side) and fuel pump unit.

(7) Turn the fuel pump upside down, move all the roller guides to the plunger side, and then put the pump on its side. Turn the camshaft to a position so that none of the cylinder cams hit the tappets.

(8) Put a plate against the governor end side of the camshaft and lightly tap it, and pull out the camshaft and drive side bearing.

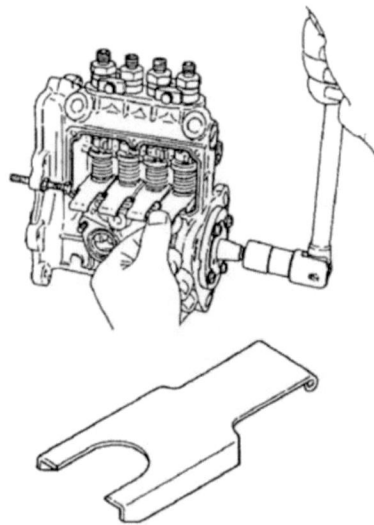

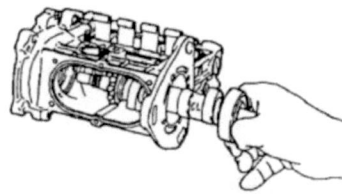

(9) Remove the roller guide stop.

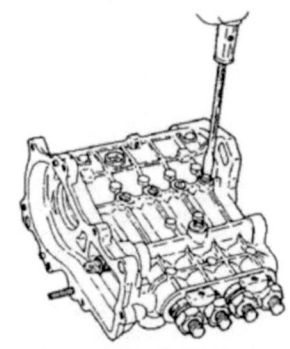

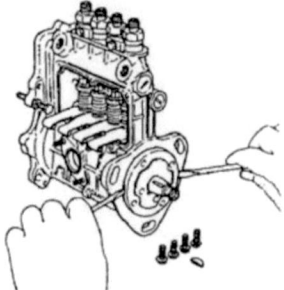

Plunger spring supportplate

NOTE : If the camshaft does not turn, put double nuts on the end of the cam shaft or remove the coupling.
(5) Remove the camshaft wood ruff key.
(6) Put a screwdriver in the two grooves on the camshaft bearing holder mounting surface, and pull out the camshaft bearing holder.

(10) Use a hammer handle or the like to push up the roller guide from the bottom of the pump, and remove the plunger spring support plate.

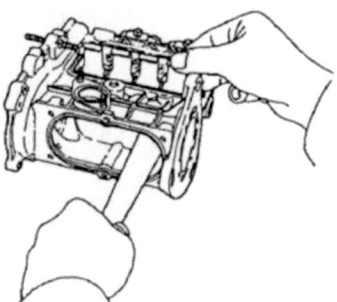

NOTE : 1. Be sure not to damage the oil seal with the threaded part of the camshaft.
2. Be careful not to loosen the shims in between the pump and bearing holder.

NOTE : The plunger spring may make the roller guide and plunger, etc. fly out when the plunger support plate is removed.

Chapter 3 Fuel Injection Equipment
3. Disassembly, Reassembly and Inspection of Fuel Injection Pump

3,4JH3(B)(C)E

(11) Remove the roller guide.

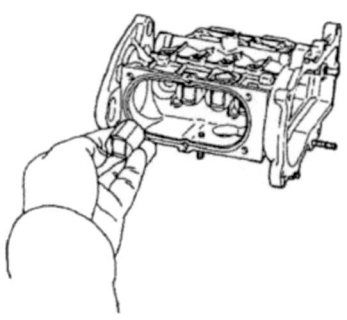

NOTE : When you stand the fuel pump up, all of the roller guides drop out at one time. Therefore, first remove the stop bolt for one cylinder at a time, and then the roller guide for each cylinder—continue this process.

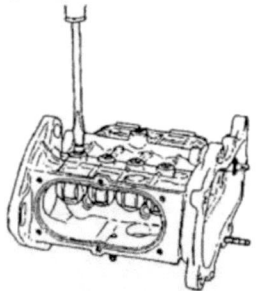

(12) Remove the plunger, plunger spring and lower washer from the lower part of the pump.

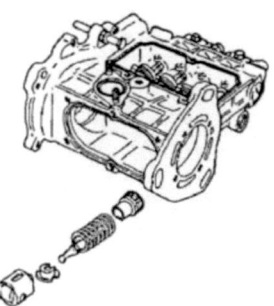

NOTE : Keep the parts separate for each cylinder.

(13) Loosen the small screw on control pinion.

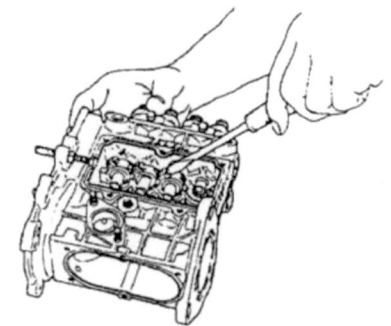

NOTE : 1. Check to make sure the match marks on the pinion/sleeve are correct before loosening the small screw on the control pinion, as the pinion and sleeve come apart when- the screw is loosened. If the mark is hard to read or off center, lightly inscribe a new mark. This will serve as a guide when adjusting injecuon volume later.

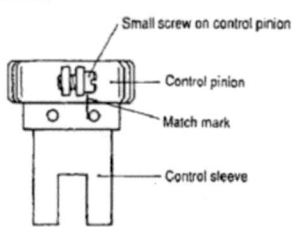

- Small screw on control pinion
- Control pinion
- Match mark
- Control sleeve

2. Keep parts separate for each cylinder.

(14) Remove the control pinion, sleeve and upper rest.

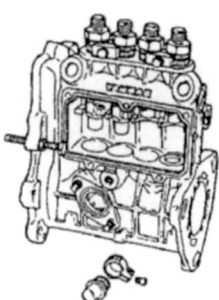

NOTE : Keep parts separate for each cylinder.

Chapter 3 Fuel Injection Equipment
3. Disassembly, Reassembly and Inspection of Fuel Injection Pump
3.4JH3(B)(C)E

(15) Remove the control rack stop bolt and remove the rack.

(17) Remove the delivery valve holder.

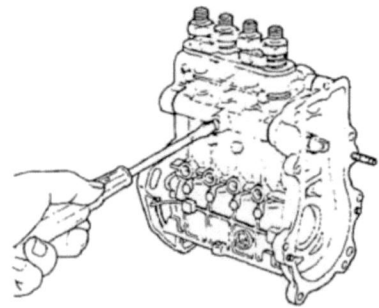

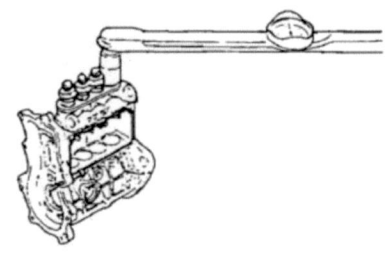

(18) Remove the delivery valve assembly.

NOTE: Be careful not to lose the spring or rest on the control rack.

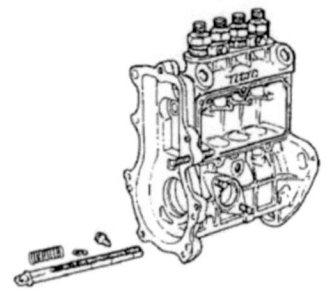

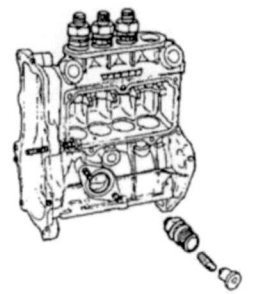

NOTE: 1. Be careful not to lose the delivery valve packing, delivery valve spring, delivery valve stopper or other small parts.
Keep the delivery valve assemblies for each cylinder clearly separated.

(16) Loosen the delivery valve retainer stop bolt, and remove the delivery valve holder stop.

(19) Take the plunger barrel out from the top of pump.

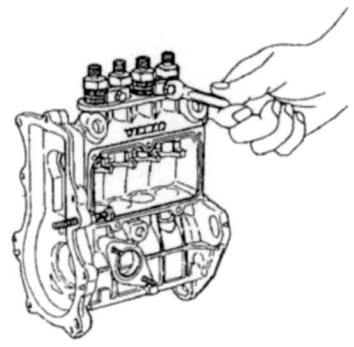

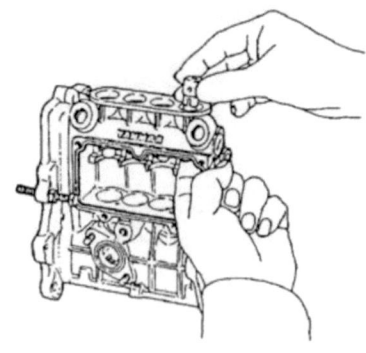

NOTE: Keep it as a set with the plunger that was removed earlier.

Chapter 3 Fuel Injection Equipment
3. Disassembly, Reassembly and Inspection of Fuel Injection Pump

3-2 Inspection of fuel injection pump

(1) Inspection of plunger
1) Thoroughly wash the plungers, and replace plungers that have scratches on the plunger lead or are discolored.
2) The plunger is in good condition if it slides down smoothly when it is tilted about 60°. Repeat this several times while turning the plunger. Repair or replace if it slides down too quickly or if it stops part way.

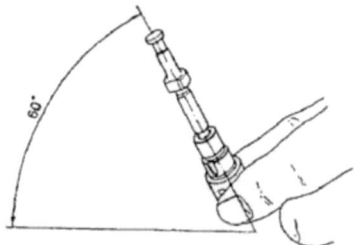

(2) Inspection of delivery valve

1) Replace as a set if the delivery valve suck-back collar or seat are scratched, scored, scuffed, worn, etc.
2) The valve is in good condition if it returns when released after being pushed it down with your finger (while the holes in the bottom of the delivery guide seat are covered). Replace if necessary.
3) Likewise, the valve should completely close by its own weight when you take your finger off the holes in the bottom of the delivery guide sheet.

NOTE : When fitting new parts, wash with diesel oil and perform the above inspection.

(3) Inspection of pump
1) Inspect for extreme wear of roller guide sliding surface. Scratches on the roller pin sliding surface are not a problem.
2) Inspect the plunger barrel seat.
If there are burn or discoloration, repair or replace as this will lead to dilution of the lubricant.

(4) Inspection of fuel camshaft and bearings
1) Fuel camshaft
Inspect for scratches or wear of camshaft, deformation of key grooves and deformation of screws on both ends, and replace if necessary.
2) Bearings
Replace if the taper rollers or outer race surface is flaked or worn.

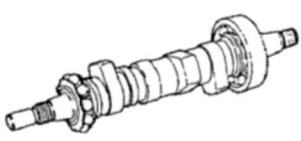

NOTE : Replace fuel camshafts and bearings together.

(5) Inspection of roller guide assembly
1) Roller

Replace if the surface is worn or flaked.
2) Roller Guide
Replace if the outer roller pin hole is extensively worn or there are many scratches.
3) Replace if the play of the roller guide assembly pin/roller is 0.2 mm or more.
4) Injection timing adjustment bolt
Replace if the surface in contact with the plunger side is unevenly or excessively worn.

(6) Inspection of rack and pinion
1) Rack

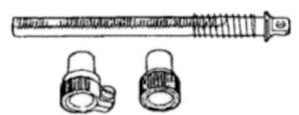

Inspect for bending of rack and wear or deformation of fit with pinion.
2) Pinion
Inspect for wear or deformation of fit with rack.

NOTE : If the tooth surface or sliding surface is not in good working order, rack resistance increases, affecting the condition of the engine (rough rpm, over running, etc.).

(7) Inspection of plunger spring and delivery spring
Inspect springs for scratches, cracks, breakage, uneven wear and rust.

Chapter 3 Fuel Injection Equipment
3. Disassembly, Reassembly and Inspection of Fuel Injection Pump — 3.4JH3(B)(C)E

(8) Inspection of oil seals
   Inspect oil seals to see if they are burred or scratched.
(9) Inspection of roller guide stop
   Inspect the side of the tip, replace if excessively worn.
(10) Inspection of O-rings
   Inspect and replace if they are burred or cracked.

3-3 Reassembly of fuel injection pump

Preparation
After inspection, put all parts in order and clean.
See Inspection of Fuel Pump for inspection procedure.

(1) Put in the plunger barrel from the top of pump.

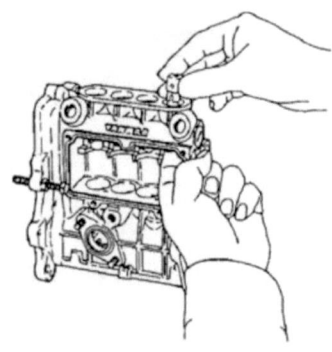

NOTE : Make sure the barrel key groove is fitted properly to the barrel stop pin.

(2) Place the delivery valve assembly, packing, spring and stopper from the top of the pump, in that order.

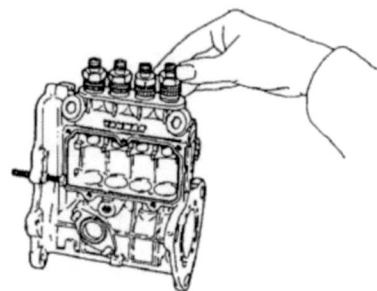

NOTE : Replace the delivery valve packing and O-ring.

(3) Place the control rack, and tighten the control rack stop bolt.

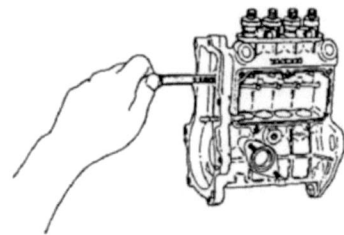

NOTE : 1. Do not forget the lack aux. spring.
       2. Make sure the rack moves smoothly through a full cycle.

(4) Place the rack set screw (using the special tool) in the rack stop bolt screw hole to fix the rack.
(5) Looking from the bottom of pump, align the match marks on the rack and pinion.

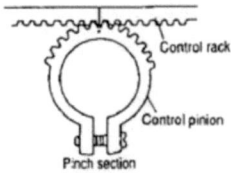

(6) While holding the pinion with one hand and keeping it aligned with the match mark, fit in the sleeve, and lightly tighten the small pinion screw.

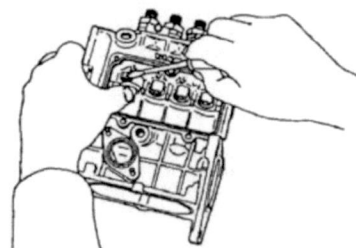

NOTE : Fitting of sleeve; Face towards small pinion screws and align with match mark.

Chapter 3 Fuel Injection Equipment
3. Disassembly, Reassembly and Inspection of Fuel Injection Pump
3.4JH3(B)(C)E

(7) Mount the plunger spring upper rest.

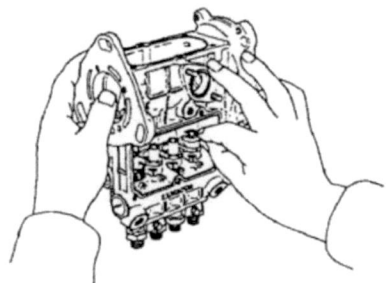

NOTE : 1. Be sure to mount the upper rest with the hollow side facing down.
2. Recheck to make sure that the lack moves easily.

(8) Mount the plunger spring.
(9) Mount the lower rest on the head of the plunger, and fit the plunger in the lower part of pump while aligning the match marks on the plunger flange and the sleeve.

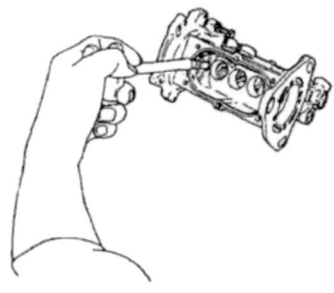

Plunger inserting tool

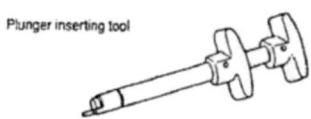

NOTE : If the plunger is mounted in the opposite direction, the injection volume will increase abnormally and cannot be adjusted.

(10) Insert the plunger spring support plate between the plunger spring seat B (lower) and fuel pump, by putting the handle of a hammer in the lower part of pump and pushing the roller guide up.

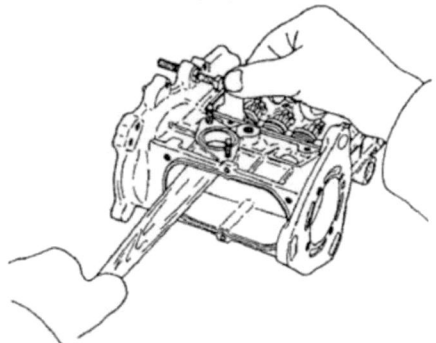

NOTE : 1. Face the roller guide stop groove upwards, and align it with the stop screw hole on the pump.

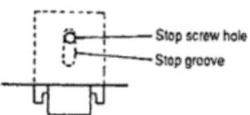

2. Check the movement of the rack. The plunger spring may be out of place if the movement is heavy — insert a acrewdriver and bring it to the correct position.
3. When replacing the roller guide assembly, fit shims and lightly tighten:

Standard shim thickness	1.2mm

(11) Make sure that the roller guide stop groove is in the correct position, and tighten the roller guide stop bolt.

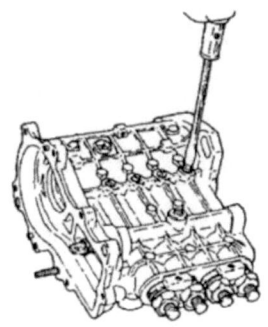

Chapter 3 Fuel Injection Equipment
3. Disassembly, Reassembly and Inspection of Fuel Injection Pump   3.4JH3(B)(C)E

(12) Fit the bearings to both ends of the camshaft and insert from the drive side by tapping lightly.

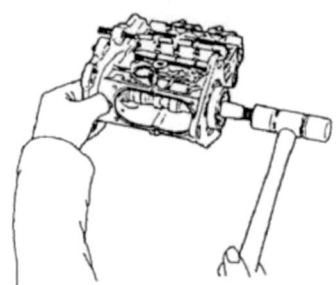

NOTE : Turn the pump upside down, and tap in the camshaft while moving the roller guide to the plunger spring side.

(13) Fit the oil seal on the inside of the bearing retainer and mount the bearing retainer.

(15) Mount the fuel pump side cover.
(16) Tap in the camshaft wood ruff key.
(17) Turn the camshaft, and pull out the plunger spring support plate.

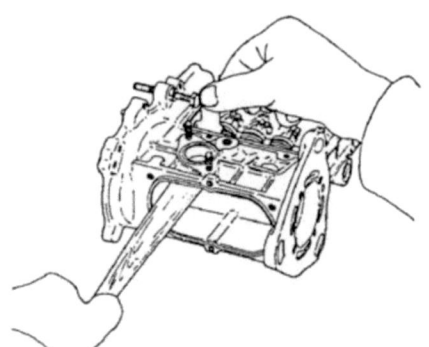

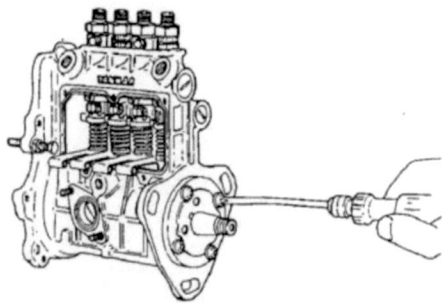

NOTE : Coat the camshaft and oil seal with oil to prevent the oil seal from being scratched.

(14) Fix the pump, lightly tap both ends of the cam shaft with a wooden hammer, and adjust the cam shaft side clearance with the adjustment shims while checking with a side clearance gauge.
mm

Camshaft side clearance	0.02~0.05

Adjusting
Pull out the adjusting shims if the clearance is too small, and add adjusting shims if it is too large.
mm

Adjusting shim thickness	0.50
	0.40
	0.30
	0.15

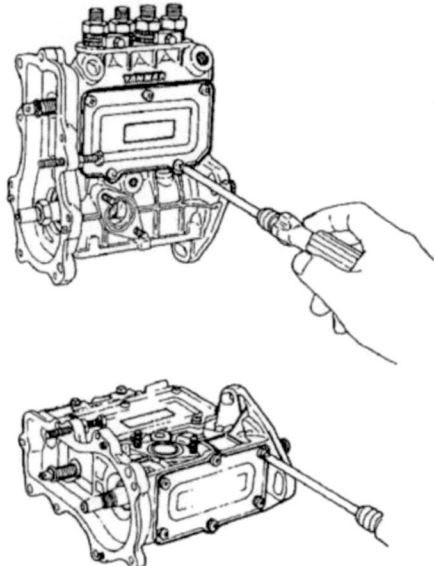

NOTE : Fit double nuts to turn the camshaft.

Chapter 3 Fuel Injection Equipment
3. Disassembly, Reassembly and Inspection of Fuel Injection Pump

(18) Tighten the delivery valve retainer.

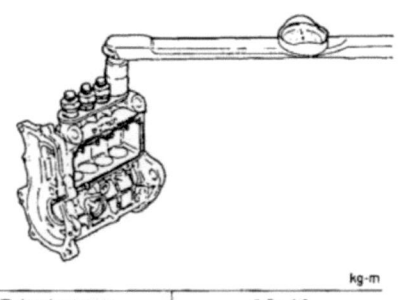

	kg-m
Tightening torque	3.5~4.0

NOTE : 1. Tighten the retainer as far as possible by hand- if the bolt gets hard to turn part way, the packing or delivery valve are out of place. Remove, correct, and start tightening again.
2. Overtightening can result in malfunctioning of the rack.

(19) Fit the delivery retainer stop and tighten the stop bolt.

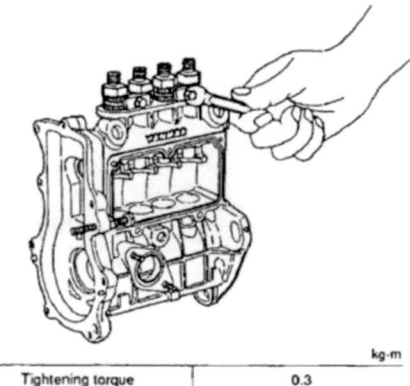

	kg-m
Tightening torque	0.3

NOTE : Overtightening can upset the delivery retainer and cause oil leakage.

(20) Mount the fuel feed pump

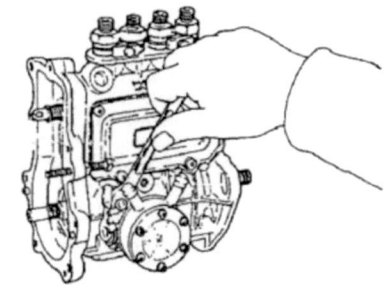

NOTE : Refer to the instructions for reassembly of the fuel feed pump.

4. Adjustment of Fuel Injection Pump and Governor

This illustration shows the fuel injection pump for model 4JH3(B)(C)E. Model 3JH3(B)(C)E differs only in the number of cylinders.

Adjust the fuel injection pump after you have completed reassembly. The pump itself must be readjusted with a special pump tester when you have replaced major parts such as the plunger assembly, roller guide assembly, fuel camshaft, etc. Procure a pump tester like the one illustrated below.

4-1 Preparations

Prepare for adjustment of the fuel injection pump as follows:
(1) Adjusting nozzle assembly and inspection of injection starting pressure

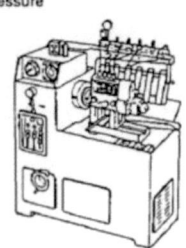

	kg/cm²
Adjusting nozzle type	DN-12SD12
Injection starting pressure	215~225

(2) Adjusting injection pipe.

Inner dia./outer dia. × length	2.0/6.0 × 600
Minimum bending radius	25 (0.9842)

(3) Mount the fuel injection pump on the pump tester platform.

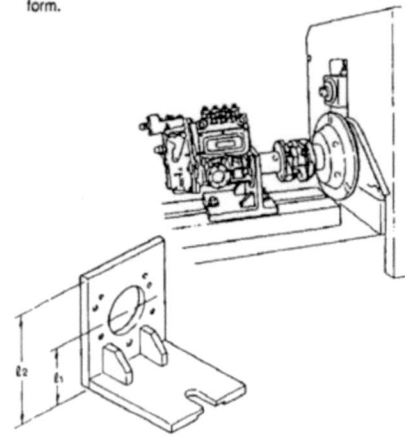

		mm
Tester used	ℓ_1	ℓ_2
Yanmar	110	150
Robert Bosch	125	165

(4) Remove the control rack blind cover and fit the rack indicator.
Next, turn the pinion from the side of the pump until the control rack is at the maximum dive side position, and set it to the rack indicator scale standard position.
Then make sure that the control rack and rack indicator slide smoothly.

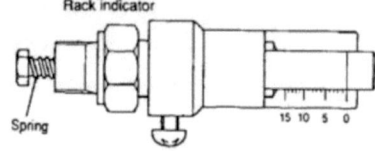

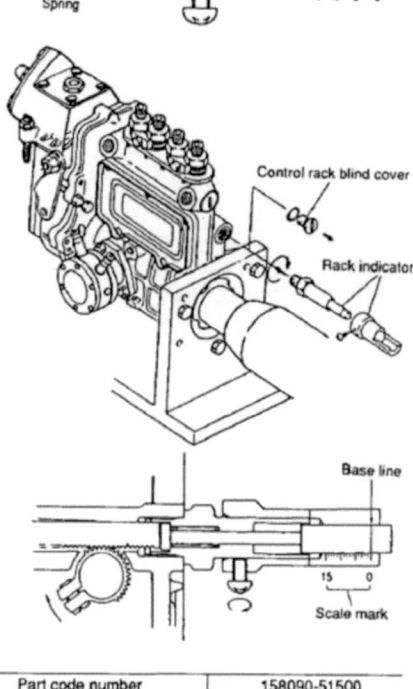

Part code number	158090-51500

Chapter 3 Fuel Injection Equipment
4. Adjustment of Fuel Injection Pump and Governor

3,4JH3(B)(C)E

(5) Check control rack stroke
Make sure the rack position is at 11.5~12.5mm (0.4527~0.4921in.) on the indicator scale when the governor control lever is set at the maximum operating position.
If it is not at this valve, change the link connecting the governor and control rack to adjust it.

NOTE : Links are availabe in 1mm (0.0394in.) increments.

(6) Remove the plug in the oil fill hole on the top of the governor case, and fill the pump with about 200cc of pump oil or engine oil.

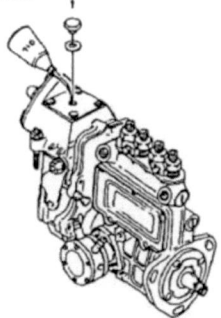

(7) Complete fuel oil piping and operate the pump tester to purge the line of air.
(8) Set the pressure of oil fed from the pump tester to the injection pump at 0.2~0.3kg/cm².

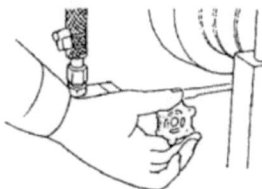

4-2 Adjustment of top clearance

Adjust the top clearance (the clearance between the top of plunger and the top of barrel with the cam at top dead center) of each cylinder plunger to bring it to the specified value by changing the thickness of the shims.

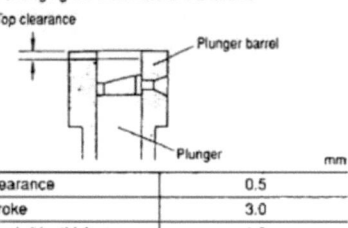

	mm
Top clearance	0.5
Pre-stroke	3.0
Standard shim thickness	1.2

Relation between top clearance, standard shim thickness and pre-stroke.

mm

Adjusting shim thickness	1.0
	1.2
	1.3
	1.4
	1.5
	1.6
Part Code No.	129155-51600

(1) Place the top clearance gauge on a level surface and set the gauge to zero.

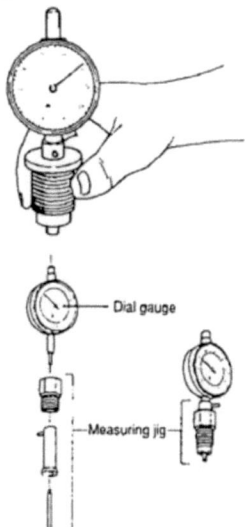

(2) Remove the injection pump delivery retainer, take out the delivery valve assembly, insert the top clearance gauge and tighten by hand.

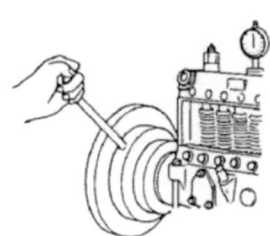

(3) Turn the camshaft, and bring the cam to the top dead center while watching the gauge needle.

Chapter 3 Fuel Injection Equipment
4. Adjustment of Fuel Injection Pump and Governor
_3.4JH3(B)(C)E_

(4) Read the gauge at this position, and adjust until the clearance is at the specified value by changing adjusting shims.
Tighten the adjusting screw after completing adjustment.

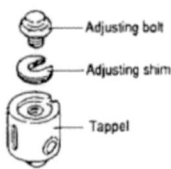

(Greater shim thickness decreases top clearance and smaller shim thickness increases top clearance).

NOTE : Adjust while watching gauge, and then tighten.

(5) After adjustment is completed, insert the delivery valve assembly and tighten the delivery retainer.

	kg-m
Delivery retainer tightening torque	3.5~4.0

Repeat the above procedure to adjust the top clearance of each cylinder.

4-3 Adjusting of injection timing

After adjusting the top clearance for all cylinders, check/adjust the injection timing.

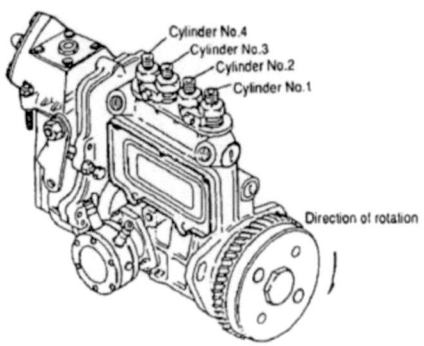

(1) Set the governor control lever to the operating position and fix (bring plunger to the effective injection range), turn the camshaft clockwise, and check the injection starting time (FID) of cylinder No.1 (start of discharge of fuel from the delivery retainer).

Cylinder no.	Count from the drive side
Direction of rotation	Right boking from drive side

(2) In the above state, set the tester needle to a position easy to read on the flywheel scale, and check the injection timing several times by reading the flywheel scale, according to the injection order.

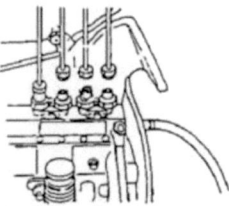

Engine model	3JH3(B)(C)E	4JH3(B)(C)E
Injection order	1-2-3-1	1-3-4-2-1
Injection timing	120°	90°
Allowable deviation	±30°	

(3) Readjust the top clearance of cylinders that are not within the allowable deviation (increasing adjusting shim thickness makes injection timing faster, and decreasing makes it slower).
The change in injection timing effected by adjusting shims is as follows :

Change in shim thickness	Change in injection timing	
	Cam angle	Crank angle
0.1mm	0.5°	1.0°

(4) When you have readjusted top clearance, make sure it is within allowable values after completing letin adjustment.

	mm
Allowable top clearance	0.3

NOTE : 1. All cylinders must be readjusted if any one shows less than the allowable value.
2. If the top clearance is less than the allowable value, the plunger will hit the delivery valve or the plunger flange will hit the plunger barrel.

Chapter 3 Fuel Injection Equipment
4. Adjustment of Fuel Injection Pump and Governor

4-4 Plunger pressure test

(1) Mount the pressure gauge to the delivery retainer of the cylinder to be tested.

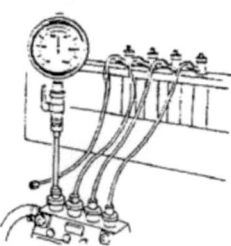

Max. pressure gauge reading	1000 kg/cm²
Connecting screw dimensions	M12×1.5

(2) Set the governor control lever to the stop position, operate the injection pump at about 200 rpm, and make sure that the pressure gauge reading is 500 kg/cm² (7110 lb/in.²) or more while lightly moving the control pinion gear towards full throttle (drive side) from the pump.
Replace the plunger if the pressure does not reach this value.

(3) Immediately release the gear after the pressure rises to stop injection.
At the same time, check to see that oil is not leaking from the delivery retainer or fuel injection piping, and that there is no extreme drop in pressure.

4-5 Delivery valve pressure test

(1) Perform the plunger pressure test in the same way, bringing the pressure to about 120kg/cm² (1706 lb/in.²), and then stopping injection.

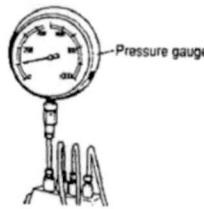
Pressure gauge

(2) After pressure rises to the above value, measure the time it takes to drop from 100~90 kg/cm³.

100→90 kg/cm²	5 seconds

If the pressure drops faster than this, wash the delivery valve, and retest. Replace the delivery valve if the pressure continues to drop rapidly.

4-6 Adjusting injection volume (uniformity of each cylinder)

The injection volume is determined by the fuel injection pump rpm and rack position. Check and adjust to bring to specified value.

4-6.1 Measuring injection volume

(1) Preparation
Set the pump rpm, rack position and measuring stroke to the specified value and measure:

Engine model	3JH3(B)(C)E	4JH3(B)(C)E
Pump RPM	1900 rpm	
Pump rotating direction	Right looking from drive side	
Rack indicator scale reading	7 mm	8 mm

Remove the rack stop bolt behind the pump and screw in the rack fixing bolt to fix the rack.

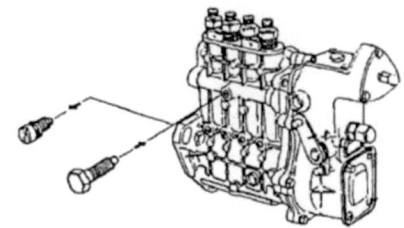

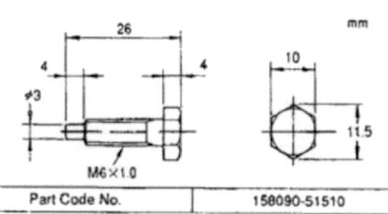

Part Code No.	158090-51510

(2) Measuring injection volume
Measure the injection volume at the standard stroke, and adjust as follows if it is not within the specified value.

Measuring stroke	1,000 st
Specified injection volume at standard rack position	See injection pump service data
Nonuniformity of cylinders	±3%

4-6.2 Adjustment of injection volume

Measure the injection volume in measuring cylinders for each cylinder, and adjust if necessary to obtain the specified values.

(1) Push the control rack all the way to the driveside, stop with the rack fixing bolt, and loosen the pinion/sleeve fixing bolt 1/3 of a revolution.

Chapter 3 Fuel Injection Equipment
4. Adjustment of Fuel Injection Pump and Governor

3,4JH3(B)(C)E

(2) When the control sleeve is turned to the right or left, the plunger is turned through the same angle to increase or decrease injection volume.
The injection volume is increased when the control sleeve is turned in the → direction and decreased when turned in the ← direction in the following figure.

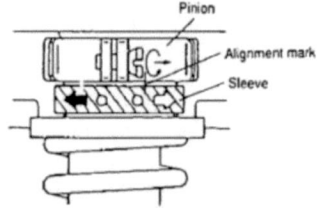

(3) Measure the injection volume of each cylinder again. Repeat this process until the injection volume for every cylinder is the same (within the specified limit).
(4) Next, measure the injection volumes under different conditions, and make sure the injection volume for every cylinder is within the specifications.
Replace the plunger if the injection volume is not within specifications.

NOTE: See adjustment data for the specified injection volume value at other measuring points.

(5) After completing measurement, firmly tighten the piston/sleeve fixing screw.
(6) If not aligned with the match mark, make a new match mark.

4-7 Adjustment of governor
4-7.1 Adjusting fuel limit bolt

(1) Adjust the tightness of the fuel limit bolt to bring the rack position to the specified value (R_1) with the governor control lever all the way down towards the fuel increase position, while keeping the pump at rated rpm N_1.

[For 3JH3(B)(C)E]

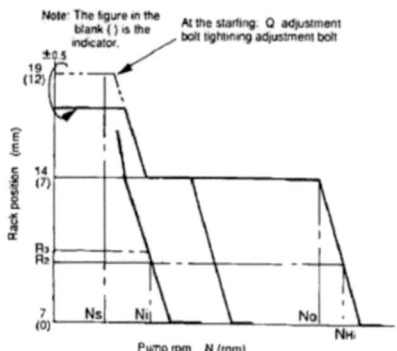

[For 4JH3(B)(C)E]

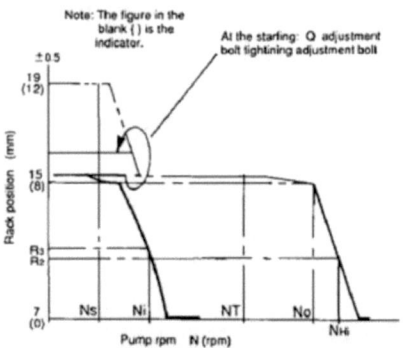

(2) Measure fuel injection volume at rack position (R_i). Tightening of fuel limit bolt.
(3) If the injection volume is at the specified value, tighten the fuel limit bolt lock nut at that position.

4-7.2 Adjusting RPM limit bolt

(1) Gradually loosen the governor control lever while keeping the pump drive condition in the same condition as when the fuel limit bolt was adjusted, and adjust the tightness of the RPM limit bolt to the point where the rack position just exceeds the specified value (R_i).

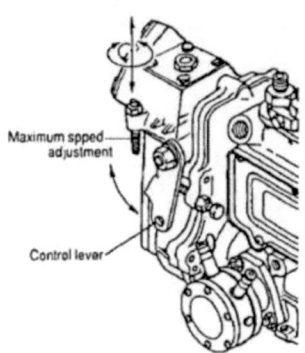

(2) Check maximum RPM at no load
Further increase rpm, and make sure that rack position ($R_2 = R_1 - L$) corresponding to maximum rpm at no load is within specified value (NHi).

4-7.3 Adjusting idling

(1) Maintain the pump rpm at specified rpm (Ni).

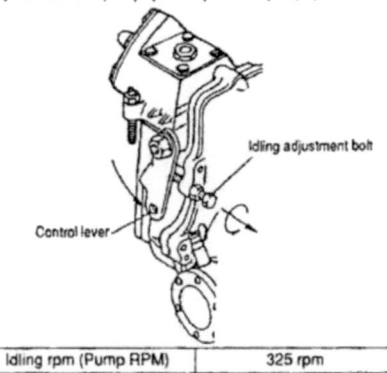

Idling rpm (Pump RPM)	325 rpm

(2) Measure the injection volume while lowering the governor control lever to the idling position, and adjust the position of the control lever with the idling adjustment bolt to bring it to the specified value.

Measuring stroke	1000 st
Idling injecion volume	See injection pump service data

4-7.4 Check injection volume when starting

(1) Make sure the control rack moves smoothly while gradually reducing idling rpm.
(2) Next, fix the governor control lever at the full load position with the pump at the specified rpm (R_4). Make sure that control rack is at the maximum rack position (11.05~12.05).
Measure the injection volume and check to make sure it is within the specified value.

Pump rpm (N_1)	200 rpm
Rack indicator scale	11.5~12.5 mm
Measuring stroke	1000 st
Injection volume	See injection pump service data

Checking injection stop
Drive the pump at rated rpm (N_1) and standard rack position (R_1) with the governor control lever at the full load position, operate the stop lever on the back of the governor case, and make sure that injection to all cylinders is stopped.

NOTE : Be sure to remove the rack fixing bolt when doing this.

5. Fuel Feed Pump

The fuel feed pump pumps fuel from the fuel tank, passes it through the fuel filter element, and supplies it to the fuel injection pump.

The fuel feed pump is mounted on the side of this engine and is driven by the (eccentric) cam of the fuel pump camshaft. It is provided with a manual priming lever so that fuel can be supplied when the engine is stopped.

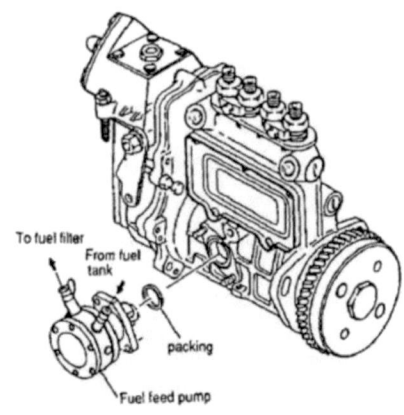

5-1 Construction of fuel feed pump

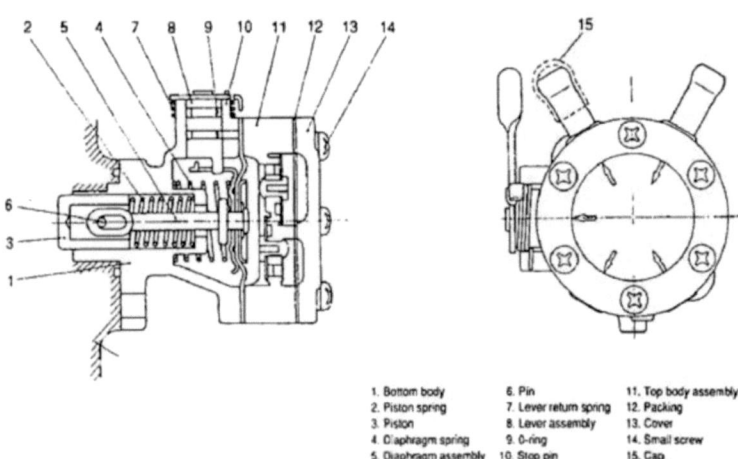

1. Bottom body
2. Piston spring
3. Piston
4. Diaphragm spring
5. Diaphragm assembly
6. Pin
7. Lever return spring
8. Lever assembly
9. O-ring
10. Stop pin
11. Top body assembly
12. Packing
13. Cover
14. Small screw
15. Cap

5-2 Fuel feed pump specifications

Head	1m
Discharge volume	230 cc/min at 1500 cam rpm, discharge pressure of 0.2 kg/cm^2
Closed off pressure	0.3 kg/cm^2 or more (at 400 cam rpm)

5-3 Disassembly and reassembly of fuel feed pump

5-3.1 Disassembly
(1) Remove the fuel feed pump mounting nut, and take the fuel feed pump off the fuel injection pump.
(2) Clean the fuel feed pump assembly with fuel oil.
(3) After checking the orientation of the arrow on the cover, make match marks on the upper body and cover, remove the small screw, and disassemble the cover, upper body and lower body.

5-3.2 Reassembly
(1) Clean all parts with fuel oil, inspect, and replace any defective parts.
(2) Replace any packings on parts that have been disassembled.
(3) Make sure that the intake valve and discharge valve on upper body are mounted in the proper direction, and that you don't forget the valve packing.
(4) Assemble the diaphragm into the body, making sure the diaphragm mounting holes are lined up (do not force).
(5) Align the match marks on the upper body of the pump and cover, and tighten the small screws evenly.

	kg·cm
Tightening torque	15~25

(4) Valve contact/mounting
Clean the valve seat and valve with air to remove any foreign matter.

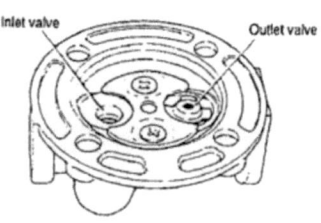

(5) Inspect the diaphragm spring and piston spring for settling and the piston for wear, and replace as necessary.

NOTE : Replace parts as an assembly.

5-4 Fuel feed pump inspection
(1) Place the fuel feed pump in kerosene, cover the discharge port with your finger, move the priming lever and check for air bubbles (Repair or replace any part which emits air bubbles).

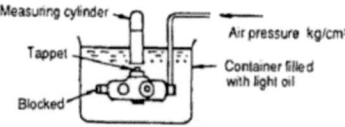

(2) Attach a vinyl hose to the fuel feed pump intake, keep the pump at the specified depth from the fuel oil surface, move the priming lever by hand and check for sudden spurts of fuel oil from the discharge port. If oil is not spurted out, inspect the diaphragm and diaphragm spring and repair/replace as necessary.
(3) Diaphragm inspection
Parts of the diaphragm that are repeatedly burned will become thinner or deteriorate over a long period of time. Check the diaphragm and replace if necessary.

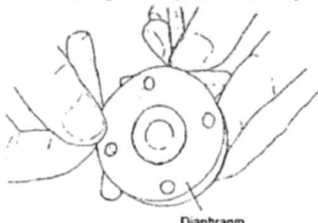

Diaphragm

6. Fuel Injection Nozzle

When fuel oil pumped by the fuel injection pump reaches the injection nozzle, it pushes up the nozzle valve (held down by spring), and is injected into the combustion chamber at high pressure

The fuel is atomized by the nozzle to mix uniformly with the air in the combustion chamber. How well the fuel is mixed with high temperature air directly affects combustion efficiency, engine performance and fuel economy. Accordingly, the fuel injection nozzles must be kept in top condition to maintain performance and operating efficiency.

6-1 Functioning of fuel injection nozzle

Fuel from the fuel injection pump passes through the oil port in the nozzle holder, and enters the nozzle body reservoir

When oil reaches the specified pressure, it pushes up the nozzle valve (held by the nozzle spring), and is injected through the small hole on the tip of the nozzle body.

The nozzle valve is automatically pushed down by the nozzle spring and closed after fuel is injected.

Oil that leaks from between the nozzle valve and nozzle body goes from the hole on top of the nozzle spring through the oil leakage fitting and back into the fuel tank.

Adjustment of injection starting pressure is effected with the adjusting shims

(1) Hole type fuel injection nozzle

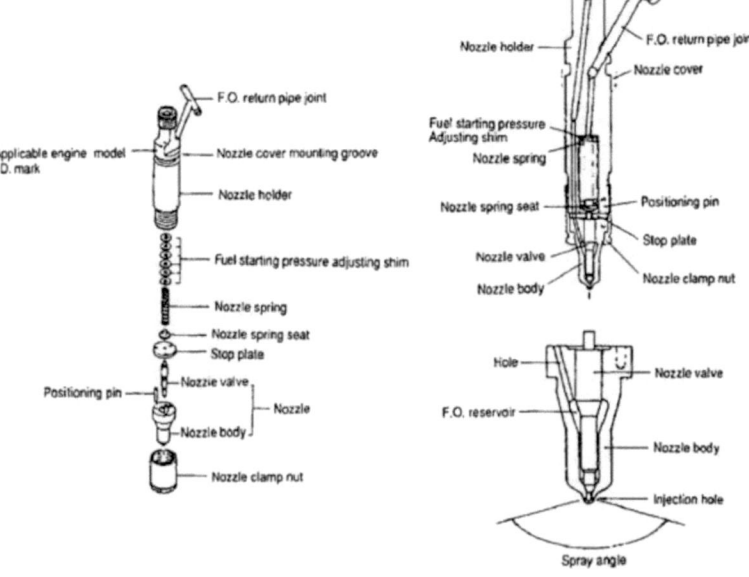

Nozzle I.D. Mark	155P225TCO
Spray angle	150°
No. of injection hole × dia	5 × 0.22mm
Nozzle opening pressure	215~225kg/cm²

Chapter 3 Fuel Injection Equipment
6. Fuel Injection Nozzle _____ 3,4JH3(B)(C)E

Nozzle body identification number
The type of nozzle can be determined from the number inscribed on the outside of the nozzle body.
1) Hole type fuel injection nozzles
Sample

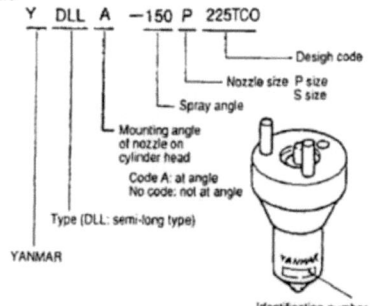

Y DLL A −150 P 225TCO
- Design code
- Nozzle size P size / S size
- Spray angle
- Mounting angle of nozzle on cylinder head
  Code A: at angle
  No code: not at angle
- Type (DLL: semi-long type)
YANMAR

Identification number

6-2 Fuel injection nozzle disassembly

NOTE : 1. Disassemble fuel injection nozzle in a clean area as for the fuel injection pump.
2. When disassembling more than one fuel injection nozzle, keep the parts for each injection nozzle separate for each cylinder (i.e. the nozzle for cylinder 1 must be remounted in cylinder 1).

(1) When removing the injection nozzle from the cylinder head, remove the high pressure fuel pipe, fuel leakage pipe, etc., the injection nozzle retainer nut, and then the fuel injection nozzle.

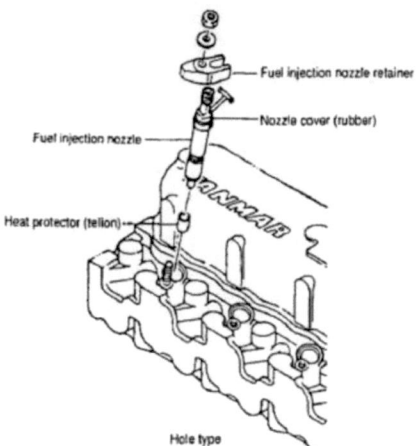

Fuel injection nozzle retainer
Nozzle cover (rubber)
Fuel injection nozzle
Heat protector (tellion)
Hole type

(2) Put the nozzle in a vise
NOTE : Use the special nozzle holder for the hole type injection nozzle so that the high pressure mounting threads are not damaged.

(3) Remo.ve the nozzle nut

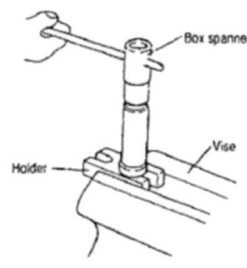

Box spanner
Vise
Holder

NOTE : Use a special box spanner for the hole type (the thickness of the two nozzle nuts is 15mm).

(4) Remove the inner parts
NOTE : Be careful not to loosen the spring seat, adjusting shims or other small parts.

6-3 Fuel injection nozzle inspection
6.3.1 Washing
(1) Be sure to use new diesel oil to wash the fuel injection nozzle parts
(2) Wash the nozzle in clean diesel oil with the nozzle cleaning kit.

Nozzle cleaning kit

1) Zexel nozzle cleaning kit:
   Type NP-8486B No.5789-001
2) Anzen Jidosha Co., Ltd. nozzle cleaning kit:
   Type NCK-001

(3) Clean off the carbon on the outside of the nozzle body with a brass brush.

Chapter 3 Fuel Injection Equipment
6. Fuel Injection Nozzle

3,4JH3(B)(C)E

(4) Clean the nozzle seat with cleaning spray.

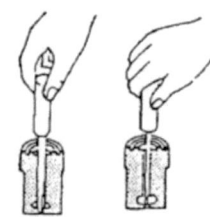

(5) Clean off the carbon on the tip of nozzle with a piece of wood.
(6) Clean hole type nozzles with a nozzle cleaning needle.

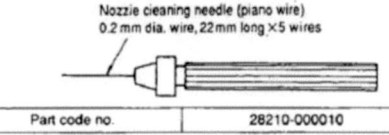

Nozzle cleaning needle (piano wire)
0.2 mm dia. wire, 22 mm long ×5 wires

Part code no.	28210-000010

6-3.2 Nozzle inspection

(1) Inspect for scratches/wear
   Inspect oil seals for abnormal scratches or wear and replace the nozzle if the nozzle sliding surface or seat are scratched or abnormally worn.
(2) Check nozzle sliding
   Wash the nozzle and nozzle body in clean diesel oil, and make sure that when the nozzle is pulled out about half way from the body, it slides down by itself when released.
   Rotate the nozzle a little; replace the nozzle/nozzle body as a set if there are some places where it does not slide smoothly

(3) Inspecting stop plate (inter-piece)
   Check for scratches/wear in seals on both ends. check for abnormal wear on the surface where it comes in contact with the nozzle; replace if the stop plate is excessively worn.

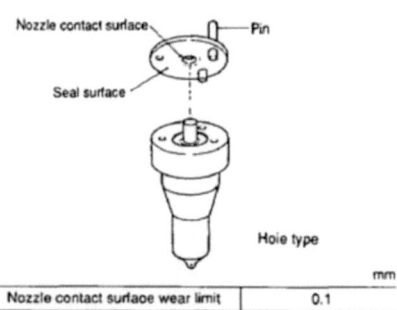

mm

Nozzle contact surface wear limit	0.1

(4) Inspecting nozzle spring
   Replace the nozzle spring if it is extremely bent, or the surface is scratched or rusted.

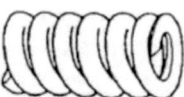

(5) Nozzle holder
   Check the oil seal surface for scratches/wear; replace if the wear is excessive.

6-4 Fuel injection nozzle reassembly

The fuel injection nozzle is reassembled in the opposite order to disassembly
(1) Insert the adjusting shims, nozzle spring and nozzle spring seat in the nozzle holder, mount the stop plate with the pin, insert the nozzle body/nozzle set and tighten the nut.
(2) Use the special holder when tightening the nut for the hole type nozzle as in disassembly.

Nozzle nut tightening torque		kg·m
	Hole type nozzle	4~4.5

6-5 Adjusting fuel injection nozzle

6-5.1 Adjusting opening pressure

Mount the fuel injection nozzle on the nozzle tester and use the handle to measure injection starting pressure If it is not at the specified pressure. use the adjusting shims to increase/decrease pressure (both hole and pintle types).

Correct

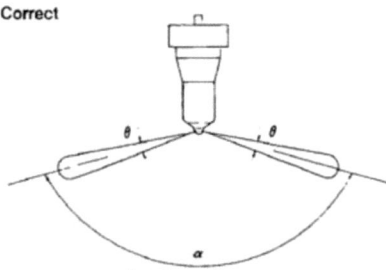

Spray from each nozzle hole is uniform

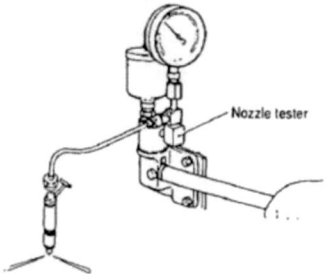

Nozzle tester

Poor

Injection starting pressure

Injection starting pressure	195~205 kg/cm²

6-5.2 Injection test

After adjusting the nozzle to the specified starting pressure, check the fuel spray condition and seat oil tightness.

(1) Check seat oil tightness

After two or three injections, gradually increase the pressure up to 20 kg/cm²(284 lb/in²) before reading the starting pressure, maintain the pressure for 5 seconds, and make sure that no oil is dripping from the tip of the nozzle.

Test the injection with a nozzle tester; retighten and test again if there is excessive oil leakage from the overflow coupling.

Replace the nozzle as a sat if oil leakage is still excessive.

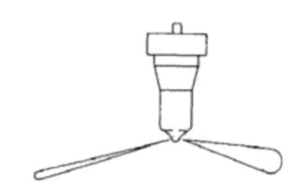

- Excessive difference in apray angle(θ)
- Excessive difference in injection angle (α)
- Incomplete atomization
- Sluggish starting/stopping of injection

(2) Injection spray condition

Operate the nozzle tester lever once to twice a second and check for abnormal injection.

1) Hole type nozzles

Replace hole type nozzles that do not satisfy the following conditions:
- Proper spray angle (θ)
- Correct injection angle (α)
- Complete atomization of fuel
- Prompt starting/stopping of injection

7. Trouble shooting of fuel injection pump

7-1 Troubleshooting of fuel injection pump

Complete repair means not only replacing defective parts, but finding and eliminating the cause of the trouble as well. The cause of the trouble may not necessarily be in the pump itself, but may be in the engine or the fuel system. If the pump is removed prematurely, the true cause of the trouble may never be known Before removing the pump from the engine, at least go through the basic check points given here.

Basic check points
- Check for breaks or oil leaks throughout the fuel system, from the fuel tank to the nozzle.
- Check the injection timings for all cylinders. Are they correctly adjusted? Are they too fast or too slow?
- Check the nozzle spray.
- Check the fuel delivery Is it in good condition? Loosen the fuel pipe connection at the injection pump inlet, and test operate the fuel feed pump.

7-2 Major faults and troubleshooting

Fault		Causa	Remedy
1. Engine won't start	Fuel not delivered to injection pump	(1) No fuel in the fuel tank.	Resupply
		(2) Fuel tank cock is closed.	Open
		(3) Fuel pipe system is clogged	Clean
		(4) Fuel filter element is clogged	Disassemble and clean, or replace element
		(5) Air is sucked into the fuel due to defective connections in the piping from the fuel tank to the fuel pump.	Repair
		(6) Defective valve contact of feed pump	Repair or replace
		(7) Piston spring of feed pump is broken.	Replace
		(8) Inter-spindle or tappets of feed pump are stuck	Repair or replace
	Fuel delivered to injection pump.	(1) Defective connection of control lever and accel. rod of injection pump.	Repair or adjust
		(2) Plunger is worn out or stuck.	Repair or replace
		(3) Delivery valve is stuck	Repair or replace
		(4) Control rack doesn't move	Repair or replace
		(5) Injection pump coupling is damaged, or the key Is broken.	Replace
	Nozzle doesn't work.	(1) Nozzle valve doesn't open or close normally	Repair or replace
		(2) Nozzle seat is defective.	Repair or replace
		(3) Case nut is loose.	Inspect and tighten
		(4) Injection nozzle starting pressure is too low	Adjust.
		(5) Nozzle spring is broken.	Replace
		(6) Fuel oil filter is clogged.	Repair or replace
		(7) Excessive oil leaks from the nozzle sliding area.	Replace the nozzle assembly
	Injection timing is defective.	(1) Injection timing is retarded due to failure of the coupling.	Adjust
		(2) Camshaft is excessively worn.	Replace camshaft
		(3) Roller guide incorrectly adjusted or excessively worn.	Adjust or replace
		(4) Plunger is excessively worn.	Replace plunger assembly
2. Engine starts, but immediately stops.		(1) Fuel pipe is clogged.	Clean
		(2) Fuel filter is clogged.	Disassemble and clean, or replace the element
		(3) Improper air-tightness of the fuel pipe connection. or pipe is broken and air is being sucked in.	Replace packing repair pipe
		(4) Insufficient fuel delivery from the feed pump	Repair or replace

Chapter 3 Fuel Injection Equipment
7. Trouble shooting of fuel injection pump

3,4JH3(B)(C)E

Fault		Cause	Remedy
3. Engine's output is insufficient.	Defective injection timing, and other failures.	(1) Knocking sounds caused by improper (too fast) injection timing. (2) Engine overheats or emits large amount of smoke due to improper (to slow) injection timing. (3) Insufficient fuel delivery from feed pump.	Inspect and adjust Inspect and adjust Repair or replace
	Nozzle movements is defective.	(1) Case nut loose. (2) Defective injection nozzle performance. (3) Nozzle spring is broken. (4) Excessive oil leaks from nozzle.	Inspect and retighten Repair or replace nozzle Replace Replace nozzle assembly
	Injection pump is defective.	(1) Max delivery limit boll is screwed in too far. (2) Plunger is worn (3) Injection amount is not uniform. (4) Injection timings are not even. (5) The 1st and 2nd levers of the governor and the control rack of the injection pump are improperly lined up (6) Delivery stopper is loose. (7) Delivery packing is defective (8) Delivery valve seat is defective. (9) Delivery spring is broken.	Adjust Replace Adjust Adjust Repair Inspect and retighten Replace packing Repair or replace Replace

4. Idling is rough.		(1) Movement of control rack is defective.
		  1) Stiff plunger movement or sticking.
		  2) Rack and pinion fitting is defective.
		  3) Movement of governor is improper
		  4) Delivery stopper is too tight.
		(2) Uneven injection volume.
		(3) Injection timing is defective.
		(4) Plunger is worn and fuel injection adjustment is difficult..
		(5) Governor spring is too weak.
		(6) Feed pump can't feed oil at low speeds.
		(7) Fuel supply is insufficient at low speeds due to clogging of fuel filter.
			
			Repair or replace
			Repair
			Repair
			Inspect and adjust
			adjust
			adjust
			Replace
			Replace
			Repair or replace
			Disassemble and clean, or replace element

5. Engine runs at high speeds, but cuts out at low speeds.		(1) The wire or rod of the accel. is caught. (2) Control rack is caught and can't be moved.	Inspect and repair Inspect and repair
6. Engine doesn't reach max. rpm.		(1) Governor spring is broken or excessively worn. (2) Injection performance or nozzle is poor	Replace Repair or replace
7. Loud knocking.		(1) Injection timing is too fast or too slow. (2) Injection from nozzle is improper. Fuel drips after each injection (3) Injection nozzle starting pressure is too high (4) Uneven injection. (5) Engine overheats, or insufficient compression.	Adjust Adjust Adjust Adjust Repair
8. Engine exhausts too much smoke.	When exhaust smoke is black:	(1) Injection timing is too fast. (2) Air volume intake is insufficient. (3) The amount of injection is uneven. (4) Injection from nozzle is improper.	Adjust Inspect and repair Adjust Repair or replace
	When exhaust smoke is white:	(1) Injection timing is too slow. (2) Water is mixed in fuel. (3) Shortage or lube oil in the engine. (4) Engine is over-cooled.	Adjust Inspect fuel system, and clean Repair Inspect

8. Tools

Name of tool	Shape and size	Application
Pump mounting scale for Yanmar tester 158090-51010 for Bosch (tester) 158090-51020		
Measuring device (cam backlash) 158090-51050		
Plunger insert 158090-51100		
Tappet holder 158090-51200		
Weight extractor 158090-51400		

Chapter 3 Fuel Injection Equipment
8. Tools

3,4JH3(B)(C)E

Name of tool	Shape and size	Application
Rack indicator 158090-51500		
Rack lock screw 158090-51010		
Dummy nut 158090-51520		
Nozzle plate 158090-51700		
Plunger gauge 121820-92540		
Top clearance gauge 158090-51300		
Timer extraction tool		

Chapter 3 Fuel Injection Equipment
9. Fuel Filter 3,4JH3(B)(C)E

9. Fuel Filter

The fuel filter is installed between the fuel feed pump and fuel injection pump, and removes dirt/foreign matter from the fuel pumped from the fuel tank.
The fuel filter element must be changed periodiically. The fuel pumped by the fuel feed pump goes around the element, is fed through the pores in the filter and discharged from the center of the cover. Dirt and foreign matter in the fuel are deposited in the element.

9-1 Fuel filter specifications

Filtering method	filter paper
Filtering area	840cm²
Maximum flow	1.5 ℓ/min
Pressure loss	20mm Hg or less
Max. dia. or unfiltered particle	10 μ

9-2 Fuel filter inspection

The fuel strainer must be cleaned occasionally If there is water or foreign matter in the strainer bowl, disassemble the strainer and wash with clean fuel oil to completely remove foreign matter. Replace the element every 300 hours of operation.
Replace the filter prior to this if the filter is very dirty, deformed or damaged.

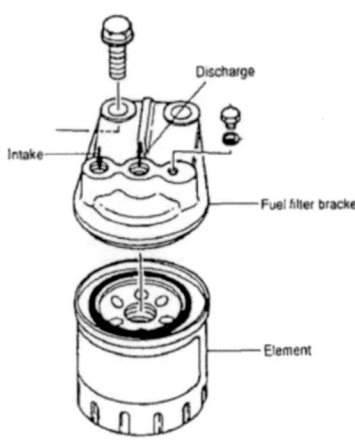

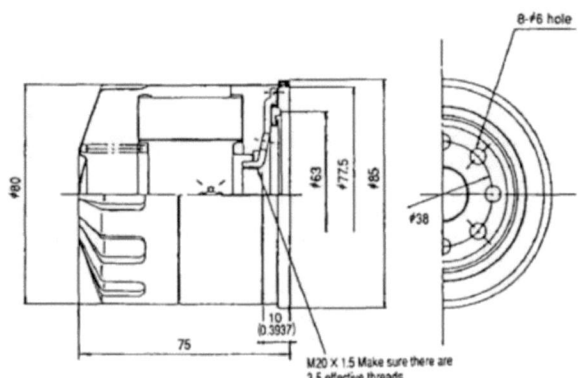

3-40

Printed in Japan
HINSHI-H8009

10. Fuel Tank

A triangular 30 liter fuel tank with a 2000mm (78.7402 in.) rubber fuel hose to fit all models is available as an option.
A fuel return connection is provided on top of the tank to which a rubber hose can be connected to retun fuel from the fuel nozlles.

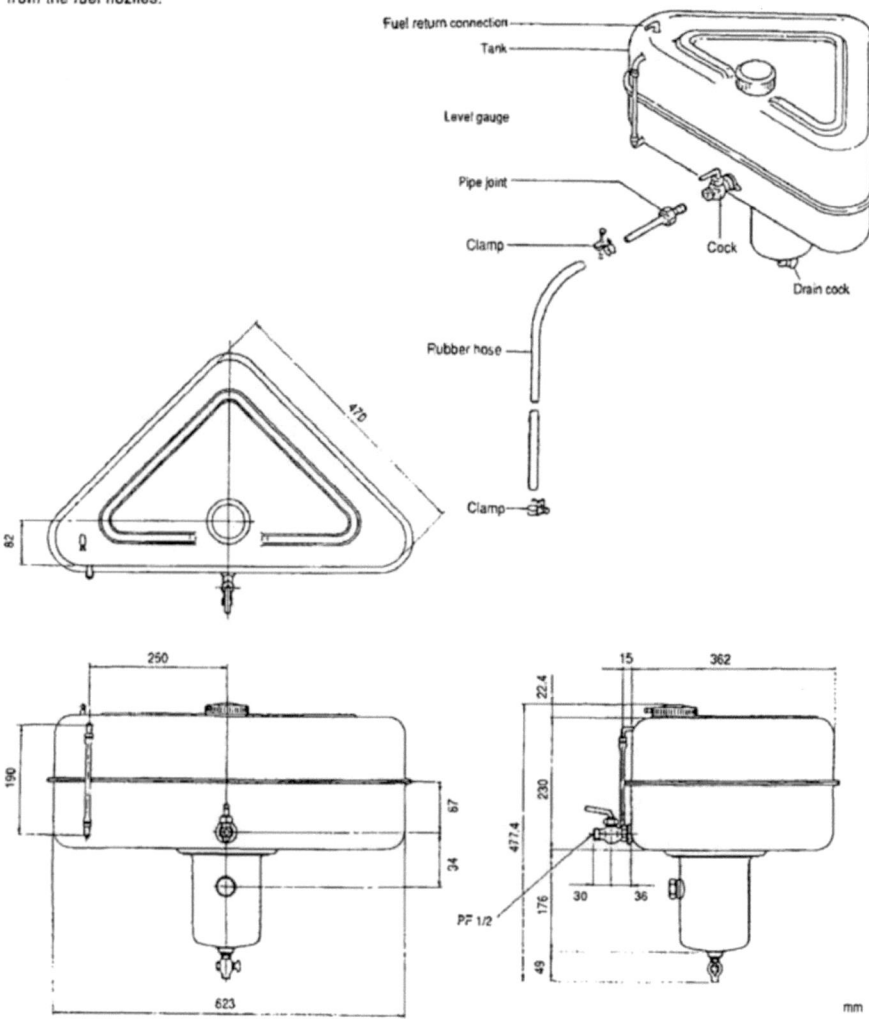

11. Troubleshooting (Concerning engine and fuel injection equipment)

Malfunctions	Causes	Remedies
The engine does not operate		
1. Fuel Oil is not injected from the injection pump	1. There is no fuel oil in the fuel tank	Supply fuel and bleed the system
	2. The fuel line from the fuel tank is blocked	Clean or replace
	3. The fuel filter is clogged	Clean or replace
	4. There is air in the fuel filter or the pump chamber	Bleed the system
	5. The accelerator linkage is not properly connected	Repair
	6. The magnet valve wiring is broken or its armature is Sticking	Repair or replace
	7. The feed pump blades are sticking, and therefore not operating	Repair or replace
	8. The drive gear or woodruff key is broken	Replace
2. Injection timing is incorrect	1. The drive gear or belt connections are incorrect	Repair
	2. The injection pump is incorrectly installed on the engine	Repair and adjust injection timing
	3. The roller holder assembly's roller or pin is worn excessively	Replace the assembly
	4. The plunger is worn excessively	Replace the distributor assembly
3. The nozzle does not operate	1. The nozzle or nozzle holder is functioning incorrectly	Inspect, then repair or replace
The engine operates, but only for a short time	1. The pipe(s) to the injection pump is blocked, or the fuel filter is clogged	Clean or replace the pipe(s) or fuel filter
	2. The fuel oil contains air or water	Bleed of air or replace the fuel oil
	3. The feed pump's delivery quantity (or pressure) is insufficient	Repair or replace
The engine "knocks"	1. The injection timing is too advanced	Readjust the timing
	2. The nozzle or nozzle holder is functioning incorrectly	Inspect, then repair or replace

Chapter 3 Fuel Injection Equipment
11. Troubleshooting (Concerning engine fuel injection equipment)   3,4JH3(B)(C)E

Malfunctions	Causes	Remedies
The engine exhaust contains smoke and the engine "knocks"	1. The injection timing is incorrect 2. The nozzle or nozzle holder is functioning incorrectly 3. The injection quantity is excessive	Readjust the timing Inspect, then repair or replace Readjust
The engine output is unstable	1. The fuel filter element is clogged and fuel oil delivery is poor 2. The amount of fuel or pressure delivered by the feed pump is too little 3. The injection pump is sucking air 4. The regulating valve is stuck in the open position 5. The plunger is sticking and does not travel its full stroke 6. The plunger spring IS broken 7. The control sleeve is not sliding smoothly 8. The governor lever is not operating properly or is worn excessively 9. The delivery valve spring is broken 10. The delivery valve is not sliding properly 11. The nozzle or the nozzle holder is not functioning properly 12. The injection timing is incorrect	Clean or replace Inspect and repair Inspect and repair Replace Replace the distributor assembly Replace Repair or replace Repair or replace Replace Repair or replace Inspect, and then repair or replace Readjust
Insufficient output 1. The injection quantity is insufficient	1. The specified full-load injection quantity is not delivered 2. The control lever is not reaching the maximum speed position 3. The governor spring is weak and therefore the governed speed is too low 4. The plunger is worn 5. The delivery valve seating portions are damaged	Readjust Readjust Replace Replace the distributor assembly Replace
2. The injection timing is too advanced and the engine is "knocking"		Readjust

Chapter 3 Fuel Injection Equipment
11. Troubleshooting (Concerning engine fuel injection equipment) _3,4JH3(B)(C)E_

Malfunctions	Causes	Remedies
3. The injection timing is too retarded and the engine is overheating or the exhaust contains smoke		Readjust
4. The nozzle or the nozzle holder is not functioning properly		Inspect and then repair or replace
The engine cannot reach its maximum speed	1. The governor spring is too weak or is improperly adjusted	Readjust or replace
	2. The control lever is not reaching the maximum-speed position	Readjust
	3. The nozzle's injection operation is poor	Repair or replace
The engine's maximum speed is too high	1. The governor spring is too strong or is improperly adjusted	Readjust or replace
	2. The governor flyweights or governor sleeve movement is not smooth	Repair or replace
Idling is unstable	1. The injection quantities are not uniform (the delivery valve is not operating properly)	Inspect or replace
	2. The governor's idling adjustment is improperly adjusted	Readjust
	3. The plunger is worn	Replace the distributor assembly
	4. The plunger spring IS broken	Replace
	5. The rubber damper is worn.	Replace
	6. The governor lever shaft pin is worn excessively	Replace
	7. The feed pump blades are not operating properly	Repair or replace
	8. The regulating valve is stuck in the open position	Replace
	9. The fuel filter element is clogged and therefore fuel oil delivery is poor	Clean or replace
	10. The nozzle or the nozzle holder is not functioning properly	Inspect and then repair or replace

12. Fuel Injection Timing Adjustment for EPA/ARB Certified Engine (3JH3E series)

12-1 Driving Part Structure of Fuel Injection Pump

(1) Current production engine model
- Structure of driving parts: A driving gear is installed directly at the end of the fuel pump cam shaft.
- Fuel injection timing adjustment.
FID method, adjusted by turning the fuel pump to the right or lefthand around the fuel pump cam shaft.

Fig. 1 Current production engine.

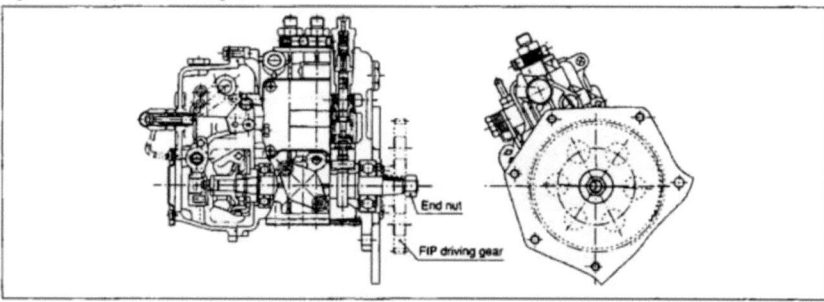

(2) EPA/ARB certified engine (3JH3E series) (EPA certified E/# A01158 and after, ARB (EPA) certified engine installed the tamper resistance device as shown illustration Fig.2.

- Driving part structure : the FIP coupling is fitted to the end of the fuel pump cam shaft. After the FIC is adjusted, the FIP coupling is locked to the pump body not to turn the fuel pump cam shaft using the lock bolts. (Adjusted by fuel pump manufacturing plant of Yanmar)

> **[NOTICE]**
> Never remove the 4 fixing bolts (E marked) installing the FIP driving gear on the FIP coupling. Refer to 12.2

- Fuel injection timing adjustment : Adjusted by using the FIC fixed method. (coupling flange-gear system)

Fig. 2 EPA/ARB certified engine (3JH3E series) (EPA certified E/# A01158 and after, ARB(EPA) certified engine installed the tamper resistance device as shown bellow.

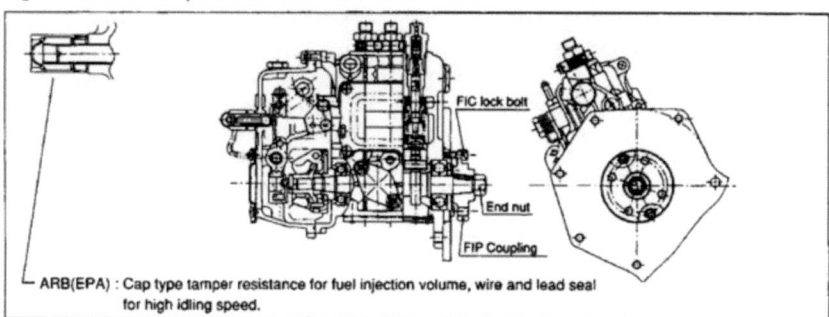

ARB(EPA) : Cap type tamper resistance for fuel injection volume, wire and lead seal for high idling speed.

Chapter 3 Fuel Injection Equipment
12. Fuel Injection Timing Adjustment for EPA/ARB Certified Engine (3JH3E series) 3,4JH3(B)(C)E

12-2 Fuel Injection Timing Adjustment

(1) Installing the fuel pump in factory (Nagahama Factory)

Procedure

① Align the fuel injection pump with the mark shown in figure 3 and install on to the gear case.

Fig.3 Aligning the marks on the fuel pump and gear case

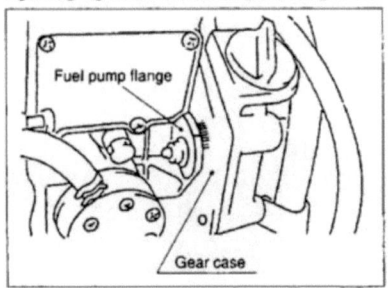

-[NOTICE]-
Align the mark on the fuel pump with the center mark (5th mark from the top) on the gear case.

-[NOTICE]-
● Before installing the fuel injection pump, confirm that the FIC lock is still attached. The correct FIP cam shaft on the assembly line side does not turn. Do not use the pump if there is the problem.

(● The marks on the gear case and the fuel pump have no relation to the fuel injection timing and are the same on all engine models.
The installing angle for the pump is fixed (all the engines are same).)

② Temporarily attach the FIP driving gear to the FIP coupling to allow rotating freely on its outer surface without bolt fixing.

③ Align the timing mark of each gear, crank, idler, cam and FIP drive gear and install them.

Fig. 4 Aligning the timing mark of the gear train.

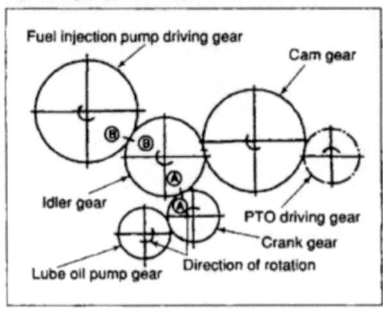

-[NOTICE]-
When aligning the timing marks, put the piston for the No.1 cylinder in the top compression position, align the letters on the gears and assemble. No.1 cylinder is from the flywheel side.

3-46

Chapter 3 Fuel Injection Equipment
12. Fuel Injection Timing Adjustment for EPA/ARB Certified Engine (3JH3E series) 3,4JH3(B)(C)E

④ Align the crankshaft with the FIC fuel injection angle (b,TDC) using the special assembling tool.

⑤ Keeping the no gear backlash, fix the FIP driving gear to the FIP coupling by tightening the 2 bolts (marked E) in the factories.
- Tightening torque (not apply lube oil): 34.32±1.96N·m(3.5±0.2kgf·m)

Fig.5 FIP Coupling Driving Gear Unit

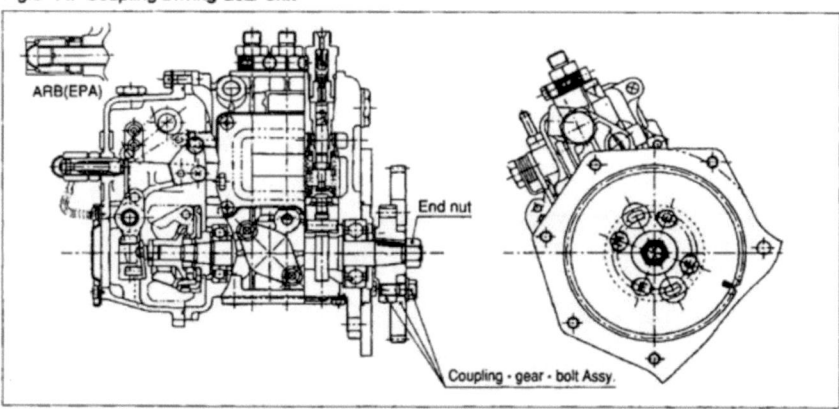

⑥ Tighten the remaining 2 fixing bolts for the FIP driving gear.
- Tightening torque (not apply lube oil) : 34.32±1.96N·m(3.5±0.2kgf·m)

⑦ Remove the FIC lock bolt. (See figure 2.)
The injection timing adjustment is completed.

[NOTICE]
- After removing the FIC lock bolts, do not separate the FIP coupling and the FIP driving gear. If they are separated, this will confuse the FIC setup and it will be necessary to adjust the fuel injection timing from the beginning.
- If the fuel pump should have to be removed the fuel injection pump, loosen the end nuts to do it.

Chapter 3 Fuel Injection Equipment
12. Fuel Injection Timing Adjustment for EPA/ARB Certified Engine (3JH3E series)   3,4JH3(B)(C)E

(2) Replacing the fuel injection pump on the local. (For EPA/ARB certified engine) (E/# A01158 and after)

When need to replace the pump, service the pump in the following manner.

> **[NOTICE]**
> The fuel injection pump as the service part is supplied with the same style (without coupling) as the service part for current engine. (see fig.1)

Procedure

① Remove the current pump from the gear case.
Loosen the end nuts to remove the fuel injection pump.
(Leave the FIP coupling and driving gear as a semi-assembly in the gear case.)

> **[NOTICE]**
> Do not separate the FIP coupling and driving gear.
> Do not touch the fixing bolts (4 bolts with E marked).

② Align the aligning mark on the fuel injection pump (FIP) flange for service part to the aligning mark on the gear case to install the FIP on the gear case. (See Fig.3)
③ Attach the FIP coupling and driving gear semi-assembly to the pump.
  • Tightening torque (apply lube oil) : 63.8 ± 5 N·m(6.5 ± 0.5 kgf·m)
  Replacing the FIP is completed. Check the fuel injection timing with the FID method.
              (Injection timing : $14 \pm 1°$ b.T.D.C, FID)

(3) Replacing the fuel injection pump of the current production engine (E/# A01157 and before).
  • Incase of replacing with the fuel injection pump for EPA/ARB certified engine as the service part.

Procedure

① Remove the current pump from the gear case. (The same manner as the procedure (2) ①) [Before remove the current pump, confirm the aligning position on the gear case (pin point mark or aligning line marks).

② Align the mark on the FIP flange to the same position on the aligning mark of the gear case (Aligning line mark or pin point mark had been aligned current FIP) to install the service part FIP. (I/T :$12 \pm 1°$ FID)

> **[NOTICE]**
> For the engine having A01157 or less E/#, service part FIP has two aligning line marks on its flange. So, align the outside line mark of two aligning line marks on the FIP flange to the gear case mark to install the FIP. (Shown in Fig.6)

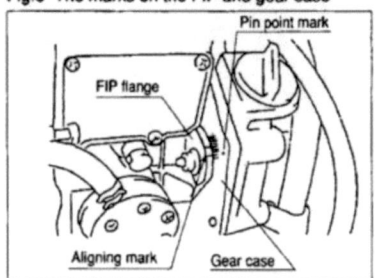

Fig.6 The marks on the FIP and gear case

CHAPTER 4
INTAKE AND EXHAUST SYSTEM

1. Intake System ·· 4-1
2. Exhaust system ·· 4-2
   2-1 Construction ··· 4-2
   2-2 Mixing elbow inspection ······························· 4-2

Chapter 4 Intake and Exhaust System
1. Intake and Exhaust System   3,4JH3(B)(C)E

1. Intake System

Air enters in the intake silencer mounted at the end of the intake manifold, is fed to the intake manifold and then on to each cylinder.
Exhaust gas goes into the exhaust manifold (in the fresh water tank) mounted on the cylinder head discharge. After cooling it enters the mixing elbow which is directly connected with the exhaust manifold, and is discharged from the ship along with waste cooling water.

When the inside of the intake manifold becomes dirty, intake resistance is created reducing engine power. Periodically check the inside of the intake manifold. In the same way, the net portion of the intake air silencer should be checked for dirt periodically and cleaned.
When the intake manifold is being attached to the cylinder head, the attachment surfaces should be checked for dirt and cleaned. Care should also be taken to insure there is no air leakage.
Do not operate with the intake air silencer removed.

Intake system

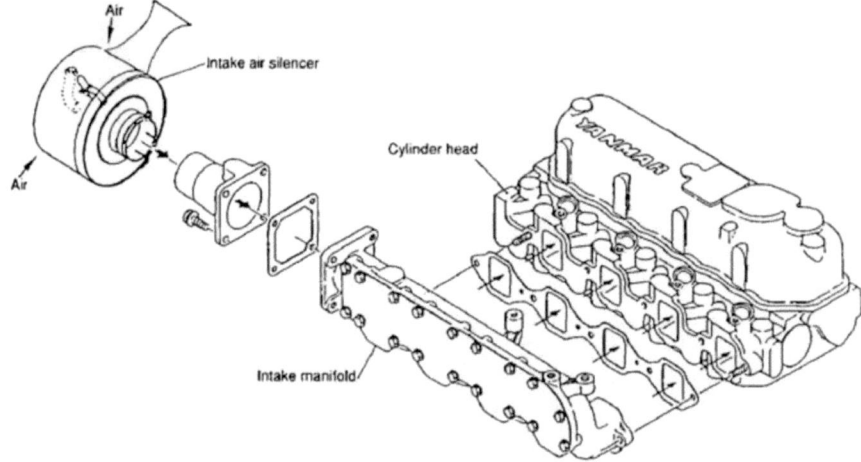

4–1

2. Exhaust System

2-1 Construction
There are two types of mixing elbows, the L-type and the U-type. The mixing elbow is attached to the exhaust manifold. Refer to the exterior diagrams included here.

2-2 Mixing elbow inspection
(1) Clean dirt and scale out of the air and cooling water lines.
(2) Repair crach or damage to welds, or replace.
(3) Inspect the gasket packing and replace as necessary.

[Example assembly diagram : L-type mixing elbow.]

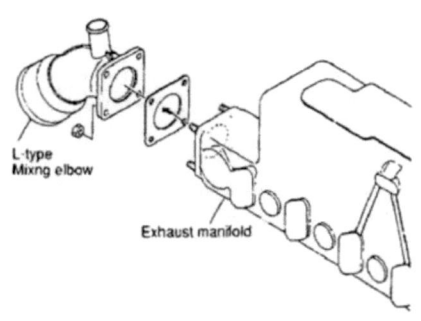

L-type Mixng elbow
Exhaust manifold

(Option)

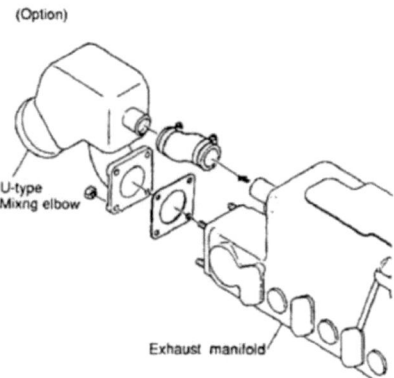

U-type Mixng elbow
Exhaust manifold

CHAPTER 5
LUBRICATION SYSTEM

1. Lubrication system ···5-1
2. Lube Oil Pump ··5-2
   2-1 Lube oil pump construction ·····················5-2
   2-2 Specifications of lube oil pump ···············5-3
   2-3 Lube oil pump disassembly ····················5-4
   2-4 Lube oil pump inspection ······················5-4
   2-5 Oil pressure regulating valve construction ······5-5
3. Lube Oil Filter··5-6
   3-1 Lube oil filter construction ·····················5-6
   3-2 Lube oil filter replacement ·····················5-7
4. Lube Oil Cooler ···5-8
   4-1 Lube oil cooler construction ···················5-8
   4-2 Inspecting the lube oil cooler ··················5-8
5. Rotary Waste Oil Pump (Optional)···················5-9
   5-1 Construction ·······································5-9
   5-2 Inspecting the waste oil pump ···············5-9

Chapter 5 Lubrication System
1. Lubrication System

3.4JH3(B)(C)E

1. Lubrication System

The lube oil in the oil pan is pumped up through the intake filter and intake piping by the lube oil pump, through the holes in the cylinder body and on to the discharge filter.

The lube oil which flows from the holes in the cylinder body through the bracket to the oil element is filtered and sent to the oil cooler. It returns from the oil cooler to the bracket, the pressure is regulated, and it is fed back to main gallery in the cylinder body.

The lube oil which flows in the main gallery goes to the crankshaft journal, lubricates the crank pin from the crankshaft journal, and a portion of the oil is fed to the camshaft bearings.

Oil is sent from the gear case camshaft bearings through the holes in the cylinder body and cylirder head to the valve arm shaft to lubricate the valve arm and valves.

Oil is also sent from the main gallery to the piston cooling nozzle to cool the piston surface, and is sent through the intermediate gear bearing (oil) holes to lubricate the intermediate gear bearings and respective gears.

Lube oil for the fuel injection pump is sent by pipe from the main gallery to the fuel injection pump.

Part of the lube oil is sent from the oil cooler discharge to the supercharger in engines fitted with one, and is then piped backfrom the supercharger to the oil pan.

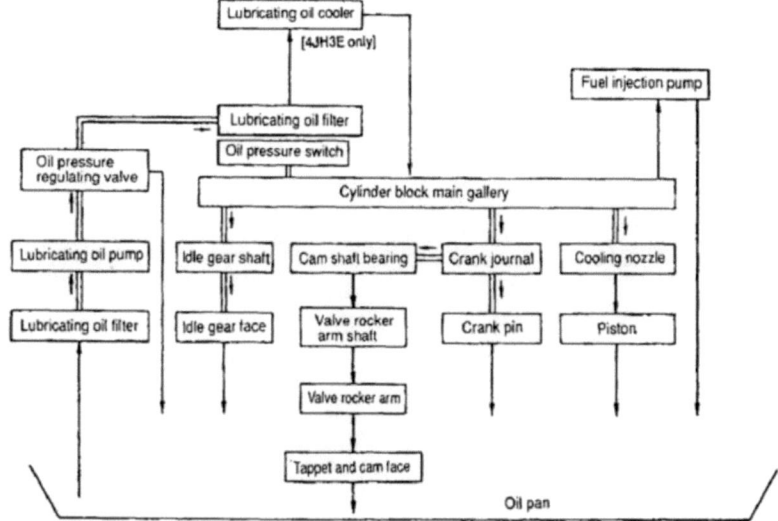

5-1

2. Lube Oil Pump

2-1 Lube oil pump construction

The trochoid type lube oil pump is mounted on the gear case side engine plate, and the rotor shaft gear is driven by the crankshaft gear.

The lube oil flows from the intake filter mounted on the bottom of the cylinder body through the holes in the cylinder body and engine plate, and out from the holes in the engine plate and cylinder body to the discharge filter. The lube oil pump is fitted with a pressure regulating valve which maintains the discharge pressure at 3kg/cm².

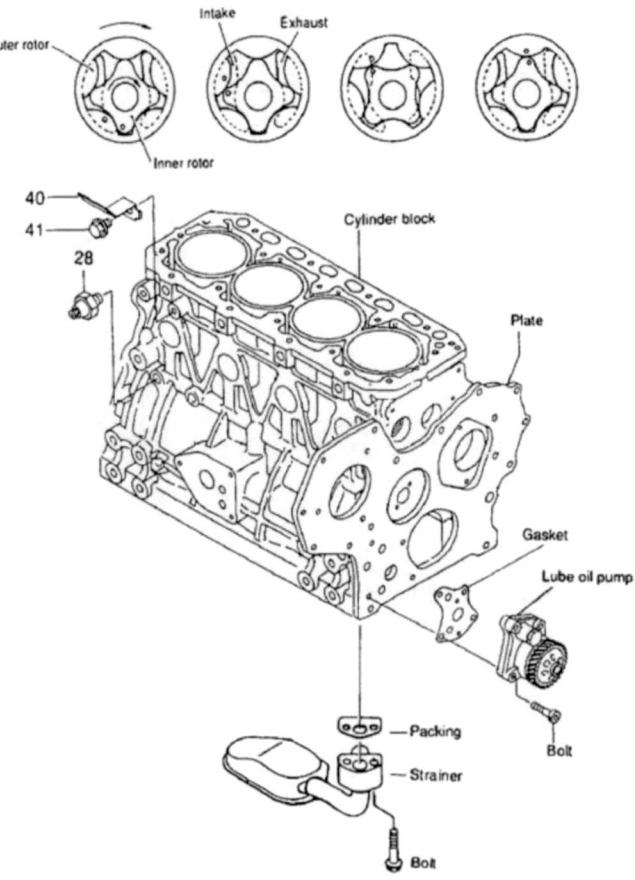

Chapter 5 Lubrication System
2. Lube Oil Pump

3,4JH3(B)(C)E

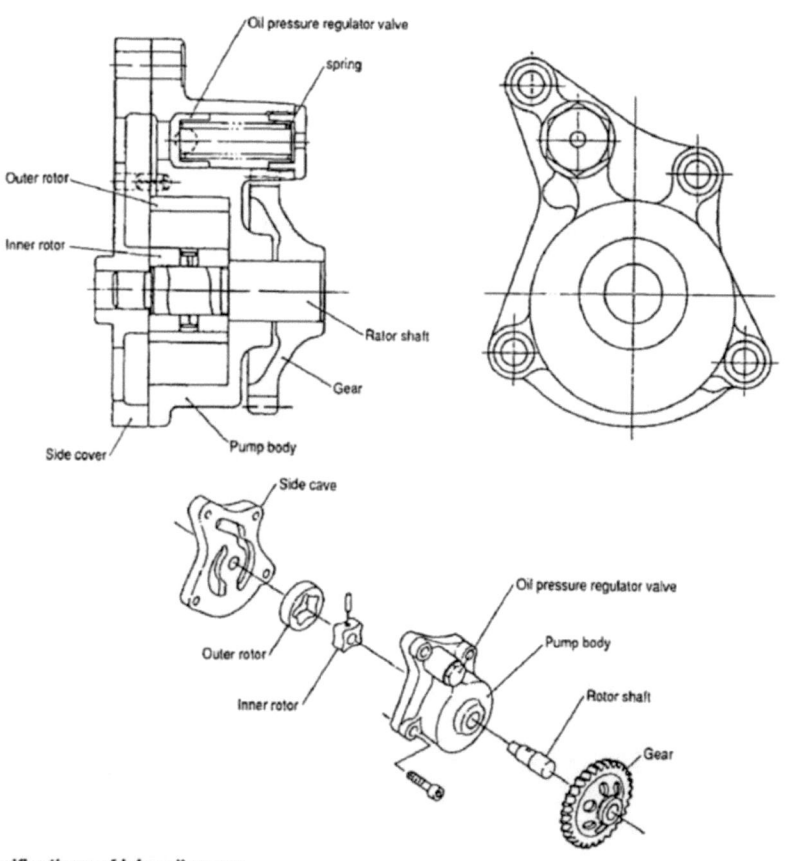

2-2 Specifications of lube oil pump

Table of helical gear					
Precision(JIS)		Class 4	Standard pitch dia.		⌀61.722
Gear teeth shape		Standard	Transposition factor		−0.0866
Tool	Gear teeth shape	Gear teeth average	Finishing method		shaving
	Module	2.0	Crowning		None
	Angle of pressure	20°	Other gear	Number of teeth	28
Number of teeth		29		Transposition factor	−0.025
Gear thickness	Straddle (Reference)	4(21.516)		Finishing method	shaving
			Distance to center		60.65±0.05
	Overpin dia.	67.956±0.04 (Pin dia.=3.969)	Backlash		0.15±0.04
			Remarks	Tough-ride surface treatment Hardness: HV570~680	
Distortion angle		20°			
Distortion direction		RIGHT			

L/O pump specifications		
Engine speed	3600(rpm)	800(rpm)
Pump speed	3477(rpm)	772(rpm)
Delivery theory	≧19.0(l/min)	≧8.0(l/min)
Delivery pressure	4.4 (kgf/cm^2)	≧0.5(kgf/cm^2)
Oil temp.	60±5(°C)	←
Suction head	1/28-40cm	←
Lube oil	SAE#30	←

Chapter 5 Lubrication System
2. Lube Oil Pump

2-3 Lube oil pump disassembly
(1) Remove the lube oil pump assembly from the engine plate
(2) The lube oil pump cover may be disassembled. but do not disassemble the rotor, rotor shaft or drive gear. The oil pressure regulating valve plug is coated with adhesive and screwed in, so it cannot be disassembled. These parts cannot be reused after disassembly. Replace if necessary as an assembly.

2-4 Lube oil pump inspection
(1) Clearance between outer rotor and pump body
Insert a feeler gauge between the outer rotor and pump body to measure the clearance, and replace if it exceeds the limit.

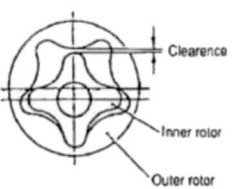

mm
	Standard	Wear limit
Outer rotor and inner rotor clearance	0.050~0.105	0.15

(3) Clearance between pump body and inner rotor side of outer rotor.
Place a straight-edge against the end of the pump body and insert a feeler gauge between the straight-edge and the rotor to measure side clearance. Replace the assembly if the clearance exceeds the limit.

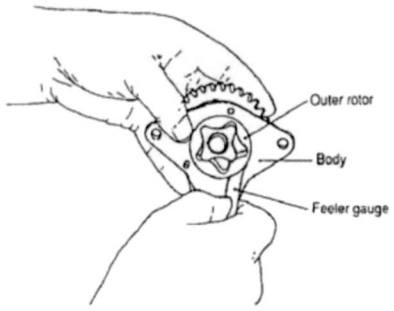

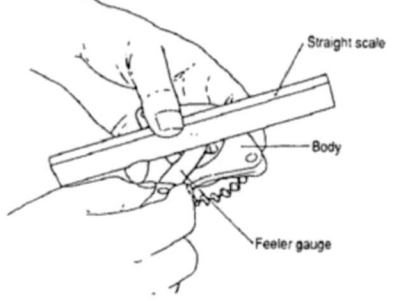

mm
	Standard	Wear limit
Outer rotor and pump body clearance	0.09~0.16	0.25

(2) Clearance between outer rotor and inner rotor
To measure clearance, insert a feeler bauge between the top of the inner rotor tooth and the top of the outer rotor tooth, and replace if it exceeds the limit.

mm
	Standard	Wear limit
Pump body and inner rotor, outer rotor clearance	0.05~0.10	0.13

(4) Clearance between rotor shaft and Side cover
Measure the rotor shaft outer diameter and the side cover hole diameter, and replace the entire assembly if the clearance exceeds the limit.

mm
	Standard	Wear limit
Rotor shaft and body clearance	0.016~0.049	0.25

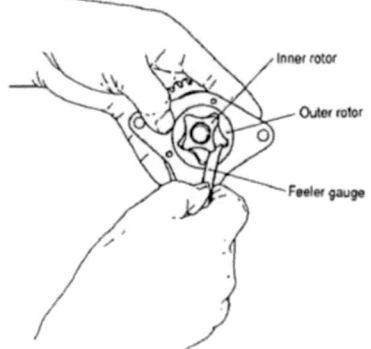

(5) Check for looseness of driver gear/rotor shaft fitting, and replace the entire assembly if loose or wobbly
(6) Push the oil pressure regulating valve piston from the oil hole side, and replace the assembly if the piston does not return due to spring breakage, etc.
(7) Make sure that the rotor shaft rotates smoothly and easily when the drive gear is. rotated.

Turning torque	less than 1.5 kg-cm

2-5 Oil pressure regulating valve construction

The oil pressure regulating valve attached with lube oil pump controls the oil pressure from the time the lube oil leaves the filter and is cooled in the lube oil cooler until just before it enters the cylinder body main gallery.

When the pressure of lube oil entering the cylinder body main gallery exceeds the setting, the regulating valve piston opens the bypass hole and lube oil flows back into the oil pan.

Regulating pressure	$3.5 \sim 4.5 \text{ kg/cm}^2$

3. Lube Oil Filter

3-1 Lube oil filter construction

The lube oil filter is a full-flow paper element type, mounted to the side of the cylinder body with the filter bracket. The cartridge type filter is easy to remove.
To prevent seizure in the event of the filter clogging up, a bypass circuit is provided in the oil filter. The bypass valve in the filter element opens when the difference in the pressure in front and behind the paper element reaches 0.8~1.2 kg/cm².

Chapter 5 Lubrication System
3. Lube Oil Filter

Type	Full flow, paper element
Filtration area	$0.10 m^2$
Discharge volume	30 ℓ/min
Pressure loss	$0.3 \sim 0.5$ kwcm^2
By-pass valve regulating pressure	$0.8 \sim 1.2$ kg/cm^2

3-2 Lube oil filter replacement

(1) Period

The paper element will get clogged up with dirt after long hours of usage, and eventually unfiltered oil will be fed to the engine through the bypass circuit. Replace the filter according to the following standard, as the dirt in unfiltered oil will of course have a detrimental effect on the engine.

(2) Replacement
1) Remove the lube oil filter with the special tool
2) Clean the filter mounting surface on the filter bracket and mounting screws.
3) Coat the filter rubber packing with lube oil
4) Screw in the filter until the rubber packing comes in contact with the bracket mounting surface, and then $2 \sim 3$ turns more.
5) Run the engine after mounting the filter, and make sure that there is no oil leakage.

4. Lube oil Cooler

4-1 Lube oil cooler construction
The lube oil coole'r is comprised of 36 cooling pipes and 9 internal baffle plates.
The lube oil flows through this passageway and is cooled by the cooling water (sea water) flowing through the inner pipe.

[4JH3E only]

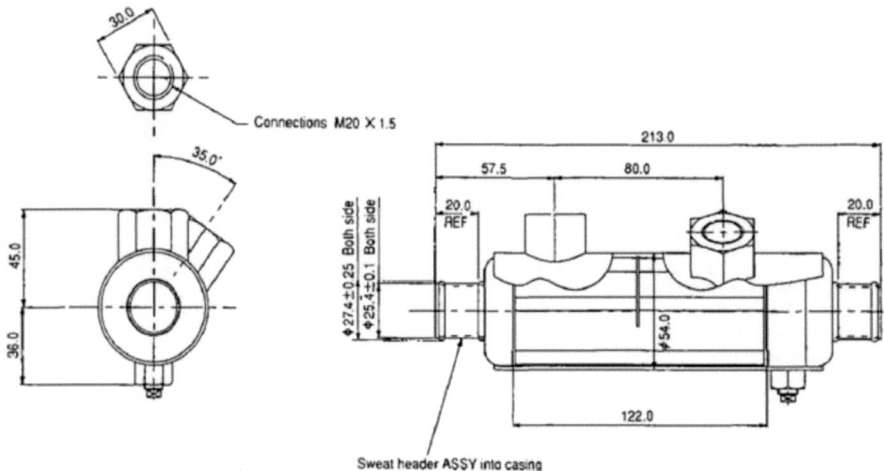

Sweat header ASSY into casing

NOTES
1. TUBE THICKNESS : 0.355 (MATERIAL 90/10 CuNi)
2. PNEUMATIC TEST
   SEA WATER SIDE : 0.4 MPa (4 kgf/cm^2)
   OIL SIDE : 1.0 MPa (10 kgf/cm^2)
3. MATERIAL (EXCEPT TUBES) : BRASS

4-2 Inspecting the lube oil cooler
(1) Clean the inside of the sea water pipes with a wire brush to prevent the build.up of saale
(2) If the rubber hose connection or welds are corroded, repair or replace the cooler
(3) Apply the following water pressures to the sea water and lube oil lines to check for any leakage. Repair or replace the cooler if there are any leaks.

	Test pressure
Lubricating oil circuit	1.5 kg/cm^2
Sea water circuit	4 kg/cm^2

5. Rotary Waste Oil Pump (Optional)

A rotary waste oil pump to pump out waste oil during oil changing is available as an option.
This is a vane type pump. Turning the handle rotates the vanes and pumps out lube oil.

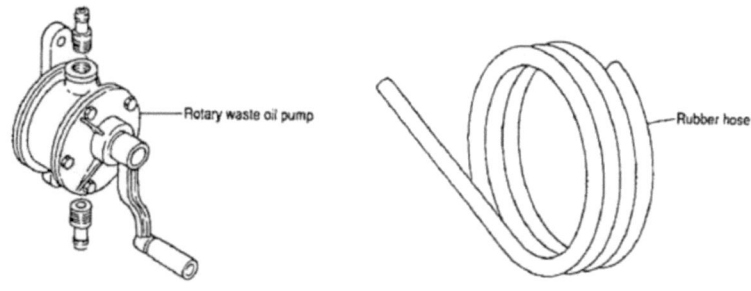

5-1 Construction

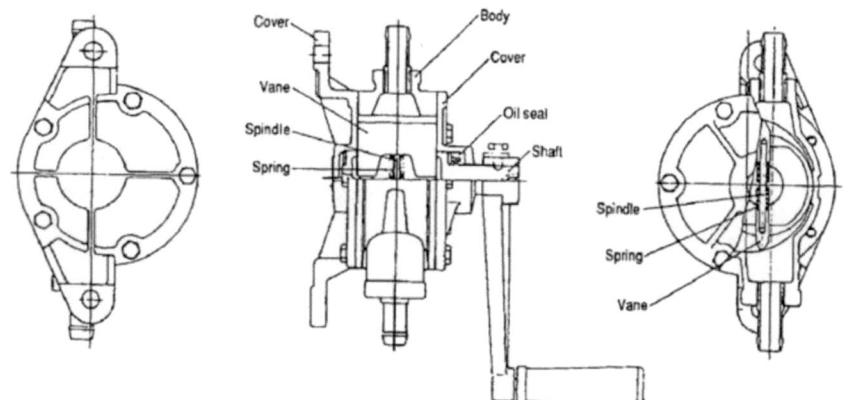

Rotary waste oil pump

Delivery capacity of one stroke	0.13 ℓ
Delivery pressure	1.5 kg/cm² or below
Suction head	less than 1m
Part No.	43600-002311

Rubber hose

Inner dia. × length	∅12×1000mm
Part No. of rubber hose	43720-001220

5-2 Inspecting the waste oil pump

(1) Disassemble the waste oil pump and check for spring breakage or vane damage when there is an extreme drop in discharge volume, and replace it necessary.
(2) Replace the oil seal if there is excessive oil leakage from the handle shaft.
(3) Replace the impeller if there is an excessive gap between the impeller and the covers on both sides of casing. This will cause a drop in discharge volume.
(4) The hose coupling is coated with adhesive and screwed in it therefore cannot be disassembled

CHAPTER 6
COOLING WATER SYSTEM

1. Cooling Water System ···················6-1
2. Sea Water Pump ···················6-3
   - 2-1 Specifications of sea water pump ···········6-3
   - 2-2 Sea water pump disassembly ············6-3
   - 2-3 Sea water pump Inspection ············6-3
   - 2-4 Sea water pump reassembly············6-4
   - 2-5 Current characeristics···············6-4
3. Fresh Water Pump ···················6-5
   - 3-1 Fresh water pump construction············6-5
   - 3-2 Specifications of fresh water pump ·········6-6
   - 3-3 Fresh water pump disassembly············6-6
   - 3-4 Fresh water pump inspection ···········6-6
4. Heat Exchanrger ···················6-8
   - 4-1 Heat exchanger construction············6-8
   - 4-2 Specifications of heat exchanger ···········6-9
   - 4-3 Disassembly and reassembly of the heat exchanger ···6-9
   - 4-4 Heat exchanger inspection············6-9
5. Pressure Cap and Sub Tank ············6-10
   - 5-1 Pressure cap construction ············6-10
   - 5-2 Pressure cap pressure control ·········6-10
   - 5-3 Pressure cap inspection ············6-10
   - 5-4 Function of the sub tank ············6-10
   - 5-5 Specifications of sub tank ············6-11
   - 5-6 Mounting the sub tank ············6-11
   - 5-7 Precautions on usage of the sub tank ······6-11
6. Thermostat ···················6-12
   - 6-1 Functioning of thermostat············6-12
   - 6-2 Thermostat construction ············6-12
   - 6-3 Characteristics of thermostat ···········6-12
   - 6-4 Thermostat inspection ············6-13
   - 6-5 Testing the thermostat ············6-13
7. Bilge Pump and Bilge Strainer (Optional) ······6-14
   - 7-1 Introduction ···················6-14
   - 7-2 Description ···················6-14
   - 7-3 Cautions ···················6-14

1. Cooling Water System

The cooling water system is of the indirect sea water cooled, fresh water circulation type. The cylinders, cylinder heads and exhaust manifold are cooled with fresh water, and fresh water cooler (heat exchanger) use sea water.

Sea water pumped in from the sea by the sea water pump cools the lube oil in the lube oil cooler and then goes to the heat exchanger, where it cools the fresh water. Then it is sent to the mixing elbow and is discharged from the ship with the exhaust gas.

Fresh water is pumped by the fresh water pump from the fresh water tank to the cylinder jacket to cool the cylinders, and the cylinder head. The fresh water pump body also serves as a discharge passageway (line) at the cylinder head outlet. and is fitted with a thermostat.

The thermostat is closed when the fresh water temperature is low, immediately after the engine is started and during low load operation, etc. Then the fresh water flows to the fresh water pump inlet, and is circulated inside the engine without passing through the heat exchanger.

When the temperature of the fresh water rises, the thermostat opens, fresh water flows to the heat exchanger, and it is then cooled by the sea water in the tubes as it flows through the cooling pine. The temperature of the fresh water is thus kept within a constant range by the thermostat.

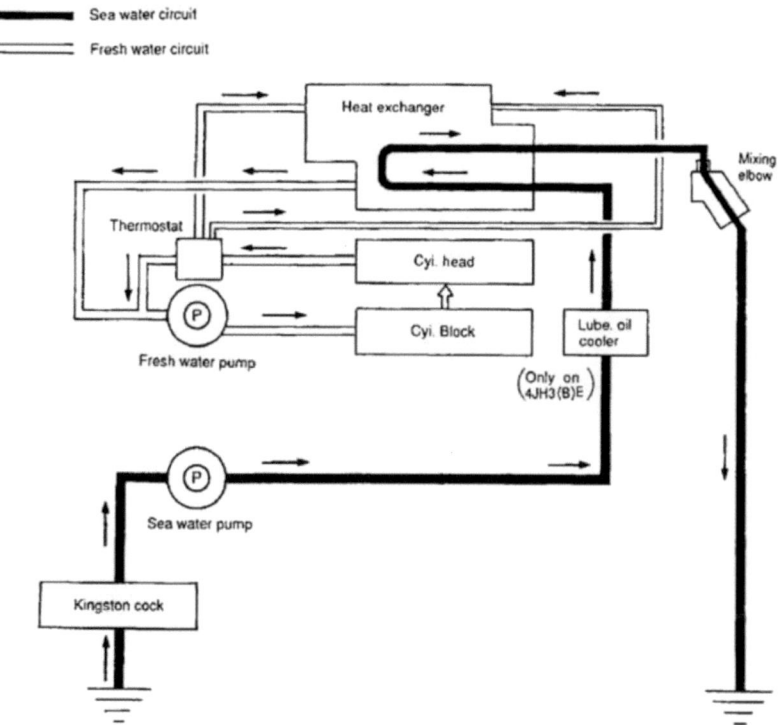

Chapter 6 Cooling Water System
1. Cooling Water System

3,4JH3(B)(C)E

Fresh water line

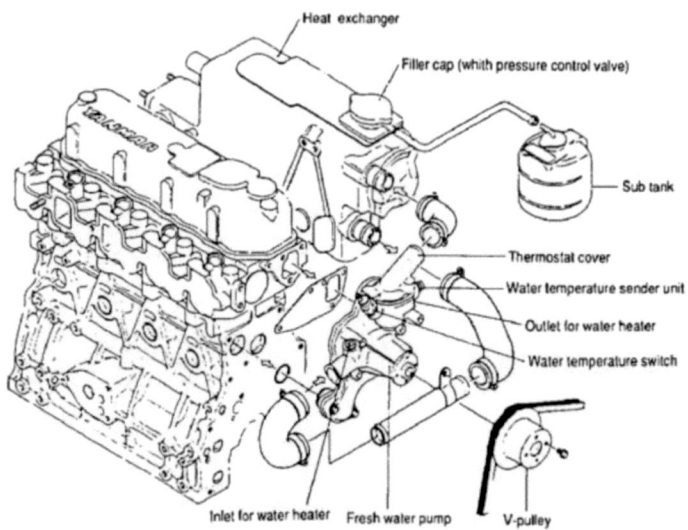

Sea water line

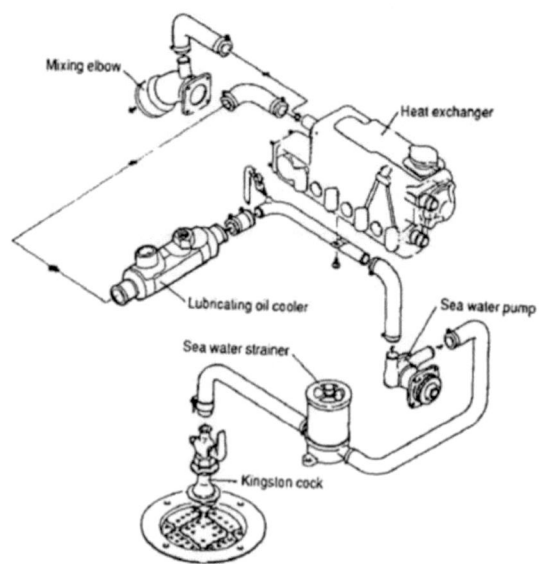

2. Sea water pump

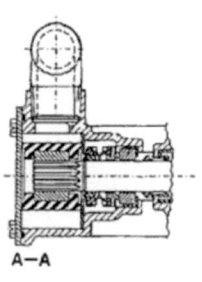

A-A

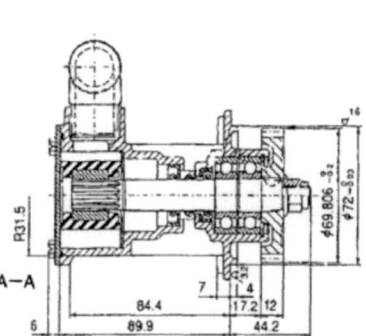

A-A

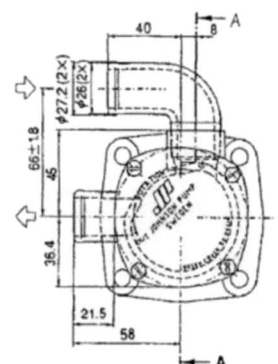

2-1 Specifications of aea water pump

1. Performance

Flow	min 3800 ℓ/h at pin=—0.05 bar pout=0.95 bar n=3250rpm after1500h duty
Selfpriming ability	max 10 s at suctionhead=0.5m length of pipe=0.6m n=500rpm
Thightness test	4bar

2. Durability

Impeller Flow drop	min1500h max10% after 1000h
Leakage from seal Lipseal,water Lipseal,oil	max3cc/h 1000h 3000h
Endcover, wear plate	min3000h
Other parts	min6000h

2-2 Sea water pump disassembly

(1) Remove the rubber hose from the sea water pump outlet and then the sea water pump assembly from the gear case.
(2) Remove the sea water pump cover and take out the O-ring, impeller and wear plate.
(3) Remove the mechanical seal side stop ring.
(4) Insert pliers from the drive gear long hole and remove the stop ring that holds the bearings.
(5) Lightly tap the pump shaft from the impeller side and remove the pump shaft, bearings, and drive gear as a set.
(6) Remove the oil seal and mechanical seal if necessary.

2-3 Sea water pump Inspection

(1) Inspect the rubber impeller, checking for splitting around the outside, damage or cracks, and replace if necessary.

Chapter 6 Cooling Water System
2. Sea Water Pump

3,4JH3(B)(C)E

(2) Inspect the mechanical seal and relace if the spring is damaged, or the seal is corroded. Also replace the mechanical seal if there is considerable water leakage during operation.

Cooling water leakage	less than 3 cc/h

(3) Make sure the ball bearings rotate smoothly. Replace if there is excessive play.

2-4 Sea water pump reassembly
(1) When replacing the mechanical seal, coat the No.1101 oil seal and pressure fit Coat the sliding surface with a good quality silicon oil, taking sufficient care not to cause any scratches.
(2) When replacing the oil seal, coat with grease and insert.
(3) Mount the pump shaft, ball bearing and gear assembly to the pump unit and fit the bearing stop ring. Be sure not to forget the water O-ring when doing this.

NOTE : Coat the shaft with grease.

(4) After inserting the mechanical seal stop ring, mount the wear plate and impeller.
(5) Mount the O-ring side cover.

NOTE : Replace the O.ring.

2-5 Current characteristics

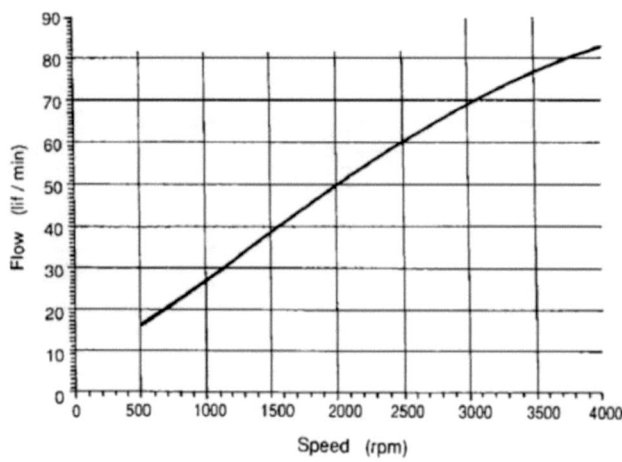

3. Fresh Water Pump

3-1 Fresh water pump construction

The fresh water pump is of the centrifugal (volute) type, and circulates water from the fresh water tank to the cylinders and cylinder head.
The fresh water pump consists of the pump body, impeller, pump shaft, bearing unit and mechanical seal. The V pulley on the end of the pump shaft is driven by a V belt from the crankshaft.
The bearing unit assembled in the pump shaft uses grease lubricated ball bearings and cannot be disassembled.
The totally enclosed mechanical seal spring presses the impeller seal mounted on the impeller side away from the pump body side. This prevents water from leaking along the pump shaft.
As the impeller and pulley flanges are press fit assembled, they cannot be disassembled.

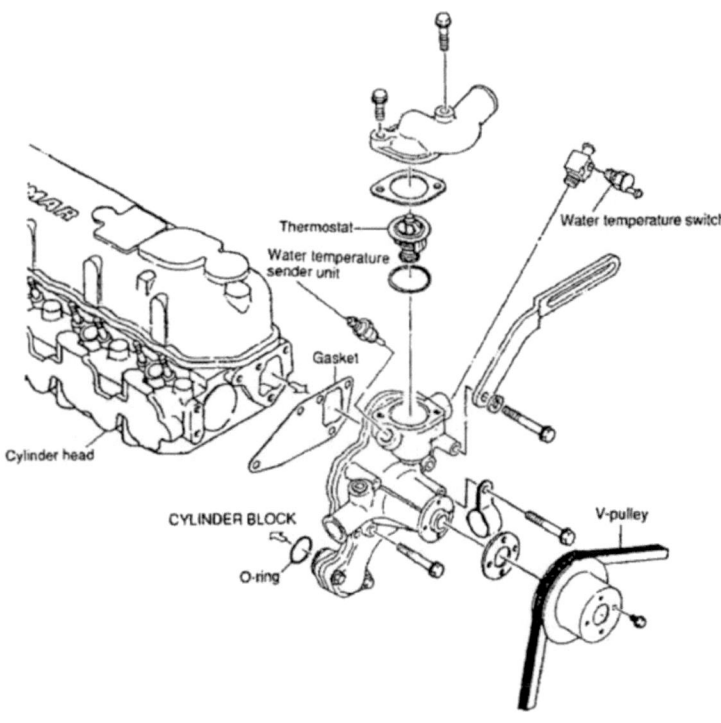

Chapter 6 Cooling Water System
3. Fresh Water Pump

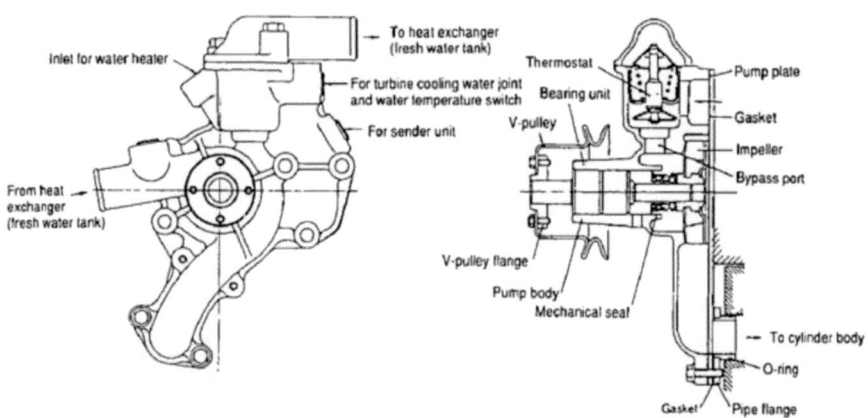

3-2 Specifications of fresh water pump

Pulley ratio (crank shaft/pump shaft)	⌀134/⌀120
Pump shaft speed(Max)	4020 rpm
Delivery capacity	70 ℓ/min
Total head	4m

3-3 Fresh water pump disassembly
(1) Do not disassemble the fresh water pump. It is difficult to disassemble and, once disassembled, even more difficult to reassemble. Replace the pump as an assembly in the event of trouble.
(2) When removing the fresh water pipe as an assembly from the cylinder and cylinder head, replace the cylinder intake pipe O-ring.
(3) When the fresh water pump body and cylinder intake flange and/or fresh water pump and pump plate are disassembled, retighten to the specified torque.

Tightening torque for pump setting bolts	70~110 kg·cm

3-4 Fresh water pump inspection
(1) Bearing unit inspection
Rotate the impeller smoothly. If the rotation is not smooth or abnormal noise is heard due to excessive bearing play or contact with other parts, replace the pump as an assembly.
(2) Impeller inspection
Check the impeller blade, and replace if damaged or corroded, or if the impeller blade is worn due to contact with pump body.

(3) Check the holes in the cooling water and bypass lines, clean out any dirt or other foreign matter and repair as necessary.
(4) Replace the pump as an assembly if there is excessive water leakage due to mechanical seal or impeller seal wear or damage.
(5) Inspect the fresh water pump body and flange, clean off scale and rust, and replace if corroded.
(6) Measure the clearance between the impeller and the pump body, and the impeller and the plate.
Measure the clearance between the impeller and the pump body by pushing the impeller all the way towards the body, and inserting a thickness gauge diagonally between the impeller and the body.
Measure the clearance between the impeller and the plate (pump body bracket) by placing a straight-edge against the end of the pump body and inserting a thickness gauge between the impeller and the straight-edge.

Chapter 6 Cooling Water System
3. Fresh Water Pump

Measuring clearance between impeller and pump body.

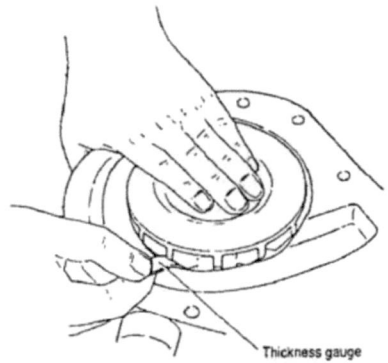

Measuring clearance between impeller and pump body bracket.

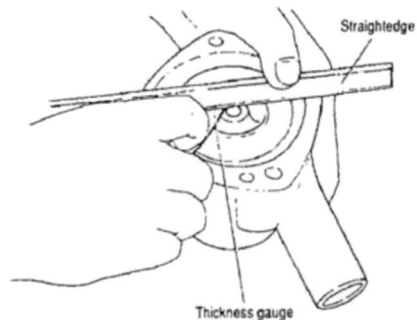

mm

	Standard	Wear limit
Clearance between impeller and body	0.3~1.1	1.5
Clearance between impeller and plate	15	—

4. Heat Exchanger

4-1 Heat exchanger construction

The heat exchanger cools the hot fresh water that has cooled the inside of the engine with sea water.
The inside of the heat exchanger cooling pipe consists of 36 small dia. tubes and baffle plates.
The sea water flows through the small dia tubes and the fresh water flows through the maze formed by the baffle plates.

There is a reservoir at the bottom of the cooling pipe which serves as the fresh water tank. There is an exhaust water passageway (line) in the reservoir which forms a water cooled exhaust gas manifold.
The filler cap on top of the heat exchanger has a pressure valve, which lets off steam through the overflow pipe when pressure in the fresh water system exceeds the specified value. It also takes in air from the overflow pipe when pressure in the fresh water system drops below the normal value.

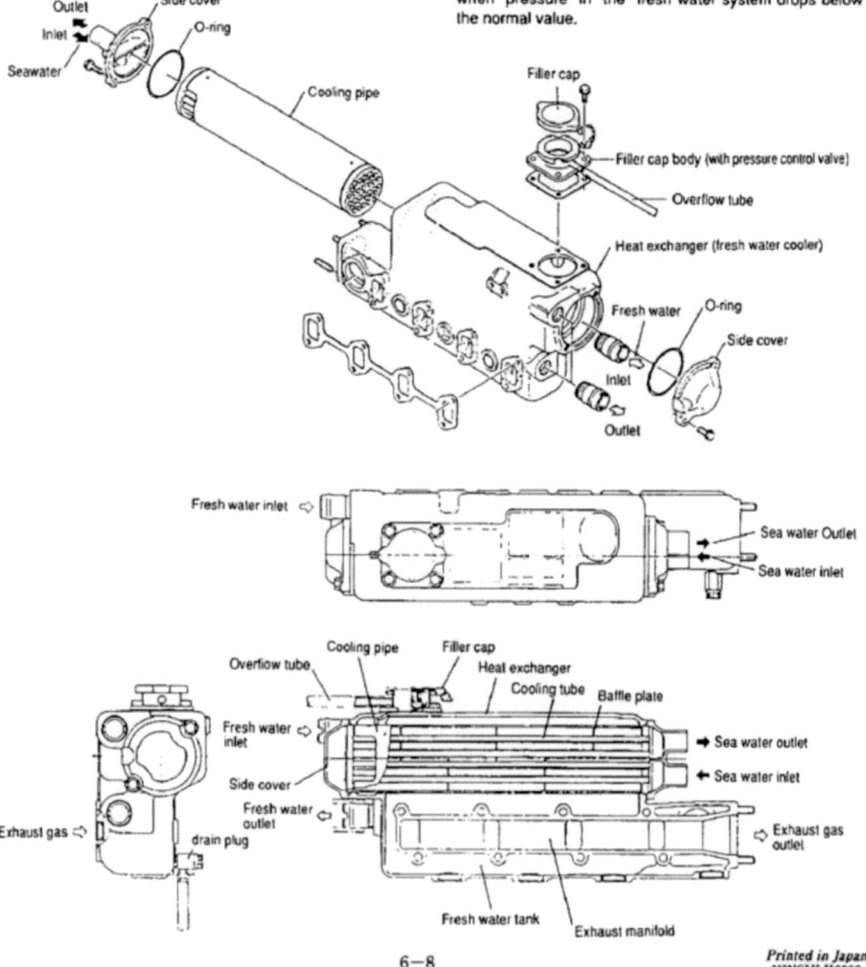

Chapter 6 Cooling Water System
4. Heat Exchanger 3,4JH3(B)(C)E

4-2 Specifications of heat exchanger

MODEL	UNIT	3JH3E	4JH3E
Tube dia.	mm	φ6/φ5×54	φ6/φ5×54
Tube surface area	m²	0.193	0.347
Tube surface area/output	m	0.0048	0.0062
Fresh water frow	ℓ/hr	4200	4200
Sea water frow	ℓ/hr	3800	3800
Fresh water velocity	m/s	1.21	1.11
Sea water velocity	m/s	1.99	1.99

4-3 Disassembly and reassembly of the heat exchanger

(1) Remove the covers on both sides and take out the cooling pipe and O-ring(s).

NOTE : Replace the O-ring(s) when you have removed the cooling pipe.

(2) Remove the filler assembly

4-4 Heat exchanger inspection

(1) Cooling pipe inspection
 1) Inspect the inside of the tubes for rust or scale buildup from sea water, and clean with a wire brush if necessary.

NOTE: Disassemble and wash when the cooling water temperature reaches 85 ℃.

 2) Check the joints at both ends of the tubes for looseness or damage, and repair if loose, Replace if damaged or corroded
 3) Check tubes and replace if leaking.
 4) Clean any scale or rust off the outside of the tubes.

(2) Heat exchanger body inspection
 1) Check heat exchanger body and side cover for dirt and corrosion. Replace if excessively corroded, or cracked.
 2) Inspect sea water and fresh water inlets and outlets, retighten any joints as necessary and clean the insides of the pipes.
 3) Check the exhaust gas intake flange and line, and replace if corroded or cracked.

(3) Heat exchanger body water Leakage test
 1) Compressed air/water tank test
 Fit rubber covers on the fresh water and sea water inlets and outlets. Place the heat exchanger in a water tank, feed in compressed air from the overflow pipe and check for any (water) leakage, (air bubbles).

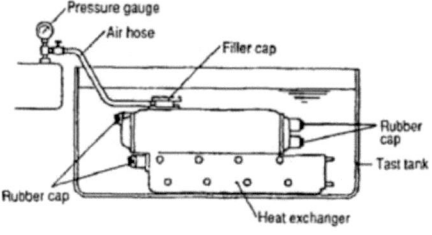

Test pressure	2kg/cm²

 2) Use of the tester
 Fit the fresh and sea water inlets and outlets with rubber covers and fill the fresh water tank with fresh water. Fit a pressure cap tester in place of the pressure cap, operate the pump for one minute and set the pressure at 1.5kg/cm² (21.33lb/in.²). If there are any leaks the pressure will not rise. If there are no leaks the pressure will not fall.

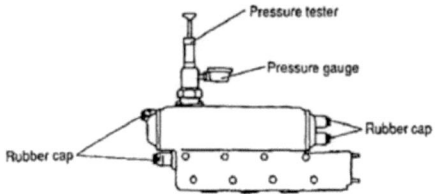

6-9

5. Pressure Cap and Sub Tank

5-1 Pressure cap construction
The pressure cap mounted on the fresh water filler neck incorporates a pressure control valve. The cap is mounted on the filler neck cam by placing it on the rocking tab and rotating. The top seal of the cap seals the top of the filler neck, and the pressure valve seals the lock seat.

5-2 Pressure cap pressure control
The pressure valve and vacuum seal both seal the valve seat when the pressure in the fresh water system is within the specified value of 0.9kg/cm². This seals the fresh water system.
When the pressure within the fresh water system exceeds the specified value, the pressure valve opens, and steam is discharged through the overflow pipe. When the fresh water is cooled and the pressure within the fresh water system drops below the normal value, atmospheric pressure opens the vacuum valve, and air is drawn in through the overflow pipe.

5-3 Pressure cap inspection
Precautions
Do not open the pressure cap while the engine is running or right after stopping because high temperature steam will be blown out. Remove the cap only after the water has had a chance to cool down.

(1) Remove scale and rust, check the seat and seat valve, etc. for scratches or wear, and the spring for corrosion or settling Replace if necessary

NOTE : Clean the pressure cap with fresh water as it will not close completely if it is dirty.

(2) Fit the adapter on the tester to the pressure cap. Pump until the pressure gauge is within the specified pressure range (0.75~1.05kg/cm²) and note the gauge reading. The cap is normal if the pressure holds for six seconds If the pressure does not rise, or drops immediately, inspect the cap and repair or replace as necessary.

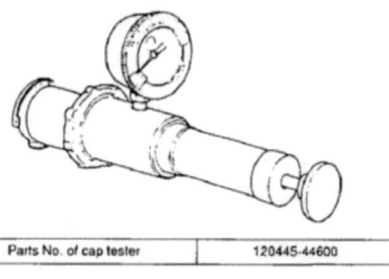

Parts No. of cap tester	120445-44600

5-4 Function of the sub tank
The pressure valve opens to discharge steam when the steam pressure in the fresh water tank exceeds 0.9kg/cm² (12.80lb/in.²).
This consumes water. The sub tank maintains the water level by preventing this discharge of water.
The steam discharged into the sub tank condenses into watch, and the water level in the sub tank rises.
When the pressure in the fresh water system drops below the normal value, the water in the sub tank is sucked back into the fresh water tank to raise the water back to its original level.
The sub tank facilitates long hours of operation without water replacement and eliminates the possibility of burns when the steam is ejected from the filler neck because the pressure cap does not need to be removed.

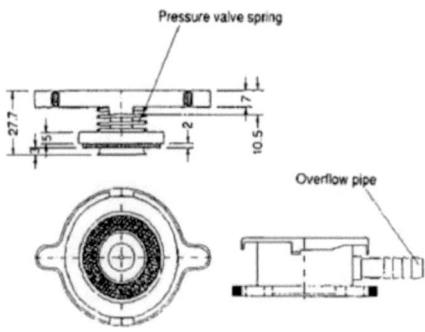

The sub tank (which will be described later), keeps the water level from dropping due to discharge of steam when the pressure valve opens.

Action of pressure control valve

Pressure valve	Open at 0.9 kg/cm²
Vacuum valve	Open at 0.05 kg/cm² or below

Chapter 6 Cooling Water System
5. Pressure Cap and Sub Tank

3,4JH3(B)(C)E

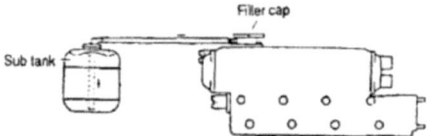

5-7 Precautions on usage of the sub tank
(1) Check the sub tank when the engine is cool and refill with fresh water as necessary to bring the water level between the low and full marks.
(2) Check the overflow pipe and replace if bent or cracked Clean out the pipe if it is clogged up.

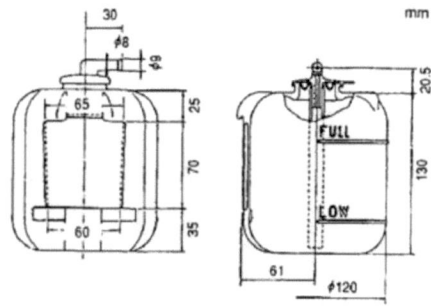

5-5 Specifications of sub tank

	Overall capacity	1.251 ℓ
Subtank capacity	Full-scale position	0.81 ℓ
	Low-scale position	0.21 ℓ

5-6 Mounting the sub tank
(1) The sub tank is mounted at approximately the same height as the heat exchanger (fresh water tank). (allowable difference in height : 300mm (11.8110 in.) or less)
(2) The overflow pipe should be less than 1000mm (39.3701in) long, and mounted so that it does not sag or bend.

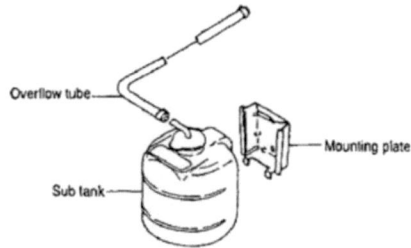

NOTE : Make sure that the overflow pipe of the sub tank is not submerged in bilge If the overflow pipe is submerged in bilge, water in the bilge will be siphoned into the fresh water tank when the water is being cooled.

6. Thermostat

6-1 Functioning of thermostat

The thermostat opens and closes a valve according to changes in the temperature of the fresh water inside the engine, controlling the volume of water flowing to the heat exchanger from the cylinder head, and in turn maintaining the temperature of the fresh water in the engine at a constant level.

The thermostat is bottom bypass type It is located in a position connected with the cylinder head outlet line at the top of the top of fresh water pump unit.

When the fresh water temperature is low (75.0°C ~78.0°C or less), the thermostat is closed, and fresh water goes from the bypass line to the fresh water pump intake and circulates in the engine.

When the fresh water temperature exceeds the above temperature, the thermostat opens, and a portion of the water is sent to the heat exchanger and cooled by sea water, the other portion going from the bypass line to the fresh water pump intake.

The bypass line is closed off as the thermostat valve opens and is completely closed when the fresh water temperature reaches 81.5°C (valve lifts 4mm (0.1575in)), sending all of the water to the heat exchanger.

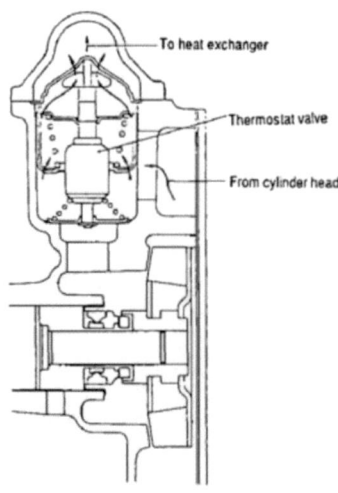

When valve is opened (by-pass passage is closed)

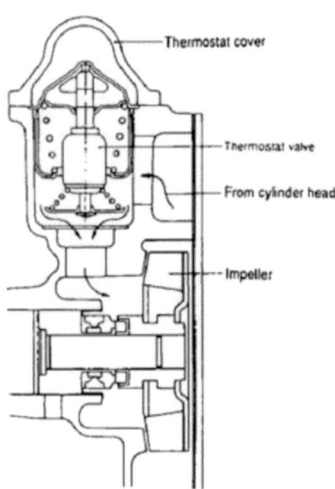

When valve is closed (by-pass passage is opened)

6-2 Thermostat construction

The thermostat used in this engine is of the wax pellet type, with a solid wax pellet located in a small chamber. When the temperature of the cooling water rises, the wax melts and increases in volume. This expansion and construction is used to open and close the valve

6-3 Characteristics of thermostat

Opening temperature	75~78°C
Full open temperature	90°
Valve lift at full open	8 mm
By.pass valve lift	3.7mm
By.pass valve close temperature	81.5°C

6. Thermostat

6-4 Thermostat inspection

Remove the thermostat cover on top of the fresh water pump and take out the thermostat. Clean off scale and rust and inspect, and replace if the characteristics (performance) have changed, or if the spring is broken, deformed ar corroded.

6-5 Testing the thermostat

(1) Put the thermostat in a Leaker with fresh water, and heat it on an electric stove. The thermostat is functioning normally if it starts to open between 75~780°C, and opens 8mm or more at 90°C Replace the thermostat if it is not functioning normally.
(2) Normally, the thermostat should be inspected every 500 hours of operation, but, it should be inspected before this if the cooling temperature rises abnormally or white smoke is emitted for a long time after engine starting.
(3) Replace the thermostat every year or 2000 hours of operation (whichever comes first).

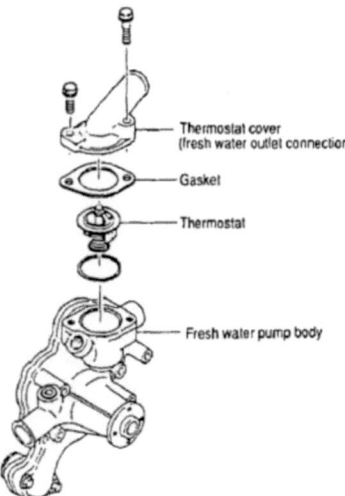

- Thermostat cover (fresh water outlet connection)
- Gasket
- Thermostat
- Fresh water pump body

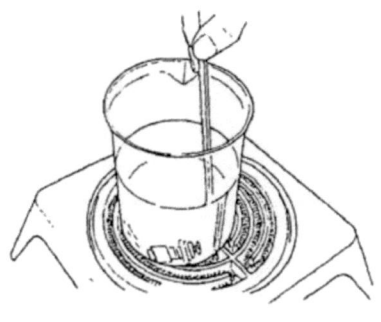

7. Bilge Pump and Bilge Strainer (Optional)

7-1. Introduction
7-1.1 General Introduction

Name	Bilge pump	
Time	10 minutes	
Rotation direction	Right (viewed from the impeller side)	
Weight	Pump	1.4kg
	Switch ASSY	0.3kg
Negative pressure detector	Diaphragm type	
Temperature	−30℃ ~ 80℃	

7-1.2 Exterior
(1) Pump dimensions

Length	225mm
Yoke diameter	ϕ 61
Assembly hole diameter	ϕ 5.3
Assembly pitch	50×90mm

For further details on the above dimensions, refer to External View (0790 001 0710).

(2) Switch ASSY dimensions

Length	64mm
Assembly hole diameter	ϕ 4.5

For further details on the above dimensions, refer to External View.

(3) Surface condition
Paint, plating, assembly, and finishing touches are well-done and without rust, scratches or other blemishes.

7-2. Description
7-2.1 Characteristics
(1) Discharge At lift : 0m discharge capacity : 20 ℓ /min. or greater.
(2) Automatic feeding height : 1m or greater
(Limit for automatic feeding height : new pump with inside parts wet, approx. 2m)
(3) Automatic feeding time : 2~5secs.
(Limit for automatic feeding time : new pump with inside parts wet, approx. 1 sec.)
(4) Automatic stopping : Air intake causes negative pressure triggering automatic stopping.

7-2.2 Insulation
(1) Insulation resistance : 500V with a megatester when the difference between the continuity point and the body is 1MΩ or greater.
(2) Insulation proof stress : AC50 between the continuity point and the body, or 60hz 500v for 1 minute when impressed current leakage is 10mA or lower.

7-2.3 Durability : Rated voltage when there is 3% salt water 60 ℓ + engine oil 3%, and operation is at 1800 cycles and there are no difficulties.

7-2.4 Vibration proof : Amplitude 0.51mm (one side of the amplitude)
Vibration frequency 10~55Hz
Sweep time 90secs.
Direction of vibration each direction 4 hours
No difficulties after test period

7-3. Cautions
(1) Attach at a position higher than the bilge water away from rain or other water, and 50~70cm above the bottom of the boat.
(2) Never run the pump dry. Be sure that the strainer is inserted in the drain water before pushing the switch. If no water is being drawn up after a period of 10 seconds or more, prime the pump. (Do not run the pump for longer than 10 seconds when no water is being drawn up.)
(3) When the pump has not been used for a long period of time, the inside of the pump will be dry and drawing ability will be lowered. Before reusing, clean the inside of the pump or prime it to insure that it is wet, and check to be sure that the pump is then operating correctly.
(4) When charging the diesel engine oil, wait a period of 30 minutes or longer from the time of stopping (oil temperature 20~70℃). Refrain from operation when the oil temperature is below 15℃, or above 50℃.
(5) When the bilge inside the pump or hose freezes, completely melt the water with a steaming towel before beginning operation. When the temperature inside the pump is low, it will take a longer amount of time for the pump to drain off the bilge.
(6) The impeller replacement kit includes one impeller and 3 washers for adjusting the side gap. If after replacing the impeller the pump does not drain, place side gap adjustment washers underneath the bottom plate to adjust. Select the number of washers used in accordance with the following. (When the pump is draining, the electric current load is about 5A. When there are too many washers, the electric current value will be too great and will blow a fuse.)

Chapter 6 Cooling Water System
7. Bilge Pump and Bilge Strainer (Optional)

3,4JH3(B)(C)E

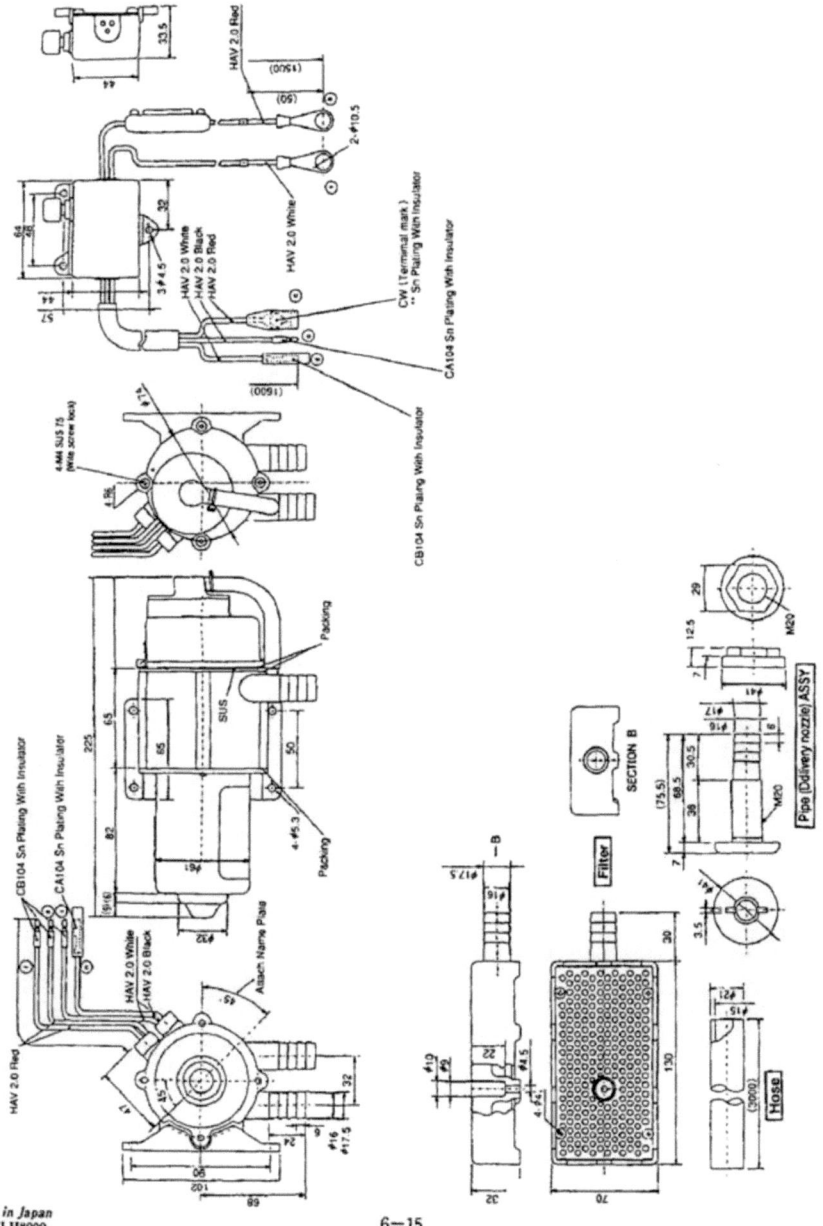

Chapter 6 Cooling Water System
7. Bilge Pump and Bilge Strainer (Optional)

3,4JH3(B)(C)E

(7) The pump cannot be used to drain off rain water or large amounts of flood water. The pump can be run continuously for a period of 10 minutes. After this time it must shut off for a period of 2 hours before reusing.

(8) Do not use the pump for showering.
If the pump outlet is deformed for showering, the increase in water pressure will increase the load on the motor and cause motor seizure.

(9) Fix the strainer so that it will not turn upside down or on its side.

(10) When sludge has built up in the bilge to be drained, position the strainer about 20mm above the sludge. When the pump is stopped, be sure there is no sludge remaining inside the pump.

(11) The specific gravity for the battery fluid is 1.25 or more.

Assembly Procedure

☆When bilge is being used, assemble in accordance with the following.

1. Assembling the bilge pump
- Select a dry place above the bilge water level.
- Select the location for the bilge pump taking into consideration the length of the switch cable (approx. 3m) and its attachment point, and the position of the battery.
- Position at a 45° angle as shown in the illustration with the nozzle facing up, and 50~70cm from the bottom of the boat.

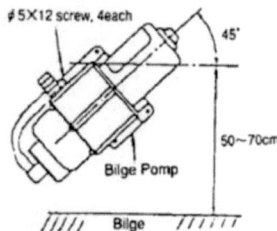

2. Assembling the switch
- Attach in a place to insure easy operation away from rainwater.
- Connect the terminal to the battery.
(When the cord will not reach the battery, an extension of no greater than 3m length suitable for AV3mm² can be attached.)

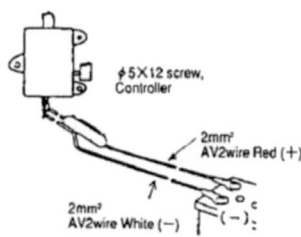

3. Positioning the strainer
- Attach at the place where the greatest amount of water is collected when the boat is stopped.
- It is best to place the strainer as close to the bilge pump as possible. Cut the 3m hose to a length of 1.2m~1.8m and attach allowing plenty of give.
- Check the strainer during a test operation before screwing firmly into place.
(When the strainer is screwed in, be especially careful not to damage the bottom of the boat.)
- The strainer contains a weight, and can be used with the weight in place.
- Always keep the strainer clean.

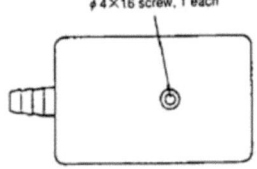

4. Attaching the delivery nozzle (outlet)
- Make a fixing hole of ø21 or less for attaching the nozzle. The hose attached at the nozzle should be 1.8m or less and should reach without any strain, therefore care should be taken in deciding on the best position.
- Fix the nozzle (outlet) in place and attach on the discharge side of the pump.

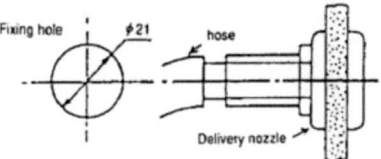

Chapter 6 Cooling Water System
7. Bilge Pump and Bilge Strainer (Optional)

3,4JH3(B)(C)E

5. Attaching the hose
- Attach the hose from the strainer to the pump inlet.
- Attach the delivery nozzle hose to the pump outlet.
- Make the hose as short as possible and avoid sharp bends.

6. Test operation
- Collect water in the bottom of the boat, and check for any problems with the hose or wiring. After doing this, connect the battery.
- Turn on the pump switch, and check to see that water is being taken in and discharged properly. The pump will stop automatically when there is no water left.
- If the inside of the pump is dry, or if the water is not being drawn up initially after a period of 10 seconds, lift the strainer above the water surface and stop the pump. Prime the pump before starting it up again.

7. Fixing the strainer
- After the test operation, fix the strainer into place with screws.
  (Be careful not to damage the bottom of the boat with the screws.)

Cautions for Assembling
Observe the following cautions for handling.

○Do not use gasoline or solvents.
  1. gasoline 2. ester 3. benzol 4. battery fluid
  5. liquids at 70°C or greater or engine oil
○Never run when there is no water in the bilge.
  Check to be sure that the strainer is in the water before turning on the switch.
○Keep the cord terminal away from the water. Water inside the motor or switch may lead to damage. When the insulation around the cord is damaged, water can seep in to the wires; thus, care should be taken not to scratch or nick the cord.
○When the pump has not been used for a long period of time, the inside of the pump will be dry and it may not operate properly at first. If after 10 seconds the pump is not working, turn off the switch and prime the pump before trying again.
  (Never run the pump dry for a period of greater than 10 seconds.)

○Replace the diesel engine oil only after the engine has been stopped for a period of 30 minutes (oil temp. 20~70°C). Whenever possible refrain from operation when the oil temperature is below 15°C or above 50°C.
○Bilge water left in the hose or inside the pump can freeze, and care should be taken to see that any excess bilge is completely discharged. If bilge water should freeze inside the hose or pump, it should be completely melted before starting up the pump. When the temperature inside the pump is low, it will take a longer time for the pump to operate. (0°C, 5~10secs.)
○Keep the pump in a dry place away from rain or other water.
○Use the regulation hose; do no use thin vinyl hose or hose which is not heat-resistant.
○The pump cannot be used to drain off rainwater or large quantities of flood water. This pump can be operated continuously for a period of 10 minutes.
○Do not use the pump for showering.
  If the pump outlet is deformed for showering, the increase in water pressure will increase the load on the motor and cause motor seizure.
○When sludge has built up in the bilge to be drained, position the strainer about 20cm above the sludge. When the pump is stopped, be sure there is no sludge remaining inside the pump housing.
○The specific gravity for the battery fluid is 1.25.
○Refer to your local dealer for impeller replacement.
  The local dealer will perform the following.
  The impeller replacement kit includes one impeller and 3 films for adjusting the side gap. If after replacing the impeller the pump does not drain, place side gap adjustment washers underneath the bottom plate to adjust. Select the number of films used in accordance with the following. (When the pump is draining, the electric current load is about 10A for 12V and 5A for 24V. The pump operates efficiently at these electric current loads.)
  *Steps for replacement
  1. Remove the impeller plate by taking out the M4 screws (4) and opening the top of the diaphragm switch and the.
     (Screw lock has been applied to the screw, and a dryer should be used to heat the screw before removing it.)
  2. Clean the inside of the pump.
  3. Grease the plate, impeller, and film for side gap adjustment, and then reassemble the pump by inserting first the film plate and then the impeller.

6-17

Chapter 6 Cooling Water System
7. Bilge Pump and Bilge Strainer (Optional)   3,4JH3(B)(C)E

Troubleshooting

Refer to the following countermeasures for difficulties that arise.

Problem	Cause	Countermeasure
1. Pump does not turn	Faulty wiring	Check the wiring between the motor and battery.
	Faulty battery	Check to see if the specific gravity of the battery fluid is greater than 1.25. Recharge or replace the battery.
	Faulty starter switch	Consult your local dealer.
	Faulty pump	Consult your local dealer.
2. Pump turns but does not draw up water.	Draws up air.	Check hose connections. Retighten pump screws.
	Low voltage in battery.	Check to see if the specific gravity of the battery fluid is greater than 1.25. Recharge or replace the battery.
	The distance between the pump and the surface of the water is too great.	Lower the pump. (Position the pump so that it is closer to the surface of the water.)
	The pump is too high.	Lower the pump. (Position the pump so that it is 50~70cm above the bottom of the boat.)
	Pump intake is weak.	If intake is still faulty after priming, consult your local dealer.
3. Pump turns, but the amount of discharge is low.	Clogged strainer	Clean strainer.
	Hose is broken or damaged.	Check for damage and repair. If incorrect hose has been used, replace with the regulation type of hose.
4. Water leakage from pump	Water leakage from packing	Retighten pump screws.
	Faulty pump seal	Consult your local dealer.
5. Pump draws up bilge, but motor stops when hand is removed from starter switch.	Faulty diaphragm switch	Check for loose wiring in diaphragm switch and correct.
	Damaged diaphragm switch	Consult your local dealer.
6. Motor does not stop when there is no bilge water left	Clogged strainer or hose	Clean strainer or hose.
	Damaged diaphragm switch	Check for continuity of diaphragm switch terminal. Consult your local dealer if there is continuity.

CHAPTER 7
REDUCTION AND REVERSING GEAR

Marine Gear Models [KM3A]

1. Construction 7-1
   - 1-1. Construction 7-1
   - 1-2. Specifications 7-2
   - 1-3. Power transmission system 7-3
   - 1-4. Drawing 7-5
   - 1-5. Sectional view 7-6
2. Shifting Device 7-7
   - 2-1. Construction of shifting mechanism 7-7
   - 2-2. Forward and reverse clutch operation 7-8
   - 2-3. Engagement and disengagement of clutch ... 7-8
   - 2-4. Clutch shifting force 7-9
   - 2-5. Adjustment of shifting device 7-9
   - 2-6. Adjustment of the remote control head 7-11
   - 2-7. Cautions 7-11
3. Inspection and Servicing 7-12
   - 3-1. Clutch case 7-12
   - 3-2. Bearing 7-12
   - 3-3. Gear 7-12
   - 3-4. Forward and reverse large gears 7-12
   - 3-5. Drive cone 7-12
   - 3-6. Thrust collar 7-14
   - 3-7. Cup spring 7-15
   - 3-8. Oil seal of output shaft 7-15
   - 3-9. Input shaft 7-15
   - 3-10. Output shaft 7-15
   - 3-11. Intermediate shaft 7-16
   - 3-12. Shifting device 7-16
   - 3-13. Damper disc 7-17
   - 3-14. Shim adjustment for output and input shafts ... 7-17
   - 3-15. Torque limiter 7-19
4. Disassembly 7-20
   - 4-1. Dismantling the clutch 7-20
   - 4-2. Removal of the output shaft 7-22
   - 4-3. Removal of the intermediate shaft. 7-24
   - 4-4. Dismantling the shifting device 7-24
5. Reassembly 7-25
   - 5-1. Reassembly of output shaft 7-25
   - 5-2. Reassembly of the clutch 7-26
   - 5-3. Reassembly of the shiating device 7-28

Marine Gear Models [KM3P4]

1. Construction 7-29
   - 1-1. Construction 7-29
   - 1-2. Specifications 7-30
   - 1-3. Power transmission system 7-31
   - 1-4. Drawing 7-33
   - 1-5. Sectional view 7-34
2. Shifting Device 7-35
   - 2-1. Construction of shifting mechanism 7-35
   - 2-2. Forward and reverse clutch operation 7-36
   - 2-3. Engagement and disengagement of clutch ... 7-36
   - 2-4. Clutch shifting force 7-37
   - 2-5. Adjustment of shifting device 7-37
   - 2-6. Adjustment of the remote control head 7-39
   - 2-7. Cautions 7-39
3. Inspection and Servicing 7-40
   - 3-1. Clutch case 7-40
   - 3-2. Bearing 7-40
   - 3-3. Gear 7-40
   - 3-4. Forward and reverse large gears 7-40
   - 3-5. Drive cone 7-40
   - 3-6. Thrust collar 7-42
   - 3-7. Cup spring and spring retainer 7-43
   - 3-8. Oil seal of output shaft 7-43
   - 3-9. Input shaft 7-43
   - 3-10. Output shaft 7-43
   - 3-11. Intermediate shaft 7-44
   - 3-12. Shifting device 7-44
   - 3-13. Damper disc 7-45
   - 3-14. Shim adjustment for output and input shafts ... 7-45
   - 3-15. Torque limiter 7-47
4. Disassembly 7-48
   - 4-1. Dismantling the clutch 7-48
   - 4-2. Removal of the output shaft 7-50
   - 4-3. Removal of the intermediate shaft. 7-51
   - 4-4. Dismantling the shifting device 7-52
5. Reassembly 7-53
   - 5-1. Reassembly of output shaft 7-53
   - 5-2. Reassembly of the clutch 7-54
   - 5-3. Reassembly of the shiating device 7-56

Chapter 7 Reduction and Reversing Gear
1. Construction   3,4JH3(B)(C)E

Marine Gear Models
KM3A , KM35A
for Engine Models 3JH3BE(A)
4JH3BE

1. Construction

1-1. Construction

These clutches are a cone-type, mechanically operated clutch. When the drive cone (which is connected to the output shaft by the lead spline) is moved forward or backward, its taper contacts with the large gear and transfers power to the output shaft.
The construction is simple when compared with other types of clutch and it serves to reduce the number of components, making for a lighter, more compact unit which can be operated smoothly. Although it is small, the power transmission efficiency is high even under a heavy load. Its durability is high and it is also reliable because high grade materials are used for the shaft and gear, and, a taper roller bearing is incorporated. Power transmission is smooth because connection with the engine is made through the damper disc.

- The drive cone is made from special aluminum bronze which has both higher wear-resistance and durability. The drive cone is connected with the output shaft through the thread spline. The taper angle, diameter of the drive cone, twist angle, and diameter of the thread spline, are designed to give the greatest efficiency, thus ensuring that the drive cone can be readily engaged or disengaged.
- Helical gears are used for greater strength. The intermediate shaft is supported at 2 points to reduce deflection and gear noise.
- The clutch case and mounting flange are made from an aluminum alloy of special composition to reduce weight.

It is also anticorrosive against seawater.

- As the damper disc is fitted to the input shaft, power can be transmitted smoothly.
- There is small clearance between the dipstick and the inside of the dipstick tube. A small hole in the dipstick works as a breather.
- When the load on the propeller is removed, the engagement of the drive cone and the large gear is maintained by the shifter and V-groove of the drive cone. Even when the drive cone's tapered area and V-groove are worn, this engagement is maintained by the shift lever device and accordingly no adjustment of the remote control cable is required.
- The cup spring on the rear of the larger gear absorbs rotational fluctuations and stabilizes the engagement of the drive cone and the larger gear. Thus, the durability of the cone against wear is enhanced.

NOTE :
- KM35A marine gear has been installed on 3JH3BE and 4JH3BE engines (Feb.,2002)
- KM35A marine gear differs from KM3A as follows.
  · No torque limiter applied to KM35A.
  · Output shaft dia. 28mm. (KM3A : 25mm).
  · Imput shaft reverse small gear width increased to strengthen.
  · Overall length of KM35A : 208mm.
    [KM3A : 246mm(with torque limiter)]
  · Marine gear oil reserve capacity up.
    0.65L (0.45L KM3A)

Chapter 7 Reduction and Reversing Gear
1. Construction

3,4JH3(B)(C)E

1-2 Specifications

Model			KM3A, KM35A			
For engine models			3JH3BE (A)		4JH3BE	
Clutch			Constant mesh gear with servo cone clutch (wet type)			
Reduction ratio	Forward		2.33	2.64	2.33	2.64
	Reverse		3.04	3.04	3.04	3.04
Propeller shaft min^{-1} (Forward)			1577	1396	1577	1396
Direction of rotation	Input shaft		Counter-clockwise, viewed from stern			
	Output shaft	Forward	Clockwise, viewed from stern			
		Reverse	Counter-clockwise, viewed from stern			
Remote control	Control head		Single lever control			
	Cable		Morse. 33-C (cable travel 76.2mm)			
	Clamp		YANMAR made, standard accessory			
	Cable connector		YANMAR made, standard accessory			
Output shaft coupling	Outer diameter		100mm			
	Pitch circle diameter		78mm			
	Connecting bolt holes i		4- 10.5mm			
Position of shift lever			Right side, viewed from stern			
Lubricating oil			API CC class, SAE 20/30			
Lubricating oil capscity			0.45L (KM3A), 0.65(KM35A)			
Dry mass			13kg			

Note
* Torque limiter should be installed on KM3A.
* No torque limiter installed on KM35A.

Reduction ratio	No. of blade	Diameter of the propeller mm	Moment of inertia N·m² (kgf·m²=GD²)	Material
2.33	3	450	$\leq$ 1.47 (0.15)	Bronze
	4	425		
2.64	3	470	$\leq$ 1.86 (0.19)	
	4	440		

1-3 Power transmission system
1-3-1 Arrangement of shafts and gears

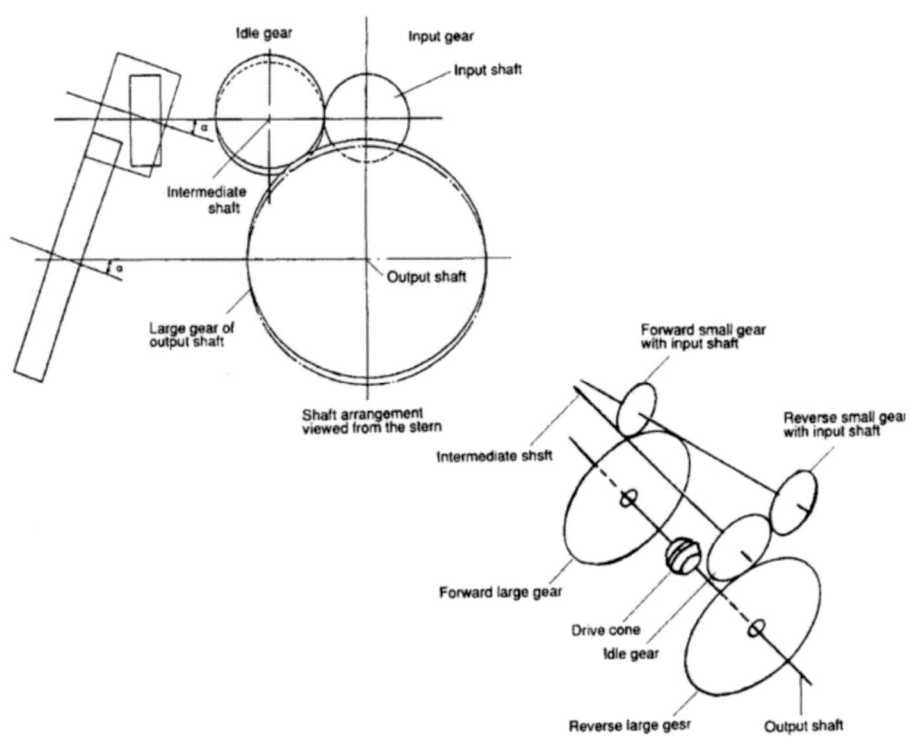

1-3-2 Reduction ratio
Forward

Model	No. of teeth of forward small gear Zif	No. of teeth of forward 18rge gear Zof	Reduction ratio Zof/Zif
KM3A, KM35A	24	56	56/24 = 2.33
	22	58	58/22 = 2.64

Reverse

Model	No. of teeth of reverse small gear Zif	No. of teeth of intemediate shaft gear Zi	No. of teeth of reverse large gear Zdr	Reduction ratio Zi/Zir · Zdr/Zl
KM3A KM35A	23	36	70	70/23 = 3.04

Chapter 7 Reduction and Reversing Gear
1. Construction

3,4JH3(B)(C)E

1-3-3 Power transmission routine-Forward

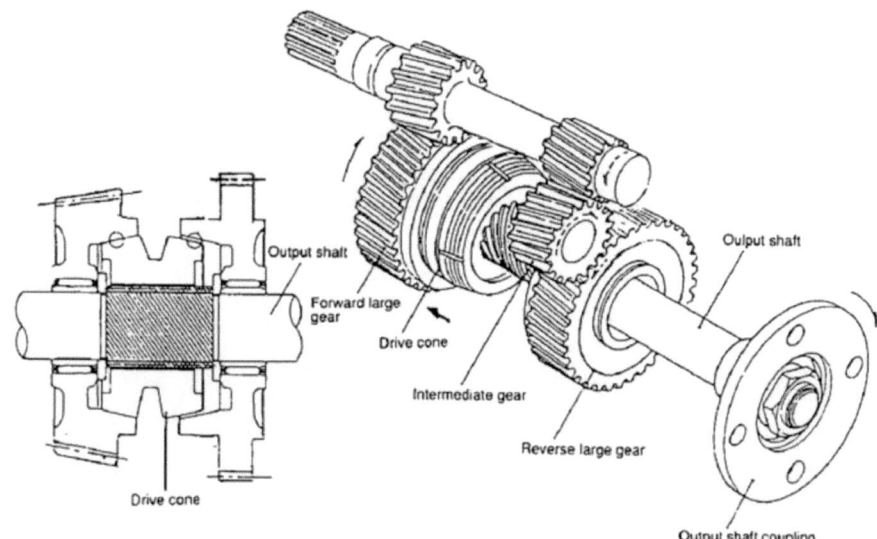

1-3-4 Power transmission routine-reverse

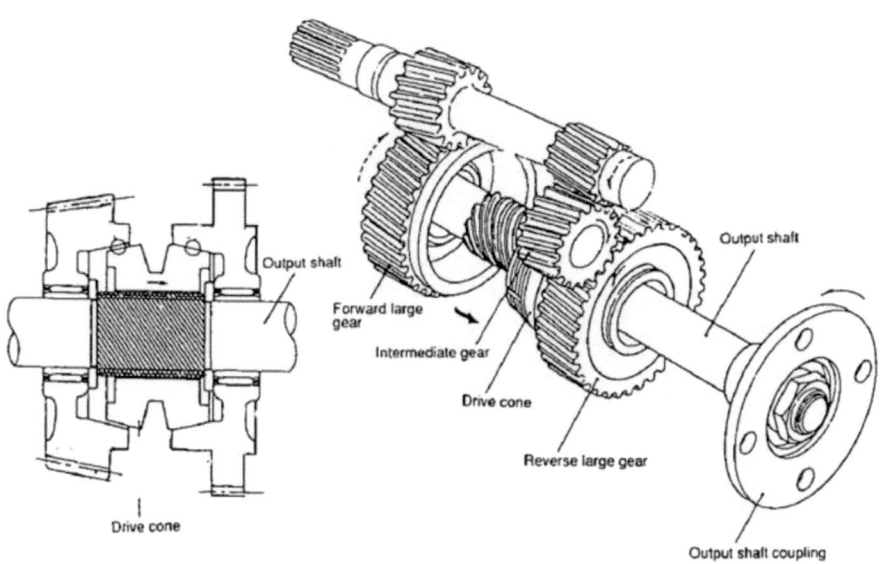

Chapter 7 Reduction and Reversing Gear
1. Construction   3,4JH3(B)(C)E

1-4 Drawing

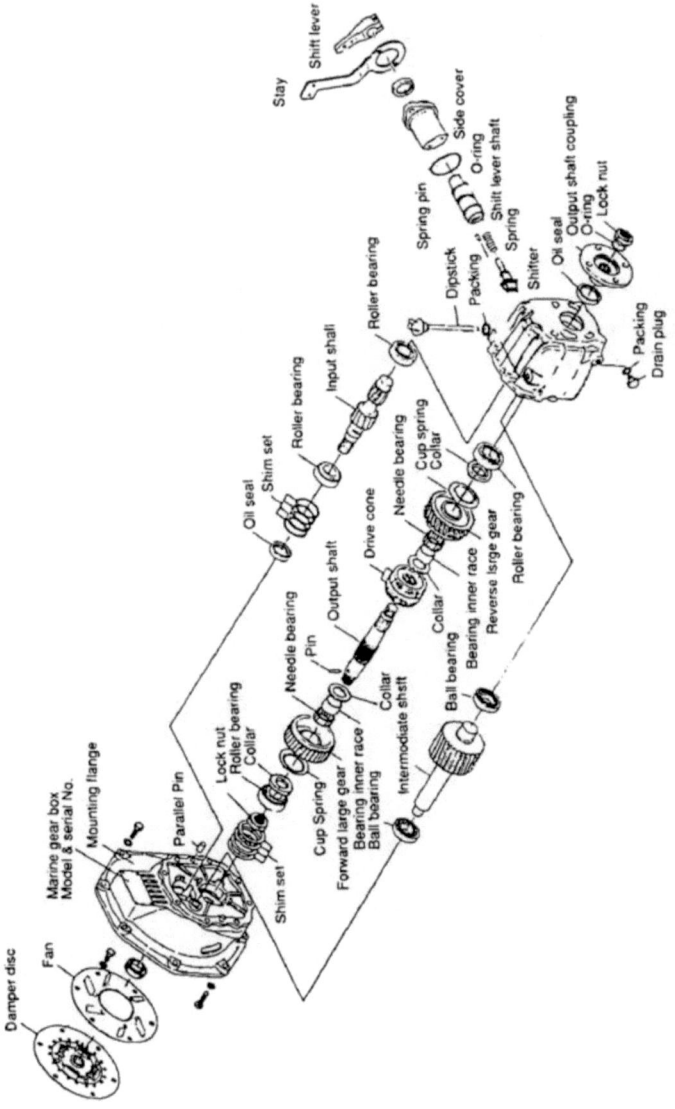

Chapter 7 Reduction and Reversing Gear
1. Construction

3,4JH3(B)(C)E

1-5 Sectional view

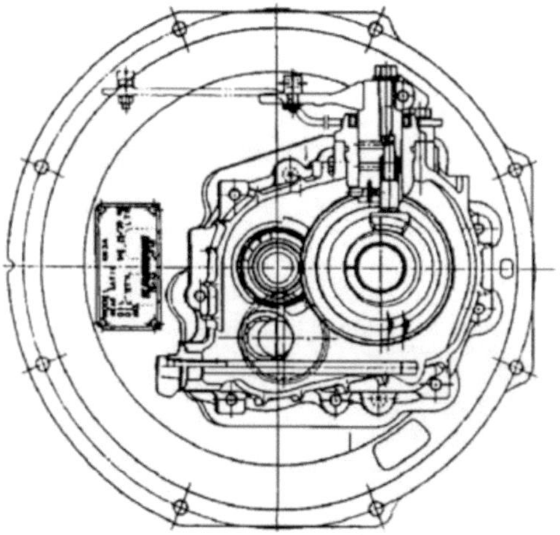

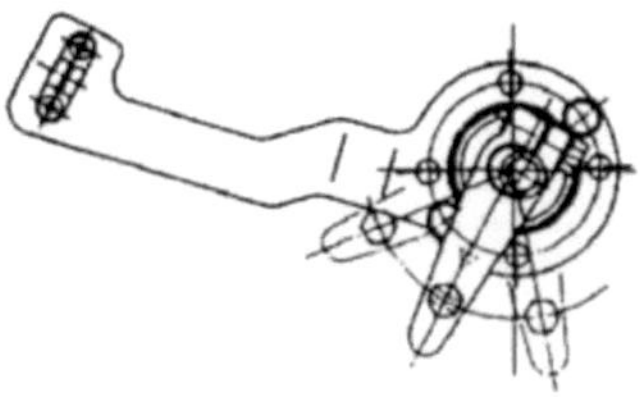

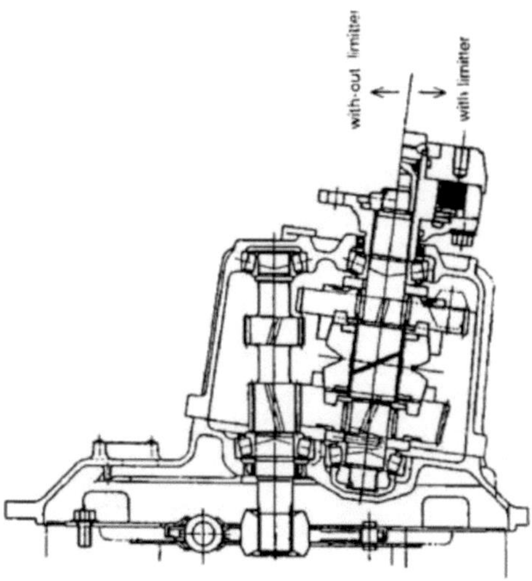

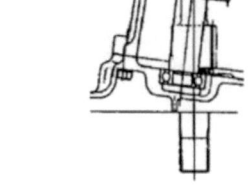

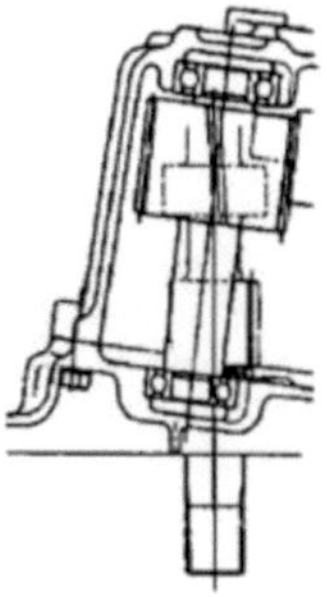

2. Shifting Device

2-1 Construction of shifting mechanism

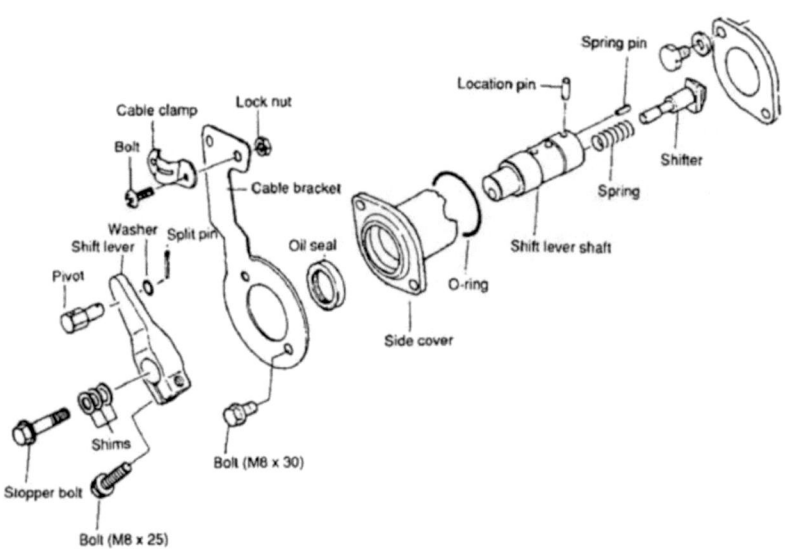

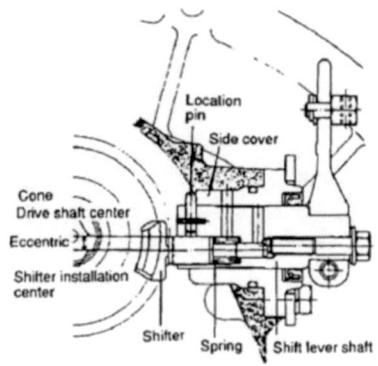

The shift lever shaft is installed on the side cover with neutral, forward and reverse positions provided on this cover. The neutral, forward and reverse location pins of the shift lever shaft are constantly inserted into their respective grooves on the shift lever by the tension of the shifter spring. The shifter is set on the eccentric hole of the shift lever shaft and moves the drive cone in the neutral position either to the forward or reverse positions, and then back to the neutral positions. (The shift lever shaft moves slightly to the shift lever or drive cone side when the shift lever is placed in the forward on reverse positions.)

Chapter 7 Reduction and Reversing Gear
2. Shifting Device

2-2 Forward and reverse clutch operation
(Neutral ⇒ Forward; Neutral ⇒ Reverse)

When the shift lever is moved to forward position from the neutral position, the shift lever shaft starts to revolve, and the location pin disengages from the neutral V-groove position of the side cover. (Shift lever moves approx. 0.5mm to the drivecone side.) At this time the shifter, moves the drive cone's V-groove to the forward large gear.

When the location pin of the shift lever shaft falls in the forward position groove of the side cover, the shift lever shaft moves approx. 3mm to the shift lever side, and the shifter stars to press the drive cone V-groove to the forward large gear side through the spring force.

2-3 Engagement and disengagement of clutch
(Forward ⇒ Neutral; Reverse ⇒ Neutral)

When the shift lever is moved to the forward position from the neutral position, the shift lever shaft starts to revolve, and the location pin disengages from the forward position groove of the side cover. (The shift lever shaft moves approx. 3mm to the drive cone side.) At this time, the shifter which is set on the eccentric hole of the shift lever shaft is moved to the neutral side (reverse large gear side). The drive cone, however, is engaged with the forward large gear through the torque force produced by the revolving centrifugal force.

Further, when the shift lever shaft starts to revolve, and the positioning pin falls in to the neutral V-groove position of the side cover (the shift lever shaft travels approx. 5mm to the shift lever side), the shifter moves to the shift lever side(to the spring side) while moving the V-groove of the drive cone to the reverse large gear side. The movement of the shifter to the shift lever side, however, is stopped when the shifter end contacts the stopper bolt. The shifter only works to press the V-groove of the drive cone to the reverse large gear side. Thus, the drive cone is disengaged from the forward large gear. After this disengagement, the transmission torque of the drive cone is decreased to zero and the shift lever is returned to the neutral position by the spring force.

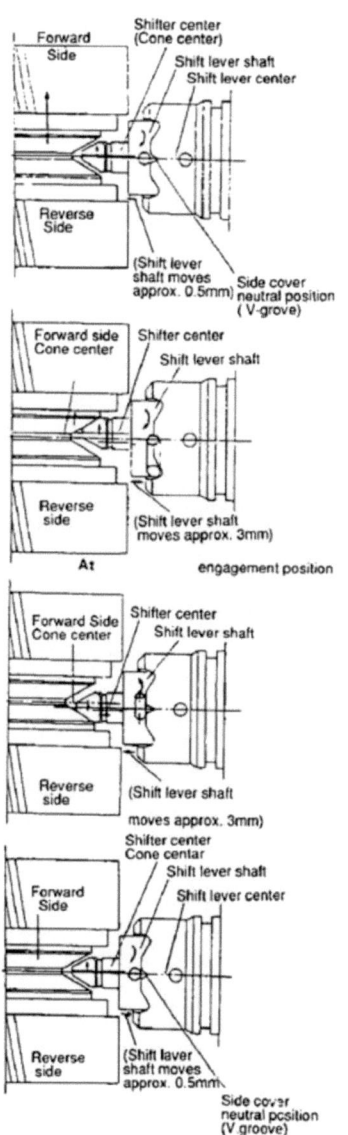

Chapter 7 Reduction and Reversing Gear
2. Shifting Device

3,4JH3(B)(C)E

2-4 Clutch shifting force

Shifting position / shifting direction	Shifting lever position at 56mm	Remote control handle postition at 170mm (Cable length, 4m)
Engaging force at 1000rpm	3~4 kg	4~5 kg
Disengaging force at 1000rpm	3.5~5 kg	4~6 kg

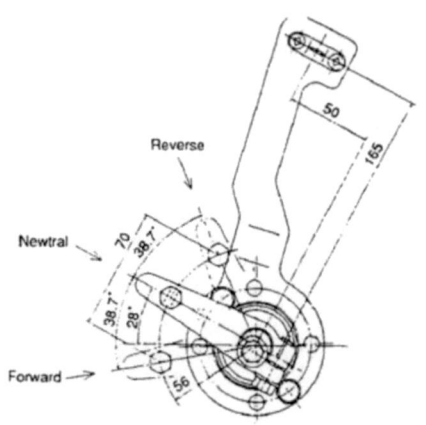

2-5 Adjustment of shifting device

Whenever the side cover, shift lever shaft, shifter, stopper bolt or drive cone is replaced, be sure to adjust the clearance between the shifter end and the stopper bolt by using shims. When the adjustment of this clearance is not proper the drive cone may be improperly fitted When the shift lever is moved to the neutral position from either the forward or the reverseposition.

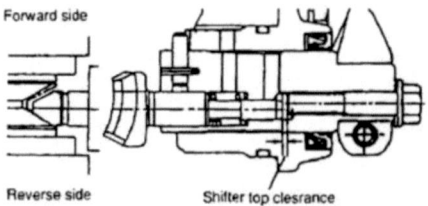

Chapter 7 Reduction and Reversing Gear
2. Shifting Device

3,4JH3(B)(C)E

2-5-1 Measurement and adjustment of clearance

(1) Assemble the shifting mechanism (without installing the stopper bolt of the shifter) to the marine gear case.

NOTE: Ensure the correct alignment of the shifter before assembly.

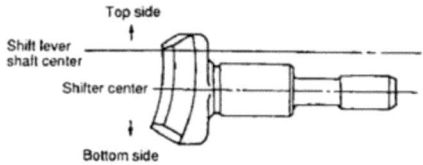

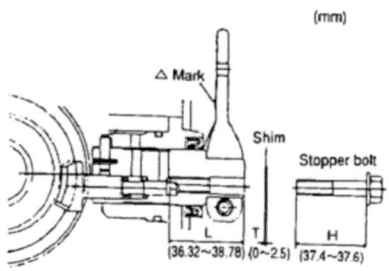

(mm)

(2) Turn the shift lever 10~15 degree either to the forward or reverse position from the neutral position.
(3) Measure the L-distance between the shift lever shaft end surface and the shifter end and measure the minimum L (Lmin).
(4) Measure the H-distance (the distance from the neck of the stopper bolt to its end).

(5) Obtain the shim thickness T" by the following formula.

$$T = (H - Lmin + 1.25) \pm 0.1mm$$

NOTE: Shim set includes one each of 1mm, 0.4mm, 0.3mm, 0.25mm shims.
(YANMAR Part No. 177088-06380)

(6) Insert shim (s) of proper thickness to the stopper bolt side and tighten to the shift lever shaft.
NOTE: When tightening the stopper bolt, apply either a non-drying type liquid packing (THREE BOND No.1215), or a seal tape around the bolt threads.

2-5-2 Inspect for the following points
(to be inspected every 2-3 months)

(1) Looseness at the connection of the cable connector and the remote control cable.
(2) Looseness of the attaching nut of the cable connector and the shift lever.

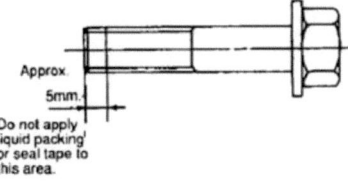

7—10

Printed in Japan
HINSHI-H8009

Chapter 7 Reduction and Reversing Gear
2. Shifting Device
3.4JH3(B)(C)E

2-6 Adjustment of the remote control head
Marine gear box control side
(1) Equal distribution of the control lever stroke.

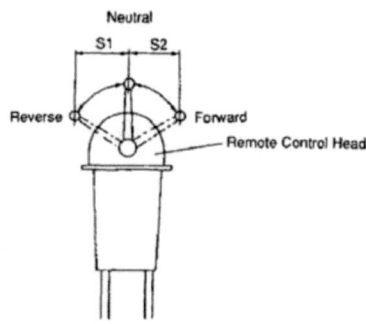

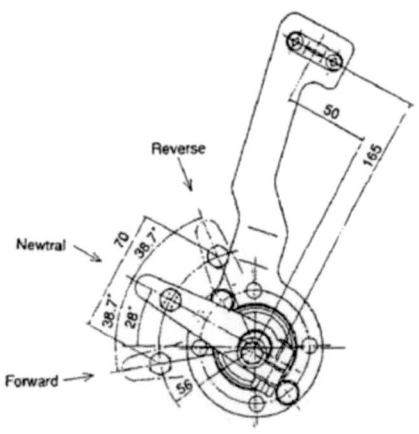

The stroke between the neutral position → forward position (S2), and the neutral position → reverse position (S1) must be equalized.
When either stroke is too short, clutch engagement becomes faulty.

(2) Equalizing the travel distance of the control cable.
After ensuring the equal distribution of the stroke described in (1), connect the cable to the control head. Adjust so that the cable shift travel of the S1 and S2 control lever strokes becomes identical.

2-7 Cautions
(1) Always stop the engine when attaching, adjusting, and inspecting.
(2) When conducting inspection immediately after stopping the engine, do not touch the clutch.
The oil temperature is often raised to around 90°C (194°F).
(3) Half-clutch operation is not possible with this design and construction. Do not use with the shift lever halfway to the engaged position.

NOTE : The dual (Two) lever remote control device cannot be usded.

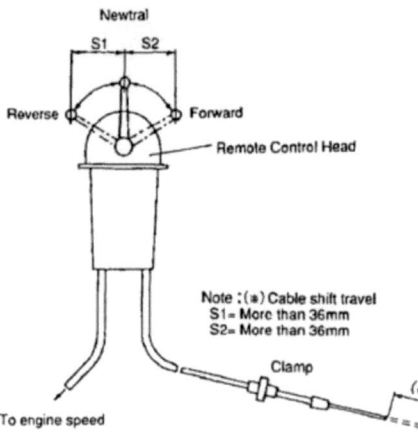

3. Inspection and Servicing

3-1 Clutch case
(1) Check the clutch case with a test hammer for cracking. Perform a color check when required.
If the case is cracked, replace it.
(2) Check for staining on the inside surface of the bearing section.
Also, measure the inside diameter of the case.
Replace the case if it is worn beyond the wear limit.

3-2 Bearing
(1) Rusting and damage.
If the bearing is rusted or the taper roller retainer is damages, replace the bearing.
(2) Make sure that the bearings rotates smoothly.
If rotation is not smooth, if there is any binding, or if any abnormal sound is evident, replace the baring.

3-3 Gear
Check the surface, tooth face conditions and backlash of each gear. Replace any defective part.
(1) Tooth surface wear.
Check the tooth surface for pitting, abnormal wear, dents, and cracks. Repair the lightly damaged gears and replace heavily damaged gears.
(2) Tooth surface contact.
Check the tooth surface contact. The amount of tooth surface contact between the tooth crest and tooth flank must be at least 70% of the tooth width.
(3) Backlash.
Measure the backlash of each gear, and replace the gear when it is worn beyond the wear limit.

mm(in)

	Maintenance standard	Wear limit
Input shaft forward gear and output shaft forward gear	0.05~0.14	0.2
Input shaft reverse gear and intermediate gear	0.06~0.12	0.2
Intermediate gear and output shaft reverse gear	0.06~0.12	0.2

3-4 Forward and reverse large gears
(1) Contact surface with drive cone.
Visually inspect the tapered surface of the forward and reverse large gears where they make contact with the drive cone to check if any abnormal condition or sign of overheating exists.
If any defect is found, replace the gear.

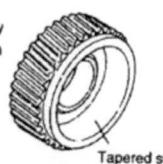
Tapered surface

(2) Forward/reverse gear needle bearing.
When an abnormal sound is produced at the needle bearing, visually inspect the rollers; replace the bearing if the rollers are faulty.

Rollers

3-5 Drive cone
(1) Visually inspect that part of the surface that comes into contact with the circumferential triangular slot to check for signs of scoring, overheating or wear. If deep scoring or signs of overheating are found, replace the cone.

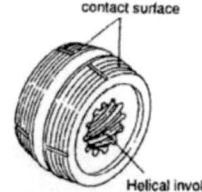
contact surface
Helical involute spline

(2) Check the helical involute spline for any abnormal condition on the tooth surface, and repair or replace the part should any defect be found.
(3) Measure the amount of wear on the tapered contact surface of the drive cone, and replace the cone when the wear exceeds the specified limit.

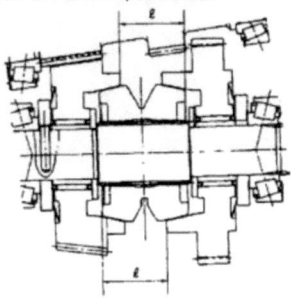

Chapter 7 Reduction and Reversing Gear
3. Inspection and Servicing

3,4JH3(B)(C)E

mm

Dimensions ℓ		Standard dimensions	Limited dimensions
	KM3A KM35A	29.2-29.8	28.1

NOTE : When dismantled, the forward or reverse direction of the drive cone must be clearly identified.

(4) If the wear of the V-groove of the drive cone is excessive, replace the part.

NOTE : When replacing the drive cone, the new drive cone and forward large gear and reverse large gear must be lapped prior to assembly.
The lapping procedure is described below.

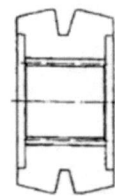

3-5-1 Lapping Procedure for Drive Cone

(1) Coat the lapping powder onto the cave of the clutch gear (Lapping powder : 67 micron silicon carbide #280)

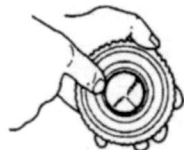

(2) Set the large gear on the output shaft with a needle bearing and then set the drive cone on the output shaft.

(3) Lap the large gear's cave and drive cone, pushing them together by hand.

(4) Push and turn the large gear about 5 times both clockwise and counter-clockwise.

(5) After lapping them, wash them with washing oil. The lapped parts should be cleaned completely.

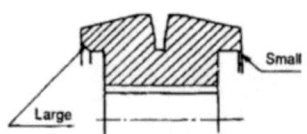

NOTE : Do not mix the combination of the lapped parts. The washing oil should be changed frequently in order to prevent residual powder being left on the parts.
When assembling the drive cone, be sure to check its alignment. The larger chamferring face should be on the forward large gear side.

Chapter 7 Reduction and Reversing Gear
3. Inspection and Servicing

3,4JH3(B)(C)E

3-6 Thrust collar

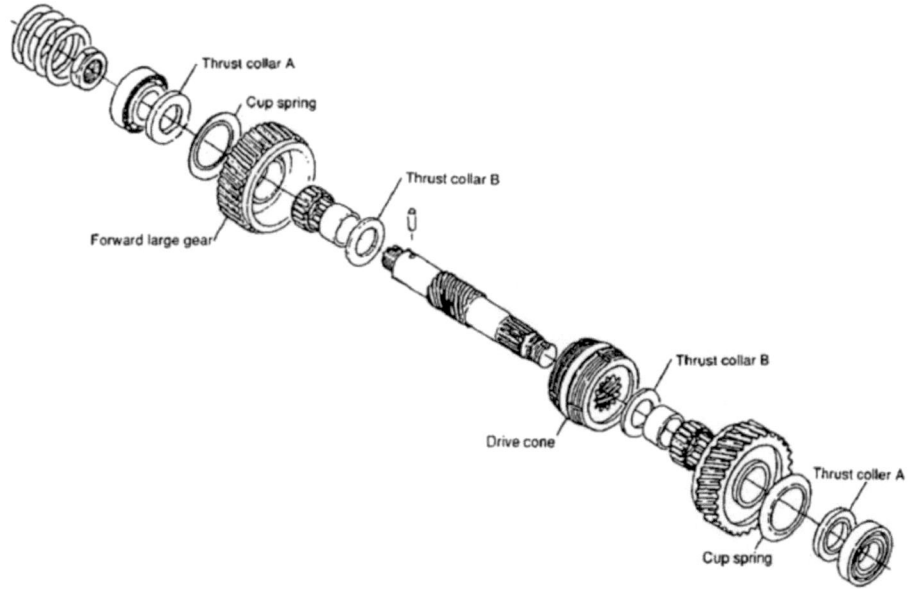

Chapter 7 Reduction and Reversing Gear
3. Inspection and Servicing
3,4JH3(B)(C)E

(1) Visually inspect the sliding surface of thrust collar A or B to check for signs of overheating, scoring, or cracks.
Replace the collar if any abnormal condition is found.
(2) Measure the thickness of thrust collar A or B, and replace it when the dimension exceeds the specified limit.

3-8 Oil seal of output shaft
Visually inspect the oil seal of the output shaft to check if there is any damage or oil leakage; replace the seal when any abnormal condition is found.

3-9 Input shaft

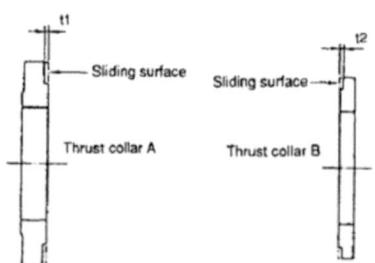

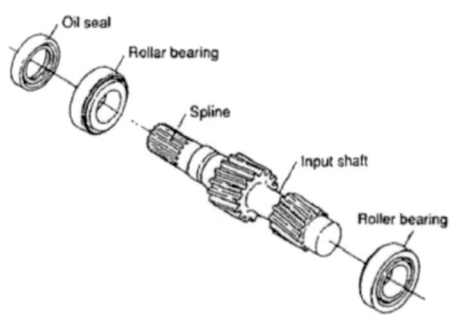

Stepped wear	Limit for use
Thrust collar A, t1	0.05
Thrust collar B, t2	0.20

3-7 Cup spring
(1) Check for cracks and damage to the cup spring. Replace the part if defective.
(2) Measure the free length of the cup spring. If the length or the thickness deviates from the standard size, replace the part.

(1) Spline part
Whenever uneven wear and/or scratches are found, replace with a new part.
(2) Surface of oil seal.
If the sealing surface of the oil seal is worn or scratched, replace.

3-10 Output shaft

Cup spring

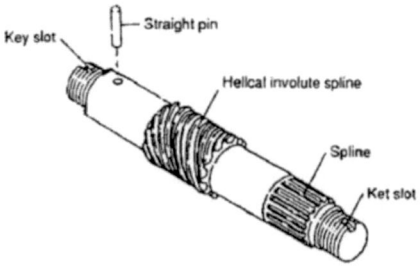

	Standard	Limit
Cup spring.T	2.8~3.1	2.6

(1) Visually inspect the spline and the helical involute spline, and repair or replace a part when any abnormal condition is found on its surface.

3-11 Intermediate shaft

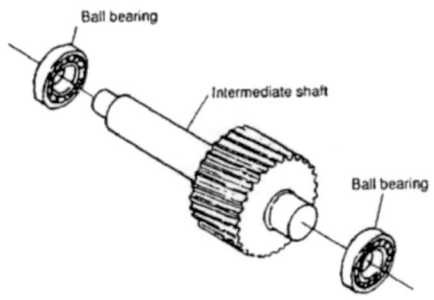

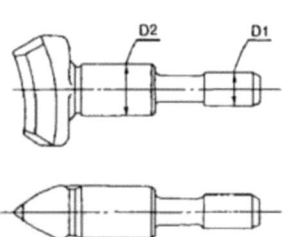

(1) Ball bearing
Check the turning condition with gently rotate, and when bearing is sticked or damaged.
Replace if necessary.

mm

	Standard	Limit
D1	6.69~6.70	6.50
D2	11.966~11.984	11.95
Shift lever shaft, Shifter insert hole	12.0~12.018	12.05

3-12 Shifting device
3-12-1 Shifter

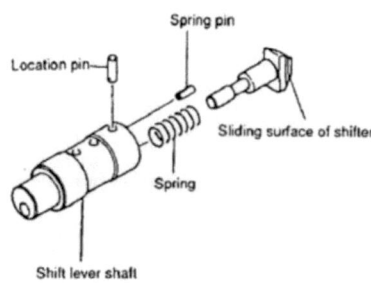

3-12-2 Shift lever shaft and location pin

(1) Check the shift lever shaft and location pin for damage or distortion, and replace defective parts. If the location pin must be replaced, replace it together with the shift lever shaft.
(2) Measure the diameter of the shift lever shaft and the shifter insertion hole. Replace the part if the size deviates from the standard value.

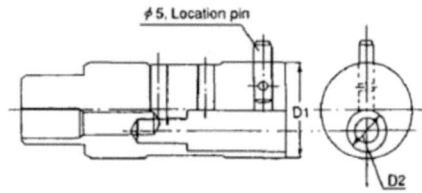

(1) Visually inspect the surface in contact with the drive cone, and replace the shifter when signs of overheating, damage or wear are found.
(2) Measure the shaft diameter of the shifter. Replace the shaft if the size deviates from the standard.

mm

	Standard	Limit
D1	27.959~27.98	27.90
D2	12.0~12.018	12.05
Side cover, Shifter insert hole	28.0~28.021	28.08

Chapter 7 Reduction and Reversing Gear
3. Inspection and Servicing

3-12-3 Shifter spring
(1) Check the spring for scratches or corrosion.
(2) Measure the free length of the spring.

Shifter spring	Standard	Limit
Free length	22.6mm	19.8mm
Spring constant	0.854kg/mm	
Length when attached	14.35mm	
Load when attached	7.046kg	6.08kg

3-12-4 Stopper bolt
Check the stopper bolt. If it is worn or stepped, replace.

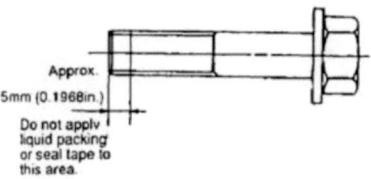

3-12-5 Side cover and oil seal
(1) Check the neutral, forward and reverse position grooves.
Replace if the grooves are worn.
(2) Measure the insertion hole of the shift lever s haft.
Replace if the size deviates from the standard value.
(3) Check the oil seal and the O-ring for damage.
Replace if the part is defective.

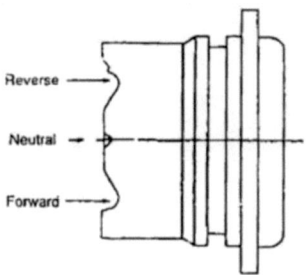

3-13 Damper disc

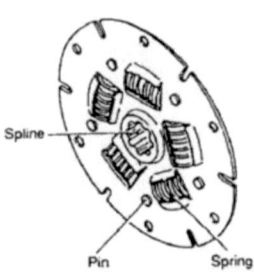

(1) Spline part.
Whenever uneven wear and/or scratches are found, replace with a new part.
(2) Spring.
Whenever uneven wear and/or scratches are found, replace with a new part.
(3) Pin wear
Whenever uneven wear and/or scratches are found, replace with a new part.
(4) Whenever a crack or damage to the spring slot is found replace the defective part with a new one.

3-14 Shim adjustment for output and input shafts

Check the thickness of shims for both input and output shafts. When the component parts are not replaced after dismantling, the same shims can be reused. When the clutch case and flange or any one of the following parts is replaced the thickness of the shim must be determined in the following manner.

For input shaft part: input shaft, bearing.
For output shaft parts: output shaft, thrust collar A, thrust-collar B, gear, bearing.

Chapter 7 Reduction and Reversing Gear
3. Inspection and Servicing

(1) Shim thickness (T2,T3) measurement of output shaft
 (a) Measure the bearing insertion hole depth (A) of the mounting flange, and the bearing insertion hole depth (A') of the clutch case.
 (b) Measure the length (B) between the bearing outer race.
 NOTE : Tighten the mounting flange nut of the output shaft assembly with the specified torque. Press-fit the inner race of the clutch case roller bearing to the large gear side.

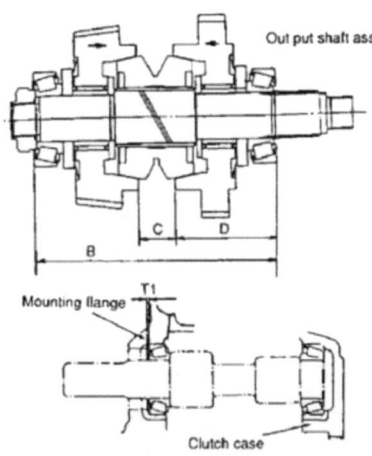

Out put shaft assy

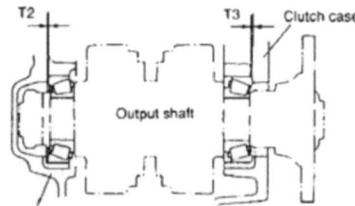

T1 : Clearance ±0.05

(c) Measure lenghts (D) and (C) from the outer race end of the clutch case bearing included in the output shaft assembly.
 NOTE : Before measuring length (D) and (C), press the forward large gear and the reverse large gear to the drive cone until there is no clearance.

(d) Obtain thicknesses (T2) and (T3) by the following formulas :

$T_2 = A + A' - B - T_3$ (T2 : Clearance $^{+0.1mm}_{0}$)

$T_3(KM3A) = A' - 50 - C/2 - D$ (Tolerance ±0.05mm)

1. Assemble the outer bearing race without inserting shims into the clutch case body and flange, and then assemble only the input shaft.
 (Caution): The outer bearing race should be inserted all the way to the bottom.
  Do not suspend it halfway.
2. Fasten the case body and the flange by tightening 2 bolts diagonally.
3. Fasten the dial gauge to the flange and fit the needle to the end face of the input shaft.
4. Move the input shaft up and down manually and read the dial gauge figure to decide the shim thickness.
 (Note): The bearing installation hole does not make a right angle to the joint face of the case and flange. Accordingly, precise measurement at the service site is not possible.

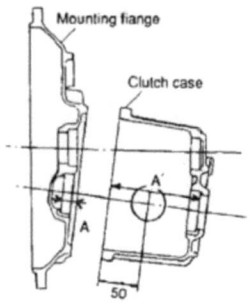

Chapter 7 Reduction and Reversing Gear
3. Inspection and Servicing

3,4JH3(B)(C)E

(2) Standard size of parts

mm

A+A'	B	C	D	Drive cone neutral center position
138.40~ 138.75	136.56~ 138.10	20.50~ 21.10	57.83~ 58.65	50

NOTE : Compare your measurements with the above standard size. If your measurements differ largely from the standard sizes, measurements may not be correct. Check and measure again.

(3) Adjusting shim set

	Part No.	Tickness. mm(in.)	No. of shims
Input and Output shaft	177088-02300	1.0	1
		0.5	1
		0.3	2
		0.1	3

3-15 Torque limiter

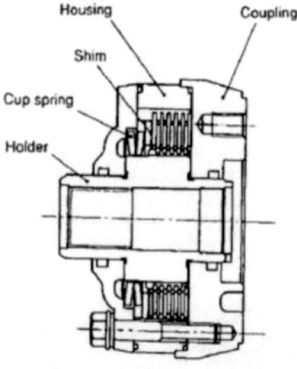
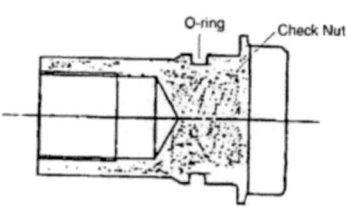

The torque limiter assembly includes these parts.
The conversion to the torque limiter specification is easy by exchanging the standard shaft coupling. (Use the check nut, not the end nut, to install the torque limiter.)

4. Disassembly

4-1. Dismantling the clutch

(1) Remove the remote control of cable.
(2) Remove the clutch assembly from the engine mounting flange.

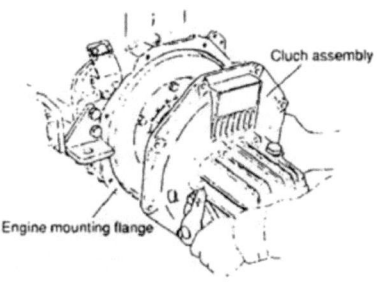

(3) Drain the lubricating oil.
Drain the lubricating oil by loosening the plug at the bottom of the clutch case.

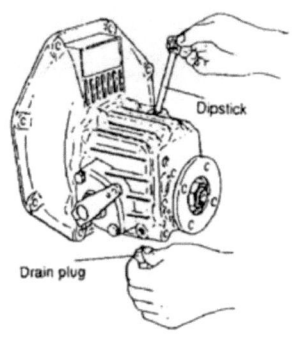

(4) Remove the end nut and output shaft coupling.

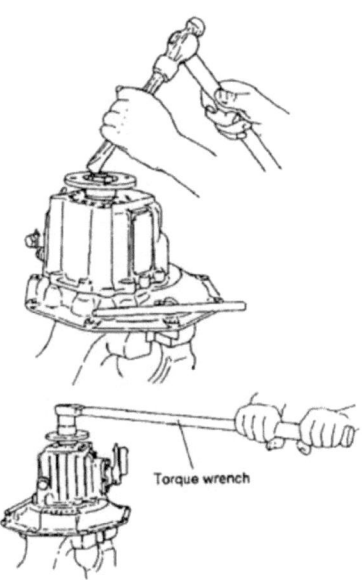

NOTE : Take care as it has a left-handed thread.

(5) Remove the oil dip stick and O-ring.
(6) Remove the fixing bolts on the side cover, and also remove the shift lever shaft, shift lever and shifter.

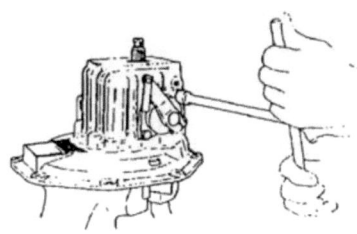

Chapter 7 Reduction and Reversing Gear
4. Disassembly
3,4JH3(B)(C)E

(7) Remove the bolts which secure the mounting flange to the case body, give light taps to the left and right with a plastic headed hammer while supporting the clutch case with your hand, then remove the mounting flange.

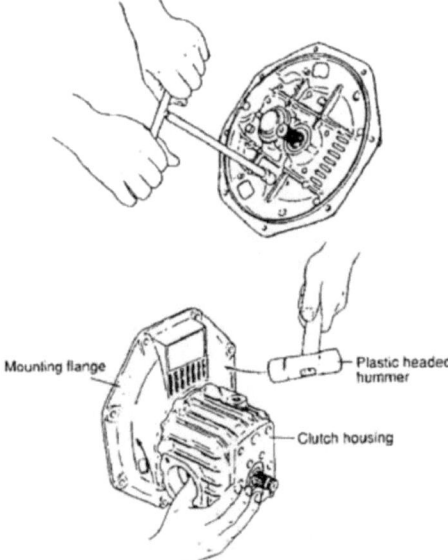

(9) Take out the intermediate shaft and input shaft and intermediate shaft.

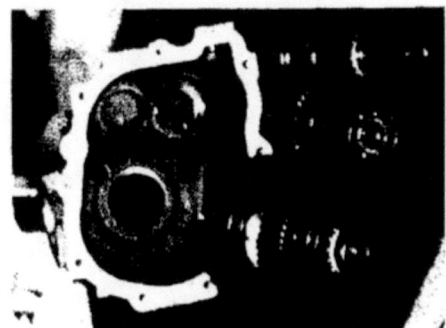

(8) Withdraw the output shaft assembly.

7—21

Chapter 7 Reduction and Reversing Gear
4. Disassembly

3,4JH3(B)(C)E

(10) Remove the oil seal of the output shaft from the case body.

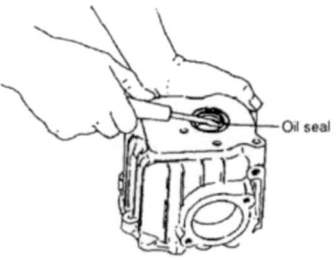
Oil seal

(11) Remove the outer bearing race from the case body by using the special tool.

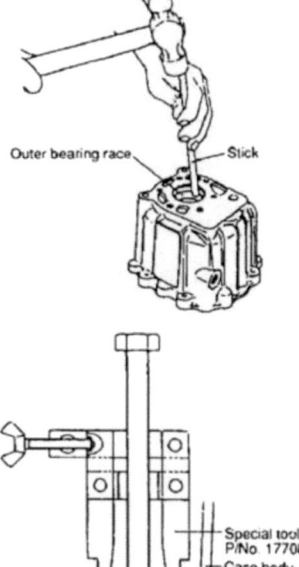
Outer bearing race — Stick
Special tool P/No. 177088-09010
Case body
Outer bearing race

(12) Remove the oil seal of the input shaft from the mounting flange.
(13) Remove the outer bearing race from the mounting flange in the same way as with the case body.
(14) Remove each adjusting plate from the input our output shaft.

NOTE : The same adjusting plates can be revsed when the following parts are not replaced.
When any part is replaced however, readjustment is necessary.

4-2 Removal of the output shaft

(1) Take out the reverse large gear, thrust collar A, cup spring and inner bearing race.
The reverse large gear must be withdrawn using a pulley extracter, by fixing the nut at the forward end in a vice.

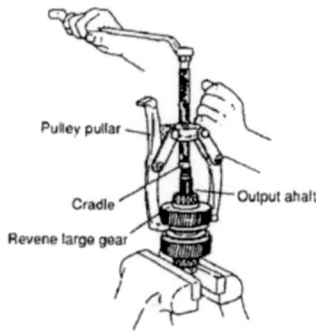
Pulley pullar
Cradle
Output ahalt
Revene large gear

(2) Loosen the calking of the forward nut and remove the nut.
Remove the nut by using a torque wrench after setting the output shaft coupling and fixing the coupling bolt in a vice.

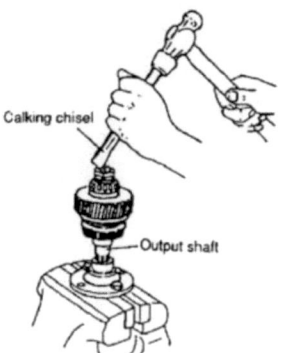
Calking chisel
Output shaft

Chapter 7 Reduction and Reversing Gear
4. Disassembly
3.4JH3(B)(C)E

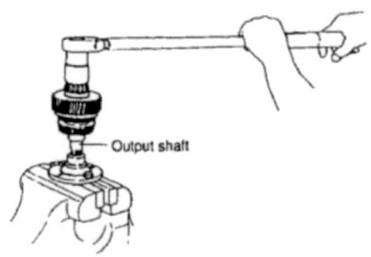

(3) Place the pulley extractor against the end surface of the forward large gear, and withdraw the forward large gear, thrust collar A, cup spring, and inner bearing race.

(4) While gripping the drive cone, tap the end of the shaft with a plastic headed hammer, and withdraw the thrust extractor may be used.

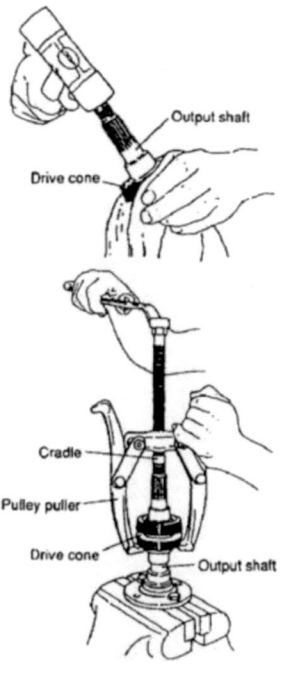

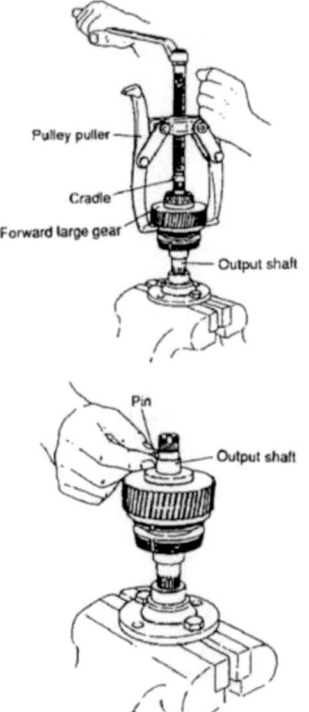

NOTE : Take care as the nut has left-handed thread.

4-3 Removal of the intermediate shaft.

(1) Remove the ball bearing using a pulley.

(2) Remove the ball bearing oppostte narrow end using screw driver.

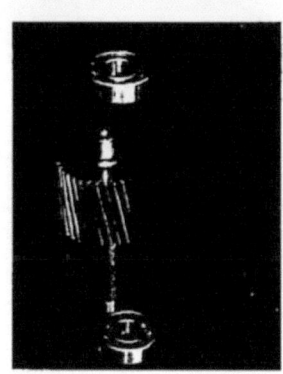

4-4 Dismantling the shifting device

(1) Take out the shifter and shifter spring.

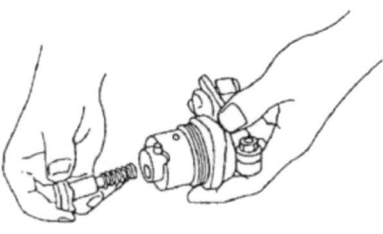

(2) Remove the stopper bolt of the shifter and shim.

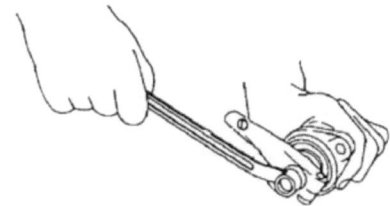

(3) Loosen the bolt of the shift lever and remove the shift lever from the shift lever shaft.

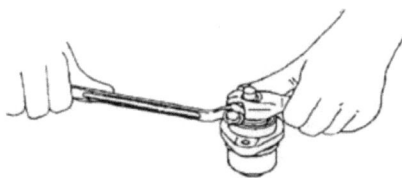

(4) Remove the shift lever to the anti-shif lever side.

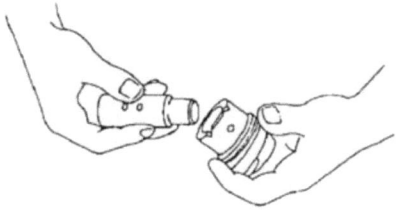

(5) Remove the oil-seal and O-ring.

5. Reassembly

5-1 Reassembly of output shaft
(1) Fit the forward side thrust collar B onto the shaft.
(2) Drive in the forward end inner needle bearing race using a jig.

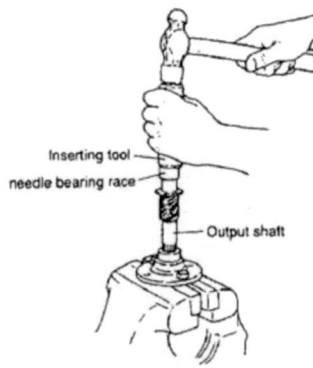

(3) Assemble the needle bearing and forward large gear.

NOTE : Check that the forward large gear rotates smoothly.

(4) Fit the cup spring, Pin and thrust collar A, and dive in the inner bearing race using a jig.

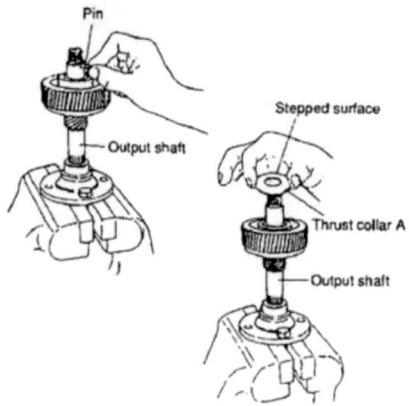

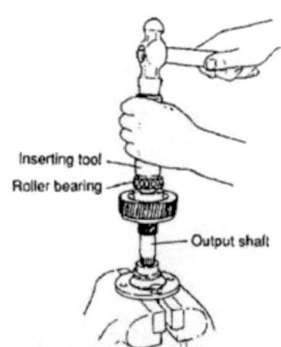

NOTE : 1) Drive in with a plastic headed hammer. Do not hit it hard.
2) When fitting the thrust collar A, note the fitting direction. Fit it keeping the stepped surface toward the roller bearing side.
3) Note that the pin cannot be fitted after the inner bearing race has been driven in.
4) Check that the forward large gear rotates smoothly.

(5) Set and tighten the forward end nut. Insert the bolt into the coupling, and fix it in a vice, keeping the spline part upward.
Insert the shaft into the spline of the coupling, fit the spacer, and tighten the nut with a torque wrench.

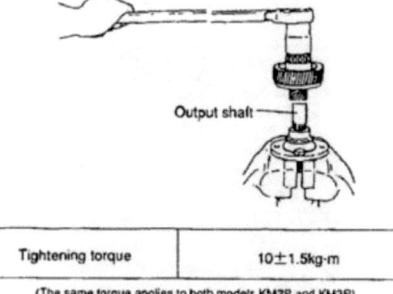

Tightening torque	10±1.5kg-m

(The same torque applies to both models KM2P and KM3P)

NOTE : 1) Take care as it is a left-handed thread.
2) Use the reverse side nut used before dismantling at the forward end. This is to provide effective calking to the nut by changing the calking position.

Chapter 7 Reduction and Reversing Gear
5. Reassembly

3.4JH3(B)(C)E

5-2 Reassembly of the clutch

(1) Fit the oil seal, bearing outer races and shim (output shaft side) in the clutch case.
(2) Insert the input shaft into the clutch case.
(3) Drive the intermediate shaft into the clutch case.

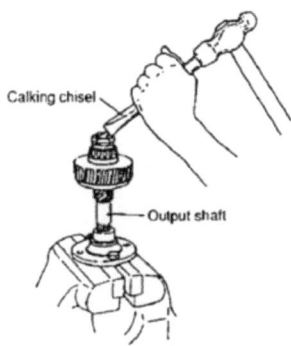

(6) Insert the drive cone while keeping the output shaft set for reverse.

(4) Insert the output shaft into the clutch case.

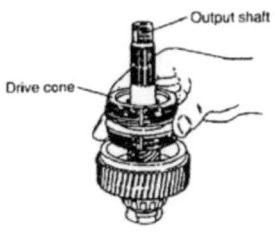

(7) Apply procedures 1 through 4 to the forward end.

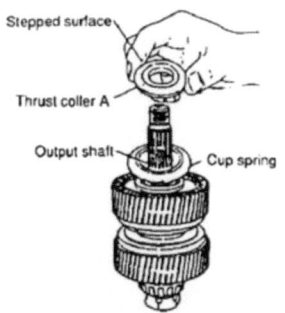

NOTE : 1) Fit thrust collar A so that the stepped surface faces the roller bearing side.
2) Check that the reverse large gear rotates smoothly.

Chapter 7 Reduction and Reversing Gear
5. Reassembly ___3,4JH3(B)(C)E

(5) Fit the adjusting plate to the mounting flange, and drive in the outer bearing race.
  NOTE : *The outer bearing race can be easily driven in by heating the mounting flange to about 100℃, or by cooling the outer race with liquid hydrogen.*
(6) Apply non-drying liquid packing around the outer surface of the oil seal, and insert the oil seal into the mounting flange while keeping the spring part of the oil seal facing the inside of the case.
(7) Apply non-drying liquid packing to the matching surfaces of the mounting flange end the case body.

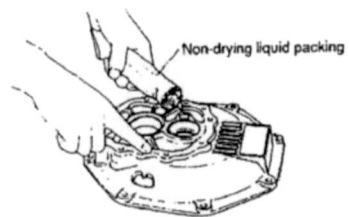
Non-drying liquid packing

(8) Insert the input shaft and output shaft into the shaft holes of the mounting flange, assemble the mounting flange on the case body, and tighten the bolt.

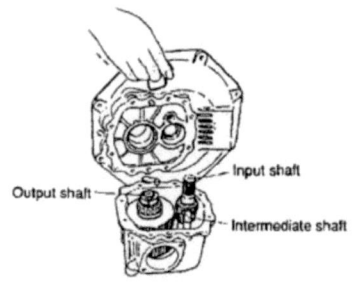
Output shaft — Input shaft — Intermediate shaft

NOTE : *Apply non-drying liquid packing to either the mounting flange or the case body.*

(9) Assemble the output shaft coupling on the output shaft, and fit the O-ring.
(10) Tighten the end nut by using a torque wrench, then calk it.

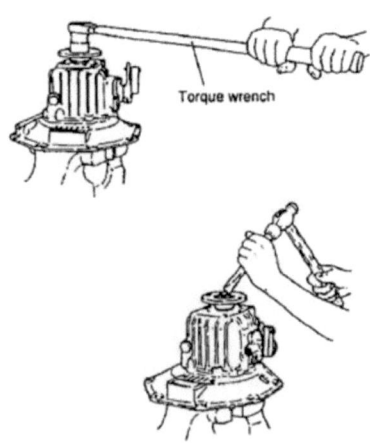
Torque wrench

NOTE : *Take care as it is a left-handed thread.*

Tightening torque	10±1.5kg-m

5. Reassembly

5-3 Reassembly of the shiating device

(1) Fit the oil seal and O-ring to the side cover.

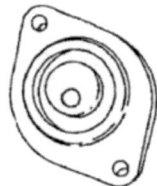

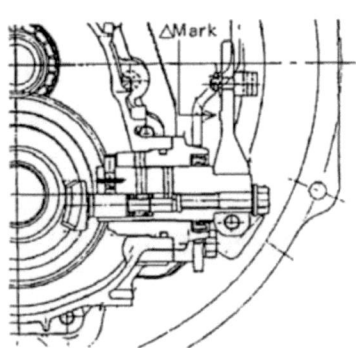
△Mark

(2) Insert the shift lever shaft to the side cover.

(4) Insert the shiater spring and shifter to the shift lever shaft.

(5) Fit the side cover assembly to the clutch case.

NOTE: 1) Check the direction of the shifter (Top and bottom side).
2) The shift lever may not turn smoothly if the clutch case is not filled with lubricating oil.

(6) Fit the shim and stopper bolt to the shift lever shaft.

NOTE: Apply non-drying liquid packing or sealtape to the thread of the stopper bolt.

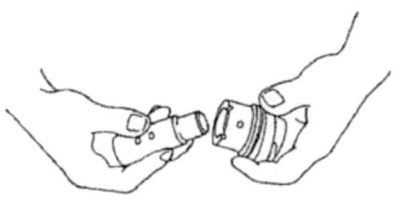

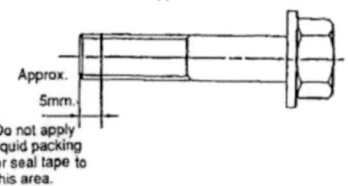

Approx. 5mm.

Do not apply liquid packing or seal tape to this area.

(3) Fit the shift lever to the shift lever shaft.

NOTE: Check the direction of the shift lever △ mark.

(7) Fit the pivot to the shift lever.

Side cover

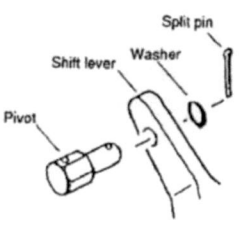
Split pin
Shift lever Washer
Pivot

Chapter 7 Reduction and Reversing Gear (KM3P)
1. Construction

3,4JH3(B)(C)E

Marine Gear Models
KM3P , KM35P
for Engine Models 3JH3E(A)
4JH3E

1. Construction

1-1. Construction

These clutches are a cone-type, mechanically operated clutch. When the drive cone (which is connected to the output shaft by the lead spline)is moved forward or backward, its taper contacts with the large gear and transfers power to the output shaft.

The construction is simple when compared with other types of clutch and it serves to reduce the number of components, making for a lighter, more compact unit which can be operated smoothly. Although it is small, the power transmission efficiency is high even under a heavy load. Its durability is high and it is also reliable because high grade materials are used for the shaft and gear, and, a taper roller bearing is incorporated. Power transmission is smooth because connection with the engine is made through the damper disc.

- The drive cone is made from special aluminum bronze which has both higher wear-resistance and durability. The drive cone is connected with the output shaft through the thread spline. The taper angle, diameter of the drive cone, twist angle, and diameter of the thread spline, are designed to give the greatest efficiency, thus ensuring that the drive cone can be readily engaged or disengaged.
- Helical gears are used for greater strength. The intermediate shaft is supported at 2 points to reduce deflection and gear noise.
- The clutch case and mounting flange are made from an aluminum alloy of special composition to reduce weight.

It is also anticorrosive against seawater.

- As the damper disc is fitted to the input shaft, power can be transmitted smoothly.
- There is small clearance between the dipstick and the inside of the dipstick tube. A small hole in the dipstick works as a breather.
- When the load on the propeller is removed, the engagement of the drive cone and the large gear is maintained by the shifter and V-groove of the drive cone. Even when the drive cone's tapered area and V-groove are worn, this engagement is maintained by the shift lever device and accordingly no adjustment of the remote control cable is required.
- The cup spring on the rear of the larger gear absorbs rotational fluctuations and stabilizes the engagement of the drive cone and the larger gear. Thus, the durability of the cone against wear is enhanced.

NOTE :
- KM35P marine gear has been installed on 3JH3E and 4JH3E engines (Feb.,2002)
- KM35P marine gear differs from KM3P as follows.
  - No torque limiter applied to KM35P.
  - Output shaft dia. 28mm. (KM3P : 25mm).
  - Drive com the same as the one for KM4A marine gear.
  - Overall length of KM35P : 209.3mm.
    [KM3P : 249mm(with torque limiter)]
  - No version of reduction gear ratio 3.20.
  - Marine gear oil reserve capacity up.
    0.5L (0.35L KM35P)

Chapter 7 Reduction and Reversing Gear
1. Construction

3,4JH3(B)(C)E

1-2 Specifications

Model			KM3P, KM35P				
For engine models			3JH3E (A)			4JH3E	
Clutch			Constant mesh gear with servo cone clutch (wet type)				
Reduction ratio	Forward		2.36	2.61	3.20	2.36	2.61
	Reverse		3.16	3.16	3.16	3.16	3.16
Propeller shaft min^{-1} (Forward)			1559	1411	1150	1559	1411
Direction of rotation	Input shaft		Counter-clockwise, viewed from stern				
	Output shaft	Forward	Clockwise, viewed from stern				
		Reverse	Counter-clockwise, viewed from stern				
Remote control	Control head		Single lever control				
	Cable		Morse. 33-C (cable travel 76.2mm)				
	Clamp		YANMAR made. standard accessory				
	Cable connector		YANMAR made, standard accessory				
Output shaft coupling	Outer diameter		100mm				
	Pitch circle diameter		78mm				
	Connecting bolt holes i		4-10.5mm				
Position of shift lever			Right side, viewed from stern				
Lubricating oil			API CC SAE 20/30				
Lubricating oil capacity			0.35L				
Dry mass			12kg				

Note
Torque limiter should be installed on KM3P.
No torque limiter installed on KM35P.

Reduction ratio	No. of blade	Diameter of the propeller mm	Moment of inertia N·m² (kgf·m²=GD²)	Material
2.36	3	450	≤ 1.49 (0.15)	Bronze
	4	425		
2.61	3	470	≤ 1.86 (0.19)	
	4	440		
3.20 (KM3P)	3	490	≤ 2.25 (0.23)	
	4	460		

Chapter 7 Reduction and Reversing Gear
1. Construction
_3,4JH3(B)(C)E_

1-3 Power transmission system
1-3.1 Arrangement of shafts and gears

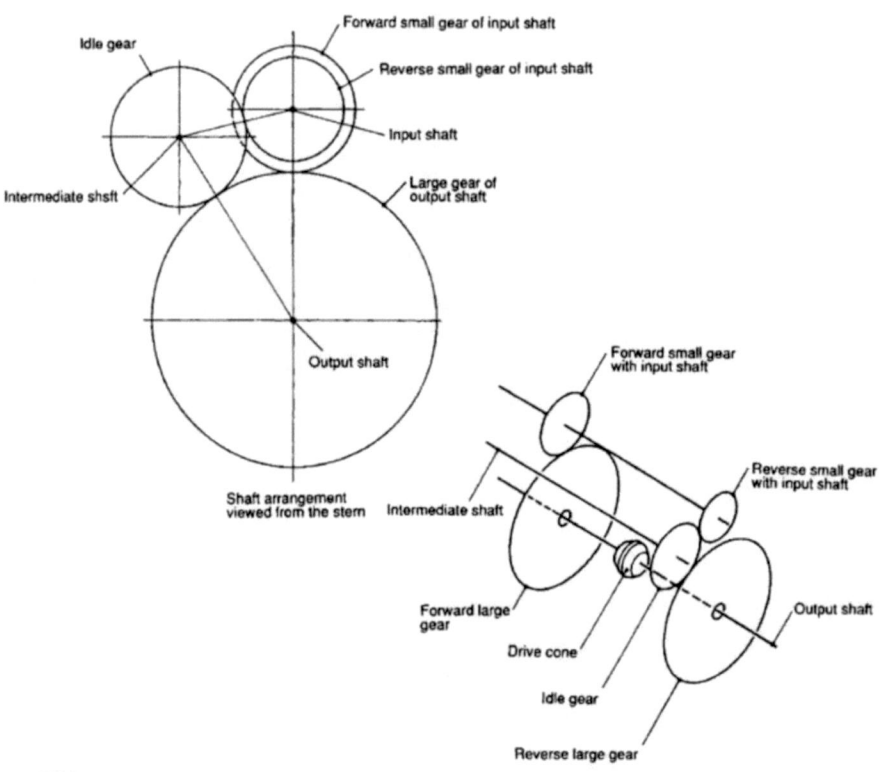

1-3-2 Reduction ratio
Forward

Model	No. of teeth of forward small gear Zif	No. of teeth of forward 18rge gear Zof	Reduction ratio Zof/Zif
KM3P4, KM35P	25	59	59/25 = 2.36
	23	60	60/23 = 2.61
KM3P4	20	64	64/20 = 3.20

Reverse

Model	No. of teeth of reverse small gear Zif	No. of teeth of intemediate shaft gear Zi	No. of teeth of reverse large gear Zdr	Reduction ratio Zi/Zir · Zdr/Zi
KM3P4 KM35P	19	26	60	60/19 = 3.16

Chapter 7 Reduction and Reversing Gear
I. Construction

3.4JH3(B)(C)E

1-3-3 Power transmission routine-Forward

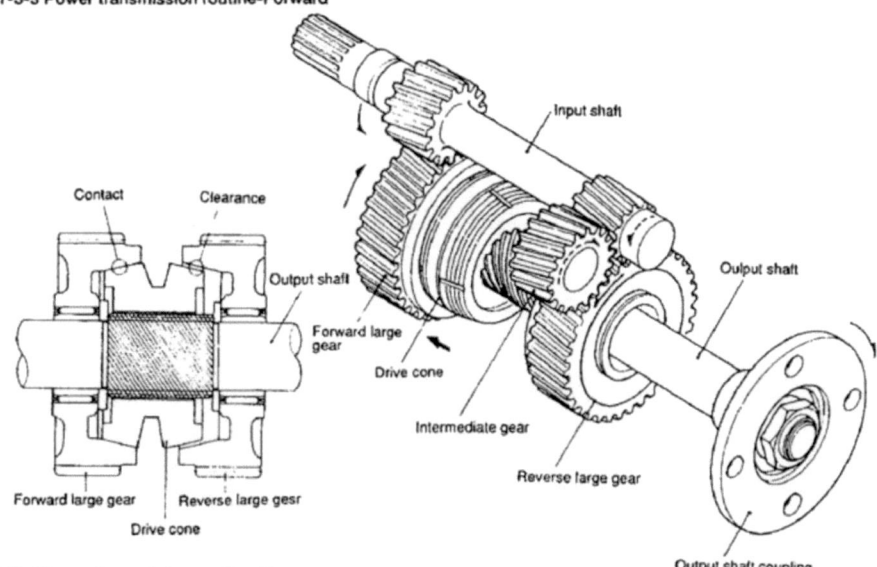

1-3-4 Power transmission routine-Reverse

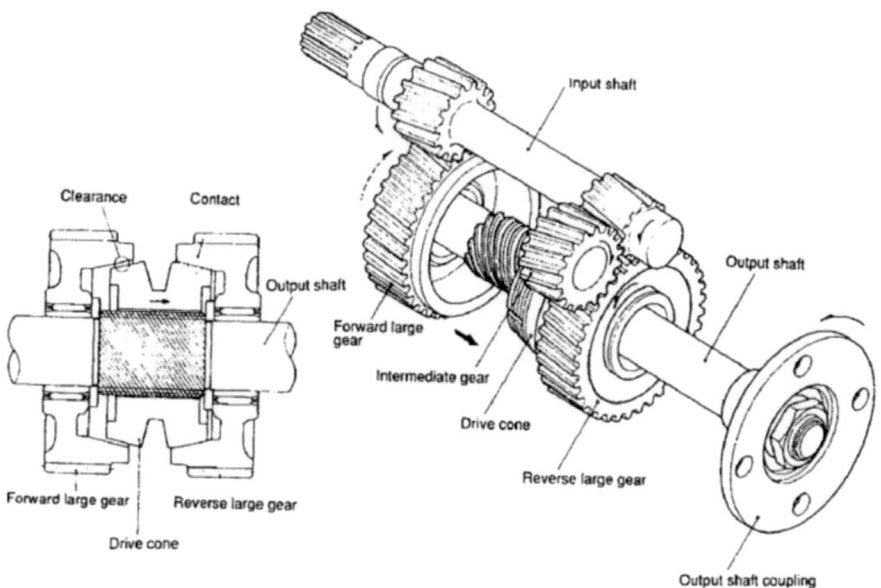

Chapter 7 Reduction and Reversing Gear
1. Construction   3,4JH3(B)(C)E

1-4 Drawing

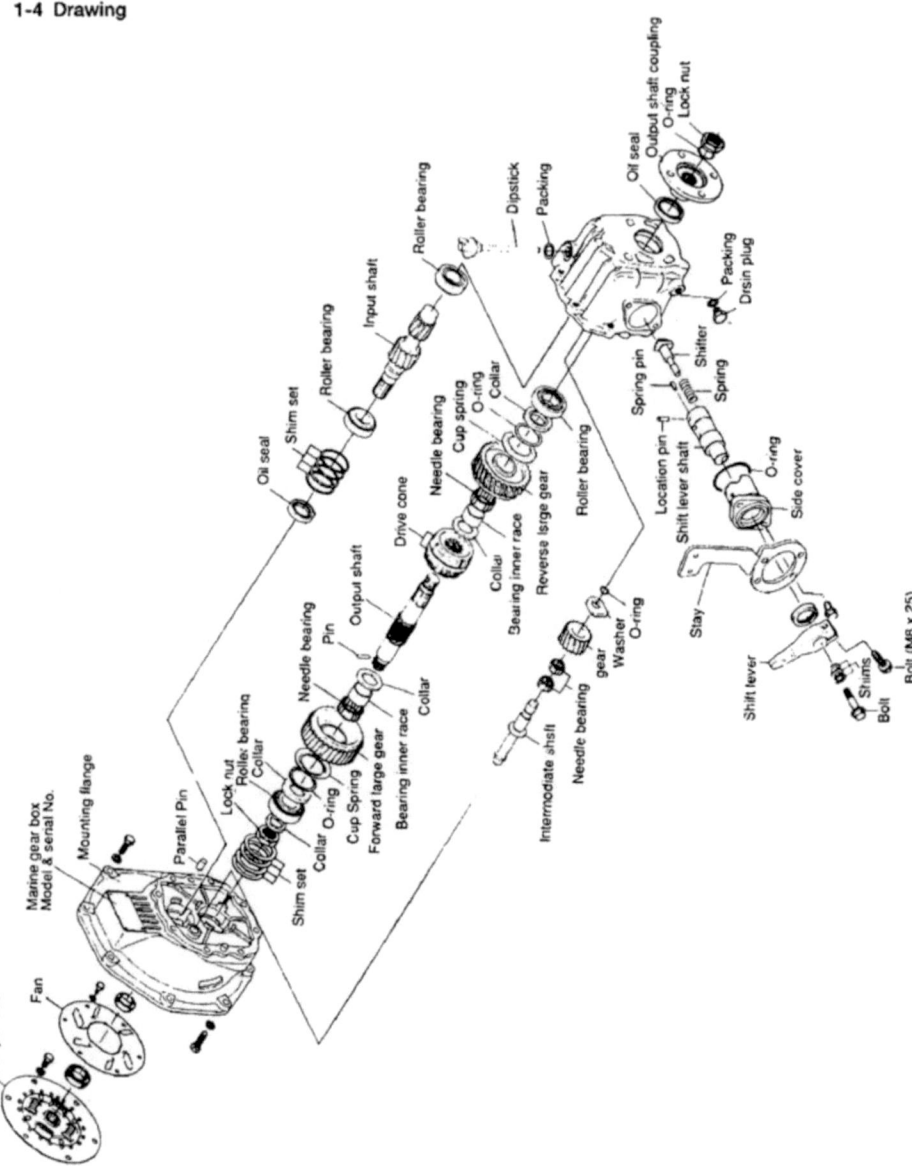

Chapter 7 Reduction and Reversing Gear
1. Construction   3,4JH3(B)(C)E

1-5 Sectional view

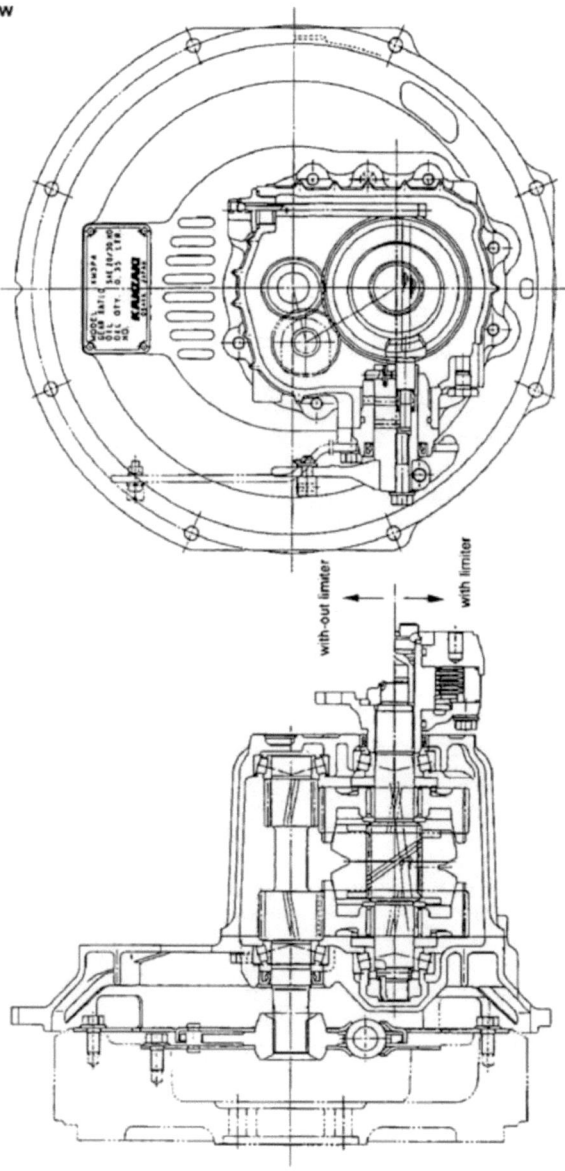

2. Shifting Device

2-1 Construction of shifting mechanism

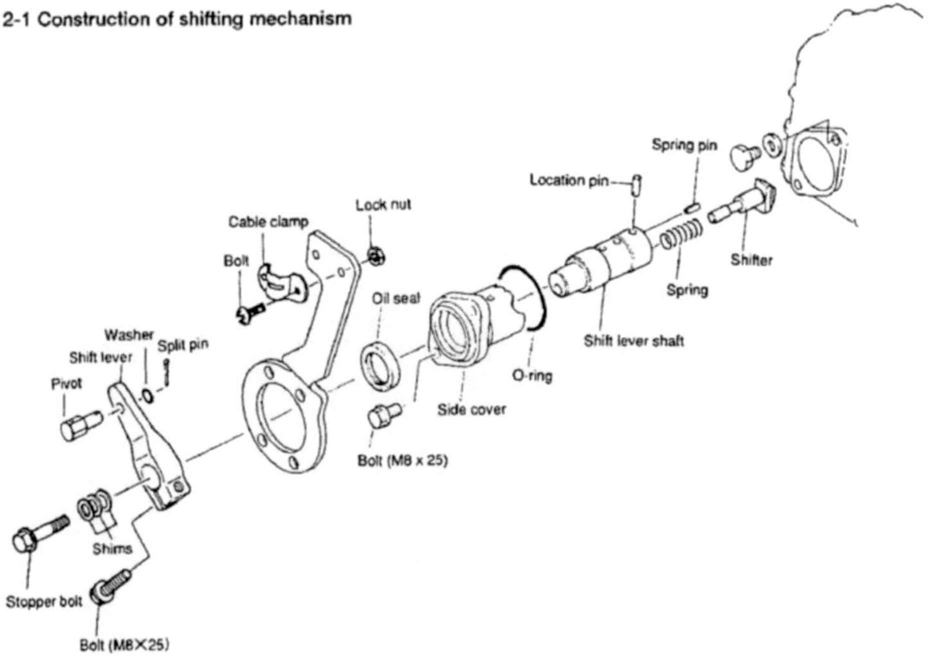

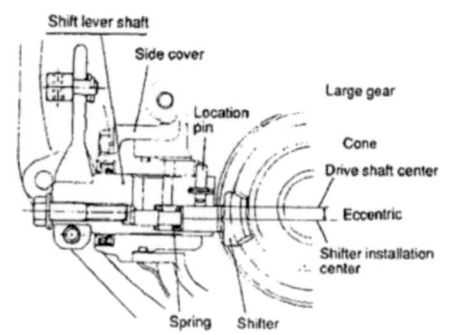

The shift lever shaft is installed on the side cover with neutral, forward and reverse positions provided on this cover. The neutral, forward and reverse location pins of the shift lever shaft are constantly inserted into their respective grooves on the shift lever by the tension of the shifter spring. The shifter is set on the eccentric hole of the shift lever shaft and moves the drive cone in the neutral position either to the forward or reverse positions, and then back to the neutral positions. (The shift lever shaft moves slightly to the shift lever or drive cone side when the shift lever is placed in the forward on reverse positions.)

Chapter 7 Reduction and Reversing Gear
2. Shifting Device

3.4JH3(B)(C)E

2-2 Forward and reverse clutch operation

(Neutral ⇒ Forward; Neutral ⇒ Reverse)

When the shift lever is moved to the forward position from the neutral position, the shift lever shaft starts to revolve, and the location pin disengages from the neutral V-groove position of the side cover. (Shift lever moves approx. 0.5mm to the drive cone side.) At this time the shifter, which is set on the eccentric hole of the shift lever shaft, moves the drive cone's V-groove to the forward large gear.

When the location pin of the shift lever shaft falls in the forward position groove of the side cover, (the shift lever shaft moves to the shift lever side approx. 3mm), and the shifter stars to press the drive cone V-groove to the forward large gear side through the spring force.

2-3 Engagement and disengagement of clutch

(Forward ⇒ Neutral; Reverse ⇒ Neutral)

When the shift lever is moved to the forward position from the neutral position, the shift lever shaft starts to revolve, and the location pin disengages from the forward position groove of the side cover. (The shift lever shaft moves approx. 3mm to the drive cone side.) At this time, the shifter which is set on the eccentric hole of the shift lever shaft is moved to the neutral side (reverse large gear side). The drive cone, however, is engaged with the forward large gear through the torque force produced by the revolving centrifugal force.

Further, when the shift lever shaft starts to revolve, and the positioning pin falls in to the neutral V-groove position of the side cover (the shift lever shaft travels approx. 5mm to the shift lever side), the shifter moves to the shift lever side(to the spring side) while moving the V-groove of the drive cone to the reverse large gear side. The movement of the shifter to the shift lever side, however, is stopped when the shifter end contacts the stopper bolt. The shifter only works to press the V-groove of the drive cone to the reverse large gear side. Thus, the drive cone is disengaged from the forward large gear. After this disengagement, the transmission torque of the drive cone is decreased to zero and the shift lever is returned to the neutral position by the spring force.

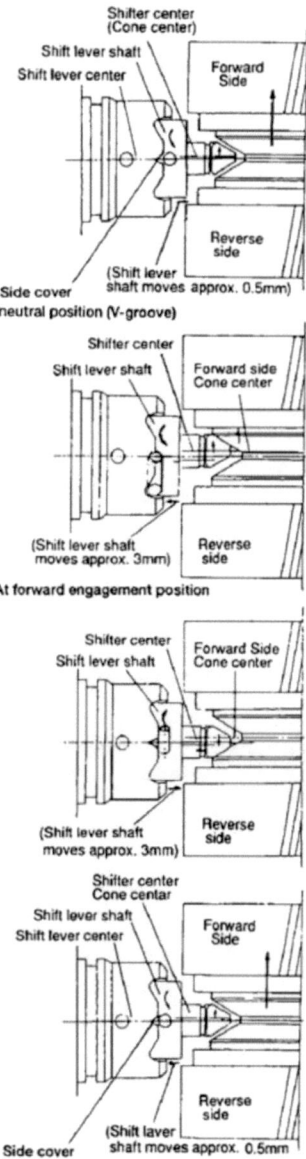

Side cover neutral position (V-groove)

At forward engagement position

Side cover neutral position (V-groove)

Chapter 7 Reduction and Reversing Gear
2. Shifting Device   3,4JH3(B)(C)E

2-4 Clutch shifting force

Shifting position / shifting direction	Shift lever position at 56mm	Remote control handle postition at 170mm (Cable length, 4m)
Engaging force at 1000rpm	3~4 kg	4~5 kg
Disengaging force at 1000rpm	3.5~5 kg	4~6 kg

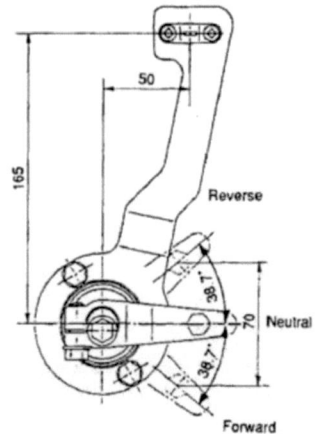

2-5 Adjustment of shifting device

Whenever the side cover, shift lever shaft, shifter, stopper bolt or drive cone is replaced, be sure to adjust the clearance between the shifter end and the stopper bolt by using shims. When the adjustment of this clearance is not proper the drive cone may be properly fitted When the shift lever is moved to the neutral position either from the forward or reverse position.

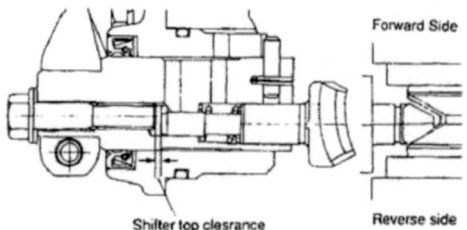

Shifter top clesrance

Chapter 7 Reduction and Reversing Gear
2. Shifting Device

3,4JH3(B)(C)E

2-5-1 Measurement and adjustment of clearance

(a) Assemble the shifting mechanism (without installing the stopper bolt of the shifter) to the marine gear case.

NOTE : Ensure the correct direction of the shifter before assembly.

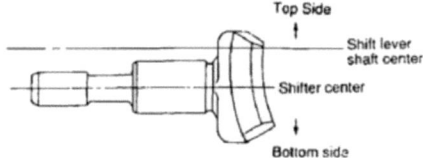

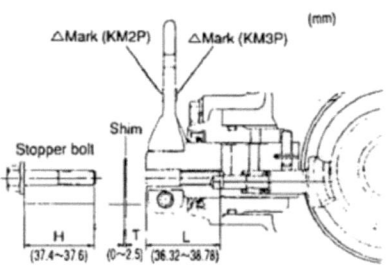

(b) Turn the shift lever 10~15 degree either to the forward or reverse position from the neutral position.
(c) Measure the L-distance between the shift lever shaft end surface and the shifter's end.
(d) Measure the H-distance (the distance from the neck of the stopper bolt to its end).

(e) Obtain the shim thickness T by the following formula.

$$T = (H - L + 1.25) \pm 0.1mm$$

NOTE : Shim set includes one piece each of 1mm, 0.4mm, 0.3mm, 0.25mm shims.
(YANMAR Part No. 177088-06380)

(f) Insert shim (s) of proper thickness to the stopper bolt side and tighten to the shift lever shaft.
NOTE : When tightening the stopper bolt, apply either a non-drying type liquid packing (TREE BOND No.1215), or a seal tape around the bolt threads.

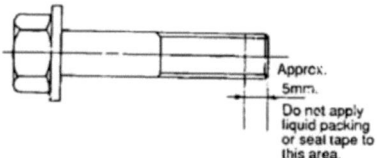

2-5-2 Inspect for the following points
(to be inspected every 2-3 months)
(1) Looseness at the connection of the cable connector and the remote control cable.
(2) Looseness of the attaching nut of the cable connector and the shift lever.

Chapter 7 Reduction and Reversing Gear
2. Shifting Device _____ 3,4JH3(B)(C)E

2-6 Adjustment of the remote control head
Marine gear box control side
(1) Equal distribution of the control lever stroke.

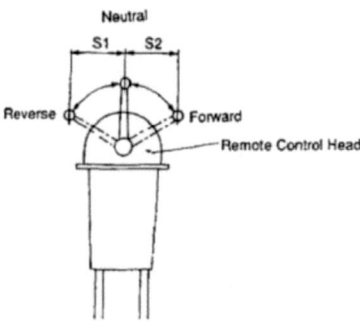

The stroke between the neutral position → forward position (S2), and the neutral position → reverse position (S1) must be equalized.
When either stroke is too short, clutch engagement becomes faulty.

(2) Equalizing the travel distance of the control cable.
Alter ensuring the equal distribution of the stroke described in (1), connect the cable to the control head. Adjust that the cable shift travel of the S1 and S2 control lever strokes becomes identical.

2-7 Cautions
(1) Always stop the engine when attaching, adjusting, and inspecting.
(2) When conducting inspection immediately after stopping the engine, do not touch the clutch.
The oil temperature is often raised to around 90°C (194°F).
(3) Half-clutch operation is not possible with this design and construction. Do not use with the shift lever halfway to the engaged position.

NOTE : *The dual (Two) lever remote control device cannot be usded.*

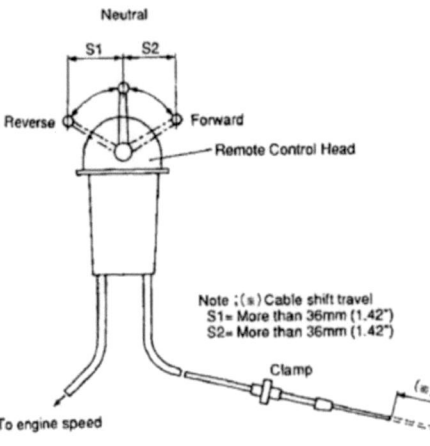

Note ;(≋)Cable shift travel
S1= More than 36mm (1.42")
S2= More than 36mm (1.42")

3. Inspection and Servicing

3-1 Clutch case
(1) Check the clutch case with a test hammer for cracking. Perform a color check when required.
If the case is cracked, replace it.
(2) Check for staining on the inside surface of the bearing section.
Also, measure the inside diameter of the case.
Replace the case if it is worn beyond the wear limit.

3-2 Bearing
(1) Rusting and damage.
If the bearing is rusted or the taper roller retainer is damages, replace the bearing.
(2) Make sure that the bearings rotates smoothly.
If rotation is not smooth, if there is any binding, or if any abnormal sound is evident, replace the baring.

3-3 Gear
Check the surface, tooth face conditions and backlash of each gear. Replace any defective part.
(1) Tooth surface wear.
Check the tooth surface for pitting, abnormal wear, dents, and cracks. Repair the lightly damaged gears and replace heavily damaged gears.
(2) Tooth surface contact.
Check the tooth surface contact. The amount of tooth surface contact between the tooth crest and tooth flank must be at least 70% of the tooth width.
(3) Backlash.
Measure the backlash of each gear, and replace the gear when it is worn beyond the wear limit. mm

	Maintenance standard	Wear limit
Input shaft forward gear and output shaft forward large gear	0.06~0.12	0.2
Input shaft reverse gear and intermediate gear	0.06~0.12	0.2
Intermediate gear and output shaft reverse large gear	0.06~0.12	0.2

3-4 Forward and reverse large gears
(1) Contact surface with drive cone.
Visually inspect the tapered surface of the forward and reverse large gears where they make contact with the drive cone to check if any abnormal condition or sign of overheating exists.
If any defect is found, replace the gear.

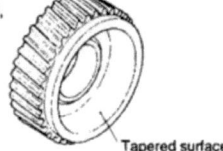

Tapered surface

(2) Forward/reverse large gear needle bearing.
When an abnormal sound is produced at the needle bearing, visually inspect the rollers; replace the bearing if the rollers are faulty.

Rollers

3-5 Drive cone
(1) Visually inspect that part of the surface that comes into contact with the circumferential triangular slot to check for signs of scoring, overheating or wear. If deep scoring or signs of overheating are found, replace the cone.

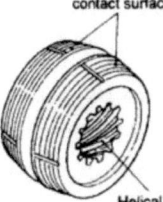

contact surface

Helical involute spline

(2) Check the helical involute spline for any abnormal condition on the tooth surface, and repair or replace the part should any defect be found.
(3) Measure the amount of wear on the tapered contact surface of the drive cone, and replace the cone when the wear exceeds the specified limit.

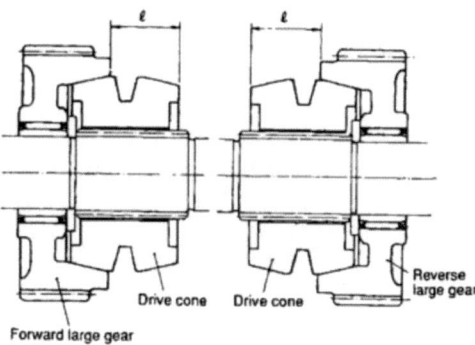

Forward large gear — Drive cone — Drive cone — Reverse large gear

Chapter 7 Reduction and Reversing Gear
3. Inspection and Servicing

3,4JH3(B)(C)E

Dimensions ℓ		Standard dimensions	Limited dimensions
	KM3P4	32.7~33.3	32.4
	KM35P	29.25~29.75	28.1

NOTE : When dismantled, the forward of reverse direction of the drive cone must be clearly identified.

(4) If the wear of the V-groove of the drive cone is excessive, replace the part.

NOTE : When replacing the drive cone, the new cone and forward large gear and reverse large gear must be lapped prior to assembly.
The lapping procedure is described below.

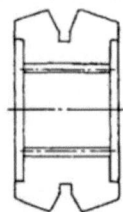

3-5-1 Lapping Procedure for Drive Cone

(1) Coat the lapping powder onto the cave of the clutch gear (Lapping powder : 67 micron silicon carbide #280)

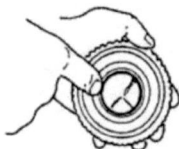

(2) Set the large gear on the output shaft with a needle bearing and then set the drive cone on the output shaft.

(3) Lap the large gear's cave and drive cone, pushing them together by hand.

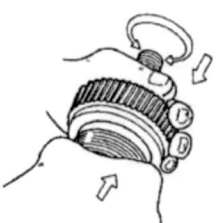

(4) Push and turn the large gear about 5 times both clockwise and counter-clockwise.

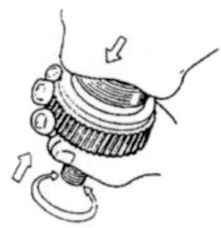

(5) After lapping them, wash them with washing oil. The lapped parts should be cleaned completely.

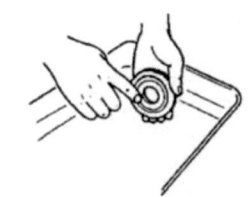

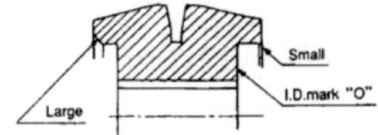

NOTE : Do not mix the combination of the lapped parts. The washing oil should be changed frequently in order to prevent residual powder being left on the parts.
When assembling the drive cone, be sure to check its alignment. The larger chamferrng face should be on the forward large gear side.

3-6 Thrust collar

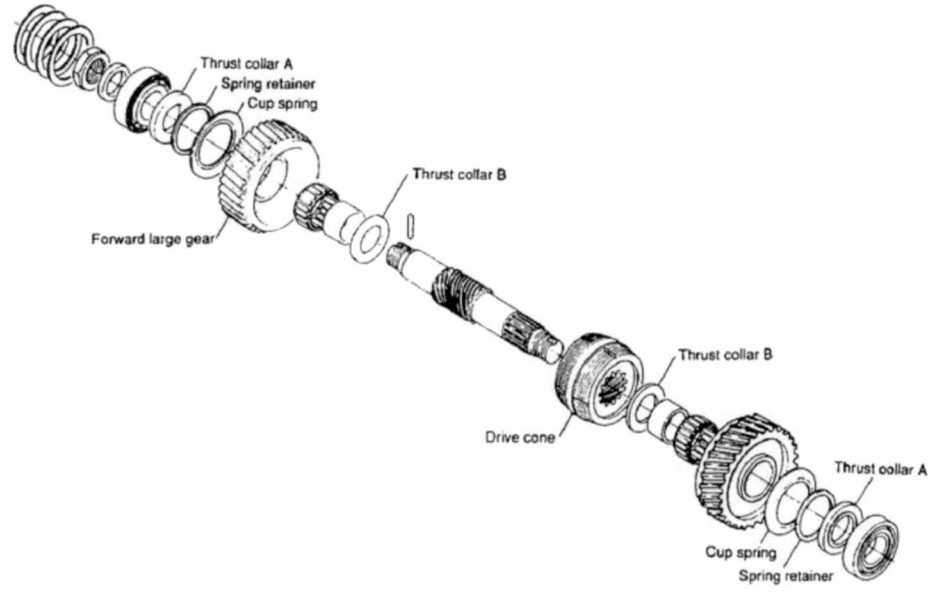

Chapter 7 Reduction and Reversing Gear
3. Inspection and Servicing

3.4JH3(B)(C)E

(1) Visually inspect the sliding surface of thrust collar A or B to check for signs of overheating, scoring, or cracks.
Replace the collar if any abnormal condition is found.
(2) Measure the thickness of thrust collar A or B, and replace it when the dimension exceeds the specified limit.

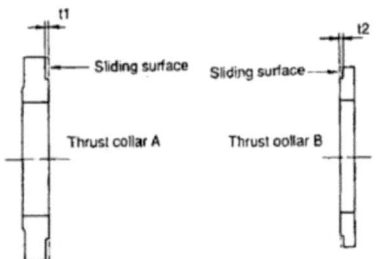

Stepped wear	Limit for use
Thrust collar A, t1	0.05
Thrust collar B, t2	0.20

(mm)

3-7 Cup spring and spring retainer
(1) Check for cracks and damage to the cup spring and spring retainer.
Replace the part if defective.
(2) Measure the free length of the cup spring and the thickness of the spring retainer. If the length or the thickness deviates from the standard size, replace the part.

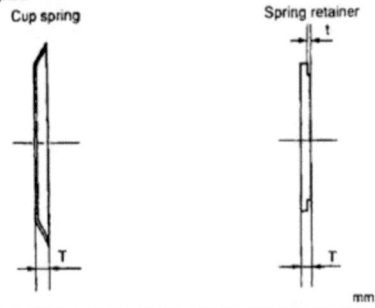

	Standard	Limit
Cup spring, T	2.8~3.1	2.6
Spring retainer, T	2.92~3.08	2.8
Spring retainer, t	—	0.1

(mm)

3-8 Oil seal of output shaft
Visually inspect the oil seal of the output shaft to check if there is any damage or oil leakage; replace the seal when any abnormal condition is found.

3-9 Input shaft

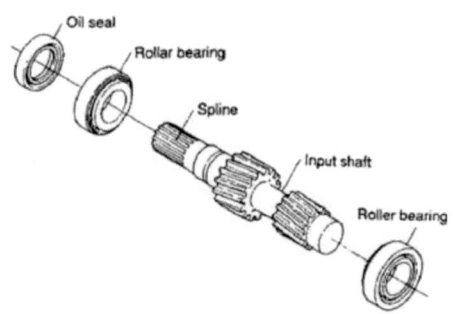

(1) Spline part
Whenever uneven wear and/or scratches are found, replace with a new part.
(2) Surface of oil seal.
If the sealing surface of the oil seal is worn or scratched, replace.

3-10 Output shaft

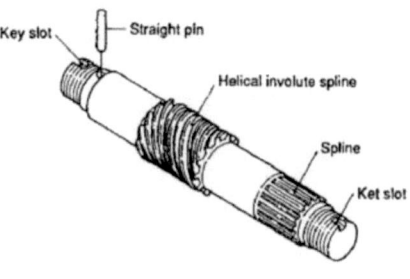

(1) Visually inspect the spline and the helical involute spline, and repair or replace a part when any abnormal condition is found on its surface.

Chapter 7 Reduction and Reversing Gear
3. Inspection and Servicing

3-11 Intermediate shaft

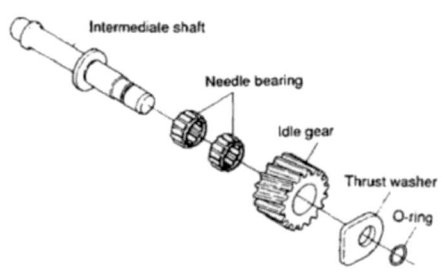

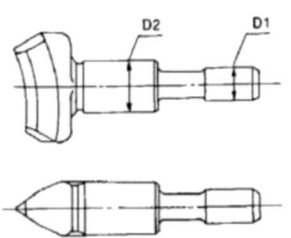

(1) Needle bearing dimensions, staining.
Check the surface of the roller to see whether the needle bearing sticks or is damaged. Replace if necessary.

	Standard	Limit
D1	66.9~67.0	65
D2	11.966~11.984	11.95
Shift lever shaft, Shifter insert hole	12.0~12.018	12.05

(mm)

3-12 Shifting device
3-12-1 Shifter

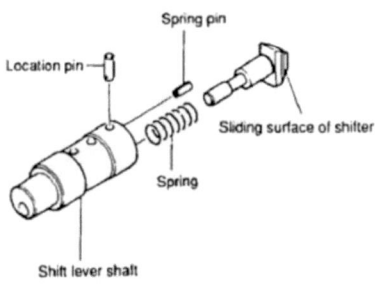

(1) Visually inspect the surface in contact with the drive cone, and replace the shifter when signs of overheating, damage or wear are found.
(2) Measure the shaft diameter of the shifter.
Replace the shaft if the size deviates from the standard.

3-12-2 Shift lever shaft and location pin

(1) Check the shift lever shaft and location pin for damage or distortion, and replace defective parts. If the location pin must be replaced, replace it together with the shift lever shaft.
(2) Measure the diameter of the shift lever shaft and the shifter insertion hole. Replace the part if the size deviates from the standard value.

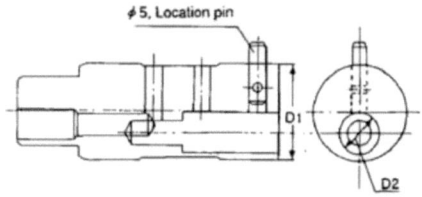

	Standard	Limit
D1	27.959~27.98	27.90
D2	12.0~12.018	12.05
Side cover, Shift insert hole	28.0~28.021	28.08

(mm)

3-12-3 Shifter spring
(1) Check the spring for scratches or corrosion.
(2) Measure the free length of the spring.

Shifter spring	Standard	Limt
Free length	22.6mm	19.8mm
Spring constant	0.854kgf/mm	—
Length when attached	14.35mm	—
Load when attached	7.046kg	6.08kg

3-12-4 Stopper bolt
Check the stopper bolt. If it is worn or stepped, replace.

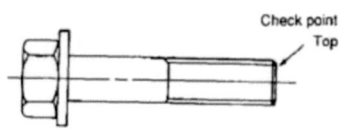

3-12-5 Side cover and oil seal
(1) Check the neutral, forward and reverse position grooves.
Replace if the grooves are worn.
(2) Measure the insertion hole of the shift lever s haft.
Replace if the size deviates from the standard value.
(3) Check the oil seal and the O-ring for damage.
Replace if the part is defective.

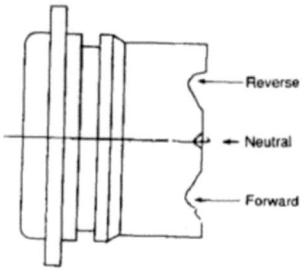

3-13 Damper disc

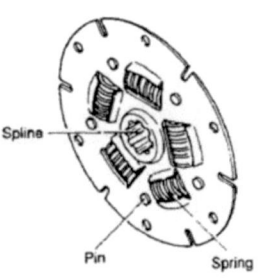

(1) Spline part.
Whenever uneven wear and/or scratches are found, replace with a new part.
(2) Spring.
Whenever uneven wear and/or scratches are found, replace with a new part.
(3) Pin wear
Whenever uneven wear and/or scratches are found, replace with a new part.
(4) Whenever a crack or damage to the spring slot is found replace the defective part with a new one.

3-14 Shim adjustment for output and input shafts

Check the thickness of shims for both input and output shafts. When the component parts are not replaced after dismantling, the same shims can be reused. When the clutch case and flange or any one of the following parts is replaced the thickness of shim must be determined in the following manner.

For input shaft part : input shaft, bearing.
For output shaft parts : output shaft, thrust collar A, thrustcollar B, gear, bearing.

Chapter 7 Reduction and Reversing Gear
3. Inspection and Servicing

(1) Shim thickness (T_1) measurement of output shaft
  (a) Measure the bearing insertion hole depth (A) of the mounting flange, and the bearing insertion hole depth (A') of the clutch case.
  (b) Measure the length (B) between the bearing outer race of the input shaft assembly.
  (c) Obtain the (T_1) thickness by the following formula :
  $T_1 = A + A' - B$ (T_1 : Clearance ±0.05mm)

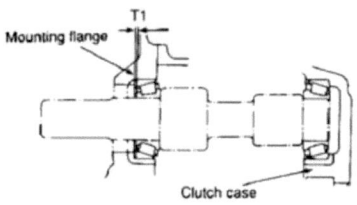
Mounting flange
Clutch case

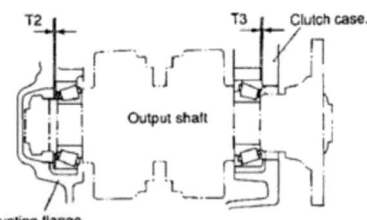
Clutch case
Output shaft

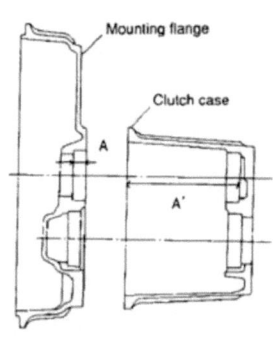
Mounting flange
Clutch case

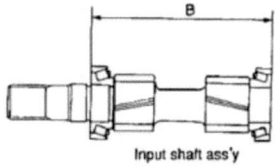
Input shaft ass'y

  (c) Measure the (F) and (E) length from the outer race end of the clutch case bearing included in the output shaft assembly.
  NOTE : Before measuring the (F) and (E) length, press the forward large gear and the reverse large gear to the drive cone until there is no clearance among them.

  (d) Obtain the (T_2) and (T_3) thicknesses by the following formulas :

  $T_2 = C + C' - D - T_3$ (Clearance $^{+0.1mm}_{0}$)

  $T_3(KM3P) = C' - 47.3 - \frac{E}{2} - F$ (Clearance ±0.05mm)

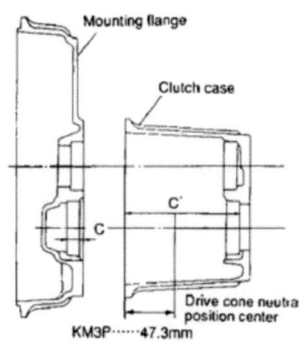
Mounting flange
Clutch case
Drive cone neutral position center
KM3P······47.3mm

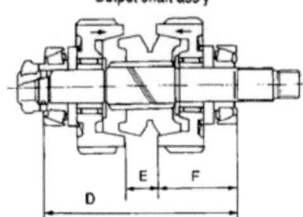
Output shaft ass'y

(2) Shim thickness (T_2, T_3) measurement of output shaft
  (a) Measure the bearing insertion hole depth (C) of the mounting flange, and the bearing insertion hole depth (C') of the clutch case.
  (b) Measure the length (D) between the bearing outer races.
  NOTE : Tighten the mounting flange nut of the output shaft assembly with the specified torque. Press-fit the inner race of the clutch case roller bearing to the large gear side .

Chapter 7 Reduction and Reversing Gear
3. Inspection and Servicing

3,4JH3(B)(C)E

(3) Standard size of parts

mm

	A+A'	B	C+C'	D	E	F	Drive cone neutral center position
KM3P	132.40~132.75	131.20~132.10	141.20~141.55	139.56~141.00	23.50~24.10	57.83~58.65	47.3

NOTE : Compare your measurements with the above standard size. If your measurements largely differ from the standard sizes, measurements may not be correct. Check and measure again.

(4) Adjusting shim set

	Tickness. mm (in.)	No. of shims
Input shaft	0.5	1
	0.4	1
	0.3	2
Output shaft	1.0	1
	0.5	1
	0.3	2
	0.1	3

3-15 Torque limiter

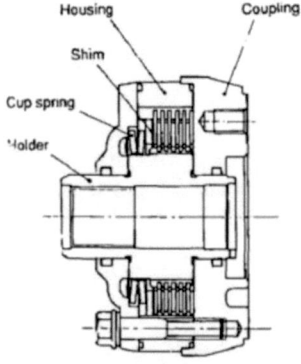
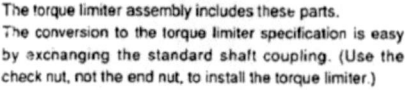
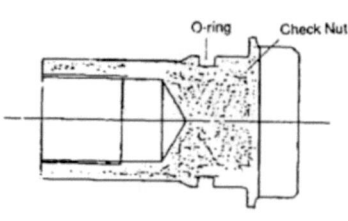

The torque limiter assembly includes these parts.
The conversion to the torque limiter specification is easy by exchanging the standard shaft coupling. (Use the check nut, not the end nut, to install the torque limiter.)

4. Disassembly

4-1. Dismantling the clutch

(1) Remove the remote control of cable.
(2) Remove the clutch assembly from the engine mounting flange.

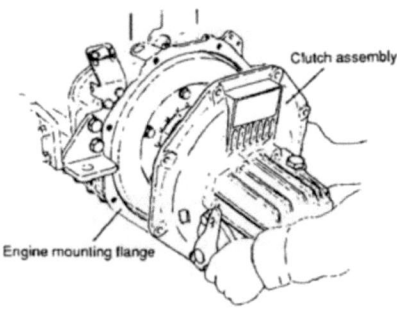

(3) Drain the lubricating oil.
Drain the lubricating oil by loosening the plug at the bottom of the clutch case.

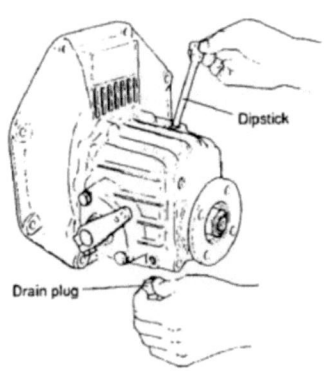

(4) Remove the end nut and output shaft coupling.

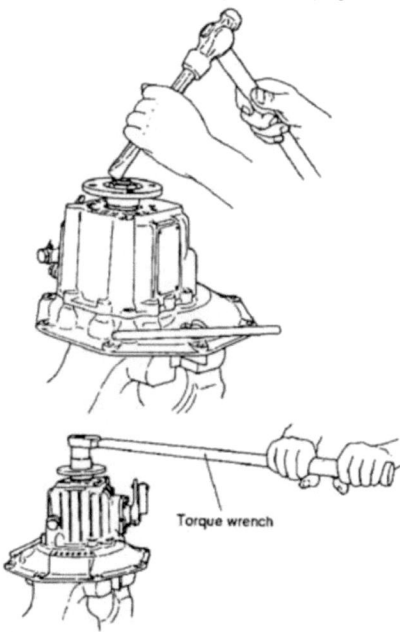

NOTE : Take care as it has a left-handed thread.

(5) Remove the oil dip stick and O-ring.
(6) Remove the fixing bolts on the side cover, and also remove the shift lever shaft, shift lever and shifter.

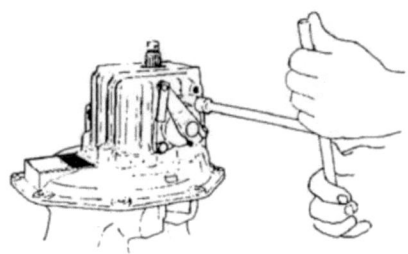

Chapter 7 Reduction and Reversing Gear
4. Disassembly
3.4JH3(B)(C)E

(7) Remove the bolts which secure the mounting flange to the case body, give light taps to the left and right with a plastic headed hammer while supporting the clutch case with your hand, then remove the mounting flange.

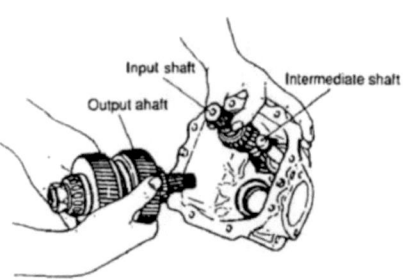

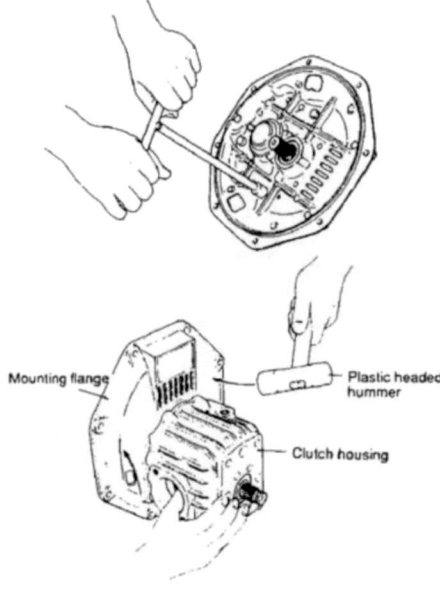

(9) Take out the intermediate shaft and input shaft. When taking out the intermediate shaft, place a bolt or spacer on the shaft hole of the case, and drive the shaft out by tapping it lightly.

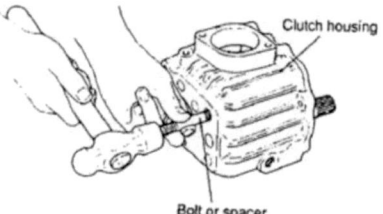

(8) Withdraw the output shaft assembly.

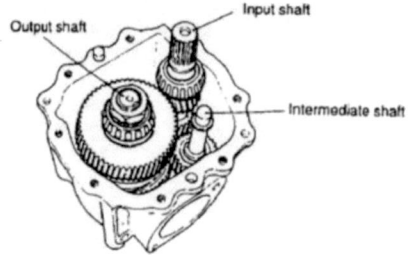

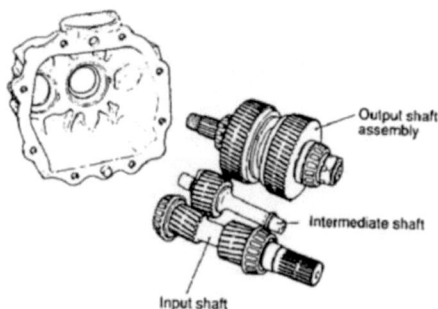

7—49

Chapter 7 Reduction and Reversing Gear
4. Disassembly
_3,4JH3(B)(C)E_

(10) Remove the oil seal of the output shaft from the case body.

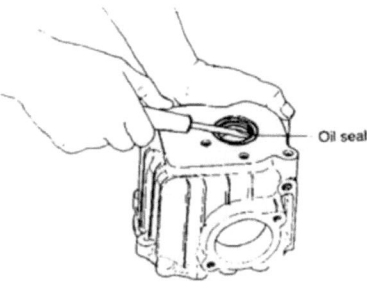
Oil seal

(11) Remove the outer bearing race from the case body by using the special tool.

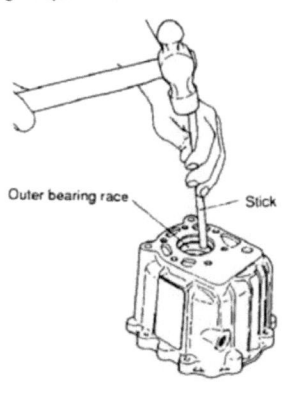
Outer bearing race — Stick

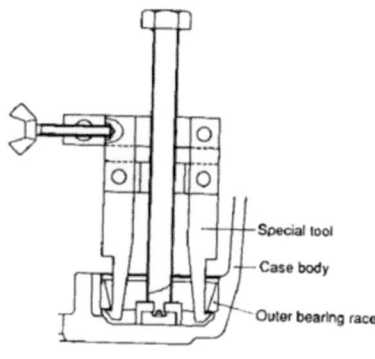
Special tool
Case body
Outer bearing race

(12) Remove the oil seal of the input shaft from the mounting flange.
(13) Remove the outer bearing race from the mounting flange in the same way as with the case body.
(14) Remove each adjusting plate from the input our output shaft.

NOTE : The same adjusting plates can be revsed when the following parts are not replaced.
When any part is replaced however, readjustment is necessary.

4-2 Removal of the output shaft

(1) Take out the reverse large gear, thrust collar A, cup spring, spring retainer and inner bearing race.
The reverse large gear must be withdrawn using a pulley extracter, by fixing the nut at the forward end in a vice.

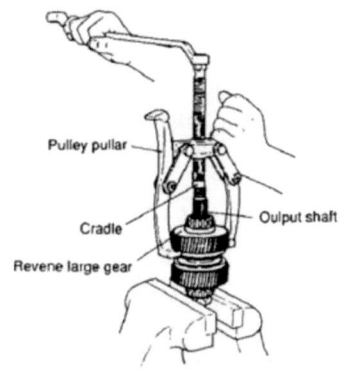
Pulley pullar
Cradle
Output shaft
Revene large gear

(2) Loosen the calking of the forward nut and remove the nut and spacer.
Remove the nut by using a torque wrench after setting the output shaft coupling and fixing the coupling bolt in a vice.

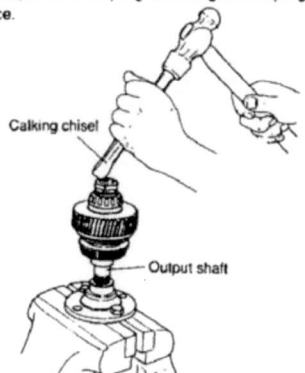
Calking chisel
Output shaft

Printed in Japan
HINSHI-H8009

Chapter 7 Reduction and Reversing Gear
4. Disassembly
3,4JH3(B)(C)E

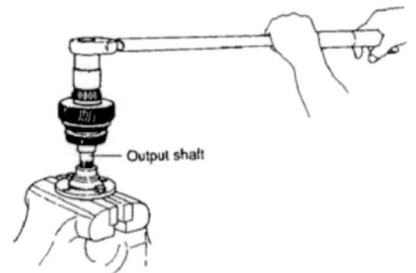

(3) Place the pulley extractor against the end surface of the forward large gear, and withdraw the forward large gear, thrust collar A, cup spring, spring retainer and inner bearing race.

(4) While gripping the drive cone, tap the end of the shaft with a plastic headed hammer, and withdraw the thrust collar B and inner needle bearing race. A pulley extractor may be used.

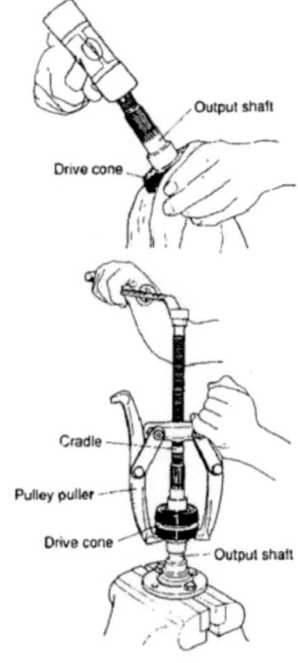

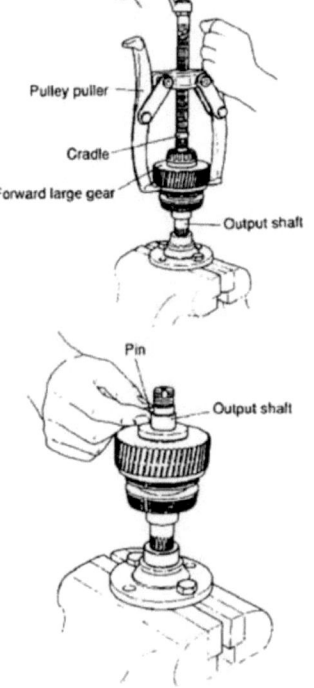

4-3 Removal of the intermediate shaft.
(1) Remove the "O" ring.
(2) Remove the thrust washer.
(3) Remove the intermediate gear and needle bearing.

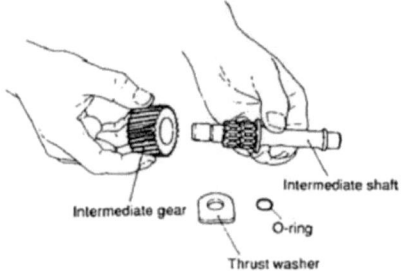

NOTE : Take care as the nut has left-handed thread.

Chapter 7 Reduction and Reversing Gear
4. Disassembly

4-4 Dismantling the shifting device
(1) Take out the shifter and shifter spring.

(4) Remove the shift lever to the anti-shif lever side.

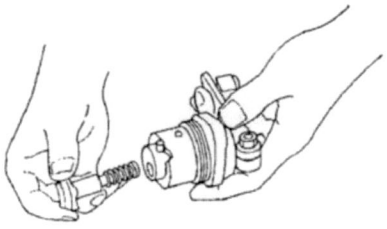

(2) Remove the stopper bolt of the shifter and shim.

(5) Remove the oil-seal and O-ring.

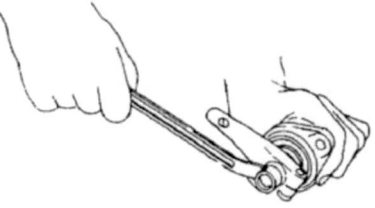

(3) Loosen the bolt of the shift lever and remove the shift lever from the shift lever shaft.

5. Reassembly

5-1 Reassembly of output shaft
(1) Fit the forward side thrust collar B onto the shaft.
(2) Drive in the forward end inner needle bearing race using a jig.

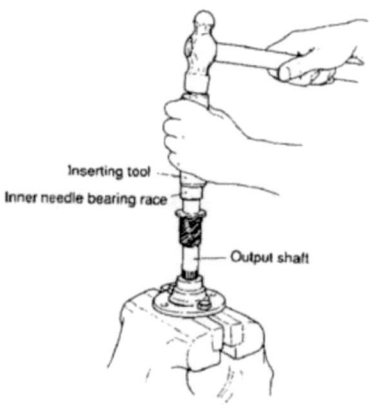

(3) Assemble the needle bearing and forward large gear.

NOTE : Check that the forward large gear rotates smoothly.

(4) Fit the cup spring, spring retainer, thrust collar A and Pin, and driven in the inner bearing race using a jig.

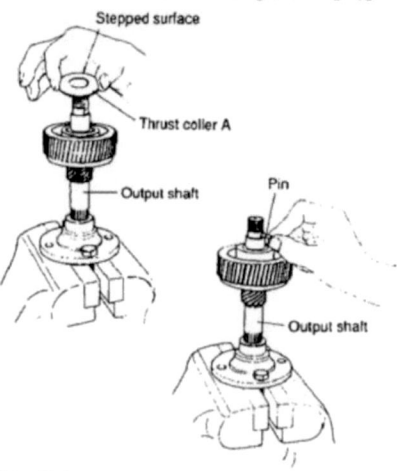

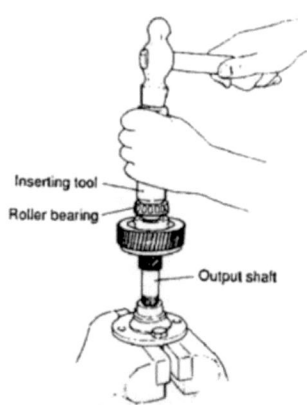

NOTE : 1) Drive in with a plastic headed hammer. Do not hit it hard.
2) When fitting the thrust collar A, note the fitting direction. Fit it keeping the stepped surface toward the roller bearing side.
3) Note that the pin cannot be fitted after the inner bearing race has been driven in.
4) Check that the forward large gear rotates smoothly.

(5) Assemble the collar and pin so that the pin is in the groove of the collar.
(6) Set and tighten the forward end nut. Insert the bolt into the coupling, and fix it in a vice, keeping the spline part upward.
Insert the shaft into the spline of the coupling, fit the spacer, and tighten the nut with a torque wrench.

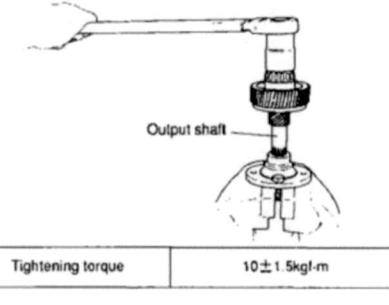

Tightening torque	10 ± 1.5 kgf-m

NOTES : 1) Take care as it is a left-handed thread.
2) Use the reverse side nut used before dismantling as the forward end nut. This is so as not to match the calked portion to the same point.

Chapter 7 Reduction and Reversing Gear
5. Reassembly _____ 3,4JH3(B)(C)E

5-2 Reassembly of the clutch

(1) Fit the oil seal, bearing outer races and shim (output shaft side) in the clutch case.
(2) Insert the input shaft into the clutch case.
(3) Drive the intermediate shaft into the clutch case.

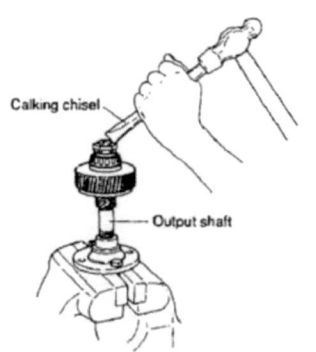

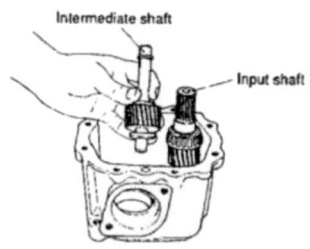

(7) Insert the drive cone while keeping the output shaft set for reverse.

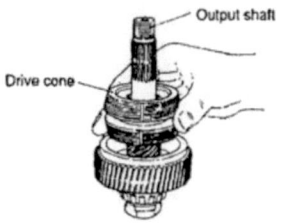

NOTES : 1) If the output shaft is not fitted into the clutch case before driving-in the intermediate shaft, it cannot be assembled.
2) Note the assembly direction of the thrust washer.

(4) Insert the output shaft into the clutch case.

(8) Apply procedures 1 through 4 to the forward end.

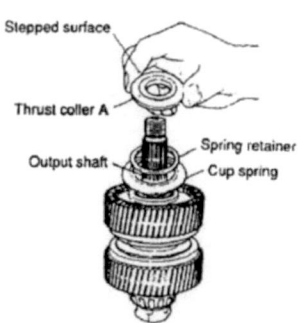

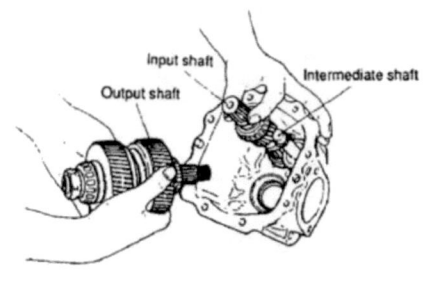

NOTE :1) Fit thrust collar A so that the stepped surface faces the roller bearing side.
2) Check that the reverse large gear rotates smoothly.

7−54

Printed in Japan
HINSHI-H8009

Chapter 7 Reduction and Reversing Gear
5. Reassembly
_____3,4JH3(B)(C)E

(5) Fit the adjusting plate to the mounting flange, and drive in the outer bearing race.
NOTE : The outer bearing race can be easily driven in by heating the mounting flange to about 100℃, or by cooling the outer race with liquid hydrogen.
(6) Apply non-drying liquid packing around the outer surface of the oil seal, and insert the oil seal into the mounting flange while keeping the spring part of the oil seal facing the inside of the case.
(7) Apply non-drying liquid packing to the matching surfaces of the mounting flange end the case body.

(8) Insert the input shaft and output shaft into the shaft holes of the mounting flange, assemble the mounting flange on the case body, and tighten the bolt.

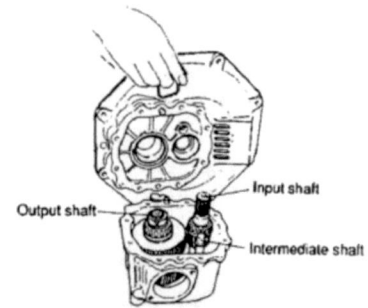

Output shaft — Input shaft — Intermediate shaft

NOTE : Apply non-drying liquid packing to either the mounting flange or the case body.

(9) Assemble the output shaft coupling on the output shaft, and fit the O-ring.
(10) Tighten the end nut by using a torque wrench, then calk it.

Non-drying liquid packing

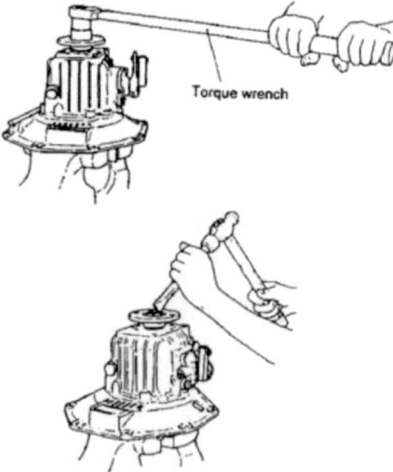

Torque wrench

NOTE : Take care as it is a left-handed thread.

Tightening torque	10±1.5kgf-m

5-3 Reassembly of the shiating device

(1) Fit the oil seal and O-ring to the side cover.

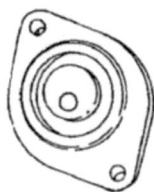

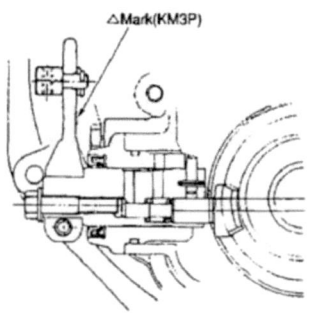
△Mark(KM3P)

(2) Insert the shift lever shaft to the side cover.

(4) Insert the shiater spring and shifter to the shift lever shaft.
(5) Fit the side cover assembly to the clutch case.

NOTE : 1) Check the direction of the shifter (Top and bottom side).
2) The shift lever may not turn smoothly if the clutch case is not filled with lubricating oil.
(6) Fit the shim and stopper bolt to the shift lever shaft.

NOTE : Apply non-drying liquid packing or sealtape to the thread of the stopper bolt.

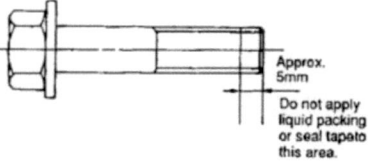

Approx. 5mm

Do not apply liquid packing or seal tapeto this area.

(3) Fit the shift lever to the shift lever shaft.

NOTE : Check the direction of the shift lever △ mark.

(7) Fit the cable connector to the shift lever.

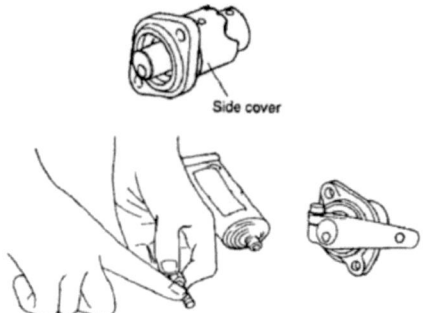
Side cover

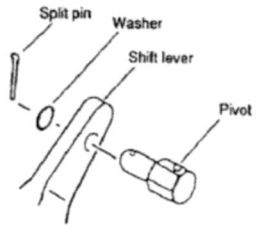
Split pin Washer
Shift lever
Pivot

CHAPTER 8
REMOTE CONTROL (OPTIONAL)

1. Remote Control system ································8-1
   1-1 Construction of remote control system ···············8-1
   1-1 Remote control device components ···················8-1
2. Remote Control Installation ·······················8-2
   2-1 Speed control ··8-2
   2-2 Clutch control ··8-2
   2-3 Engine stop ··8-3
3. Remote Control Inspection ·······················8-4
4. Remote Control Adjustment ······················8-5

Chapter 8 Remote Control
1. Remote Control System   3,4JH3(B)(C)E

1. Remote Control System

1-1 Construction of remote control system

The remote control permits one handed control of the engine speed changing from forward to reverse, and stopping.

Fittings which allow for easy connection of the remote control cables with the fuel injection pump and transmission are provided with the remote control set.

The use of Morse remote control cables, clamps and a remote control head, are also provided for The device to stop the engine is electric and will be explained under the section on electrical equipment

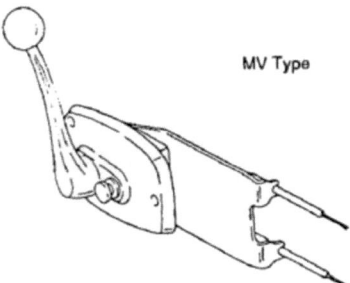

MV Type

1-2 Remote control device components

	Morse description
Remote control head	Morse MT3 top mounting single lever Morse MV side mounting single lever
Remote control cable	Morse 33C × 4m Morse 33C × 7m
Engine stop cable	Yanmar 4m Yanmar 7m

(1) Remote control handle

The MV type controller has been designed so that operation of the clutch and throttle can be effected with one lever. When the button next to the control lever is pulled out with the lever in the central position, it holds the clutch in the neutral position so that the throttle can be opened all the way and warm up the engine. When the engine is warmed up, return the handle to the central position and push the button back in. Control of the clutch and throttle is thus effected with one handle.

(2) Remote control cable

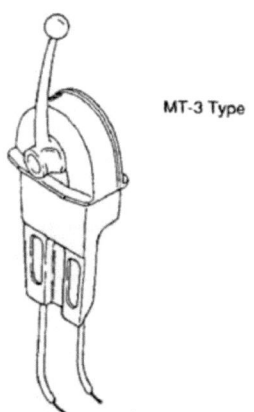

MT-3 Type

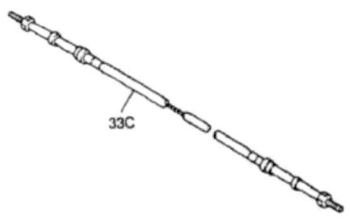

33C

Use only Super Responsive Morse Control Cables These are designed specifically for use with Morse control heads. This engineered system of Worse cables, control head and engine connection kits ensures dependable, smooth operation with an absolute minimum of backlash.

(3) Engine stop cable

The model MT-3 remote control has been designed so that operation of the clutch (shift) and governor (throttle) can be effected with one lever.

Two cables are required for the MT-2 single, one for the clutch and the other for the governor.

When warming up the engine, to freely control the governor separately from the clutch put the lever in-neutral, the central position. and pull the knob in the center of the control lever. When the lever is returned to the neutral position, the knob automatically returns to its original position, and the clutch is free. The governor can then be freely operated.

2. Remote Control Installation

2-1 Speed control

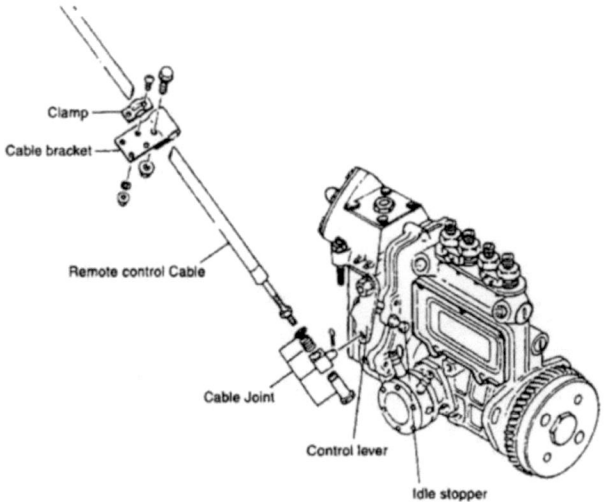

2-2 Clutch control

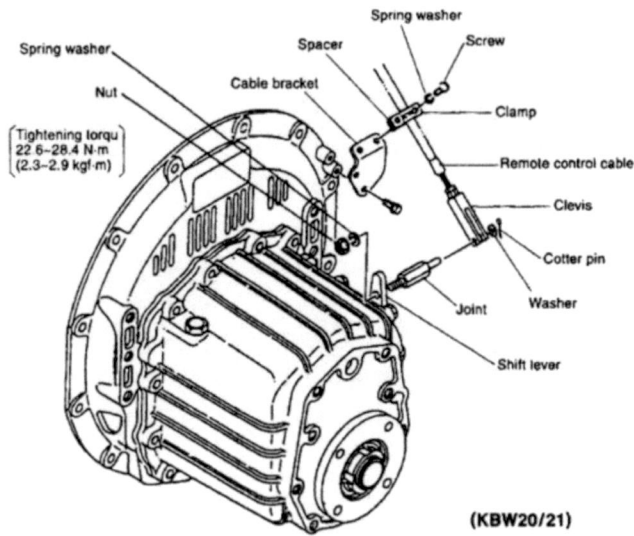

(KBW20/21)

Chapter 8 Remote Control
2. Remote Control Installation

2-3 Engine stop

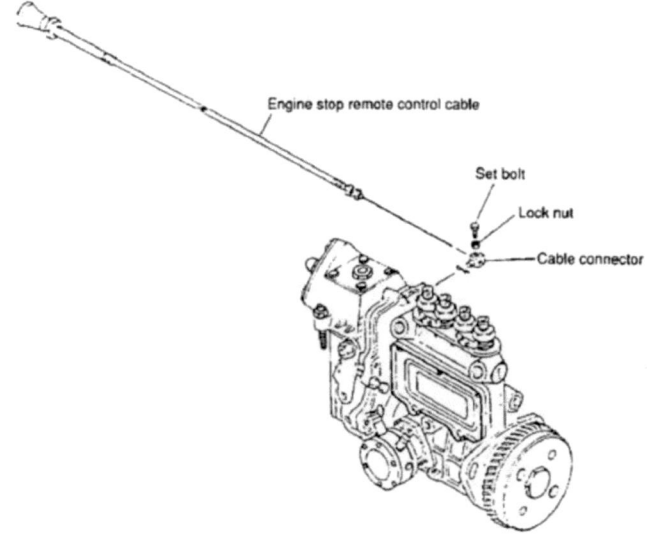

3. Remote Control Inspection

(1) When the control lever movement does not coincide with operation of the engine, check the cable end stop nut to see whether or not it is loose, and readjust/ retighten when necessary.

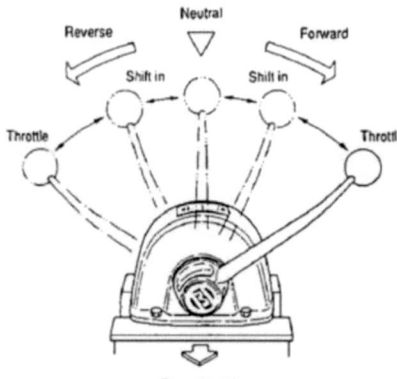

Free throttle

(2) Too many bends (turns) in the cable or bends at too extreme an angle will make it difficult to turn the handle. Reroute the cable to reduce the number of bends or enlarge the bending radius as much as possible (to 200mm or more).

(3) Check for loose cable bracket/clamp bolts or nuts and retighten as necessary.

(4) Check cable connection screwheads, cable sleeves and other metal parts for rust or corrosion. Clean off minor rust and wax or grease the parts. Replace if the parts are heavily rusted or corroded.

4. Remote Control Adjustment

(1) Shift lever adjustment

Move the lever several times—the movement of the clutch lever on the engine from forward, neutral and reverse must coincide with the forward, neutral and reverse on the control lever. If they do not coincide, adjust the fittings as necessary (first engine side, then controller side).

(2) Throttle lever adjustment

Move the control lever all the way to full throttle several times, and then return. The throttle lever on the engine must lightly push against the idle switch when it is returned If it is properly adjusted, the knob can be easily pulled out when the lever is in the neutral position, and will automatically return when the control lever is brought back to the neutral position If the control lever presses too hard against the knob, it may not return automatically, in which case the cable end must be adjusted as explained for the clutch. The knob cannot be pulled out when the lever is not in the neutral (central) position.

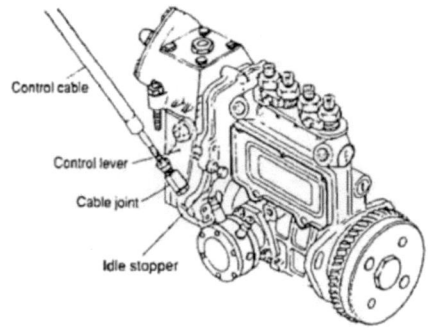

CHAPTER 9

ELECTRICAL SYSTEM

1. Electrical System ··· 9-1
   1-1 System diagram of electric parts (B-type) ················· 9-1
   1-2 Wiring diagram ··· 9-3
2. Battery ·· 9-5
   2-1 Construction ··· 9-5
   2-2 Battery capacity and battery cables ·························· 9-5
   2-3 Inspection ··· 9-5
   2-4 Charging ·· 9-7
   2-5 Battery storage precautions ······································ 9-7
3. Starter Motor ··· 9-8
   3-1 Specifications ··· 9-8
   3-2 The planetary gear starter system ···························· 9-8
   3-3 Removal ··· 9-9
   3-4 Trouble mooting the starter system ························· 9-10
   3-5 Disassembly ··· 9-11
   3-6 Inspection and Repair ··· 9-15
   3-7 Reassembly ·· 9-20
   3-8 Operation Specifications Check ······························ 9-21
4. Alternator   Standard, 12V/55A ·································· 9-22
   4-1 Features ··· 9-22
   4-2 Specifications ··· 9-22
   4-3 Characteristcs ·· 9-22
   4-4 Construction ··· 9-23
   4-5 Alternator functioning ··· 9-24
   4-6 Handling precautions ·· 9-24
   4-7 Disassembling the alternator ·································· 9-25
   4-8 Inspection and adjustment ····································· 9-26
   4-9 Reassembling the alternator ·································· 9-28
   4-10 Performance test ··· 9-29
5. Alternator   12V/80A (OPTIONAL) ··· 9-30
   5-1 Features ··· 9-30
   5-2 Specifications ··· 9-30
   5-3 Characteristcs ·· 9-30
   5-4 Construction ··· 9-31
   5-5 Alternator functioning ··· 9-32
   5-6 Handling precautions ·· 9-32
   5-7 Disassembling the alternator ·································· 9-33
   5-8 Inspection and adjustment ····································· 9-34
   5-9 Reassembling the alternator ·································· 9-36
   5-10 Performance test ··· 9-37
   5-11 Troubleshooting ··· 9-38
6. Instrument Panel ·· 9-40
   6-1 B2-type instrument panel with wiring ····················· 9-40
   6-2 C-type instrument panel ··· 9-40
   6-3 Extension codes ··· 9-41
7. Warning Devices ·· 9-42
   7-1 Oil pressure alarm ·· 9-42
   7-2 Cooling water temperature alarm ··························· 9-43
   7-3 Sender unit for lube oil pressure gauge ·················· 9-43
   7-4 Sender unit Oor the cooling water temperature gauge ··· 9-44
8. Air Heater (Optional) ·· 9-45
9. Electric type Engine Stopping Device (Optional) ·························· 9-46
   9-1 Solenoid ··· 9-46
   9-2 Relay ·· 9-47
   9-3 Wire harness of engine stop ··································· 9-47
10. Tachometer ··· 9-48
    10-1 Construction of tachometer ··································· 9-48
    10-2 Specifications and dimensions of tachometer ········ 9-48
    10-3 Measurement of sensor unit characteristics ··········· 9-49

Printed in Japan
HINSHI-H8009

1. Electrical System

1-1 System diagram of electric parts (B-type)

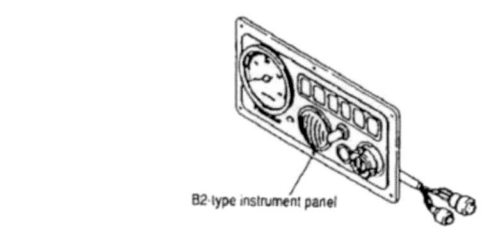

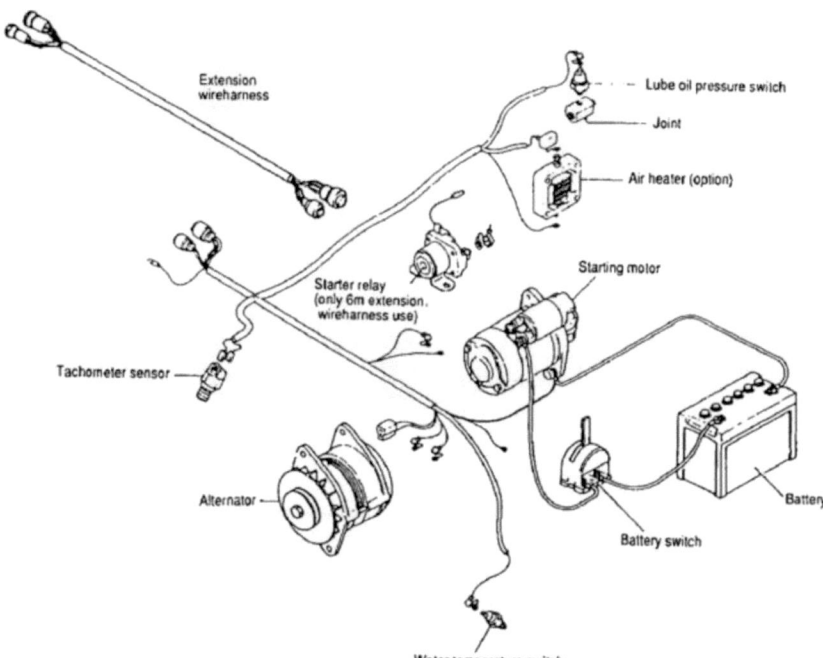

Chapter 9 Electrical System
1. Electrical System

C-type

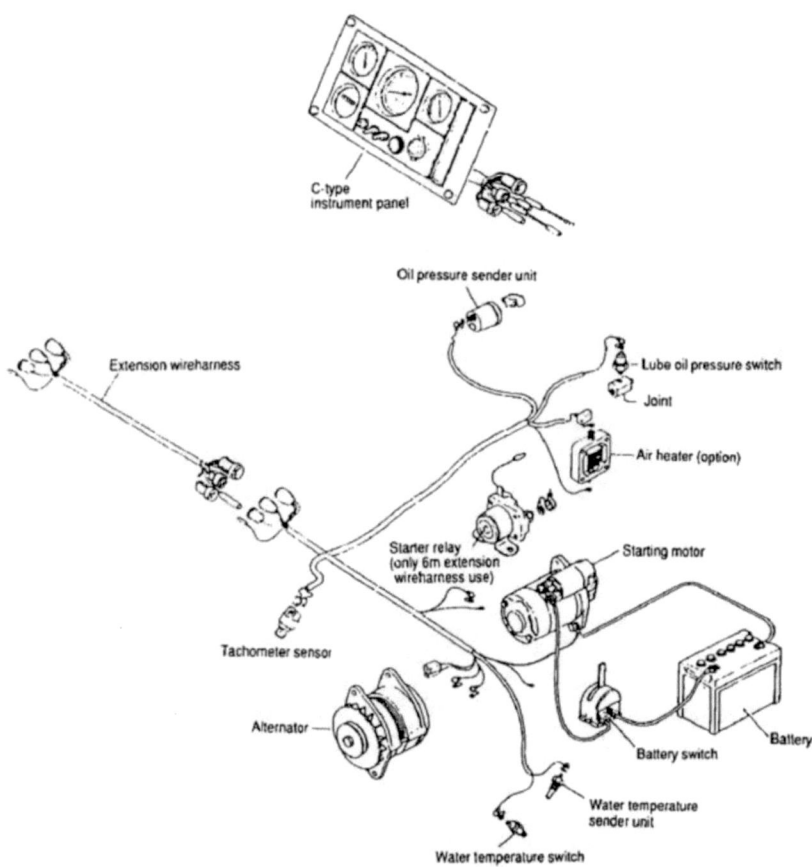

Chapter 9 Electrical System
1. Electrical System

1-2 Wiring diagram
1-2.1 For B-type instrument panel

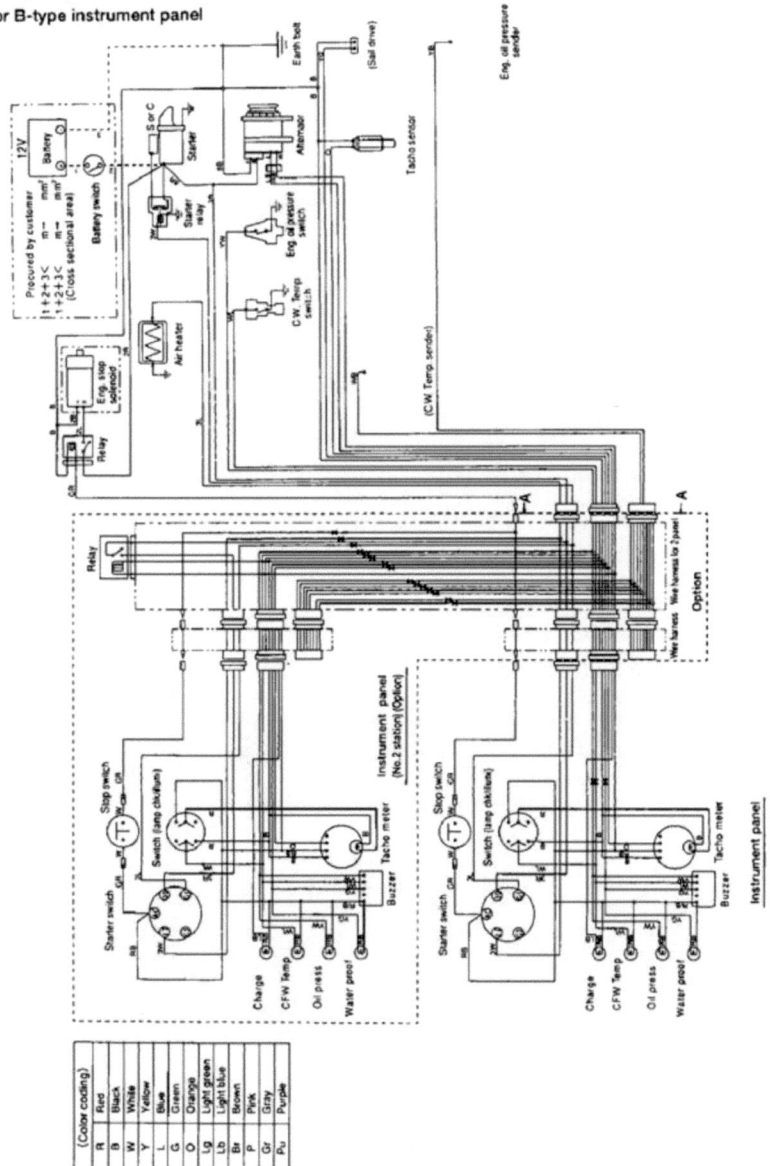

Chapter 9 Electrical System
1. Electrical System

1-2.2 For C-type instrument panel

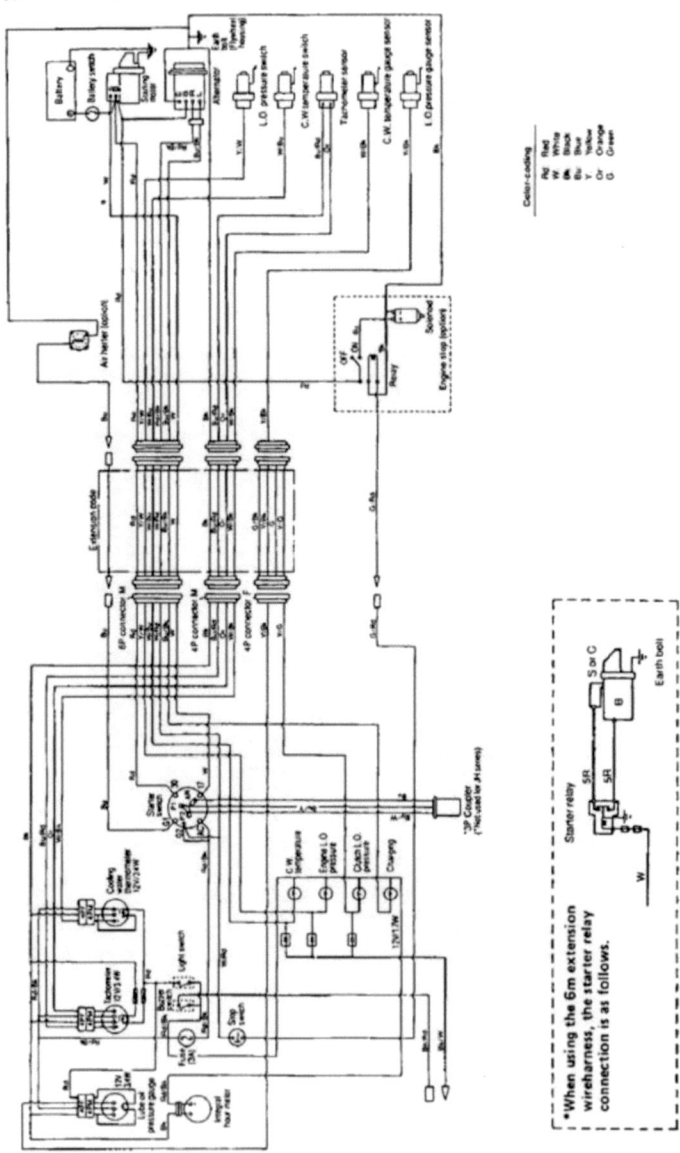

2. Battery

2-1 Construction

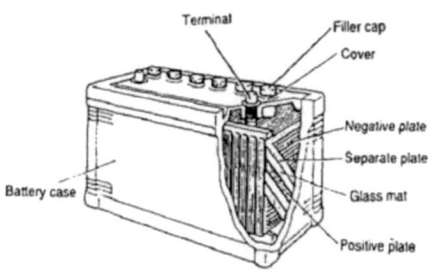

The battery utilizes chemical action to convert chemical energy to electrical energy. This engine uses a read acid battery which stores a fixed amount of power that can be used when required. After use, the battery can be recharged and used again.
As shown in the figure, a nonconductive container is filled with dilute sulfuric acid electrolyte. Lead dioxide positive plates and lead dioxide negative plates separated by glass mats are stacked alternately in the electrolyte. The positive and negative plates are connected to their respective terminals.
Power is removed from the battery by connecting the load across these two terminals.
When the battery is discharging, an electric current flows from the positive plates to the negative plates. When the battery is being charged, electric current is passed through the battery in the opposite direction by an external power source.

2-2 Battery capacity and battery cables

2-2.1 Battery capacity
Since the battery has a minimum capacity of 12V, 70AH, it can be used for 100~150AH.

Battery capacity	minimum	12V-100AH
	standard	12V-120AH
	coold weather	12V-150AH
Full charged specific gravity		1.26

2-2.2 Battery cable
Wiring must be performed with the specified electric wire. Thick, short wiring should be used to connect the battery to the starter, (soft automotive low-voltage wire [AV wire]) Using wire other than that specified may cause the following troubles:

- Wire thinner than specified
- Wire longer than specified
- High wiring resistance
- Low current
- Faulty starting

- Single conductor wire
- Open circuit caused by vibrations
- Faulty charging

The overall lengths of the wire between the battery (+) terminal and the starter (B) terminal, and between the battery (−) terminal and the starter (E) terminal, should be determined according to the following table.

Voltage system	Allowable wiring voltage drop	Conductor cross-section area	a+b+c allowable length
12V	0.2V or less/100A	20mm²	Up to 2.5m
		40mm²	Up to 5m

Note: Excessive resistance in the key switch circuit (between the battery and start [S] terminals) can cause improper pinion engagement. To prevent this, follow the wiring diagram carefully.

2-3 Inspection
The quality of the battery governs the starting performance of the engine. Therefore the battery must be routinely inspected to ensure that it functions perfectly at all times.

2-3.1 Visual inspection
(1) Inspect the case for cracks, damage and electrolyte leakage.
(2) Inspect the battery holder for tightness, corrosion, and damage.
(3) Inspect the terminals for rusting and corrosion, and check the cables for damage.
(4) Inspect the caps for cracking, electrolyte leakage and clogged vent holes.
Correct any abnormal conditions found. Clean off rusted terminals with a wire brush before reconnecting the battery cable.

Chapter 9 Electrical System
2. Battery

3,4JH3(B)(C)E

2-3.2 Checking the electrolyte
(1) Electrolyte level

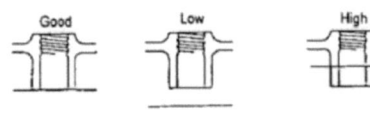

Check the electrolyte level every 7 to 10 days. The electrolyte must always be 10 ~ 20 mm (3937~ 0.7874in) over the top of the plates.

NOTES: 1. The "LEVEL" line on a transparent plastic battery case indicates the height of the electrolyte.
2. Always use distilled water to bring up the electrolyre level.
3. When the electrolyte has leaked out, add dilute sulfuric acid with the same specific gravity as the electrolyte.

(2) Measuring the specific gravity of the electrolyte
1) Draw some of the electrolyte up into a hydrometer.

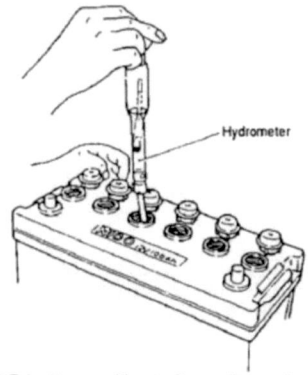

2) Take the specific gravity reading at the top of the scale of the hydrometer.

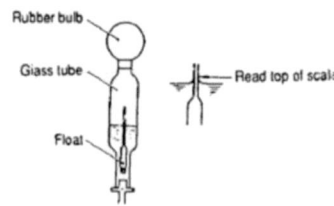

3) The battery is fully charged if the specific gravity is 1.260 at an electrolyte temperature of 20°C. The battery is discharged if the specific gravity is 1.200 (50%). If the specific gravity is below 1200, recharge the battery.
4) If the difference in the specific gravity among the cells of the battery is ±0.01, the battery is OK.
5) Measure the temperature of the electrolyte.
Since the specific gravity changes with the temperature, 20°C is used as the reference temperature.
Reading the specific Gravity at 20°C
$S_{20} = St + 0.0007(t-20)$
S_{20} : Specific gravity at the standard temperature of 20°C
St : Specific gravity of the electrolyte at t°C
0.0007 : Specific gravity change per 1 °C
t : Temperature of electrolyte

2-3.3 Voltage test
Using a battery tester, the amount of discharge can be determined by measuring the voltage drop which occurs while the battery is being discharged with a large current.

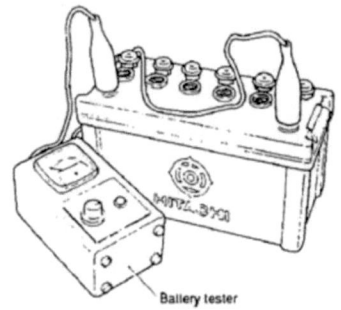

(1) Connect the tester the battery.
12V battery tester
Adjust the current (A).
(2) Connect the (+) lead of the tester to the (+) battery terminal. and the (−) tester lead to the (−) battery terminal.
(3) Push the TEST button, wait 5 seconds, and then read the meter.
● Repeat the test twice to make sure that the meter indication remains the same.

2-3.4 Washing the battery
(1) Wash the outside of the battery with a brush while running cold or warm water over the battery. (Make sure that no water gets into the battery.)
(2) When the terminals or other metal parts are corroded due to exposure to electrolyte leakage, wash off all the acid.
(3) Check the vent holes of the caps and clean if clogged.
(4) After washing the battery, dry it with compressed air, connect the battery cable, and coat the terminals with grease Since the grease acts as an insulator, do not coat the terminals before connecting the cables.

2-4 Charging

2-4.1 Charging methods
There are two methods of charging a battery: normal and rapid.
Rapid charging should only be used in emergencies.
- Normal charging···Should be conducted at a current of 1/10 or less of the indicated battery capacity (10A or less for a 100AH battery)
- Rapid charging··· Rapid charging is done over a short period of time at a current of 1/5 ~ 1/2 the indicated battery capacity (20A~50A for a 100AH battery). However, since rapid charging causes the electrolyte temperature to rise too high, special care must be exercised.

2-4.2 Charging procedure
(1) Check the specific gravity and adjust the electrolyte level.
(2) Disconnect the battery cables.
(3) Connect the red clip of the charger to the (+) battery terminal and connect the black clip to the (−) terminal.

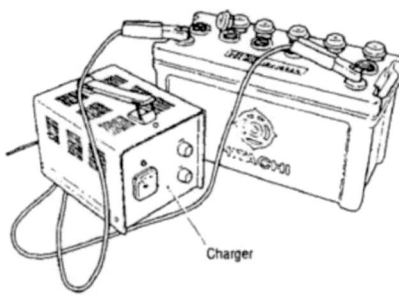
Charger

(4) Set the current to 1/10 ~1/5 of the capacity indicated on the outside the battery.
(5) Periodically measure the specific gravity during charging to make sure that the specific gravity remains at a high fixed value. Also check whether gas is being generated.

2-4.3 Charging precautions
(1) Remove the battery caps to vent the gas during charging.
(2) While charging, ventilate the room and prohibit smoking, welding, etc.
(3) The electrolyte temperature should not exceed 45°C during charging.
(4) Since an alternator is used on this engine, when charging with a charger, always disconnect the battery (+) cable to prevent destruction of the diodes.
(Before disconnecting the (+) battery cable, disconnect the (−) battery cable [ground side].)

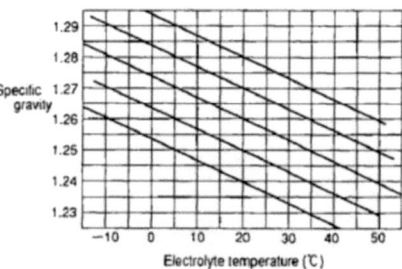
Electrolyte temperature and specific gravity

2-5 Battery storage precautions
The life of a battery depends considerably on how it is handled. Generally speaking, however, after about two years its performance will deteriorate, starting will become difficult, and the battery will not fully recover its original charge even after recharging. Then it must be replaced.

(1) Since the battery will self-discharge about 05%/day even when not in use, it must be charged 1 or 2 times a month when it is being stored.

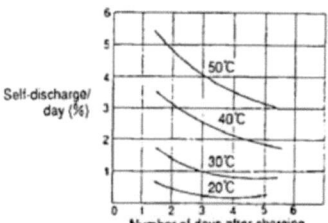

(2) If charging by the engine alternator is insufficient because of frequent starts and stops, the battery will rapidly lose power.
Charge the battery as soon as possible after it is used under these conditions.
(3) An easy-to-use battery charger that permits home charging is available from Yanmar. Take proper care of the battery by using the charger as a set with a hydrometer.
When the specific gravity has dropped to about 1.16 and the engine will not start, charge the battery up to a specific gravity of 1.26 (24 hours).
(4) Before putting the battery in storage for long periods, charge it for about 8 hours to prevent rapid aging.

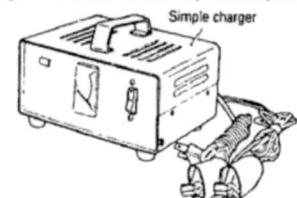
Simple charger

3. Starter Motor

3-1 Specifications

YANMAR Part No.			129698-77010
HITACHI Model No.			S114-815
Yoke diameter		(mm)	68
Nominal power		(kW)	1.2
Nominal voltage		(V)	12
Rating		(sec)	30
Direction of Rotation (Looking from the Pinion side)			Clockwise
Number of Pinion teeth			11
Weight		(kg)	3.0
No load	Terminal voltage	(V)	11
	Electric current	(A)	90 (MAX)
	Revolutions	(r/min)	2.750 (MIN)
Load	Terminal voltage	(V)	8.4
	Electric current	(A)	250
	Torque	(N·m)	7.2 (MIN)
	Revolutions	(r/min)	1.200 (MIN)

3-2. The planetary gear starter system

3-2.1 The planetary gear starter

While these only had specialized applications in the past, they currently are being widely adopted because of their compact, lightweight design.
Although smaller than the direct-drive type starter with its armatuer and pinion driven at the same speed, the planetary gear starter actually reduces the motor speed to approximately 17% prior to driving the pinion.
It does this without reducing output, hence the derivation of its name.
Furthermore, use of heat-resistant insulating materials and advanced production technology makes the compact, light weight design possible and improves its starting capabilities in cold regions.

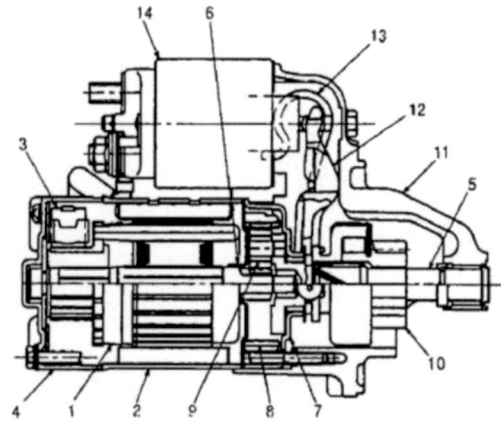

1. Armature
2. Yoke
3. Brush
4. Rear Cover
5. Pinion Shaft
6. Center Bracket (A)
7. Center Bracket (P)
8. Internal Gear
9. Planet Gear
10. Pinion
11. Eear Case
12. Shift Lever
13. Torsion Spring
14. Hagnetic Switch

Fig.1 Planetary Gear Starter Construction

Chapter 9 Electrical System
3. Starter Motor

3,4JH3(B)(C)E

3-2.2 The Engagement Mechanism

This type utilizes electromagnetic force. The pinion is engaged with the ring gear by means of the torsion spring and shift lever. The plunger is shifted by the attracting force, and depresses the pinion. When the pinion does not strike the ring gear, smooth engagement occurs, and then the contacts close to start the motor.

Also, when the pinion strikes the ring gear teeth, it compresses the torsion spring and closes the contacts. When the current flows through the motor and the armature starts rotating, the pinion is depressed strongly on the ring gear and rotated by means of the torsion spring pressure and the helical spline's force. Then, the pinion teeth are arranged in engagement with the ring gear teeth. When the key start switch is turned OFF, the magnetic switch is demagnetized, and the pinion is returned by the torsion spring force. Simultaneously, the contacts open to stop motor operation. In Fig. 2, engagement between the pinion and ring gear is illustrated.

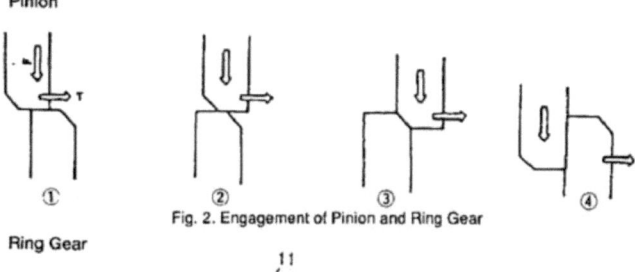

Fig. 2. Engagement of Pinion and Ring Gear

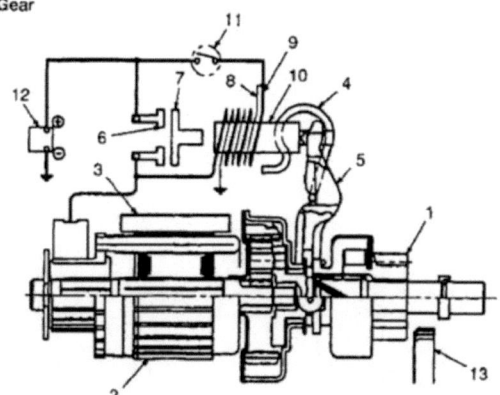

1. Pinion
2. Armature
3. Magnet
4. Torsion Spring
5. Shift lever
6. Stationary Contactor
7. Movable Contactor
8. Shunt Coil (Holding Coil)
9. Series Coil (Attracting Coil)
10. Plunger
11. Key Start Switch
12. Battery
13. Riug Gear

Fig. 3. Schematic Layout of Planetary Gear Starter's Electrical Circuit

3-3 Removal

(1) Disconnect the battery's negative or ⊖ side cable at the battery.
(2) Disconnect the battery's positive or ⊕ cable and the main harness' feed wire from the magnetic switch of the starter.
(3) Disconnect ⊖ cable at the starter.
(4) Remove the starter retaining bolts and lockwashers. Then, withdraw the starter.

Chapter 9 Electrical System
3. Starter Motor

3-4 Trouble shooting the starter system

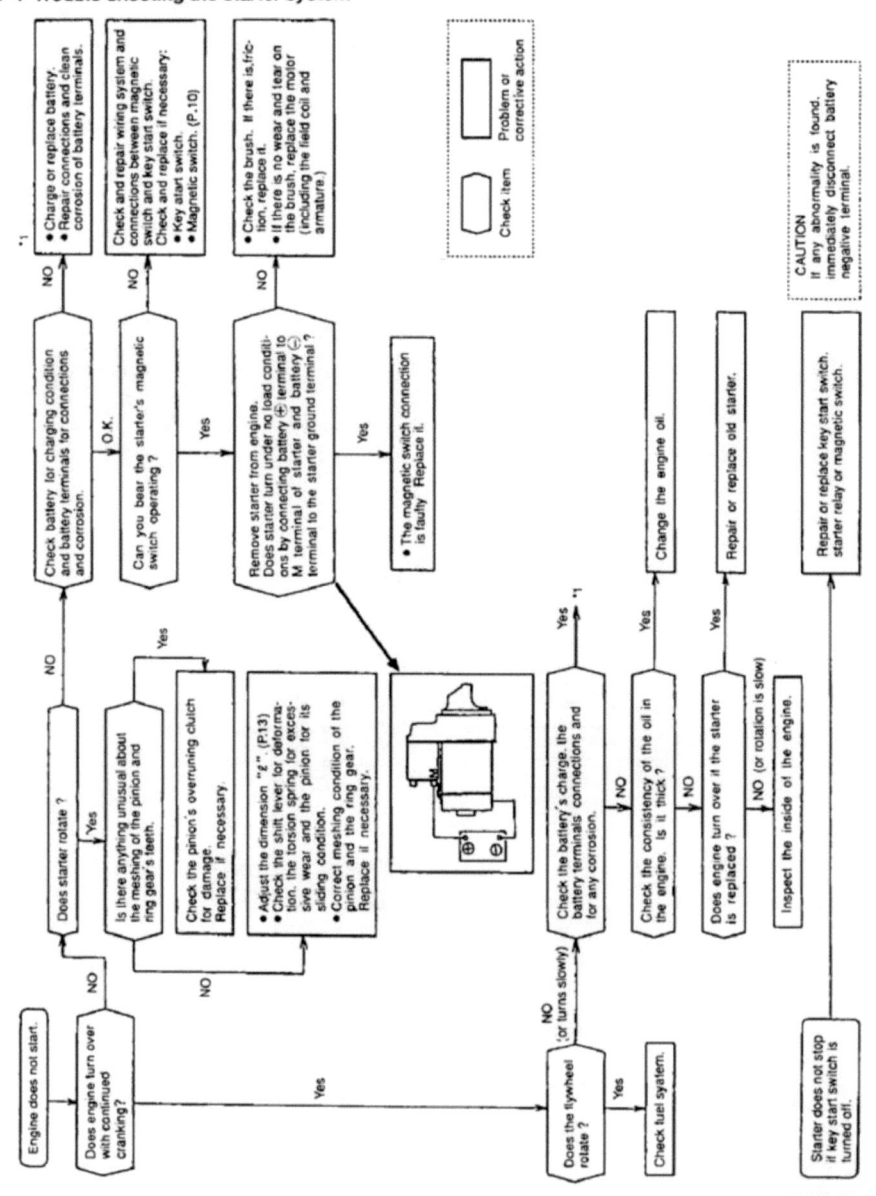

Chapter 9 Electrical System
3. Starter Motor

3,4JH3(B)(C)E

3-5 Disassembly

- ▲ 1) The Magnetic switch's 8 mm nut
- 2) The 6 mm Bolts (2)
- ▲ 3) Magnetic switch
- 4) The 4 mm Screws (2)
- 5) The 5 mm Through Bolts (2)
- ▲ 6) The Rear Covee
- 7) Thrust Washer
- ▲ 8) The Brush Holder
- 9) Yoke
- 10) Armature
- ▲ 11) Center Bracket (A)
- 12) Gear Case
- ▲ 13) Shift Lever
- 14) Dust Cover
- 15) Internal Gear
- ▲ 16) Planet Gear (3)
- ▲ 17) The Pinion Stopper clip
- 18) Pinion Stopper
- ▲ 19) Pinion
- ▲ 20) E Ring
- 21) washer (2)
- 22) Center Bracket (p)
- ▲ 23) Pinion Shaft

▲ : Disassembly reference exhibit is provided

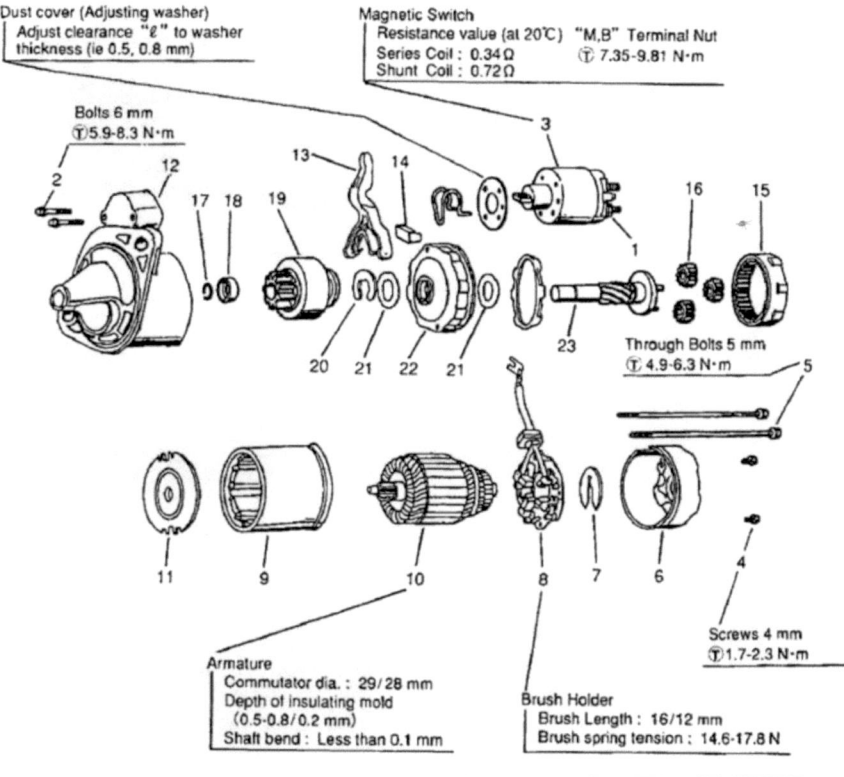

Dust cover (Adjusting washer)
Adjust clearance "ℓ" to washer thickness (ie 0.5, 0.8 mm)

Magnetic Switch
Resistance value (at 20℃)   "M,B" Terminal Nut
Series Coil : 0.34Ω   ⓣ 7.35-9.81 N·m
Shunt Coil : 0.72Ω

Bolts 6 mm
ⓣ 5.9-8.3 N·m

Through Bolts 5 mm
ⓣ 4.9-6.3 N·m

Screws 4 mm
ⓣ 1.7-2.3 N·m

Armature
Commutator dia. : 29/28 mm
Depth of insulating mold (0.5-0.8/0.2 mm)
Shaft bend : Less than 0.1 mm

Brush Holder
Brush Length : 16/12 mm
Brush spring tension : 14.6-17.8 N

Clearance "ℓ" between Pinion's front edge and pinion stopper : 0.3-1.5 mm

ⓣ : N·m
Unit : mm (Standard "New"/ Limit "Used")

Fig. 4. Exhibit of dissembled parts

Chapter 9 Electrical System
3. Starter Motor
3,4JH3(B)(C)E

1) The Magnetic switch's 8 mm nut

   Remove the magnetic switch's 8 mm nut and disconnect the connecting wire.

Fig. 5

2) The 6 mm Bolts (2)
3) Magnetic Switch

   The Magnetic Switch can be disassembled once the 6 mm Bolts are reamoved.

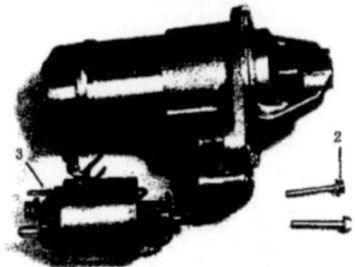
Fig. 6

4) The 4 mm Screws (2)
5) The 5 mm Through Bolts (2)
6) The Rear Cover

The Rear Cover is disassembled by removing the 4 mm screws and the 5 mm through bolts.

Fig. 7

7) Thrust Washer
The Thrust Washer is removed with a standard screwdriver.

Fig. 8

Chapter 9 Electrical System
3. Starter Motor

8) The Brush Holder

Pull the Brush Spring up with a Brush Spring lifter tool so that the Brush is separated from the surface of the Commutator.

Fig. 9

9) Yoke
10) Armature
11) Center Bracket (A)

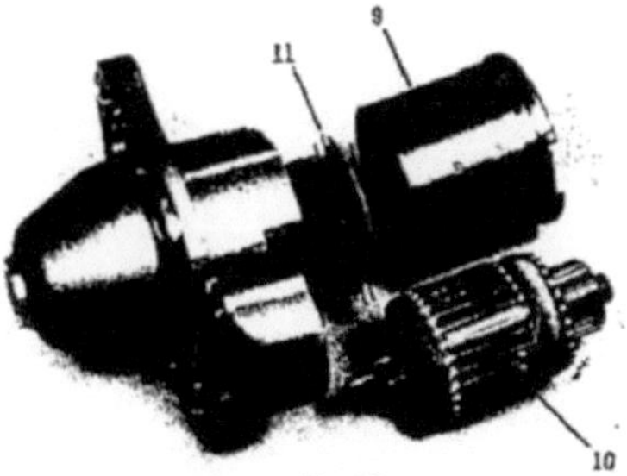

Fig. 10

12) Gear Case
13) Shift Lever
14) Dust Cover

The Shift Lever can be removed once the Dust Cover is disassembled from the Gear Case.

Fig. 11

15) Internal Gear
16) Planet Gear (3)

The Internal Gear and the Planet Gear disassemble.

Fig. 12

Chapter 9 Electrical System
3. Starter Motor
_3,4JH3(B)(C)E_

17) The Pinion Stopper Clip

The Pinion Stopper Clip is removed with a standard screwdriver while the Pinion Stopper is pushed toward the Pinion.

Fig. 13

18) Pinion Stopper
19) Pinion

The Pinion Stopper and the Pinion can be disassembled once the Pinion Stopper Clip has been removed.

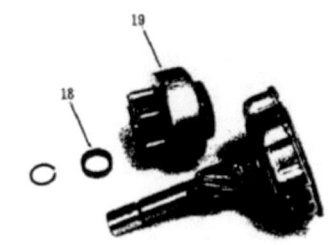

Fig. 14

20) E Ring

The E Ring is removed by hammer with special fixture.

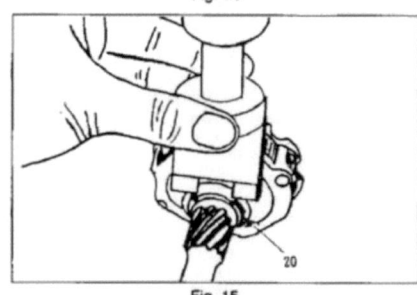

Fig. 15

21) Washer (2)
22) Center Bracket (p)
23) Pinion Shaft

The Center Bracket (P) and the Pinion Shaft can be diassembled once the E Ring is removed.

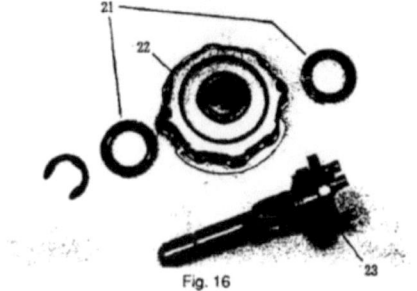

Fig. 16

3. Starter Motor

3-6. Inspection and Repair
3-6.1 Armature
(1) Check the diameter of the Commutator.

If the outside diameter of the commutator is below the minimum limit then replace it.

mm

Standard (New)	Limit (Used)
29	28

Fig. 17

(2) Continuity Test for the Armature Coil.

Use a tester to check for continuity between parallel points on the commutator. If there is continuity, the armature is still good.

No continuity : (Disconnected coil)
　　　　　　　　Replace the armature.

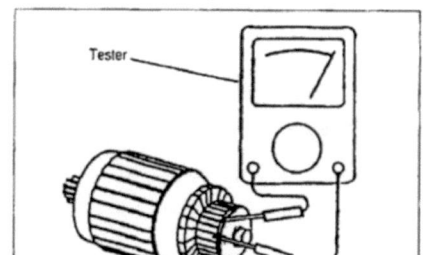

Fig. 18

(3) Insulation Test for the Armature Coil.

Use a tester to check for continuity between a point on the commutator and the shaft or the core.
If there is no continuity the armature is still good.
Continuity Exists : (Short circuited coil)
　　　　　　　　　Replace the armature.

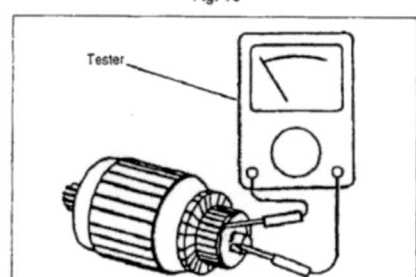

Fig. 19

(4) Check for Surface Distortion on the Armature and the Commutator.

Use a dial gauge to measure the distortion of the outside surfaces of the armature core and the commutator. If it is above the limit, then repair or replace it.

mm

	Standard (New)	Limit (Used)
Armature	0.05 (MAX)	0.1
Commutator	0.05 (MAX)	0.1

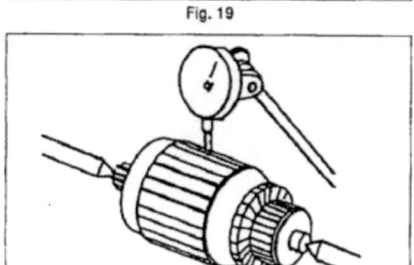

Fig. 20

Chapter 9 Electrical System
3. Starter Motor
3,4JH3(B)(C)E

(5) Check the Surface of the Commutator

If the commutator surface is rough, then please use No. 500-600 sandpaper to make it smooth.

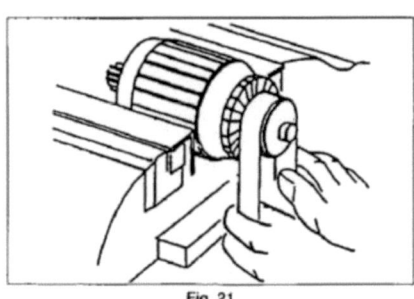

Fig. 21

(6) Check the Depth of Insulating Material from the Commutator Surface.
If the depth of the insulating material from the commutator segments is less than the limit, then please repair it by filing it down.

mm

Standard (New)	Limit (Used)
0.5~0.8	0.2

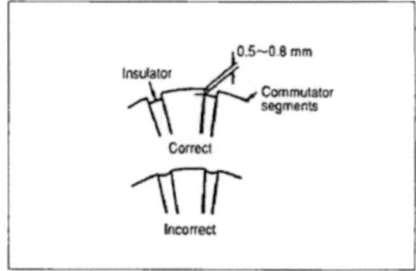

Fig. 22

3-6.2 Brush

Measure the length of the brushes and if they are under the limit, replace them.

mm

Standard (New)	Limit (Used)
16	12

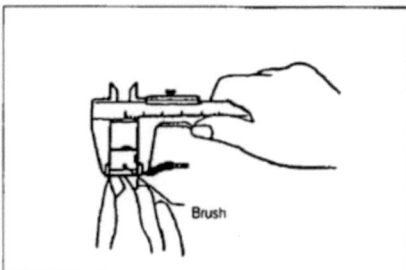

Fig. 23

3-6.3 Brush Holder

Insulation Test for the Brush Holder

Check for continuity between the brush holder's positive side and its base (negative side) with a tester. If there is no continuity the brush holder are still good.
Continuity Exists : (Unsatisfactory insulation)
　　　　　　　Replace the brush holder.

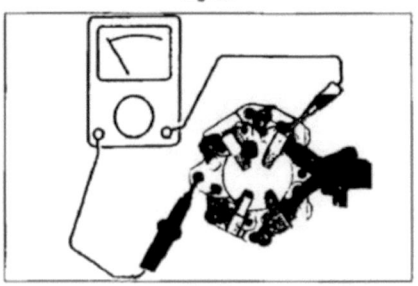

Fig. 24

9—16

Printed in Japan
HINSHI-H8009

Chapter 9 Electrical System
3. Starter Motor

(3) Inspection of the Brush Springs.

Check the weight of the brush springs.

Standard Weight (N)
14.6～17.8

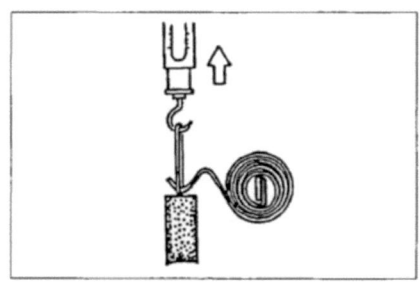

Fig. 25

3-6.4 Magnetic Switch

(1) Continuity Test for the Shunt Coil

Check for continuity between the "S" terminal and the switch body with a tester. If there is continuity, then it is still good.

No continuity : (Disconnected coil)
　　　　　　　Replace the magnetic switch.

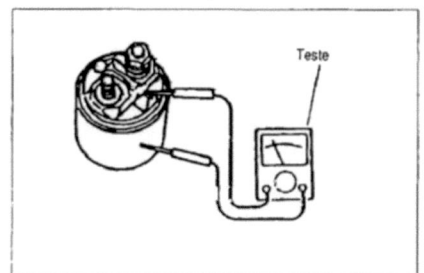

Fig. 26

(2) Continuity Test for the Series Coil

Check for continuity between the "S" and "M" terminals with a tester. If there is continuity, then it is still good.

No continuity : (Disconnected coil)
　　　　　　　Replace the magnetic switch.

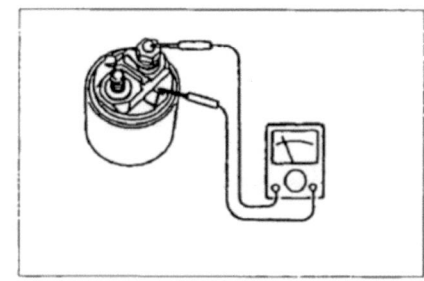

Fig. 27

(3) Continuity Test for Contact-Points

Put the plunger on the under side and then push the magnetic switch down. At this time, check for continuity between the "B" and "M" terminals with a tester. If there is continuity, then it is still good.

No continuity : (Insufficient Continuity)
　　　　　　　Replace the magnetic switch.

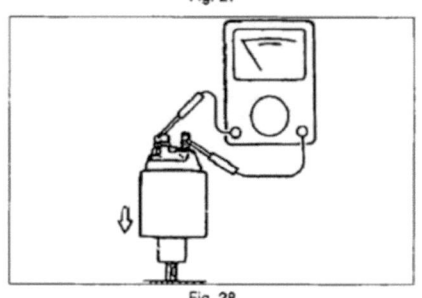

Fig. 28

3. Starter Motor

3-6.5 Pinion
(1) Inspection of the Pinion

Rotate the pinion manually. While rotating it in the direction of normal operation, smoothly reverse the direction of rotation to confirm that it locks.
In the event of any irregularity, replace it.

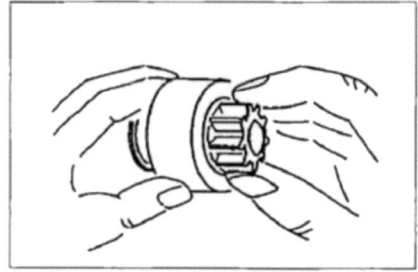
Fig. 29

3-6.6 Yoke Assembly
(1) Inspection of the Yoke
  Check the magnet of the yoke assembly for damage.

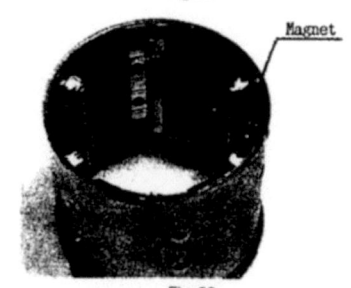
Fig. 30

3-6.7 Check the Bearing Diameter
(1) Inspection of the Gear Case
  If the diameter of the gear case is above the limit then replace it.

mm

Standard (New)	Limit (Used)
$12.5^{+0.027}_{0}$	0.1

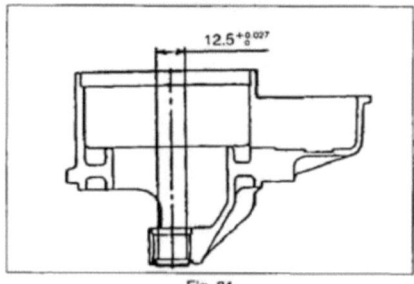
Fig. 31

(2) Inspection of the Rear Cover
  If the diameter of the rear cover is above the limit then replace it.

mm

Standard (New)	Limit (Used)
$12^{+0.027}_{0}$	0.1

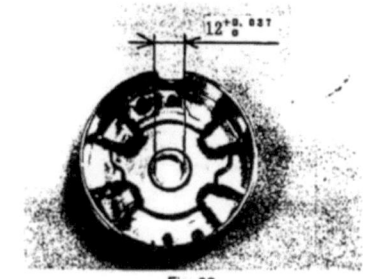
Fig. 32

Chapter 9 Electrical System
3. Starter Motor

(3) Inspection of the Center Bracket (P)

If the diameter of the center bracket (P) is above the limit then replace it.

mm

Standard (New)	Limit (Used)
$18^{+0.037}_{+0.012}$	0.1

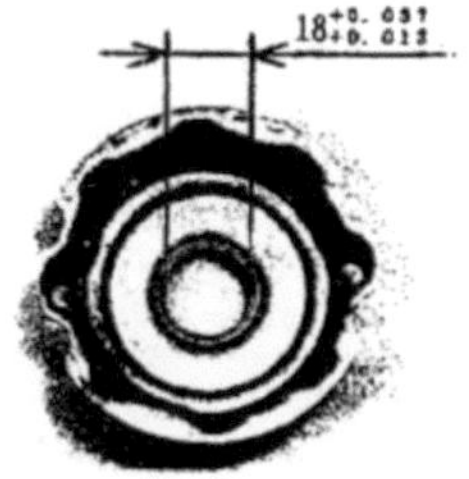

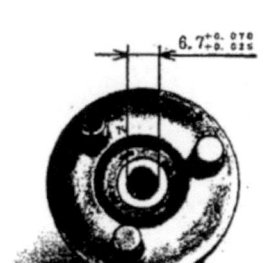

Fig. 33

(4) Inspection of the Pinion Shaft

If the diameter of the Pinion Shaft is above the limit then replace it.

mm

Standard (New)	Limit (Used)
$6.7^{+0.070}_{+0.025}$	0.1

Fig. 34

3. Starter Motor

3-7 Reassembly

Reassembly is in the reverse order of disassembly, however please note the following points.

1. Tightening Torques : Refer to page 4 of the referece materials for the tightening torques of particular screws.

2. The Places to Apply Grease :
   ① ---- The moving parts of shift lever.
   ② ---- The sliding surface of magnetic switch plunger.
   ---- The sliding surface of pinion.
   ③ ---- The tooth of Internal Gear and Planet Gear.

Part	①	②	③
Grease	Shell Alvania Grease No. 2	NPC FG-6A GREASE	Multemp SRL GREASE

(1) Measurement of the Pinion's Motion

After connecting the positive ⊕ side of the battery to the "S" terminal and the negative ⊖ side to the "M" terminal and turning the switch on, measure the amount of movement "ℓ" in the direction of the pinion's thrust.

Standard length "ℓ"
0.3~1.5mm

Note : When taking the measurement, please do so by pushing the pinion softly in the direction of the large arrow in the exhibit.

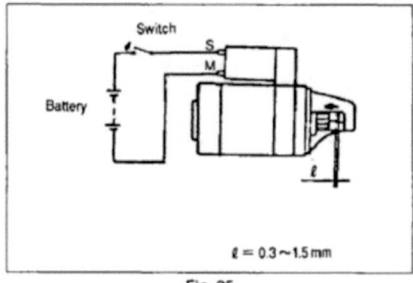

$\ell = 0.3 \sim 1.5 mm$

Fig. 35

(2) When the measurement "ℓ" is outside of the standard range, please adjust the dust cover by inserting it further or loosening it in order to achieve an acceptable measurement.

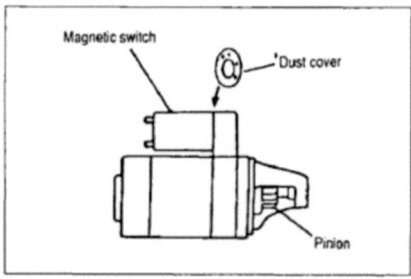

Fig. 36

3. Starter Motor

3-8. Operation Specifications Check

Please follow the directions in Performing a no-load test, since to a certain extent, it provides an easy way to confirm the specifications.
Note : The rating is 30 seconds, so please perform the test expeditiously.

(1) The No-load Test
   Set the starter securely on a test bench and lay the lines as shown in fig.37.
   When the switch is turned off, the electric current flows into the starter in noload operating conditions. With the electric current flowing, please measure the voltage and the r/min, and determine if they satisfy the specifications.

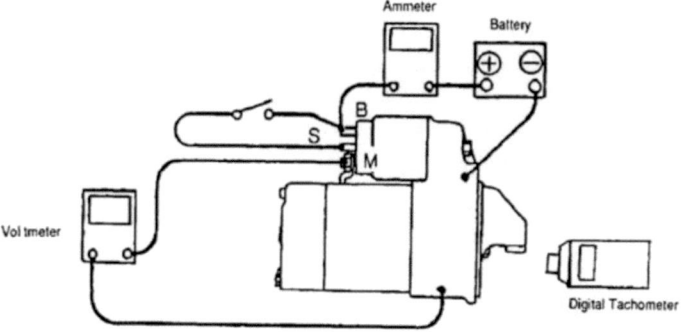

Fig. 37

4. Alternator   Standard, 12V/55A

The alternator serves to keep the battery constantly charged. It is installed on the cylinder block by a bracket, and is driven from the V-pulley at the end of the crankshaft by a V belt.
The type of alternator used in this engine is ideal for high speed engines with a wide range of engine speeds. It contains diodes that convert AC to DC, and an IC regulator that keeps the generated voltage constant even when the engine speed changes.

4-1 Features
The alternator contains a regulator using an IC, and has the following features.
(1) The IC regulator is self-contained, and has no moving parts (mechanical contact points) It therefore has superior features such as freedom from vibration, no fluctuation of voltage during use, and no need for readjustment. Also, it is of the over-heating compensation type and can automatically adjust the voltage to the most suitable level depending on the operating temperature.
(2) The regulator is integrated within the alternator to simplify external wiring.
(3) It is an alternator designed for compactness, lightness of weight and high output
(4) A newly developed U-shaped diode is used to provide increased reliability and easier checking and maintenance.
(5) As the alternator is to be installed on board, the following measures are taken to provide salt-proofing.
 1) The front and rear covers are salt-proofed.
 2) Salt-proof paint is applied to the diode.
 3) The terminal, where the inboard harness is connected to the alternator, is nickel plated.

4-2 Specifications

Model of alternator	LR155-20 (HITACHI)
Model of IC regulator	TRIZ-63 (HITACHI)
Battery voltage	12V
Nominal output	12v/55A
Earth polarity	Negative earth ($\ominus$)
Direction of rotation (viewed from pulley end)	Clockwise
Weight	4.3kg
Rated speed	5000 rpm
Operating speed	1000 ~ 9000
Speed for 13.5V	1000 or less
Output current at 20°C	over 53A/5000 rpm
Regulated voltage	14.5±0.3V(Standard temperature voltage gradient, −0.01/°C)

4-3 Characteristcs

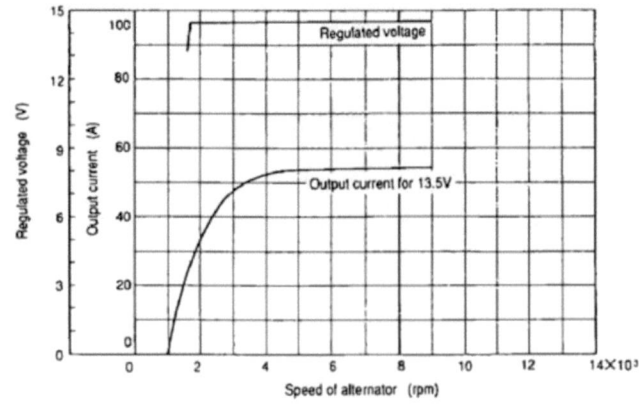

Speed of alternator (rpm)

4-4 Construction

This is a standard rotating field type three-phase alternator.

It consists of six major parts: the pulley, fan, front cover, rotor, stator and rear cover. The IC regulator is an integral part of the alternator.

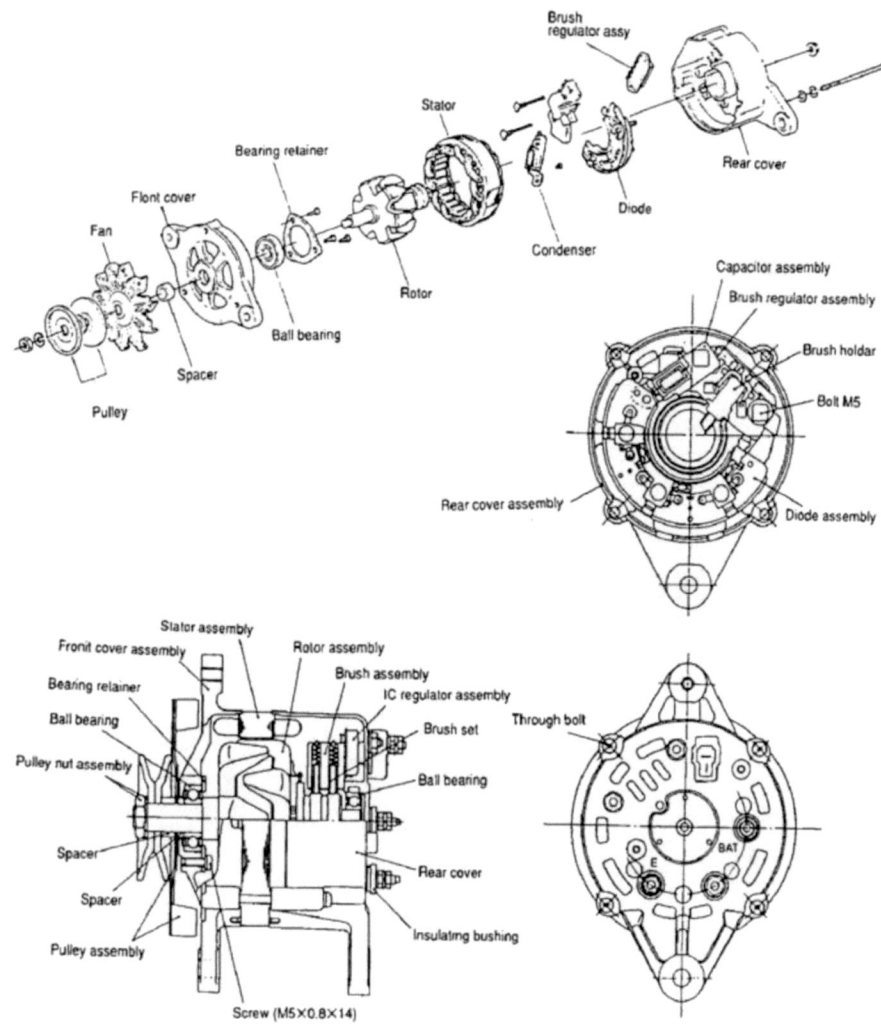

4-5 Alternator functioning

(1) IC regulator

The IC regulator is the transistor (Tr₁) which is series-connected with the rotor. The IC regulator controls the output voltage of the generator by breaking or conducting the rotor coil (exciting) current.

When the output voltage of the generator is within the standard value, the transistor (Tr₁) turns on. When the voltage exceeds the standard value, the Zener diode goes on and the transistor (Tr₁) turns off.

With the repeated turning on and off of the transistor, the output voltage is kept at the standard value. (Refer to the circuit diagram below.)

(2) Charge lamp

When the transistor (Tr₁) is on, the charge lamp key switch is turned to ON, and current flows to R₁, R₄ and to Tr₁ to light the lamp. When the engine starts to run and output voltage is generated in the stator coil, the current stops flowing to this circuit, turning off the charge lamp.

(3) Circuit diagram

4-6 Handling precautions

(1) Be careful of the battery's polarity (+, − terminals), and do not connect the wrong terminals to the wrong cables, or the battery will be short-circuited by the generator diode.
In this case too much current will flow, the IC regulator and diodes burn out, and the wire harness will burn.
(2) Make sure of the correct connection of each terminal.
(3) When quick-charging, etc., disconnect either the battery terminal on the AC generator or the terminal on the battery.
(4) Do not short-circuit the terminals
(5) Do not conduct any tests using high tension insulation resistance. (The diodes and IC regulator will burn out.)

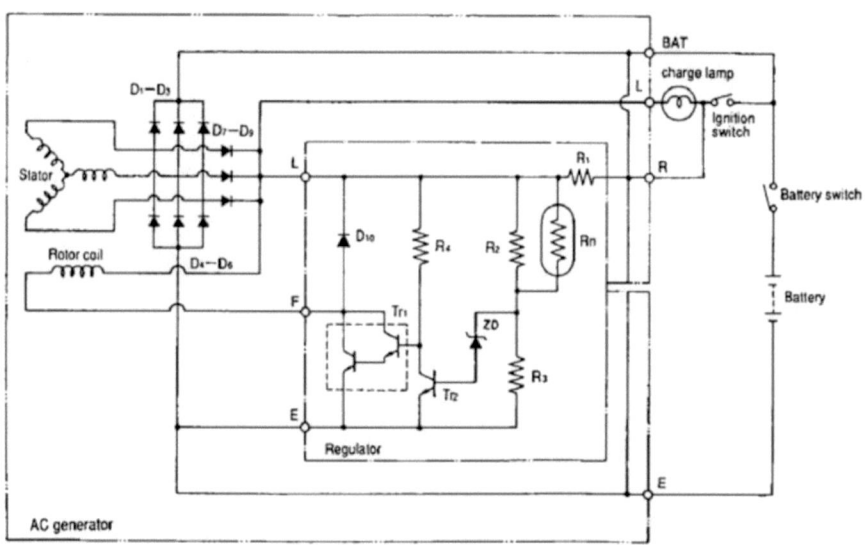

BAT:	Generator output terminal	D₁-D₆:	Output commutation diode
D₁₀:	IC protecting diode	R₁-R₄:	Resistor
L:	Charge lamp terminal	D₇-D₉:	Charging lamp switching diode
ZD:	Zener diode	F:	To supply current to rotor coil
E:	Earth	Rn:	Thermistor
Tr₁, Tr₂:	Transistor		(Temperature gradient resistance)

Chapter 9 Electrical System
4. Alternator

4-7 Disassembling the alternator
(1) Remove the through-bolt, and separate the front assembly from the rear assembly.

(4) Remove the nut, the brush-holder and diode fixing nut at the SAT, and the terminal screws of the rear cover. Separate the rear cover from the stator (with the diode and brush holder).

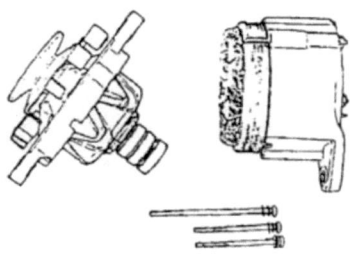

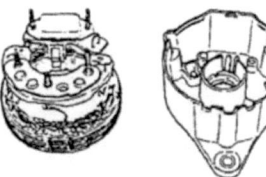 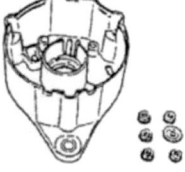

(5) Disconnect the soldered joint of the stator lead wire, and remove the diode and brush regulator assemblies from the stator at the same time.

(2) Remove the pulley nut, and pull out the rotor from the front cover.

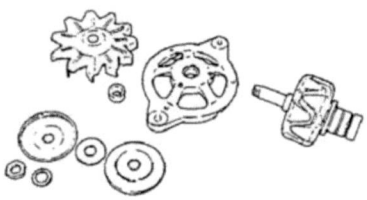

(6) Separating the regulator
1) To separate the regulator, remove the ⌀3mm (⌀0.1181 in) rivet which keeps the diode assembly and the brushless regulator in place, and the soldered joint of the L-terminal.

(3) Remove the ⌀5mm (⌀0.1969 in.) screw from the front cover, and then remove the ball bearing.

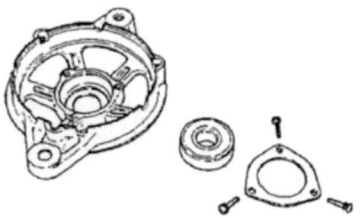

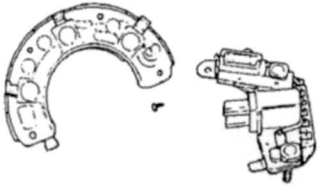

Chapter 9 Electrical System
4. Alternator
_3,4JH3(B)(C)E_

2) To replace the IC regulator, disconnect the soldered joint the IC regulator and pull out the two bolts. Do not remove these two bolts except when replacing the IC regulator.

After repeating the above test, if any diode is found to be defective, replace the diode assembly. Since there is no terminal on the auxiliary diode, check the continuity between both ends of the diode.

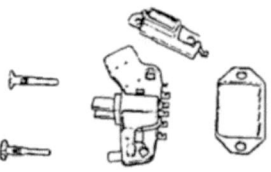

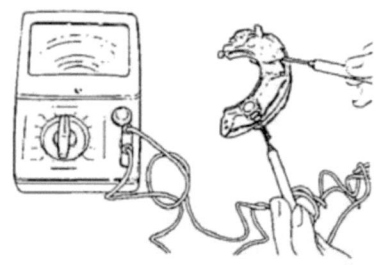

CAUTION : Do not use high tensile insulation resistance such as meggers, etc. for testing. The diode may burn out.

4-8 Inspection and adjustment
(1) Diode

Between terminals		BAT (+side diode)	
	Tester wire	+ side	− side
U.V.W.	+ side		Continuity
	− side	No Continuity	

Between terminals		E (+side diode)	
	Tester wire	− side	− side
U.V.W.	+ side		No continuity
	− side	Continuity	

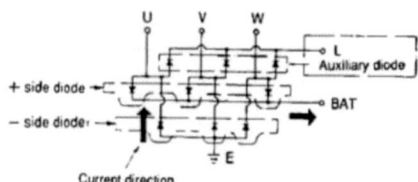

U.V.W.: terminal from the stator coil

Current flows only in one direction in the diode as shown in Fig. 181. Accordingly, when there is continuity between each terminal (e.g. BAT and U), the diode is in normal condition (photo). When there is no continuity, the diode is defective.
When the tester is connected in the reverse of above, there should be no continuity. If there is, the diode is defective.

(2) Rotor
Inspect the slip ring surface, rotor coil continuity and insulation.
1) Inspecting the slip ring surface
Check if the surface of the slip ring is sufficiently smooth. If the surface is rough, grind the surface with No. 500-600 sand paper. If it is contaminated with oil, etc., wipe the surface clean with alcohol.

	Standard	Wear limit
Slip ring outer dia.	⌀31.6mm	⌀30.6mm

2) Rotor coil continuity test
Check the continuity in the slip ring with the tester. If there is no continuity, there is a wire break. Replace the rotor coil.

Resistance value	Approx. 3.34 Ω at 20°C

Chapter 9 Electrical System
4. Alternator

3) Rotor coil insulation test
Check the continuity between the slip ring and the rotor core, or the shaft. If there is continuity, insulation inside the rotor is defective, causing a short with the earth circuit. Replace the rotor coil.

4) Check the rear side ball bearing. If the rotation of the bearing is heavy, or produces abnormal sounds, replace the ball bearing.

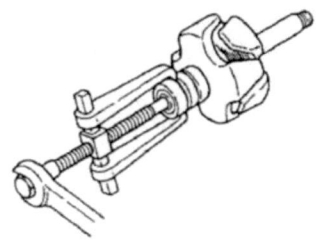

(3) Stator
1) Stator coil continuity test
Check the continuity between each terminal of the stator coil. If there is no continuity, there is a wire break in the stator coil. Replace the stator coil.

Resistance value	Approx. 0.077Ω at 20°C 1-phase resistance

2) Stator coil insulation test
Check the continuity between the terminals and the stator core. If there is continuity, insulation of the stator coil is defective. This will cause a short-circuit with the earth core. Replace the stator coil.

(4) Brush
The brush is hard and wears slowly, but when it is worn beyond the allowable limit, replace it. When replacing the brush, also check the strength of the brush spring.
To check, push the spring down to 2mm (0.0787in.) from the end surface of the brush holder, and read the gauge.

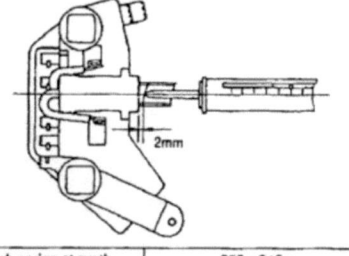

Brush spring strerath	255—345g

(5) Brush wear
Check the brush length.
The brush wears very little, but replace the brush if worn over the wear limit line printed on the brush.

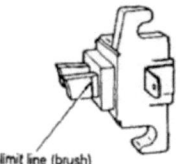

Wear limit line (brush)

	Maintenance standard	Wear limit mm
Brush length	16	9

Chapter 9 Electrical System
4. Alternator

3,4JH3(B)(C)E

(6) IC regulator
   Connect the variable resistance, two 12V batteries, resistor, and voltmeter as shown in the diagram.

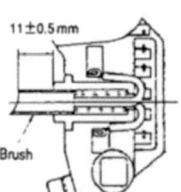

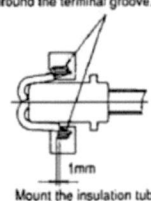

11±0.5mm

Brush

Wind the wire 1.5 times around the terminal groove.

1mm

Mount the insulation tube on the terminal surface.

1) Use the following measuring devices.
   Resistor (R1)   100Ω, 2W, 1pc.
   Variable resistor (Rv) 0–300Ω, 12W, 1pc.
   Battery (BAT1, BAT2)   12V, 2pcs
   DC voltmeter   0–30V, 0.5 class 1pc.
                           (measure at 3 points)

2) Check the regulator in the following sequence, according to the diagram.
   a) Check V_3, (BAT_1+BAT_2 voltage). If the voltage is 20-26V, both BAT_1, and BAT_2, are normal.
   b) While measuring V_2 (F-E terminal voltage), move Rv gradually from the O-position. Check if there is a point where the V_2, voltage rises sharply from below 2.0V to over 2.0V. If there is no such point, the regulator is defective. Replace the regulator. If there is a sharp voltabe rise when testing, return the Rv to the 0-position, and connect the voltmeter to the V_1, position.
   c) While measuring V_1, (voltage between L-E terminals), move RV gradually from the O-position. There should be a point where the voltage of V_1, rises sharply by 2-6V. Measure the voltabe of V_1, just before this sharp voltage rise. This is the regulating voltage of the regulator. If this voltage of V_1, is within the standard limit, the regulator is normal. If the voltage deviates from the limit, the regulator is defective. Replace the regulator.

NOTES : 1. Use non-acid type paste.
        2. The soldering iron temperature is 300~350°C.

2) Mount the IC regulator on the brush holder as illustrated, and press in the M5 bolt. Do not forget to assemble the bushing and the connecting plate at the same time.
   (If the bushing is left out, the output terminal will be earthed and the battery short-circuited).

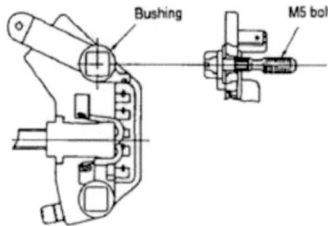

Bushing   M5 bolt

NOTES : 1. Insertion pressure is 100kg
        2. Insert vertically.

(2) Connecting the brush regulator assembly and diode
   1) Check the rivets
      Place the rivets as shown in the figure, and then calk them using the calking tool.

Calking torque	500kg

2) Connect the brush to the diode.
   Insert the brush side terminal into the diode terminal, calk it, and then solder into place.

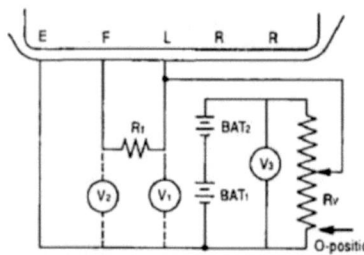

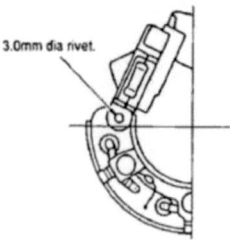

3.0mm dia rivet.

4-9 Reassembling the alternator
Reassembly is done in the reverse order of disassembly. For reassembly, be careful of the following points (Refer to 4-7 disassembling alternator.)
(1) Assembling the brush regulator
  1) Solder the brush.
     Position the brush as shown in the drawing and solder it. Be careful not to let the solder drip into the pig tail (lead wire).

Rivetting pressure	500kg

Chapter 9 Electrical System
4. Alternator

(3) Assembling the rear cover
Insert pins from the outsice of the rear cover. Install the brush on the brush holder, then attach the rear cover.
After assembly, pull out the pins.

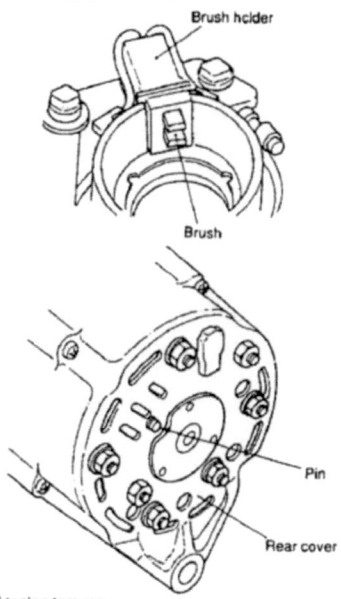

(4) Tightening torques

Positions	Tightening torque kg·cm
Brush holder fixing	32—40
Diode fixing	32—40
Bearing retainer fixing	32—40
Pulley nut tightening	400—600
Through-bolt tightening	32—40

4-10 Performance test
Conduct a performance test on the reassembled AC generator as follows. The following is the circuit for the performance test.

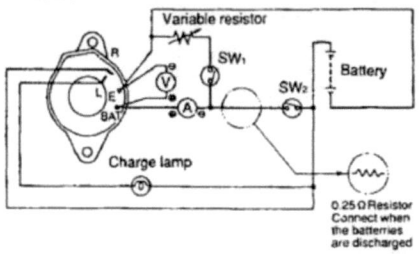

(1) Measuring devices

DC voltmeter	0—15V or 0—30V, 0.5 Class, 1pc.
DC ammeter	0—100A, 1.0 Clsss 1pc.
Variable resistor	0—0.25Ω. 1kW, 1pc.
Lamp	12V, 3W
100Ω resistor	3W
0.25Ω resistor	25W

(2) Measuring the regulating voltage
1) When measuring devices are connected in the performance test circuit as shown above, the charge lamp lights.
2) Close SW₂ while keeping SW₁ open and run the AC generator. When the revolutions of the generator are gradually raised, the charge lamp goes off.
3) Raise the revolutions of the AC generator, and read the voltmeter gauge when the revolutions reach about 5,000 rpms.

NOTES : 1. Make sure that the ammeter indication at this time is less than 5A If the indication is over 5A, connect the 0.25Ω resistor. The voltmeter indication at this time must be within the prescribed regulating voltage value.
2. Raise the AC generator revolutions high to make sure the regulating voltage does not fluctuate along with changes in the revolution speed.

(3) Precautions for measuring the regulating voltage
1) When measuring the voltage, measure the voltage between the AC generator BAT terminal, or Battery + terminal, and AC generator E-terminal.
2) Use a fully charged battery.
3) Measure the voltage quickly.
4) Keep SW, open for measurement.

5. Alternator 12V/80A (OPTIONAL)

The alternator serves to keep the battery constantly charged. It is installed on the cylinder block by a bracket, and is driven from the V-pulley at the end of the crankshaft by a V belt.
The type of alternator used in this engine is ideal for high speed engines with a wide range of engine speeds. It contains diodes that convert AC to DC, and an IC regulator that keeps the generated voltage constant even when the engine speed changes.

5-1 Features

The alternator contains a regulator using an IC, and has the following features.
(1) The IC regulator is self contained, and has no moving parts (mechanical contact points) It therefore has superior features such as freedom from vibration, no fluctuation of voltage during use, and no need for read-justment.
Also, it is of the over-heating compensation type and can automatically adjust the voltage to the most suitable level depending on the operating temperature.
(2) The regulator is integrated within the alternator to simplify external wiring.
(3) It is an alternator designed for compactness, lightness of weight, and high output.
(4) A newly developed U-shaped diode is used to provide increased reliability and easier checking and maintenance.
(5) As the alternator is to be installed on board, the following measures are taken to provide salt-proofing.
  1) The front and rear covers are salt-proofed.
  2) Salt-proof paint is applied to the diode.
  3) The terminal, where the inboard harness is connected to the alternator, is nickel plated.

5-2 Specifications

Model of alternator	LR160-03 (HITACHI)
Model of IC regulator	TRIZ-63 (HITACHI)
Battery voltage	12V
Nominal output	12V/80A
Earth polarity	Negative earth (⊖)
Direction of rotation (viewed from pulley end)	Clockwise
Weight	5.8kg
Rated speed	5000 rpm
Operating speed	1000 ~ 9000
Speed for 13.5V	1000 or less
Output current at 20℃	over 78A/5000 rpm
Regulated voltage	14.5±0.3V (Standard temperature voltage gradient, −0.01/℃)

5-3 Characteristcs

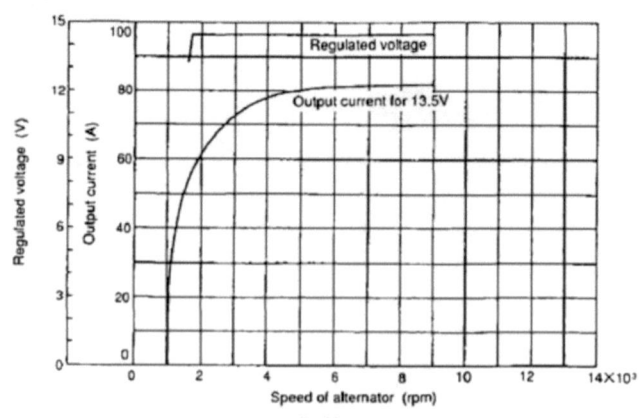

5. Alternator (OPTIONAL)

5-4 Construction

This is a standard rotaing field type three-phase alternator.

It consists of six major parts: the pulley, fan, front cover, rotor, stator and rear cover. The IC regulator is an integral part of the alternator.

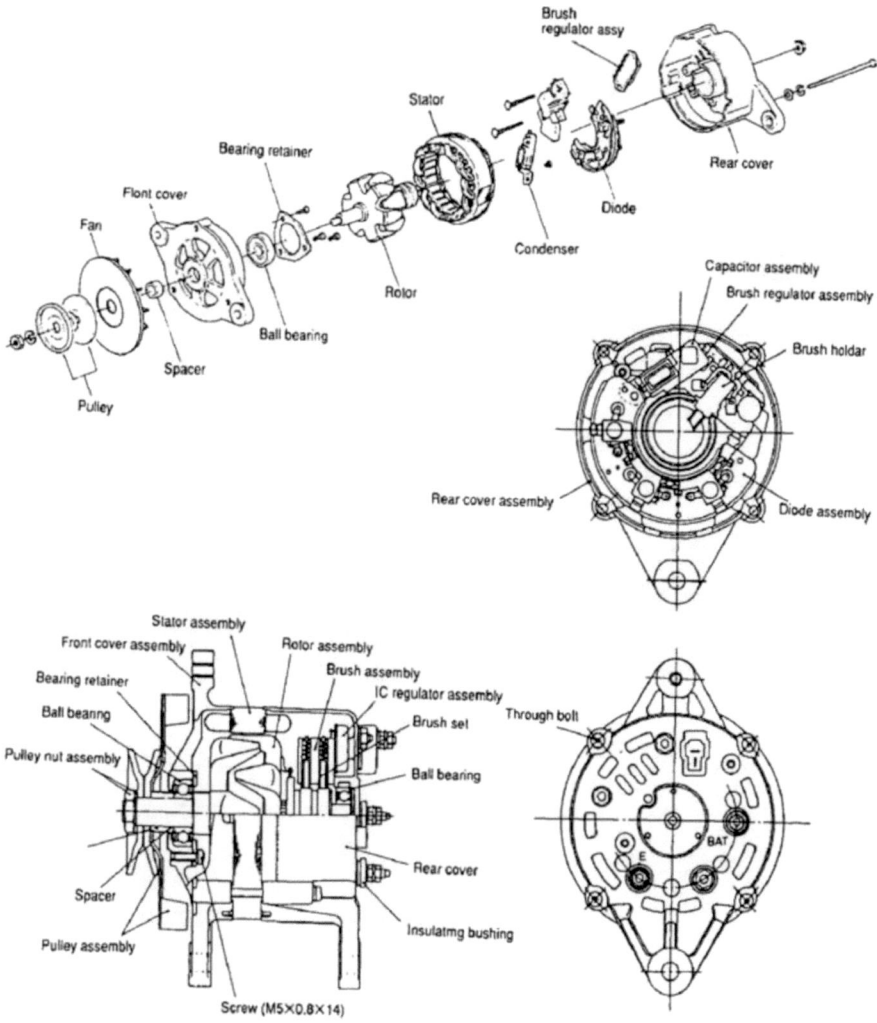

Chapter 9 Electrical System
5. Alternator (OPTIONAL)
_3,4JH3(B)(C)E_

5-5 Alternator functioning

(1) IC regulator
 The IC regulator is the transistor (Tr1) which is series-connected with the rotor. The IC regulator controls the output voltage of the generator by breaking or conducting the rotor coil (exciting) current.
 When the output voltage of the generator is within the standard value, the transistor (Tr1) turns on. When the voltage exceeds the standard value, the Zener diode goes on and the transistor (Tr1) turns off.
 With the repeated turning on and off of the transistor, the output voltage is kept at the standard value (Refer to the circuit diagram below.)

(2) Charge lamp
 When the transistor (Tr1) is on, the charge lamp key switch is turned to ON, and current flows to R_1, R_4 and to Tr1 to light the lamp. When the engine starts to run and output voltage is generated in the stator coil, the current stops flowing to this circuit, turning off the charge lamp.

(3) Circuit diagram

5-6 Handling precautions

(1) Be careful of the battery's polarity (+, −terminals), and do not connect the wrong terminals to the wrong cables, or the battery will be short-circuited by the generator diode.
 In this case too much current will flow, the IC regulator and diodes burn out, and the wire harness will burn.
(2) Make sure of the correct connection of each terminal.
(3) When quick-charging, etc., disconnect either the battery terminal on the AC generator or the terminal on the battery.
(4) Do not short-circuit the terminals
(5) Do not conduct any tests using high tension insulation resistance. (The diodes and IC regulator will burn out.)

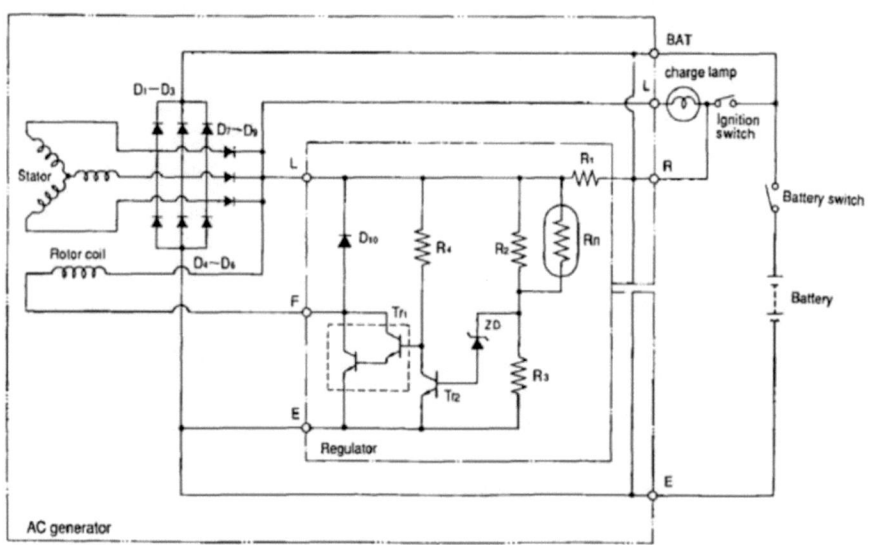

BAT:	Generator output terminal	D_1-D_6:	Output commutation diode
D_{10}:	IC protecting diode	R_1-R_4:	Resistor
L:	Charge lamp terminal	D_1-D_9:	Charging lamp switching diode
ZD:	Zener diode	F:	To supply current to rotor coil
E:	Earth	Rn:	Thermistor
Tr1, Tr2:	Transistor		(Temperature gradient resistance)

Chapter 9 Electrical System
5. Alternator (OPTIONAL) 3.4JH3(B)(C)E

5-7 Disassembling the alternator

(1) Remove the through-bolt, and separate the front assembly from the rear assembly.

(4) Remove the nut, the brush-holder and diode fixing nut at the SAT, and the terminal screws of the rear cover. Separate the rear cover from the stator (with the diode and brush holder).

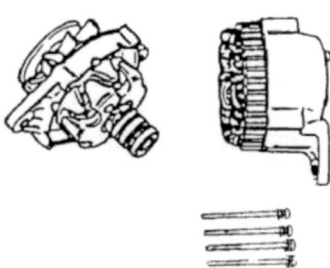

(2) Remove the pulley nut, and pull out the rotor from the front cover.

(5) Disconnect the soldered joint of the stator lead wire, and remove the diode and brush regulator assemblies from the stator at the same time.

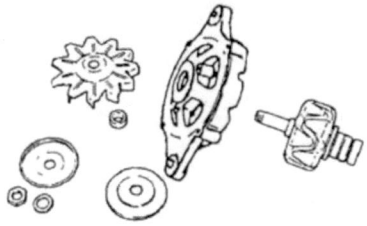

(3) Remove the ϕ5mm (ϕ0.1969 in.) screw from the front cover, and then remove the ball bearing.

(6) Separating the regulator
1) To separate the regulator, remove the ϕ3mm (ϕ0.1181 in) rivet which keeps the diode assembly and the brushless regulator in place, and the soldered joint of the L-terminal.

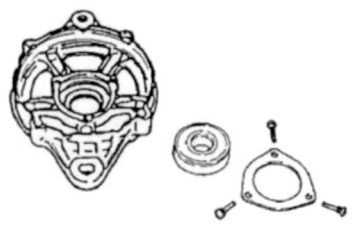

 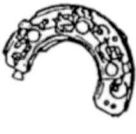

Chapter 9 Electrical System
5. Alternator (OPTIONAL) 3,4JH3(B)(C)E

2) To replace the IC regulator, disconnect the soldered joint the IC regulator and pull out the two bolts. Do not remove these two bolts except when replacing the IC regulator.

After repeating the above test, if any diode is found to be defective, replace the diode assembly. Since there is no terminal on the auxiliary diode, check the continuity between both ends of the diode.

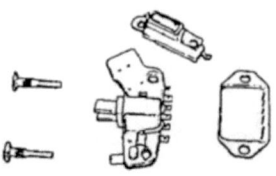

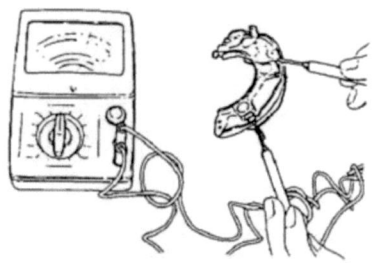

5-8 Inspection and adjustment
(1) Diode

Between terminals		BAT (+side diode)	
	Tester wire	+ side	− side
U.V.W.	+ side		No continuity
	− side	Continuity	

Between terminals		E (−side diode)	
	Tester wire	+ side	− side
U.V.W.	+ side		continuity
	− side	No Continuity	

CAUTION: Do not use high tensile insulation resistance such as meggers, etc. for testing. The diode may burn out.

(2) Rotor
Inspect the slip ring surface, rotor coil continuity and insulation.
1) Inspecting the slip ring surface
Check if the surface of the slip ring is sufficiently smooth. If the surface is rough, grind the surface with No. 500−600 sand paper. If it is contaminated with oil, etc., wipe the surface clean with alcohol.

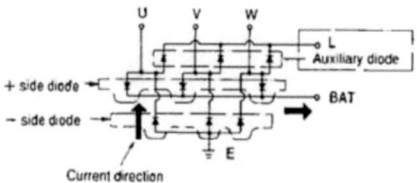

U.V.W.: terminal from the stator coil

	Standard	Wear limit
Slip ring outer dia.	⌀31.6mm	⌀30.6mm

2) Rotor coil continuity test
Check the continuity in the slip ring with the tester. If there is no continuity, there is a wire break. Replace the rotor coil.

Current flows only in one direction in the diode as shown in Fig. 181. Accordingly, when there is continuity between each terminal (e.g. BAT and U), the diode is in normal condition. When there is no continuity, the diode is defective.
When the tester is connected in the reverse of above, there should be no continuity. If there is, the diode is defective.

Resistance value	Approx. 2.58Ω at 20°C

Chapter 9 Electrical System
5. Alternator (OPTIONAL) — 3,4JH3(B)(C)E

3) Rotor coil insulation test
   Check the continuity between the slip ring and the rotor core, or the shaft. If there is continuity, insulation inside the rotor is defective, causing a short with the earth circuit. Replace the rotor coil.

4) Check the rear side ball bearing. If the rotation of the bearing is heavy, or produces abnormal sounds, replace the ball bearing.

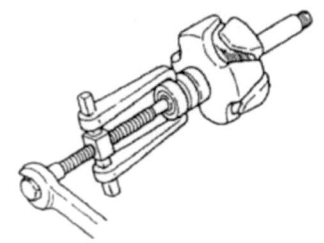

(3) Stator
1) Stator coil continuity test
   Check the continuity between each terminal of the stator coil. If there is no continuity, there is a wire break in the stator coil. Replace the stator coil.

Resistance value	Approx. 0.04 Ω at 20°C u,v-phase resistance
	Approx. 0.036 Ω at 20°C w-phase resistance

2) Stator coil insulation test
   Check the continuity between the terminals and the stator core. If there is continuity, insulation of the stator coil is defective. This will cause a short-circuit with the earth core. Replace the stator coil.

(4) Brush
   The brush is hard and wears slowly, but when it is worn beyond the allowable limit, replace it. When replacing the brush, also check the strength of the brush spring.
   To check, push the spring down to 2mm (0.0787in.) from the end surface of the brush holder, and read the gauge.

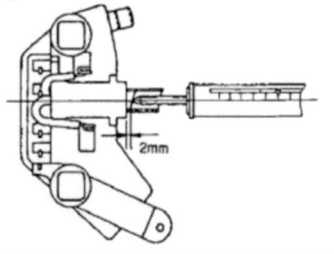

Brush spring strerath	255–345g

(5) Brush wear
   Check the brush length.
   The brush wears very little, but replace the brush if worn over the wear limit line printed on the brush.

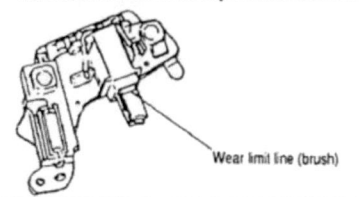

Wear limit line (brush)

mm

	Maintenance standard	Wear limit
Brush length	16	9

Chapter 9 Electrical System
5. Alternator (OPTIONAL)

3,4JH3(B)(C)E

(6) IC regulator
Connect the variable resistance, two 12V batteries, resistor, and voltmeter as shown in the diagram.

1) Use the following measuring devices.
   Resistor (R_1)   100Ω, 2W, 1pc.
   Variable resistor (Rv)   0–300Ω, 12W, 1pc.
   Battery (BAT_1, BAT_2)   12V. 2pcs
   DC voltmeter   0–30V, 0.5 class 1pc.
                                (measure at 3 points)

2) Check the regulator in the following sequence, according to the diagram.
   a) Check V_3, (BAT_1+BAT_2 voltage). If the voltage is 20-26V, both BAT_1, and BAT_2, are normal.
   b) While measuring V_2 (F-E terminal voltage), move Rv gradually from the O-position. Check if there is a point where the V_2, voltage rises sharply from below 2.0V to over 2.0V. If there is no such point, the regulator is defective. Replace the regulator if there is a sharp voltabe rise when testing, return the Rv to the 0-position, and connect the voltmeter to the V_1, position.
   c) While measuring V_1 (voltage between L-E terminals), move RV gradually from the O-position. There should be a point where the voltage of V_1, rises sharply by 2-6V. Measure the voltabe of V_1, just before this sharp voltage rise. This is the regulating voltage of the regulator. If this voltage of V_1, is within the standard limit, the regulator is normal. If the voltage deviates from the limit, the regulator is defective.
   Replace the regulator.

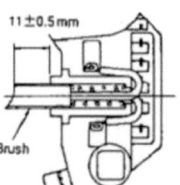
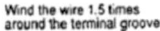
Wind the wire 1.5 times around the terminal groove.
11±0.5mm
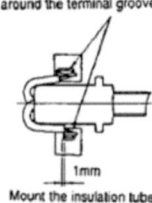
Brush
1mm
Mount the insulation tube on the terminal surface.

NOTES : 1. Use non-acid type paste.
        2. The soldering iron temperature is 300~350℃.

2) Mount the IC regulator on the brush holder as illustrated, and press in the M5 bolt. Do not forget to assemble the bushing and the connecting plate at the same time.
(If the bushing is left out, the output terminal will be earthed and the battery short-circuited).

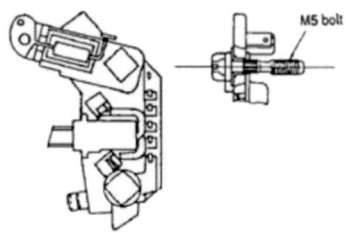
M5 bolt

NOTES : 1. Insertion pressure is 100kg
        2. Insert vertically.

(2) Connecting the brush regulator assembly and diode
1) Check the rivets
   Place the rivets as shown in the figure, and then calk them using the calking tool.

Calking torque	500kg

2) Connect the brush to the diode.
   Insert the brush side terminal into the diode terminal, calk it, and then solder into place.

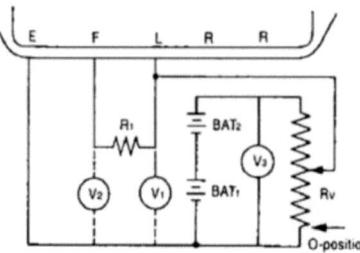

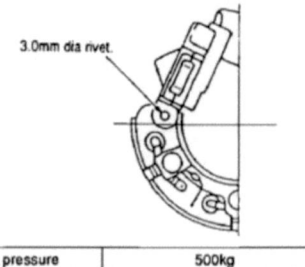
3.0mm dia rivet.

Rivetting pressure	500kg

5-9 Reassembling the alternator
Reassembly is done in the reverse order of disassembly. For reassembly, be careful of the following points (Refer to 4-7 disassembling alternator.)
(1) Assembling the brush regulator
1) Solder the brush.
   Position the brush as shown in the drawing and solder it. Be careful not to let the solder drip into the pig tail (lead wire).

Chapter 9 Electrical System
5. Alternator (OPTIONAL)

(3) Assembling the rear cover
Insert pins from the outsice of the rear cover. Install the brush on the brush holder, then attach the rear cover.
After assembly, pull out the pins.

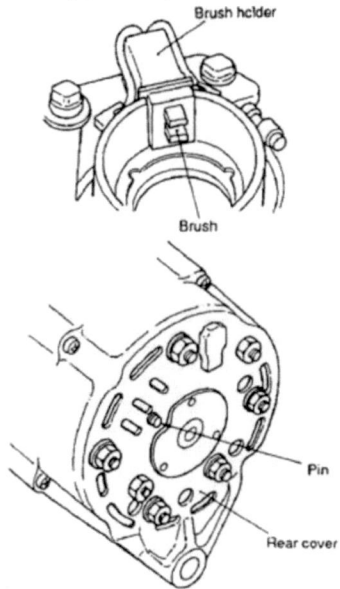

(4) Tightening torques

Positions	Tightening torque kg-cm
Brush holder fixing	32—40
Diode fixing	60—70
Bearing retainer fixing	32—40
Pulley nut tightening	400—600
Through-bolt tightening	32—40

(1) Measuring devices

DC voltmeter	0—15V or 0—30V, 0.5 Class, 1pc.
DC ammeter	0—100A, 1.0 Clsss 1pc.
Variable resistor	0—0.25Ω, 1kW, 1pc.
Lamp	12V, 3W
100Ω resistor	3W
0.25Ω resistor	25W

(2) Measuring the regulating voltage
1) When measuring devices are connected in the performance test circuit as shown above, the charge lamp lights.
2) Close SW$_2$ while keeping SW$_1$ open and run the AC generator. When the revolutions of the generator are gradually raised, the charge lamp goes off.
3) Raise the revolutions of the AC generator, and read the voltmeter gauge when the revolutions reach about 5,000 rpms.

NOTES : 1. Make sure that the ammeter indication at this time is less than 5A. If the indication is over 5A, connect the 0.25Ω resistor. The voltmeter indication at this time must be within the prescribed regulating voltage value.
2. Raise the AC generator revolutions high to make sure the regulating voltage does not fluctuate along with changes in the revolution speed.

(3) Precautions for measuring the regulating voltage
1) When measuring the voltage, measure the voltage between the AC generator BAT terminal, or Battery + terminal, and AC generator E-terminal.
2) Use a fully charged battery.
3) Measure the voltage quickly.
4) Keep SW, open for measurement.

5-10 Performance test
Conduct a performance test on the reassembled AC generator as follows. The following is the circuit for the performance test.

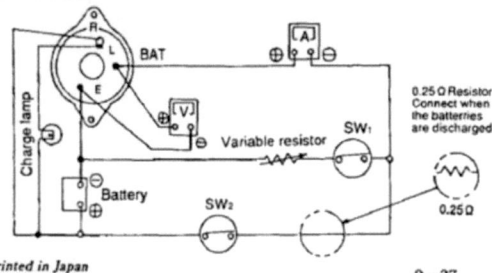

5-11 Troubleshooting

(1) Charging failure

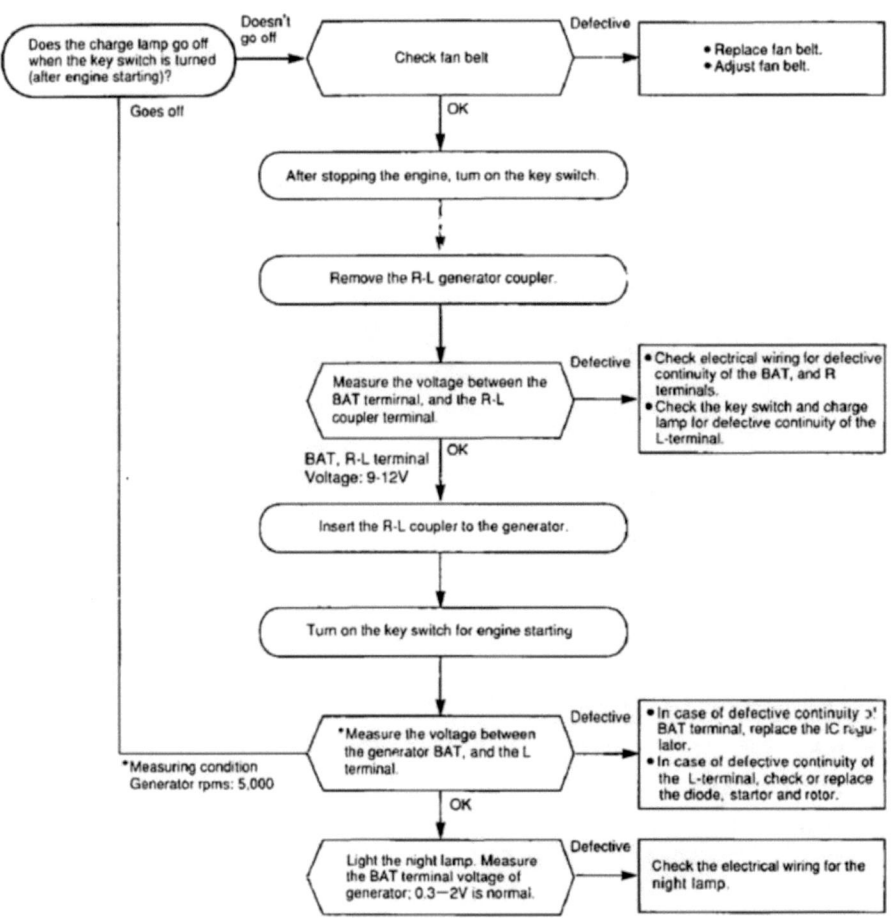

Chapter 9 Electrical System
5. Alternator (OPTIONAL) _____ 3.4JH3(B)(C)E

(2) Overcharging

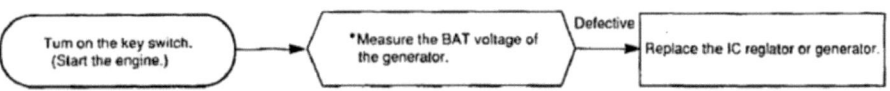

(3) Charge lamp failure

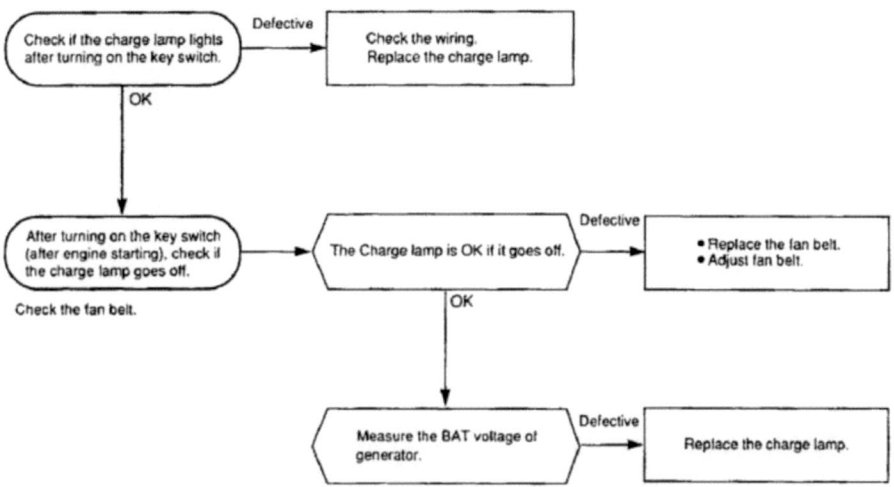

6. Instrument Panel

6-1 B2-type instrument panel with wiring

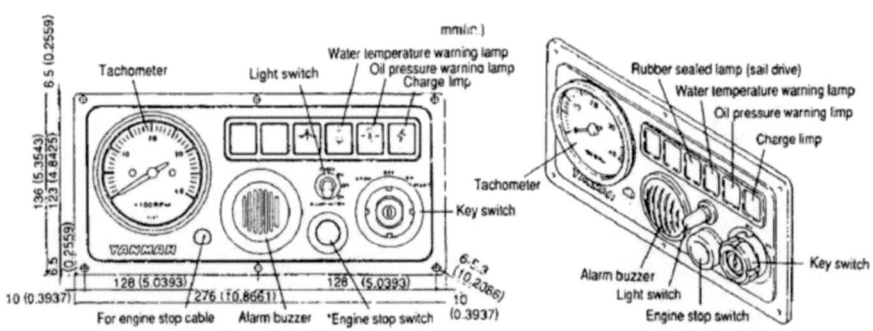

6-2 C-type instrument panel

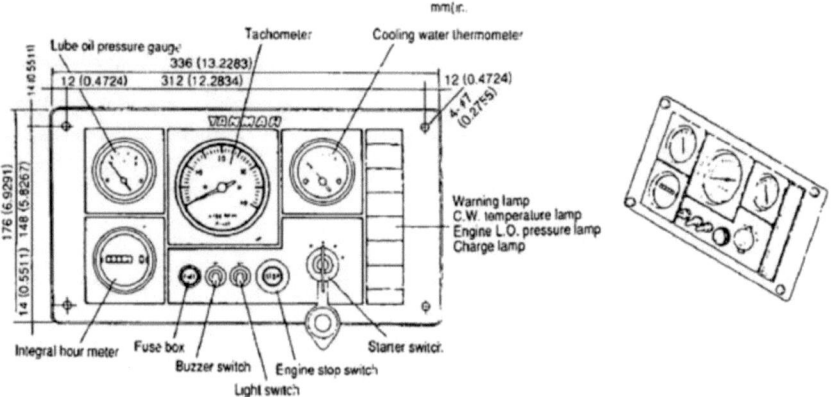

6-3 Extension codes

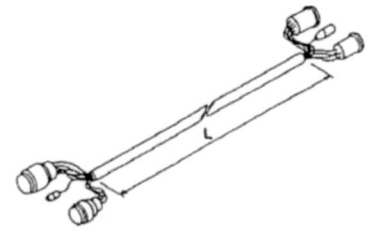

	Part code No.	L
Extension cord 4M	129574-77710	3750 ~ 3850
Extension cord 6M	129574-77720	5750 ~ 5850

mm

7. Warning Devices

7-1 Oil pressure alarm

If the engine oil pressure is below 0.1~0.3 kg/cm² (1.42~4.26 lb/in.²), with the main switch in the ON position, the contacts of the oil pressure switch are closed by a spring, and the lamp is illuminated through the lamp → oil pressure switch → ground circuit system. If the oil pressure is normal, the switc contacts are opened by the lubricating oil pressure and the lamp remains off.

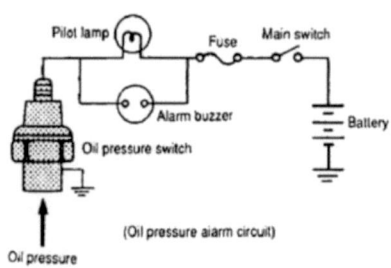

(Oil pressure alarm circuit)

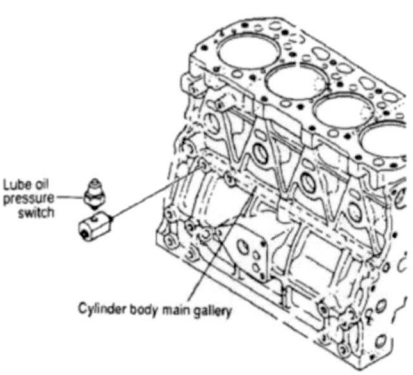

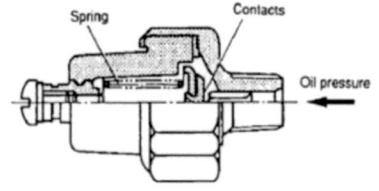

Rated voltage	12V
Operation pressure	0.1~0.3kg/cm²
Lamp capacity	5W

Inspection

Problem	Inspection Item	Inspection method	Corrective action
Lamp not illuminated when main switch set to ON	1. Oil pressure lamp blown out	(1) Visual inspection	Replace lamp
		(2) Lamp not illuminated even when main switch set to ON position and terminals of oil pressure switch grounded	
	2. Operation of oil pressure switch	Lamp illuminated when checked as described in (2) above	Replace oil pressure switch
Lamp not extinguished while engine running	1. Oil level low	Stop engine and check oil level with dipstick	Add oil
	2. Oil pressure low	Measure oil pressure	Repair bearing wear and adjust regulator valve
	3. Oil pressure faulty	Switch faulty if abnormal at (1) and (2) above	Replace oil pressure switch
	4. Wiring between lamp and oil pressure switch faulty	Cut the wiring between the lamp and switch and wire with separate wire	Repair wiring harness

7-2 Cooling water temperature alarm

A water temperature lamp and water temperature gauge, backed up by an alarm in the instrument panel, are used to monitor the temperature of the engine cooling water. A high thermal expansion material is set on the end of the water temperature unit. When the cooling water temperature reaches a specified high temperature, the contacts are closed, and an alarm lamp and buzzer are activated at the instrument panel.

Operating temperature	ON	97~103°C
	OFF	87°C or high
Electric capacity		DC 12V, 1A
Response time		with in 60 sec.
Indication color		Green
Tightening torque		2.40~3.20kg-m

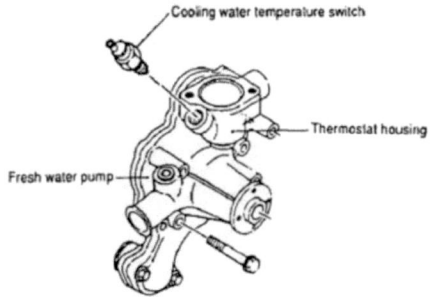

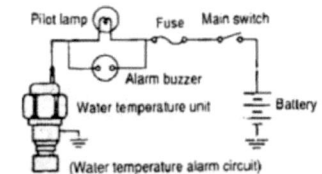

(Water temperature alarm circuit)

7-3 Sender unit for lube oil pressure gauge

The sender unit for the lube oil pressure gauge has a mounting seat for mounting on the lube oil filter bracket. Oil pressure is measured when the oil enters into the main gallery after being fed from the lube oil cooler and passing through the oil pressure control valve. Be sure to mount a vibration damper when mounting the oil pressure sender unit.

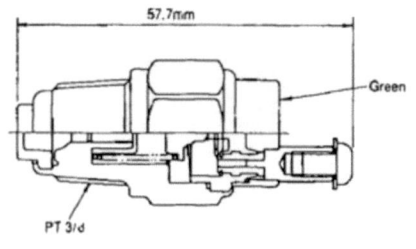

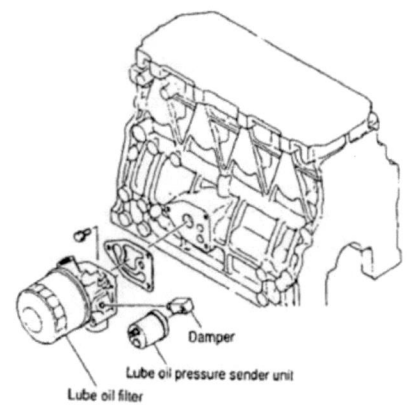

7. Warning Devices

Lube oil pressure sender unit

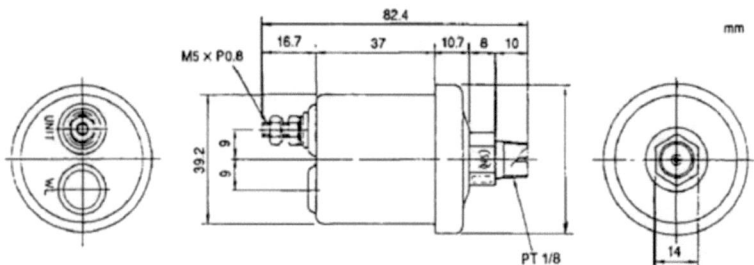

Damper

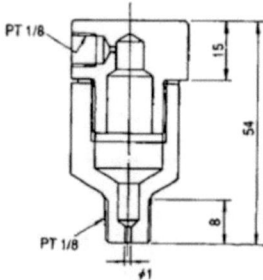

Type	Resistance switch
Rated voltage	DC 12/DC 24
Max. operating pressure	8kg/cm²

7-4 Sender unit Oor the cooling water temperature gauge

The water temperature sender unit has a mounting seat for mounting on the fresh water pump unit. Water temperature is measured when the cooling water flows into the thermostat housing after leaving the cylinder head.

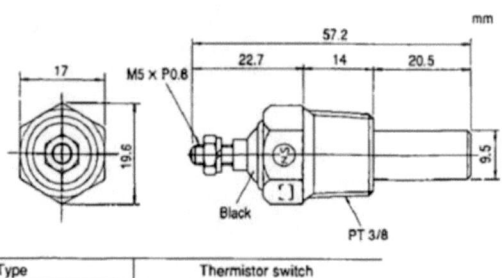
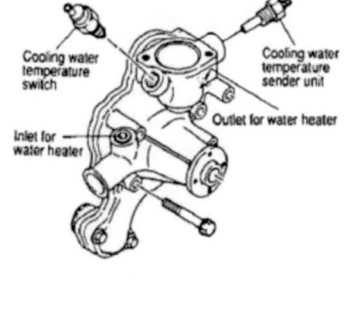

Type	Thermistor switch
Rated voltage	12V/24V

8. Air Heater (Optional)

An air heater is available for warming intake air when starting in cold areas in winter. The air heater is mounted between the intake manifold and intake manifold coupling. The device is operated by the glow switch on the instrument panel.

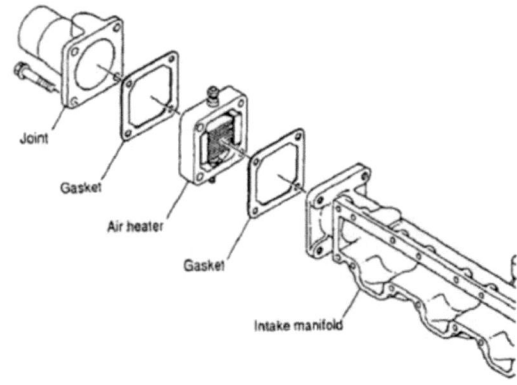

Joint
Gasket
Air heater
Gasket
Intake manifold

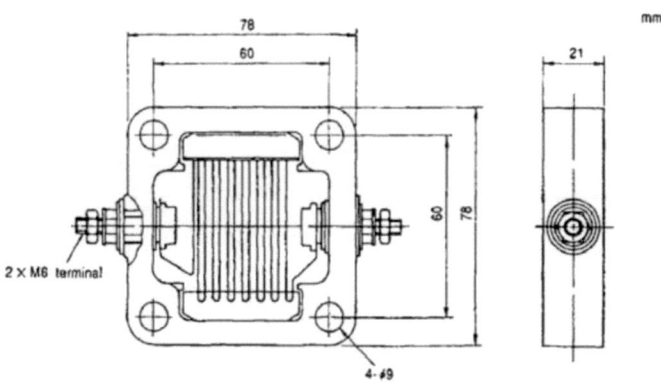

Rated output	400W
Rated current	33.3A
Rated voltage	DC 12V
Rated operating time	Engine operation : 60 sec. Engine stop : 30 sec.
Range operating temperature	+50℃~-30℃ (122°F~-22°F)

9. Electric type Engine Stopping Device (Optional)

To employ the eletric engine stop device, the stop lever of the fuel injection pump is connected to the solenoid with a connection metal.
The device is operated by the stop switch on the instrument panel.

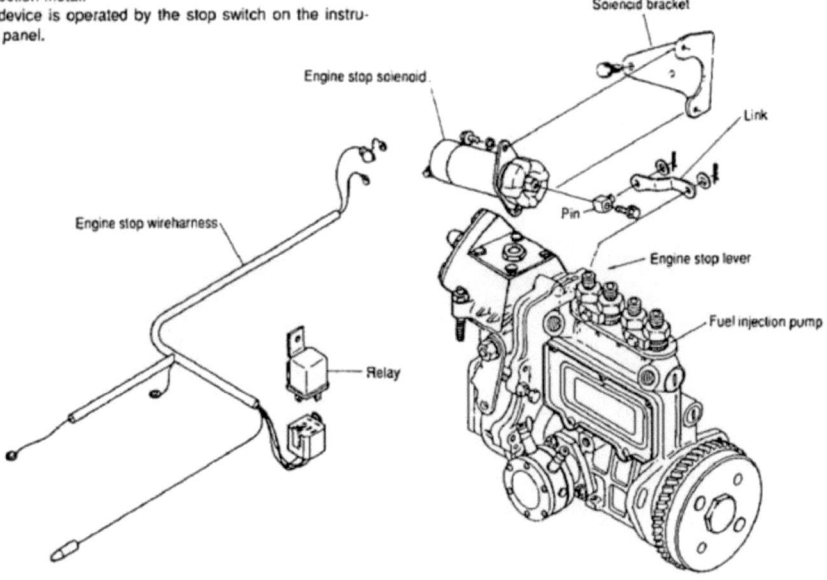

9-1 Solenoid

Solenoid model	1504-12AU1B
Rated voltage	12V
Taking current	41A
Taking force	5.0kg
Holding force	9.0kg
Holding current	0.75A

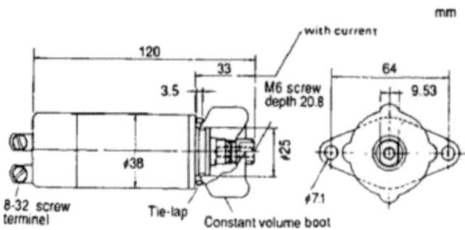

Chapter 9 Electrical System
9. Electric Type Engine Stopping Device (Optional)

3,4JH3(B)(C)E

9-2 Relay

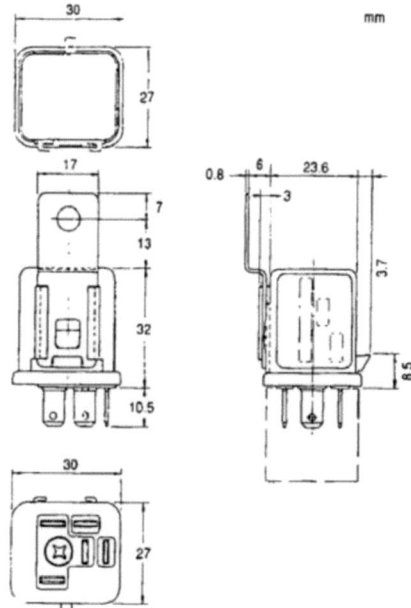

Rated voltage	12V
Contact current	Lamp: 20A, extra-lamp : 25A
Range of operation	−30°C ~ +90°C

9-3 Wire harness of engine stop

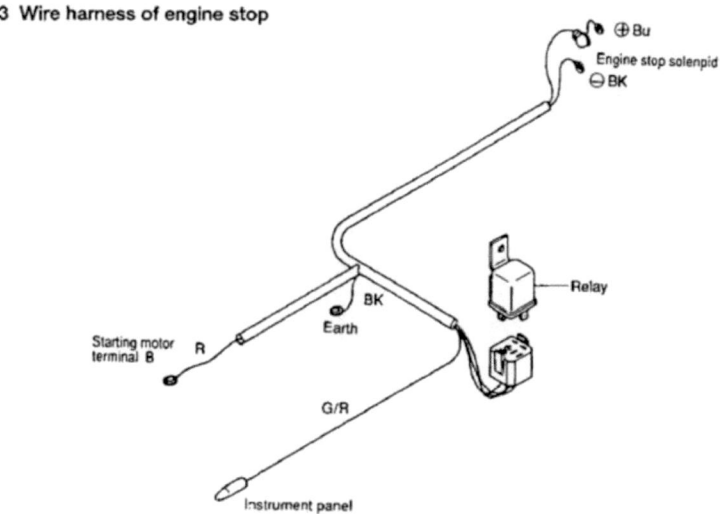

10. Tachometer

10-1 Construction of tachometer

The tachometer indicates the number of revolutions per minute by means of an electrical input signal which is generated as a pulse signal from the magnetic pickup sender (MPU sender).
The function of the sender is to convert the rotary motion into an electrical signal by counting the number of teeth of the ring gear connecting with the flywheel housing.

(2) Sensitivity limit of sender unit

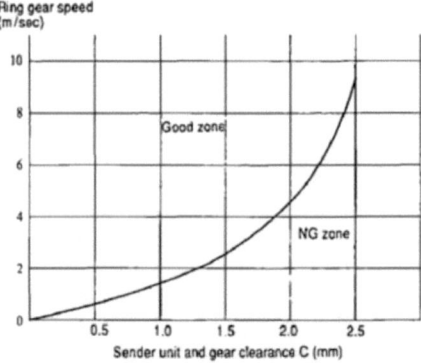

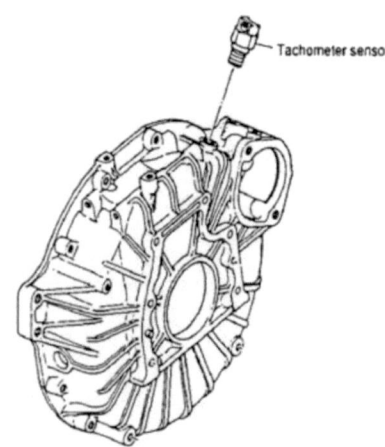

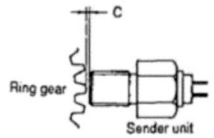

(3) Dimensions of sender unit

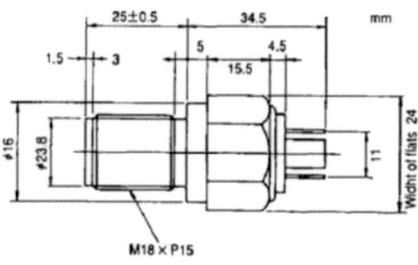

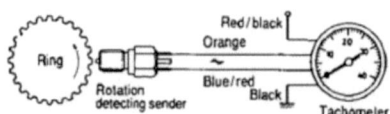

(4) Dimensions and shape of tachometer

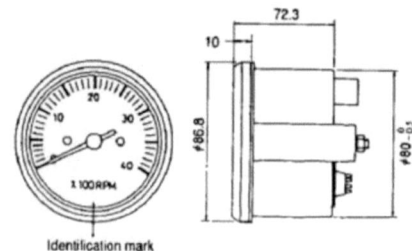

10-2 Specifications and dimensions of tachometer

(1) Specifications

Rated voltage		DC 12V
Range of operating voltage		10~15V
illumination		3.4W / 12V
Ring gear	No. of teeth	116
	Module	2.54
Part No. of sender unit		128170-91160

Chapter 9 Electrical System
10. Tachometer

10-3 Measurement of sender unit characteristics

(1) Measurement of output voltage

Output voltage	1.0V or higher

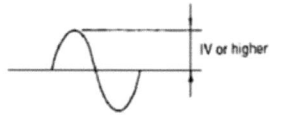

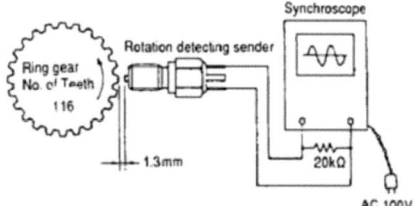

*Check the output wave pattern and number of pulses when carrying out the output voltage measurement.

Measuring conditions

Number of teeth of ring gear	116
Gap between the ring gear and sender	1.3mm
Resistance	20kΩ
Speed of ring gear	500 rpm
Measuring temperature	20℃
Measuring instrument	Synchroscope

(2) Measurement of internal resistance

Measuring conditions

Measuring temperature	20℃
Measuring instrument	Digital tester

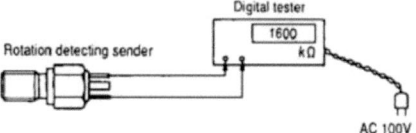

Fault	Diagnosis	Remedy
Does not function well. 1) Pointer does not move. 2) Functions intermittently.	Check if there is an open-circuit cable connection at the rear of the meter, a loose or disconnected terminal or bad continuity due to corrosion. ↓	Yes Make good the connection.
	Disconnect at the instrument terminals, and measure the voltage between the cable terminals. (To be 10~16V) ↓ Satisfactory	No If the input voltage is abnormal, check the cause. (e.g. short-circuit, disconnection, or blown fuse, etc.)

Chapter 9 Electrical System
10. Tachometer
_____ 3,4JH3(B)(C)E

	Check if the sender is loosely fitted. ↓ No	Yes	Fix the sender securely.
	Measure the internal resistance of the sender. (To be 1.6±0.1kΩ at 20℃) ↓	No	Replace the sender.
	Measure the output voltage of the sender. (To be or higher at 20℃)	No	Replace the sender.

CHAPTER 10

DISASSEMBLY AND REASSEMBLY

1. Disassembly and Reassembly Precautions 10-1
2. Disassembly and Reassambly Tools 10-2
   - 2-1 General Handtools 10-2
   - 2-2 Special Handtools 10-5
   - 2-3 Measuring Instruments 10-7
   - 2-4 Other material 10-8
   - 2-5 Measuring Instruments 10-11
3. Disassembly and Reassembly 10-14
   - 3-1 Disassembly 10-14
   - 3-2 Reassembly 10-23
4. Table of Standard Measurements for Maintenance ... 10-35
   - 4-1 Cylinder head 10-35
   - 4-2 Cylinder block 10-36
   - 4-3 Valve equipment 10-36
   - 4-4 Piston 10-37
   - 4-5 Piston ring 10-37
   - 4-6 Connecting rod 10-38
   - 4-7 Cam shaft 10-38
   - 4-8 Crank shaft 10-38
   - 4-9 Side clearance and backlash 10-39
   - 4-10 Miscellaneous 10-39
5. Tightening torque 10-40
   - 5-1 Main Bolt and Nut 10-40
   - 5-2 Standard Bolts and Nuts (without lubricant) ... 10-40
6. Test Running 10-41
   - 6-1 Preliminary Precautions 10-41
   - 6-2 Check Points and Precautions During Running ... 10-41

1. Disassembly and Reassembly Precautions

(1) Disassembly
- Take sufficient time to accurately pin-point the cause of the trouble, and disassemble only those parts which are necessary.
- Be careful to keep all disassembled parts in order.
- Prepare disassembly tools.
- Prepare a cleaner and cleaning can.
- Clear an adequate area for parts and prepare a container(s)
- Drain cooling water (sea water, fresh water) and lube oil.
- Close the Kingston cock

(2) Reassembly
- Sufficiently clean and inspect all parts to be assembled.
- Coat sliding and rotating parts with new engine oil when assembling.
- Replace all gaskets and O-rings.
- Use a liquid packing agent as necessary to prevent oil/water leaks.
- Check the oil and thrust clearances, etc. of parts when assembling
- Make sure you use the correct bolt/nut/washer. Tighten main bolts/nuts to the specified torque. Be especially careful not to overtighten the aluminum alloy part mounting bolts.
- Align match marks (if any) when assembling. Make sure that the correct sets of parts are used for bearings, pistons, and other parts where required.

2. Disassembly and Reassembly Tools

The following tools are required when disassembling and reassembling the engine.
Please use them as instructed.

2-1. General Handtools

Name of tool	Illustration	Remarks
Wrench		Size : 10×13
Wrench		Size : 12×14
Wrench		Size : 17×19
Wrench		Size : 22×24
Screwdriver		
Steel hammer		Local supply

Chapter 10 Disassembly and Reassembly
2. Disassembly and Reassembly Tools
3,4JH3(B)(C)E

Name of tool	Illustration	Remarks
Copper hammer		Local supply
Mallet		Local supply
Nippers		Local supply
Pliers		Local supply
Offset wrench		Local supply 1 set
Box spanner		Local supply 1 set
Scraper		Local supply

Chapter 10 Disassembly and Reassembly
2. Disassembly and Reassembly Tools _____ 3,4JH3(B)(C)E

Name of tool	Illustration	Remarks
Lead rod		Local supply
File	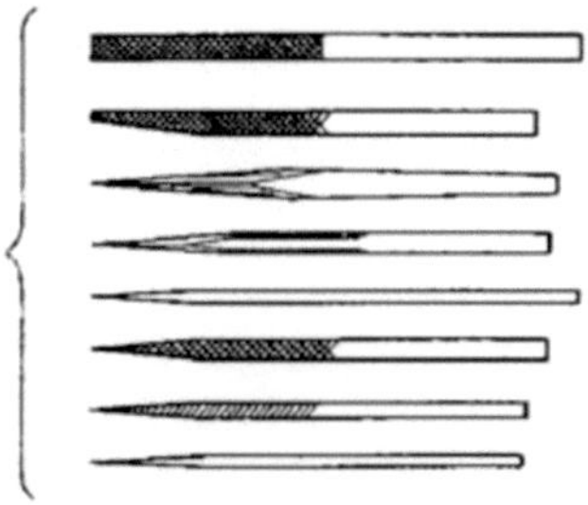	Local supply 1 set
Rod spanner for hexagon socket head screws		Local supply Size : 6 mm 8 mm 10 mm
Starting Pliers Hole type Shaft type	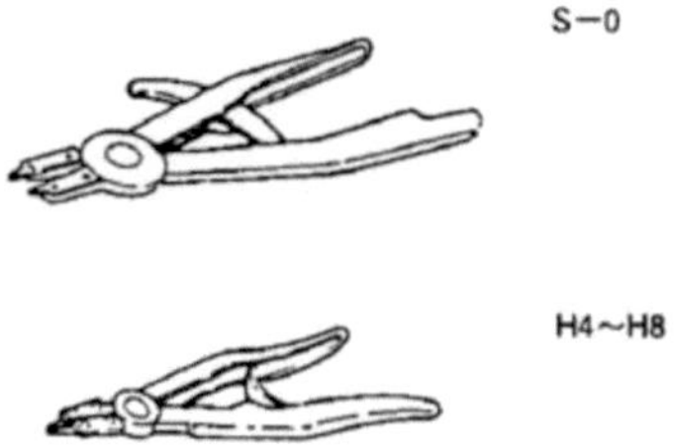 S—0 H4~H8 S = Hole type H = Shaft type	Local supply

10—4

Printed in Japan
HINSHI-H8009

Chapter 10 Disassembly and Reassembly
2. Disassembly and Reassembly Tools   3.4JH3(B)(C)E

2-2 Special Handtools

Name of tool	Shape and size	Application
Piston pin insertion/ extraction tool	20, 80; 12, 25 (mm)	Piston pin extractor — Extraction of piston pin; Insertion of piston pin
Connecting rod small end bushing insertion/ extraction tool	20, 80; 25.4~25.7, 28.4~28.7	Extraction
Intake and exhaust valve insertion/ extraction tool	20, 75; 7.5, 11	
Lubricating oil No.2 filter case remover		

Printed in Japan
HINSHI-H8009

10−5

Chapter 10 Disassembly and Reassembly
2. Disassembly and Reassembly Tools

3,4JH3(B)(C)E

Name of tool	Shape and size	Application
Piston ring compressor		Piston insertion guide
Valve lapping handle		Lappira tool
Valve lapping powder		
Feeler gauge		
Pulley puller	Local supply	Removing the coupling

10−6

Printed in Japan
HINSHI-H8009

2-3 Measuring Instruments

Name of tool	Shape and size	Application
Vernier calipers		0.05mm 0~150mm
Micrometer		0.01mm 0~25mm 25~50mm 50~75mm 75~100mm 100~125mm 125~150mm
Cylinder gauge		0.01mm 18~35mm 35~60mm 50~100mm
Thickiness gauge		0.05~2mm
Torque wrench		0~13kg-m
Nozzle tester		0~500kg/cm²

2-4 Other material

	Items	Usual Contents	Features and application
Liquid gasket	Three Bond No.1 TB1101	200g (1kg also aviable)	Non-drying liquid gasket; solventless type, easy to remove, superior in seawater resistance, applicable to various mating surfaces.
	Three Bond No.2 TB1102	200g (1kg also aviable)	Non-drying liquid gasket; easy to apply, superior in water resistance and oil resistance, especially superior in gasoline resistance.
	Three Bond No.3 TB1103	150g	Drying film, low viscosity and forming of thin film, appropriate for mating surface of precision parts.
	Three Bond No.4 TB1104	200g (1kg also aviable)	Semi-drying viscoelastic material, applicable to non-flat surface having many indentations and protrusions, superior in heat resistance, water resistance, and oil resistance.
	Three Bond No.10 TB1211	100g	Solventless type silicone-base sealant, applicable to high temperature areas. ($-50°C$ to 250)
	Three Bond TB1212	100g	Silicone-base, non-fluid type, thick application possible.
Adhesive	Three Bond TB1401	200g	Prevention of loose bolts, gas leakage, and corrosion. Torque required to loosen bolt: 10 to 20% larger than tightening torque.
	Lock tight SUPER TB1324	50g	Excellent adhesive strength locks bolt semipermanently.
	Seal Tape	5m round tape	Sealing material for threaded parts of various pipes. Ambient temperature range: $-150°C$ to $200°C$
	O-ring kit	ϕ 1.92-m dia.:1 ϕ 2.42-m dia.:1 ϕ 3.12-m dia.:1 ϕ 3.52-m dia.:1 ϕ 5.72-m dia.:1	O-ring of any size can be prepared, whenever required. (Including adhesive, release agent, cutter, and jig)
EP lubricant (molybdenum disulfate)	Brand name (LOWCOL PASTE)	50g	For assembly of engine cylinders, pistons, metals, shafts, etc. Spray type facilitates application work.
	Brand name (PASTE SPRAY)	330g	
	Brand name (MOLYPASTE)	50g	Prevention of seizure of threaded parts at high temperature. Applicable to intake and exhaust valves. (stem, guide, face)

Chapter 10 Disassembly and Reassembly
2. Disassembly and Reassembly Tools

3,4JH3(B)(C)E

Items		Usual Contents	Features and application
Scale solvent	Scale solvent	1 box (4kg×4removers)	• The scale solvent removes scale in a short time. (1 to 10 hours) • Prepare water (seawater is possible) in an amount that is about 10 times the weight of the solvent. Mix the solvent with water. • Just dipping disassembled part into remover mixture removes scale. To shorten removal time, stir remover mixture. • If cleaning performance drops, replace remover mixture with new remover mixture. • Neutralize used mixture, and then dispose of it. To judge cleaning performance of mixture, put pH test paper into mixture. If test paper turns red, remover mixture is still effective.
	Neutralizer (caustic soda)	1 box (2kg×4 neutralizers)	
	pH test paper		
Antirust		2 ℓ	Add antirust to fresh water system. Then operate engine for approximately 5 minutes. Antirust will be effective for 6 months.
Anti freeze		2 ℓ	Add antirust to fresh water system at the cold area to engine operate.
Cleaning agent		1kg×20	• The cleaning agent removes even carbon adhering to disassembled parts. • If a cleaning machine is used, prepare 4 to 6% mixture of 60° to 80°C to ensure more effective cleaning.

Chapter 10 Disassembly and Reassembly
2. Disassembly and Reassembly Tools

Items	Usual Contents	Features and application
Cleaning agent for turbocharger	4 ℓ×4	Special cleaning agent that requires no watar, specially designed for blower of turbocharger and intercooler.
	18 ℓ×1	
	15sets : 1, 500cc×6	

Cautions:
It is recommended that the liquid gasket of Three Bond TB1212 should be used for service work.

Before providing service, observe the cautions below:
(1) Build up each gasket equally.
(2) For a bolt hole, apply liquid gasket to the inside surface of the hole.
(3) Conventionally, Three Bond TB1104(gray) or Three Bond

  TB1102(yellow) is used for paper packings though single use of one of these bonds is not effective.
(4) If conventional packings are used, do not use a liquid packing.

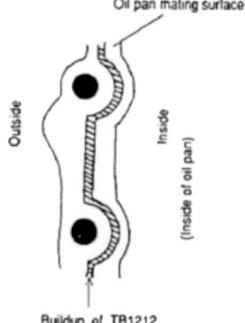
Buildup of TB1212

Chapter 10 Disassembly and Reassembly
2. Disassembly and Reassembly Tools

3,4JH3(B)(C)E

2-5 Measuring Instruments

No.	Name of tool	Use	Illustration
1	Dial gauge	Measures shaft bending, distortions of levelness, and gaps.	
2	Test indicator	Measures narrow and deep places which cannot be measured with dial gauge.	
3	Magnetic stand	Keeps the dial gauge firmly in position, thereby permitting it to be used at various angles.	
4	Micrometer	Measures the outer diameter of the crank shaft, piston, piston pin, etc.	
5	Cylinder gauge	Measure the inner diameter of the cylinder liner and rod metal.	
6	Vernier calipers	Measures various outer diameters, thicknesses, and widths.	
7	Depth micrometer	Measures sinking of valves.	
8	Square	Measures distortion in position of springs and perpendicularity of parts.	
9	V Block	Measures shaft distortion.	

Chapter 10 Disassembly and Reassembly
2. Disassembly and Reassembly Tools

3,4JH3(B)(C)E

No.	Name of tool		Use	Illustration
10	Torque wrench		Used to tighten bolts and nuts to standard torque.	
11	Thickness gauge		Measures the distance between the ring and ring groove, and between the shaft and shaft joint at time of assembling.	
12	Cap tester		Checks for leakage in the fresh water system.	
13	Battery current tester		Checks density of antifreeze and charging condition of battery fluid.	
14	Nozzle tester		Checks the shape and pressure of spray emitted from the fuel injection valve at the time of injection.	
15	Digital thermostat		Measures temperature of various parts.	Detector
16	Rotation gauge	Contact type	Measures rotation speed by placing at the indenta-tion hole of the revolving shaft.	
		Photoelectric type	Measures rotation speed by using a reflector seal which is placed on the exterior of the revolving shaft.	Revolving part / Reflector seal
		High pressure fuel pipe clamp type	Measures rotation speed without reference to revolving shaft center or the exterior of the revol.	High pressure pipe

10−12

Chapter 10 Disassembly and Reassembly
2. Disassembly and Reassembly Tools

3,4JH3(B)(C)E

No.	Name of tool	Use	Illustration
17	Circuit tester	Measures the resistance, voltage, and continuity of the electric circuit.	
18	Compression gauge	Measures the pressure of the compression. | Model	Yanmar code no.
---	---
All models	TOL–97190080		

3. Disassembly and Reassembly

3-1 Disassembly
For engines mounted in an engine room, remove the piping and wiring connecting them to the ship.

(1) Remove the remote control cable (from engine and marine gearbox).
(2) Uunplug the extension cord for the instrument panel from the engine.
(3) Remove the wiring between the starting motor and the battery.
(4) Remove the exhaust rubber hose from the mixing elbow.
(5) Remove the fresh water sub-tank rubber hose from the filler cap.
(6) Remove the cooling water (sea water) pump sea water intake hose (after making sure the Kingston cock is closed).
(7) Remove the fuel oil intake rubber hose from the fuel feed pump.
(8) Remove the body fit (reamer) bolts and disassemble the propeller shaft coupling and thrust shaft coupling.
(9) If a driven coupling is mounted to the front drive coupling, disassemble.
(10) Remove the flexible mount nut, lift the engine, and remove it from the engine base.
(Leave the flexible mount attached to the engine base.)

3-1.1 Drain cooling water
(1) Open the sea water drain cock between the sea water pump and lube oil cooler to drain the sea water.
(2) Open the cylinder body drain cock to drain the fresh water from the cylinder head and cylinder body.
(3) Open the fresh water drain cock on the lower part of the fresh water tank to drain the fresh water.

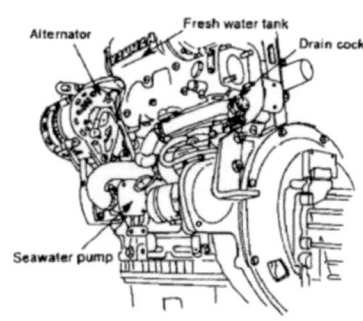

3-1.2 Drain lube oil
(1) Remove the pipe coupling bolt which holds the lube oil dip stick guide, and drain the lube oil from the engine.
(2) Remove the drain plug on the lower part of the crank case contron side, and drain the lube oil from the marine gearbox.

NOTE: *If a lube oil supply/discharge pump is used for the engine, the intake hose is placed in the dip stick guide, and for the clutch side (gearbox) it is placed in the oil hole on top of the case.*

3-1.3 Removing (electrical) wiring
Remove the wiring from the engine.

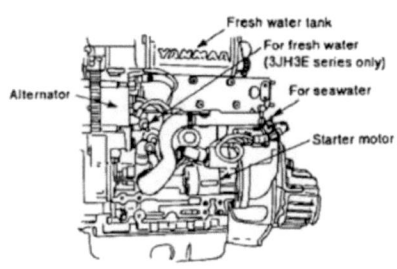

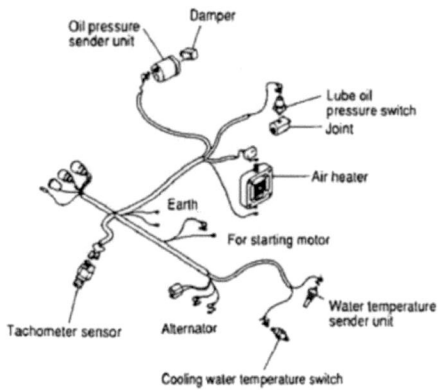

Chapter 10 Disassembly and Reassembly
3. Disassembly and Reassembly

3,4JH3(B)(C)E

3-1.4 Removing the fuel oil filter & fuel oil pipe
(1) Remove the fuel oil pipe (fuel oil filter-fuel feed pump, fuel oil filter-fuel injection pump)
(2) Remove the fuel oil filter (with bracket from the intake manifold.

3-1.6 Removing the mixing elbow
(1) Remove cooling water (sea water) pipe rubber (heat exchanger-mixing elbow).
(2) Remove the mixing elbow from the intake manifold intake coupling.

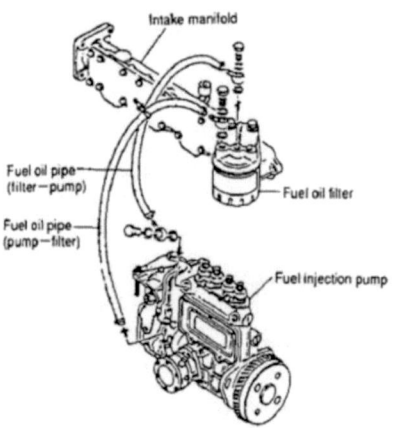

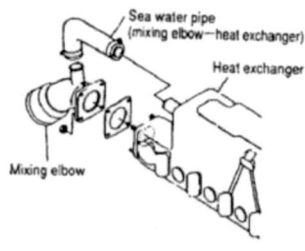

3-1.5 Removing the intake silencer
(1) Remove the breather hose attached to the intake silencer-valve rocker arm chamber cover
(2) Remove the intake silencer from exhaust manifold outlet.

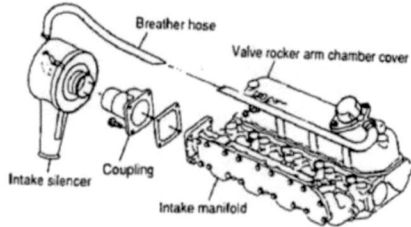

Chapter 10 Disassembly and Reassembly
1. Disassembly and Reassembly Precautions

3,4JH3(B)(C)E

3-1.7 Removing the starting motor
Remove the starting motor from the flywheel housing.

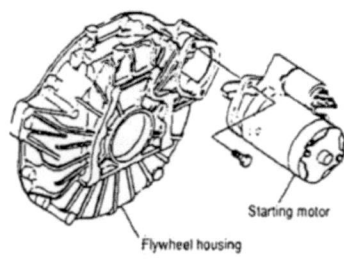

3-1.8 Removing the alternator
(1) Loosen the alternator adjuster bolt and remove the v-belt.
(2) Removing the adjuster from the fresh water pump, and remove the alternator from the gear case (with distance piece).

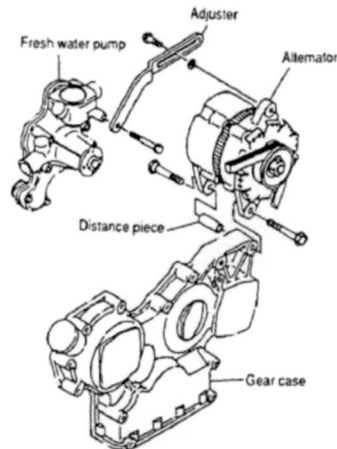

3-1.9 Removing the cooling water pipe
(1) Remove the cooling water (sea water) pipe (lube oil cooler — heat exchanger).
(2) Remove the cooling water (fresh water) pipe (heat exchanger-fresh water pump, fresh water pump—fresh water tank).
(3) Remove the cooling water pipe (lube Oil cooler — marine gearbox).

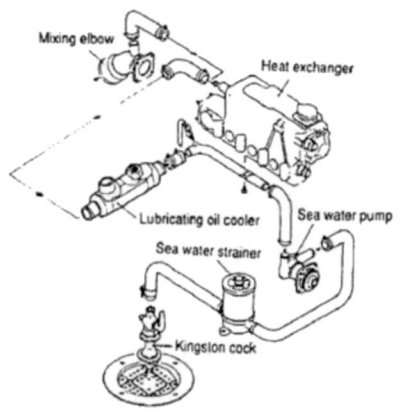

3-1.10 Removing the heat exchanger (exhaust manifold, fresh water tank unit)
Remove the heat exchanger and gasket packing.

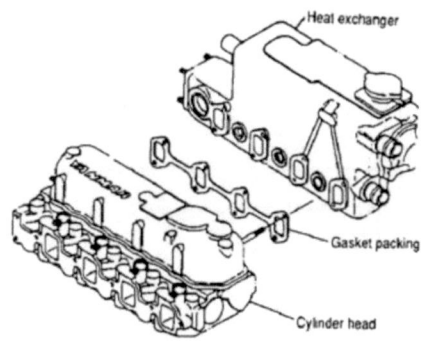

Chapter 10 Disassembly and Reassembly
3. Disassembly and Reassembly

3-1.11 Removing the cooling water (sea water) pipe (sea water pump-Lube oil cooler).

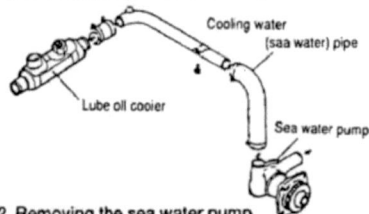

3-1.12 Removing the sea water pump
(1) Pull out the bearing mounts, receptacles from the sea water pump mounting side and from the opposite side of the gear case.
(2) Remove the sea water pump.

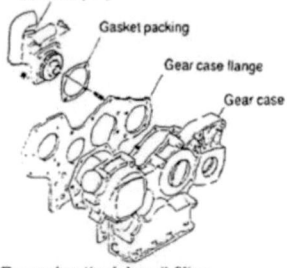

3-1.13 Removing the lube oil filter
(1) Remove the lube oil pipe (lube oil cooler-filter bracket filter bracket-lube oil cooler)
(2) Remove the filter bracket (with lube oil filter element) from the cylinder block
(3) Remove the lube oil pipe (cylinder block-fuel injection pump)
(4) Remove the tube oil dipstick and guide.

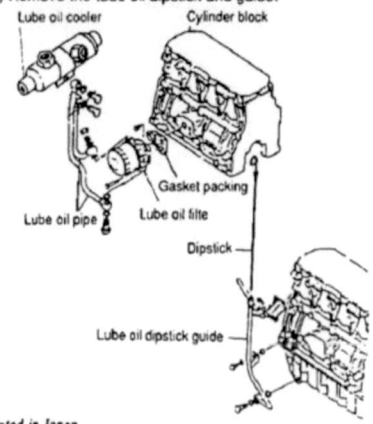

3-1.14 Removing the high pressure fuel pipe
(1) Remove the high pressure fuel pipe vibration stop from the intake manifold.
(2) Loosen the box nuts on both ends of the high pressure fuel pipe and remove the high pressure fuel pipe
(3) Remove the fuel oil return pipe (fuel injection nozzle-fuel injection pump)

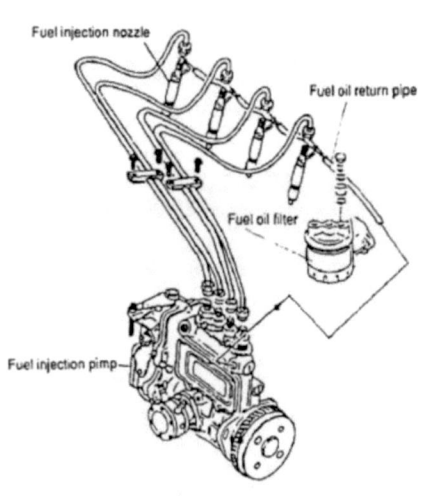

3-1.15 Removing the intake manifold
(1) Remove the governor speed remote control bracket.
(2) Remove the intake manifold and gasket packing.

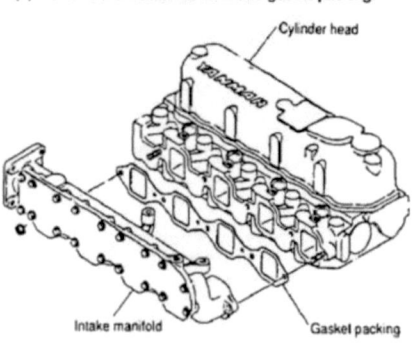

Chapter 10 Disassembly and Reassembly
3. Disassembly and Reassembly   3,4JH3(B)(C)E

3-1.16 Removing the fresh water pump
Remove the fresh witer pump, gasket packira and O-ring.

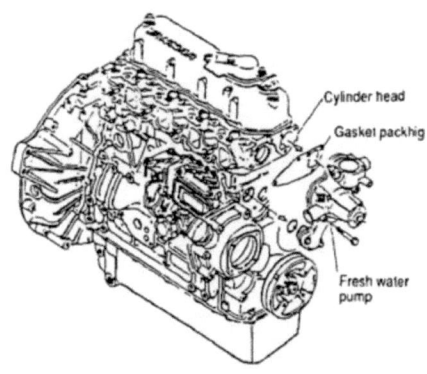

3-1.18 Removing the valve elbow shaft assembly
(1) Remove the valve elbow chamber cover.
(2) Remove the valve elbow shaft support mounting bolts(s), and remove the entire valve elbow shaft assembly.
(3) Pull out the push rods.

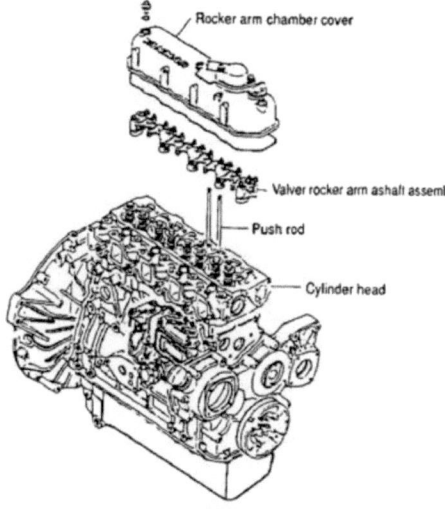

3-1.17 Removing the fuel injection nozzles
Remove the fuel injection nozzle retainer nut, and pull out the fuel injection nozzie retainer and fuel injection nozzle.

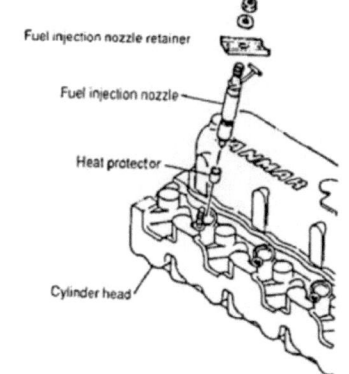

NOTE : If the heat protector stays in the cylinder head, make a note of the cylinder no. and be sure to remove it when you disassemble the cylinder head.

3-1.19 Removing the cylinder head
(1) Remove the cylinder head bolts with a torque wrench, and remove the cylinder head.
(2) Remove the cylinder gasket parking.

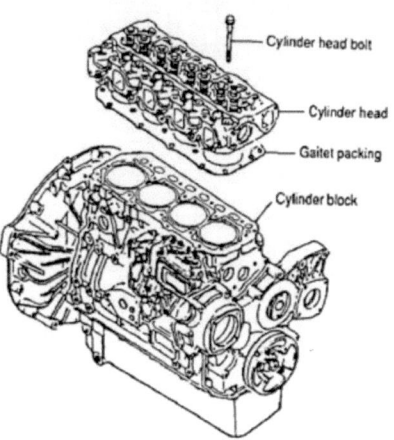

3-1.20 Removing the crankshaft V-pulley

Remove the hex bolts holding the crankshaft V pulley, and remove the crankshaft V-pulley with an extraction tool.

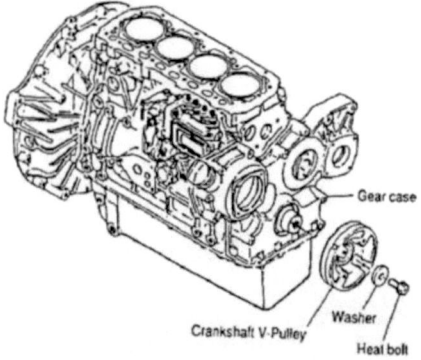

3-1.21 Removing the marine gearbox

(1) Remove the hex bolts from the clutch case flange, and remove the gearbox assembly

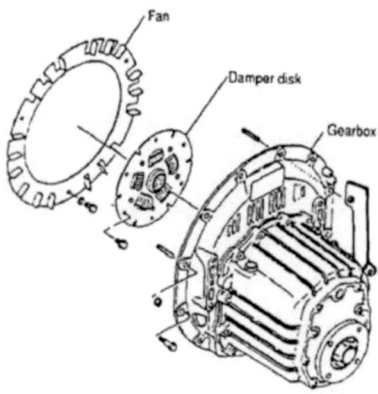

3-1.22 Removing the lube oil cooler

Remove the lube oil cooler from the upper part of the flywheel housing.

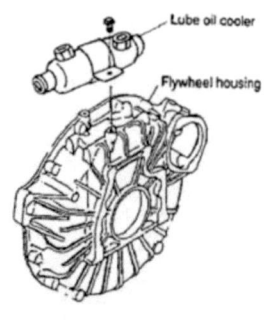

3-1.23 Removing the flywheel

Remove the flywheel mounting bolts and then the flywheel.

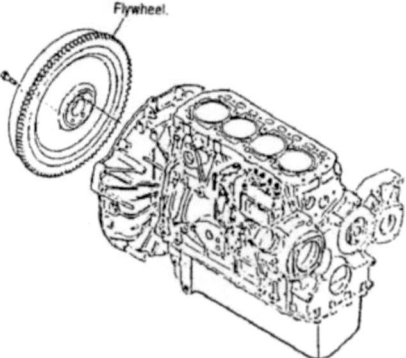

NOTE : Be careful not to scratch the ring gear.

Chapter 10 Disassembly and Reassembly
3. Disassembly and Reassembly _____ 3,4JH3(B)(C)E

3-1.24 Turning the engine over
(1) Place a wood black of appropriate size on the floor, and stand up the engine on the, flywheel housing
(2) Remove the engine mounting feet.

3-1.25 Removing the oil pan
(1) Remove the bracket holding the oil pan and clutch housing
(2) Remove the oil pan and gasket packing.

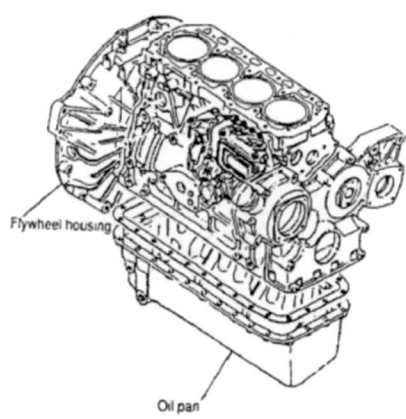

3-1.26 Removing tne lube oil intake pipe
Remove the lube oil intake pipe and gasket packin

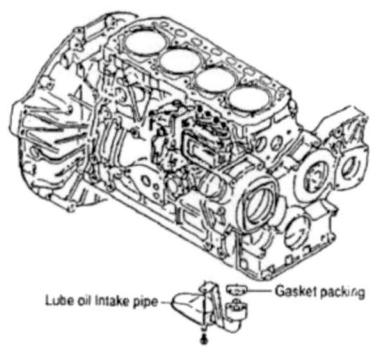

3-1.27 Removing the gear case
Remove the gear case mounting bolts, and remove the gear case from the cylinder block.

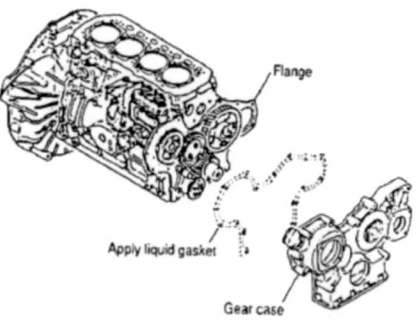

3-1.28 Removing the lube oil pump
Remove the lube oil pump and gasket packing from the gear case flange.

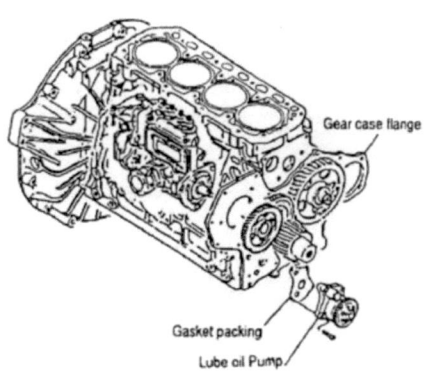

Chapter 10 Disassembly and Reassembly
3. Disassembly and Reassembly
3,4JH3(B)(C)E

3-1.29 Remove the fuel injection pump
(1) Remove the blind plug mounted to the hub of the automatic advancing timer
(2) Remove the box nut, and pull out the fuel oil pump drive gear/automatic advancing timer assembly with an extraction tool.
(3) Remove the fuel injection pump and O-ring from the gear case flange.

3-1.31 Removing the pistons and connecting rods
(1) Remove the connecting rod bolt and the large end cap.
(2) Push the connecting rod from the bottom and pull out the piston connecting rod assembly.

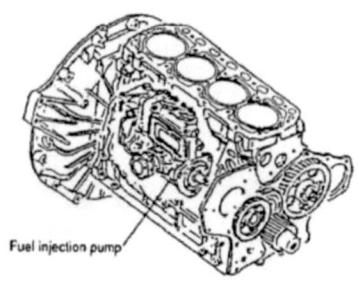

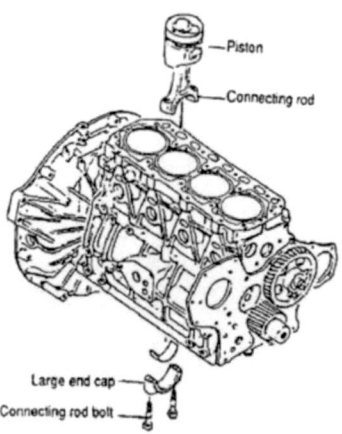

3-1.30 Removing the iding gear
Remove the two hex bolts holding the idling the idling pull out the idling gear and idling shaft.

NOTE : Place a tool against the piston cooling nozzle to make sure the nozzle position does not change and it does not get scratches.

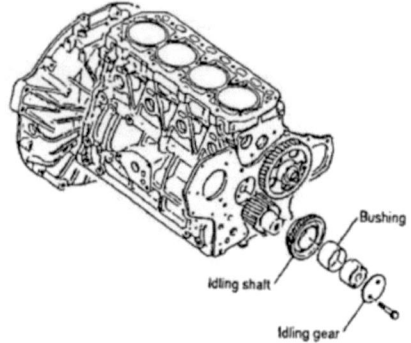

Chapter 10 Disassembly and Reassembly
3. Disassembly and Reassembly   3,4JH3(B)(C)E

3-1.32 Turning the engine over
Place a wood block of suitable size on the floor and turn the engine over, with the cylinder head mounting surface facing down.

NOTE : Make sure that the cylinder head positioning pins on the cylinder block do not come in contact with the wood block.

3-1.33 Removing the flywheel housing
Remove the flywheel housing from the cylinder black.

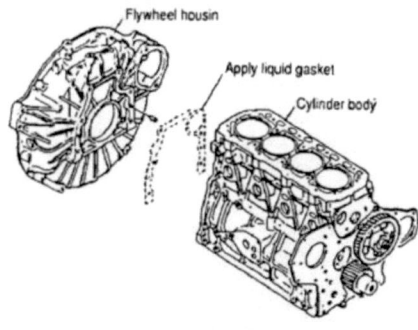

3-1.34 Removing the main bearing.
(1) Remove the main bearing bolts.
(2) Remove the main bearing cap and lower main bearing metal.

NOTE : The thrust metal (lower) is mounted to the standard main bearing cap. Be sure to differentiate between mounting surfaces.

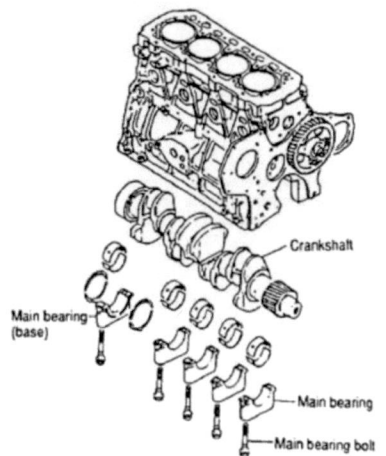

3-1.35 Removing the crankshaft
(1) Remove the crankshaft

NOTE : 1. The thrust metal (upper) is mounted to the standard main bearing. However, in some cases the thrust metal (upper) may be mounted to the crankshaft.
2. Remove the main bearing metal (upper) from the cylinder block.

3-1.36 Removing the camshaft
(1) Loosen the thrust rest mounting bolts out of the holes in the camshaft gear, and remove.
(2) Pull out the camshaft gear and camshaft assembly from the cylinder block.

NOTE : The camshaft gear and camshaft are shrunk fit They must be heated to 180-200℃ to disassemble.

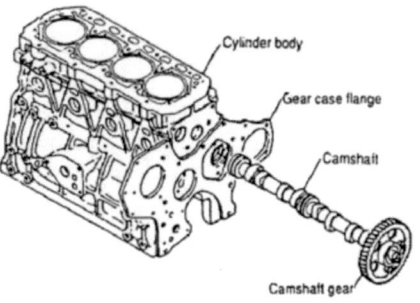

3-1.37 Removing the tappets
Remove the tappets from the tappet holes in the cylinder black

3-1.38 Removing the gear case flange
(1) Remove the gear case flange from the cylinder block.
(2) Remove the two O-rings from the lube oil passage.

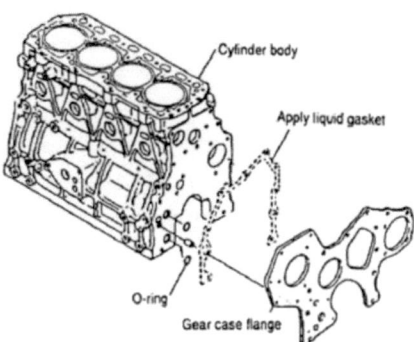

Chapter 10 Disassembly and Reassembly
3. Disassembly and Reassembly

[Precautions when disassembly]
1) Be careful to keep all disassembled parts in order.
2) Clear an adequate area for parts and prepare a container (S).
3) Prepare a cleaner and cleaning can before disassembling start.

3-2 Reassembly
3-2.1 Clean all parts
Clean all parts using by the cloth and diesel (or cleaning agent) before reassembly.

NOTE : 1. If the dust remain with the parts, engine may cause the seizing or damage.
2. The cleaning agent removes even carbon adhering to disassembled parts.

3-2.2 Mounting the gear case flange
Mount the gear case flange, gasket packing and lube oil line O-ring onto the cylinder block.

NOTE : 1. When mounting the gear case flange, match up the two cylinder block pipe knock pins.
2. Be sure to coat the cylinder block lube oil line O-ring with grease when assembling, so that it does not get out of place.

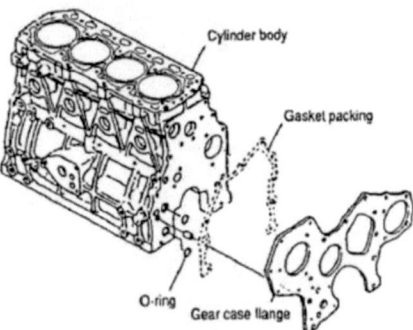

3-2.3 Inserting the tappets
Coat the inside of the cylinder block tappet holes and the outside circumference of the tappets with engine oil, and insert the tappets in the cylinder block.

NOTE : Separate the tappets to make sure that they are reassembled in the same cylinder, intake/exhaust manifold as they came from.

Chapter 10 Disassembly and Reassembly
I. Disassembly and Reassembly Precautions
3,4JH3(B)(C)E

3-2.4 Mounting the camshaft

(1) If the camshaft and camshaft gear have been disassembled, shrink fit the camshaft and camshaft gear [heat the camshaft gear to 180–200°C in the hot oil and press fit].

NOTE : When mounting the camshaft and camshaft gear, be sure not to forget assembly of the thrust rest. Also make sure they are assembled with the correct orientation.

(2) Coat the cylinder block camshaft bearings and camshaft with engine oil, insert the camshaft in the cylinder block, and mount the thrust rest with the bolt.

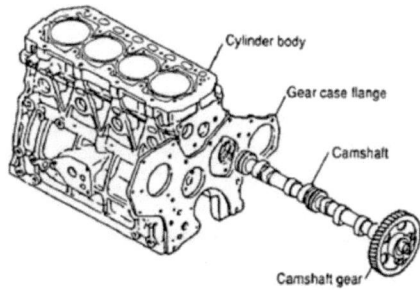

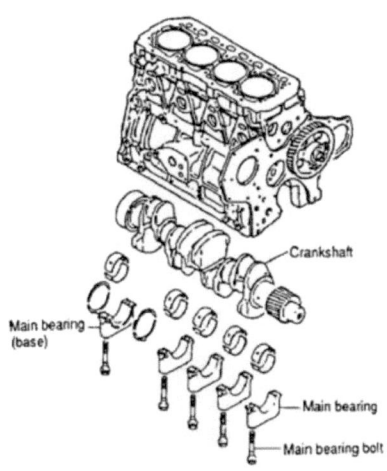

(3) Measure the camshaft side gap.

	mm
Camshaft side gap	0.05~0.20

(4) Make sure that the camshaft rotates smoothly.

3-2.5 Mounting the crankshaft

(1) The crankshaft and crankshaft gear are shrink fitted. If the crankshaft and crankshaft gear have been disassembled, they have to be shrink fitted [heat the crank shaft gear to 180°–200°C in the hot oil and press fit].
(2) Coat the cylinder block crank journal holes and upper part of the main bearing metal with oil and fit the upper main bearing metal onto the cylinder block.

NOTE : 1. Be sure not to confuse the upper and lower main bearing metals. The upper metal has an oil groove.
2. When mounting the thrust metal, fit it so that the surface with the oil groove slit faces outwards, (crankshaft side).

(3) Coat the crank pin and crank journal with engine oil and place them on top of the main bearing metal.

NOTE : 1. Align the crankshaft gear and camshaft gear with the "A" match mark.
2. Position so that the crankshaft gear is on the gear case side.
3. Be careful not to let the thrust metal drop.

3-2.6 Mounting the main bearing metal with engine oil, and mounting the main bearing cap.

NOTE : 1. The lower main bearing metal does not have an oil groove.
2. The standard bearing thrust metal is fitted with the oil groove slit facing outwards.

(1) Coat the main bearing cap bolt washer contact surface and threads with engine oil, place them on the crankshaft journal, and tighten the main bearing bolts to the specified torque.

	kg·m
Main bearing bolt tightening torque	10.5~11.5

NOTE : 1. The main bearing cap should be fitted with the arrow near the embossed letters "FW" on the cap pointing towards the flywheel.
2. Make sure you have the correct cylinder alignment no

(2) Measure the crankshaft side clearance.

	mm
Crankshaft side clearance	0.140~0.220

(3) Make sure that the crankshaft rotates smoothly and easily.

Chapter 10 Disassembly and Reassembly
3. Disassembly and Reassembly

3,4JH3(B)(C)E

3-2.7 Mounting the flywheel housing
(1) Press fit the oil seal in the flywheel housing, and coat the lip of the oil seal with engine oil
(2) mount the flywheel housing and gasket packing. matching them up with the cylinder block positioning pins.

NOTE : Trim the gasket packing if it protrudes onto the oil pan mounting surface.

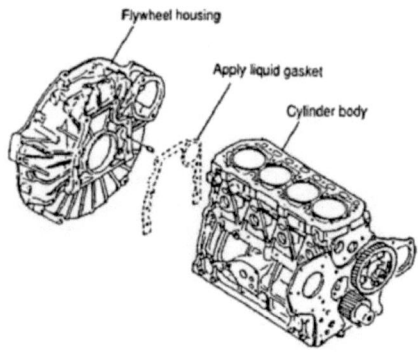

3-2.8 Stand up the cylinder block
On wood blocks, with the flywheel housing facing down. Take care that the gearbox mounting surface does not get scratched.

3-2.9 Mounting the piston and connecting rod
(1) Reassemble the piston and connecting rod.

NOTE : When reassembling the piston and connecting rod, make sure that the parts are assembled with the correct orientation.

(2) Each ring opening (piston/oil rings) should be staggered at gaps of 120°.

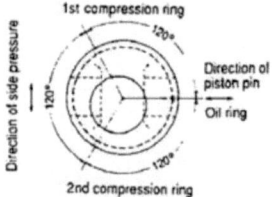

(3) Coat the outside of the piston and the inside of the connecting rod crank pin metal with engine oil and insert the piston with the piston insertion tool.

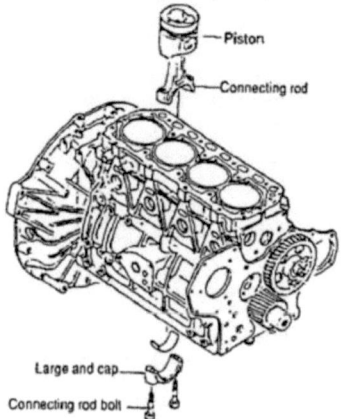

Chapter 10 Disassembly and Reassembly
3. Disassembly and Reassembly
3,4JH3(B)(C)E

NOTE : 1. Insert the piston so that the match mark on the large end of the connecting rod faces the fuel feed pump, and the manufactuers mark on the stem points toward the flywheel
2. After inserting the piston, make sure the combustion chamber hollow is facing the fuel feed pump, looking from the top of the piston.

(4) Align the large end match mark, mount the cap, and tighten the connecting rod bolts.

kg·m

Connecting rod bolt tightening torque	5.0~5.5

NOTE : If a torque wrench is not available, match up with the mark made before disassembly.

3-2.10 Mounting the idling gear
(1) Fit the idling gear so that the side of the idling shaft with two oil holes faces up.
(2) Align the "A" and "C" camshaft gear and crankshaft gear match marks, match up with idling shaft retaining plate, and tighten the bolts.
(3) Measure the idling gear, camshaft gear and crankshaft gear backlash.

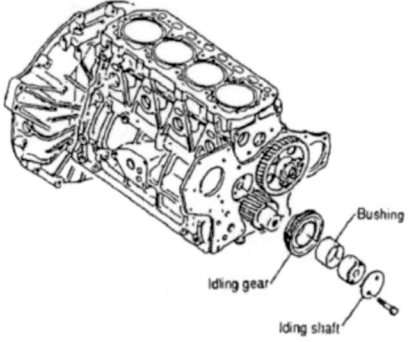

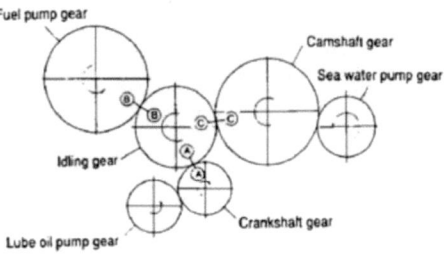

Looking from gear case side

3-2.11 Mounting the fuel injection pump
Lightly fit the fuel injection pump on the gear case.

NOTE : 1. Be careful not to scratch the O-ring between the fuel injection pump and gear case flange.
2. Tighten the fuel injection pump all the way after adjusting injection timing.

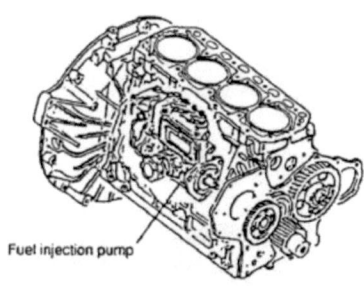

Fuel injection pump

3-2.12 Mounting the fuel feed pump drive gear and automatic advancing timer.
(1) When the drive gear and automatic advancing time have been disassembled, coat all sliding parts in bot assemblies with grease.
(2) Align the "B" match marks on the fuel pump drive gea and idling gear.
(3) Tighten all box nuts holding the fuel feed pump to the specified torque.

kg·m

Box nut tightening torque	6~7

(4) Grease parts around the box nuts (lithium grease) ar tighten the blind plug.
(5) Measure the backlash of the fuel feed pump drive gear.

3-2.13 Mounting the lube oil pump
(1) Mount the lube oil pump on the gear case flange.
(2) Measure the backlash of the lube oil pump drive gear.

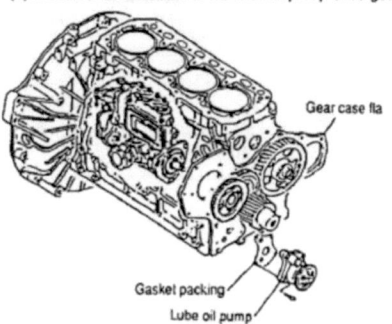

Printed in Japan
HINSHI-H8009

3-2.14 Mounting the gear case
(1) Coat the inside and outside of the oil seals with engine oil and press fit them into the gear case.
(2) Position the two pipe knock pins and tighten the bolts holding the gear case and gasket packing.

NOTE : Trim the gasket packing if it protrudes onto the oil pan mounting surface.

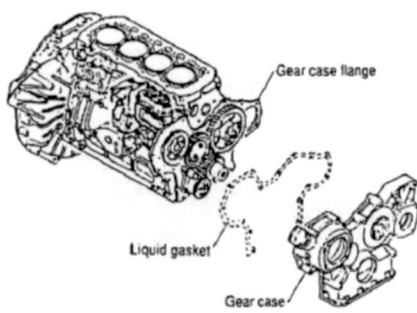

3-2.15 Mounting the lube oil intake pipe
Mount the lube oil intake pipe on the bottom of the cylinder block, using new packing.

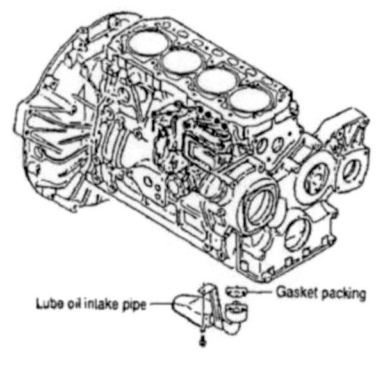

	kg·m
lube oil intake pipe tightening torque	2.6

3-2.16 Mounting the oil pan
(1) Coat with three bond (3B-1114) the surfaces of the gear case, gear case flange and flywheel that contact with the cylinder block
(2) Tighten the gasket packing/oil pan bolts.
(3) Mount the bracket that connects the flywheel with the oil pan.

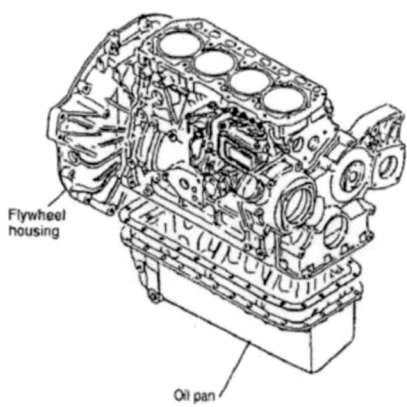

3-2.17 Mounting the engine mounting feet and turning the engine upright.
Place suitable wood blocks below the oil pan and turn the engine upright.

3-2.18 Mounting the flywheel
(1) Coat the flywheel mounting bolt threads with engine oil.
(2) Align the positioning pins, and tighten the flywheel bolts to the specified torque.

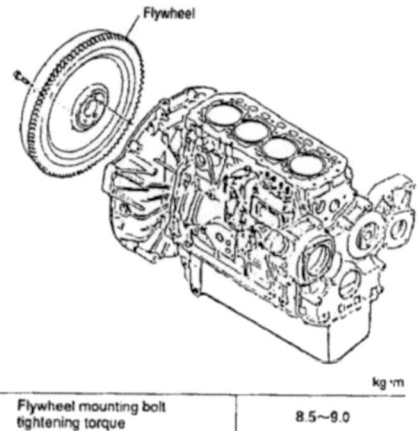

	kg·m
Flywheel mounting bolt tightening torque	8.5~9.0

Chapter 10 Disassembly and Reassembly
3. Disassembly and Reassembly

3-2.19 Mounting the marine gearbox
(1) Mount the fan and damper disk to the flywheel.
(2) Align the damper disk with the input shaft spline and insert Tighten the flywheel housing and flange.

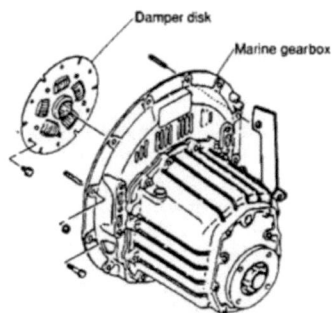

3-2.20 Mounting the crank V-pulley
(1) Coat the oil seal and the section of the shaft with which it comes in contact with oil.
(2) Make sure to wipe off oil on the taper surface.
(3) Tighten to the specfied torque.

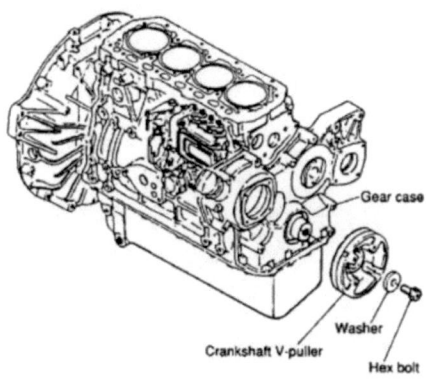

	kg·m
V-pulley tightening torque	11.5~12.5 ※
	8.5~9.5 ※※

※ For 4JH3(B)(C)E and for P·T·O V-pulley (optional) of 3JH3(B)(C)E (Material: steel).

※※ For 3JH3(B)(C)E (Material: casting iron).

3-2.21 Mounting the cylinder head
(1) Fit the Qasket packing against the cylinder block, aligning it with the cylinder block posihoning pins.

NOTE : The side on which the engine model is inscribed should face up (cylinder head side).

(2) Lift the cylinder head hoizomtally and mount aligning with the cylinder head gaskeL
(3) Coat the mounting bolt washers and threads with engine oil, and lightly tighten the bolts in the specified order Then tighten completely, in the same order.

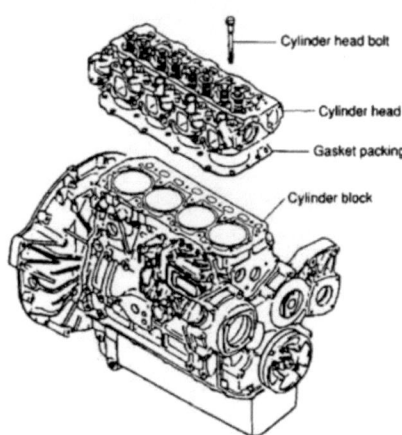

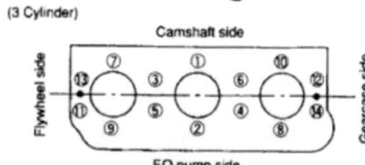

	Partial	Complete	kg·m
Cylinder bolt tightening torque	4.0~5.0	9.0~9.6	

(4) Measure the top clearance

	mm
top clearance	0.74

3-2.22 Mounting the valve rocker arm shaft assembly pushrod

(1) Fit the pushrod to the tippet.
(2) hlount the valve rxker arm shaft assembly.

	kg·m
Valve rocker arm shaft support tightening torque	2.4~2.8

(3) Adjust valve clesrance.

3-2.23 Mounting the fuel injetion nozzle

(1) Mount the injection nozzle tip heat protectar, and then the fuel injection nozzle.

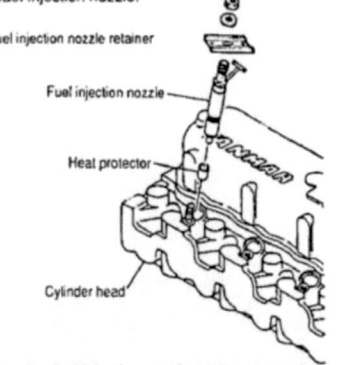

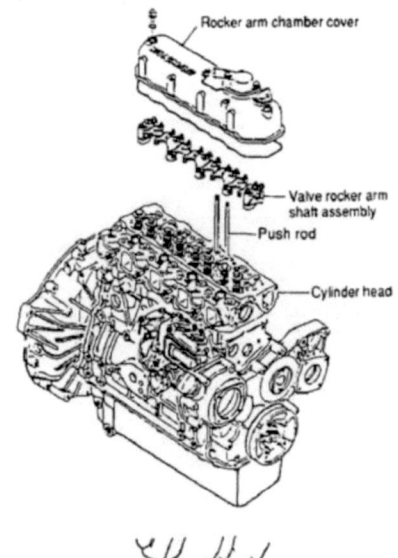

(2) Tighten the fuel injection nozzle retainer nut to the specified torque.

	kg·m
Fuel injection nozzle retainer tightening torque	0.7~0.9

3-2.24 Mounting the fresh water pump

(1) Thoroughly coat both sides of tlbe packing with adhesive.
(2) Replace the O-rirg for the connecting pipe which is inserted in the cylinder block, and tighten the fresh water pump to the specified torque.

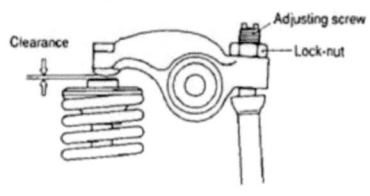

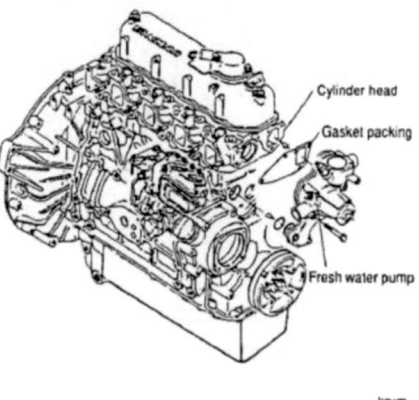

	mm
Intake/discharge valve clearance	0.2

	kg·m
Fresh water pump tightening torque	0.7~1.1

(4) Coat the valve rocker arm and valve spring with engine oil and mount lhe valve rocker arm chamber cover.

Chapter 10 Disassembly and Reassembly
3. Disassembly and Reassembly

3-2.25 Mounting the intake manifold
(1) Thoroughly clean the inside of the intake manifold, and mount the gasket packing and intake manifold.
(2) Mount the governor remote control bracket.

3-2.27 Mounting the lube oil cooler
Mount the lube oil cooler to the top of the flywheel housing with the bracket.

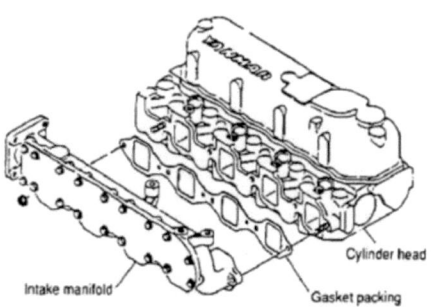

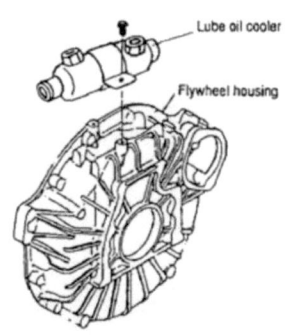

3-2.26 Mounting the high pressure fuel pipe and fuel oil return pipe
(1) Mount the high pressure fuel pipe and then the high pressure fuel pipe vibration stop.

NOTE : Lightly tighten the box nuts on both ends of the high pressure fuel pipe. Completely tighten after adjusting the injection timing.

(2) Mount the fuel oil return pipe with the hose clamp (fuel injection nozzle-fuel injection pump).

3-2.28 Mounting the lube oil filter
(1) Mount the filter bracket and packing on the cylinder block.
(2) Mount the filter element with the filter remover mounting tool.

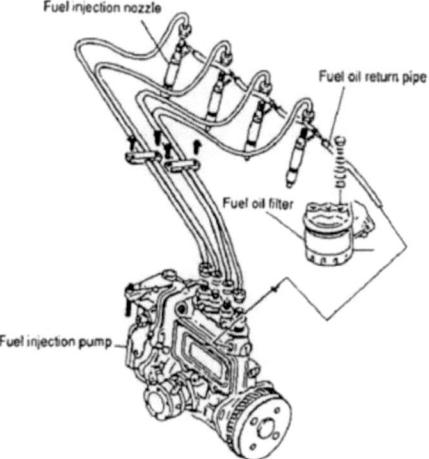

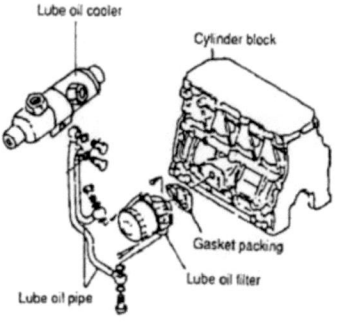

Chapter 10 Disassembly and Reassembly
3. Disassembly and Reassembly

3,4JH3(B)(C)E

3-2.29 Mounting the lube oil pipe
(1) Mount the lube Oil pipe (filter-lube oil cooler, lube oil cooler-filter).
(2) Mount the lube oil pipe (cylinder block-fuel injection pump).

3-2.30 Mounting the dipstick guide
Mount the dipstick and dipstick guide.

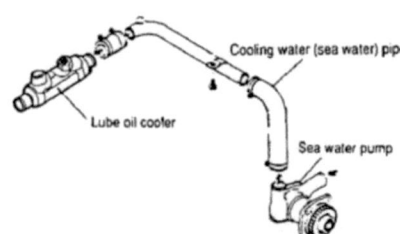

3-2.33 Mounting the heal exchanger (exhaust martifotd, fresh water tank urdt).
Mount the gasket packing and exhaust manifold.

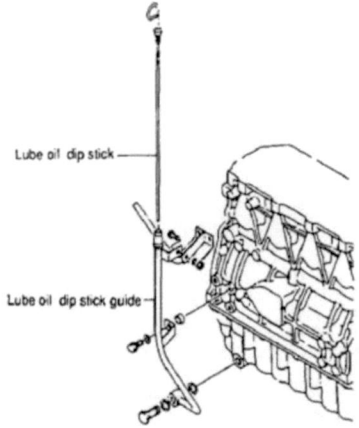

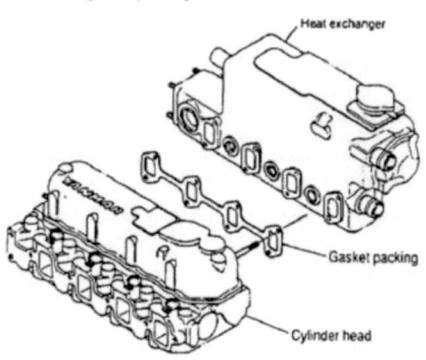

3-2.31 Mounting the sea water pump
(1) Mount the sea water pump assembly to the gear case flange.
(2) Lightly tap the gear case side bearing rest with a wood hammer, and tighten the mounting bolts.

3-2.34 Mounting the cooling water pipe
(1) Mount the cooliirg fresh water pipe with the hose clamp (fresh water tank—fresh water pump, fresh water pump heat excharger).
(2) Mount the cooling sea water pipe with tbe hose clamp (lube oil cooler—heat exchanger).
(3) Mount the cooling sea water pipe with the hose clamp (lube oil cooler—marine gearbox).

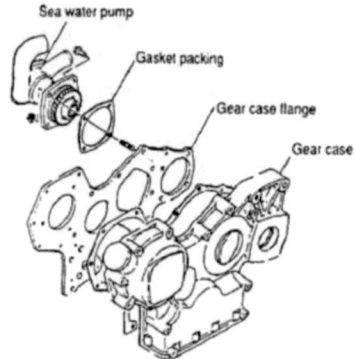

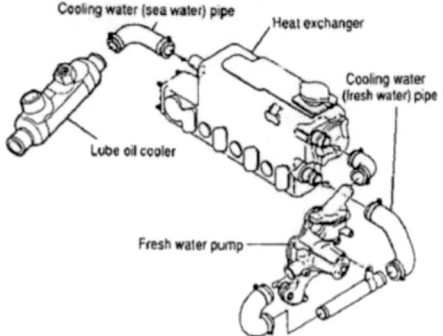

3-2.32 Mounting the cooling sea water pipe
Mount the cooling water pipe with the hose clamp (sea water pump-lube oil cooler).

10—31

Chapter 10 Disassembly and Reassembly
3. Disassembly and Reassembly

3,4JH3(B)(C)E

3-2.35 Mounting the alternator
(1) Mount the adjuster on the fresh water pump, the distance piece on the gearcase, and then the alternator.
(2) Adjust V-belt tension with the adjuster, and tighten the mounting bolts.

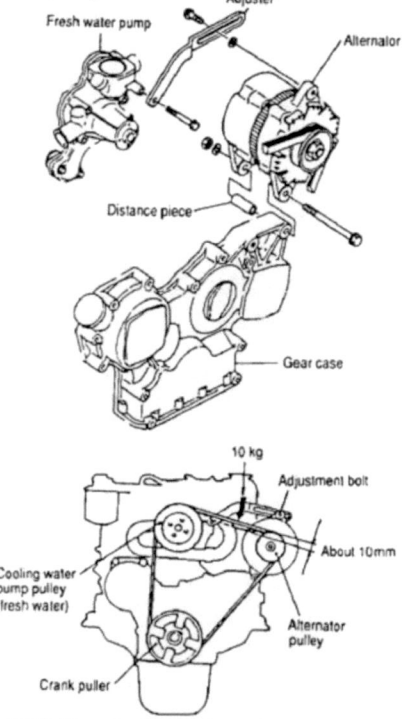

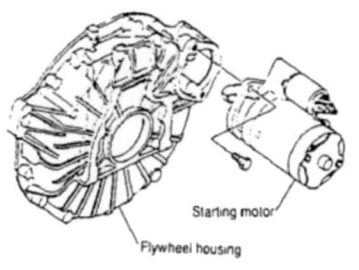

3-2.36 Mounting the starting motor
Fit the starting motor in the flywheel housing.

3-2.37 Mounting the mixing elbow
(1) Mount the mixing elbow on the exhaust manifold outlet.
(2) Mount the cooling sea water pipe rubber hose with the hose grip (heat exchanger-mixing elbow).

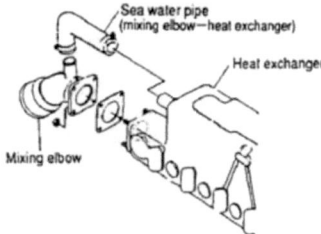

3-2.38 Mounting the intake silencer
(1) Mount the intake silencer on the intake manifold inlet coupling for model 4JHE and on the turbocharger blower side for model 4JH-TE.
(2) Mount the breather hose with the hoe clamp (intake silencer—valve rocker arm chamber cover).

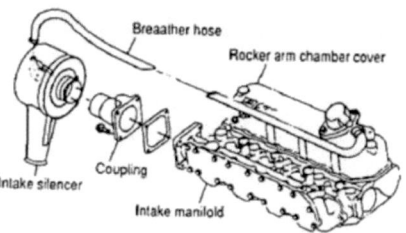

3-2.39 Mounting the fuel filter and fuel oil pipe
(1) Mount the fuel filter.
(2) Mount the fuel oil pipe (fuel feed pump-fuel filter, fuel filter-fuel injection pump).

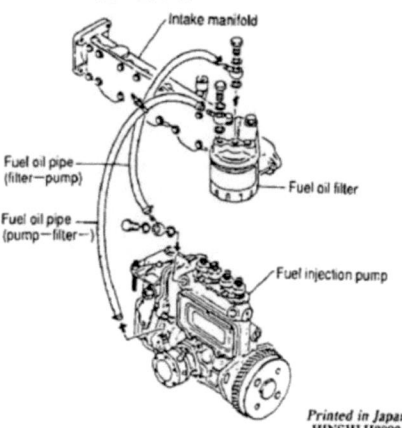

10-32

Printed in Japan
HINSHI-H8009

3-2.40 Electrical Wiring

Connect the wiring to the proper terminals, observing the color coding to make sure the connections are correct.

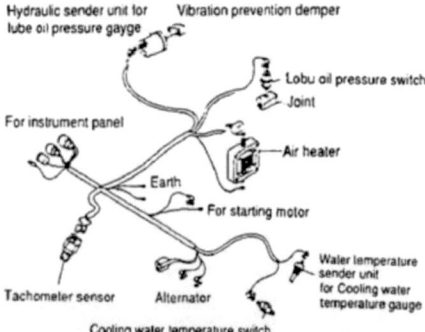

3-2.41 Installation in the ship and completion of the piping and wiring

Mount the engine in the ship after all engine assembly has been completed. Connect the cooling water, fuel oil and other piping on the ship and the exhaust hoses. Connect the battery, Instrument panel, remote control and other wiring.

3-2.42 Filling with lube oil

Fill the engine with lube oil from the supply port on top of the gear case and the marine gearbox supply port on top of the clutch case.

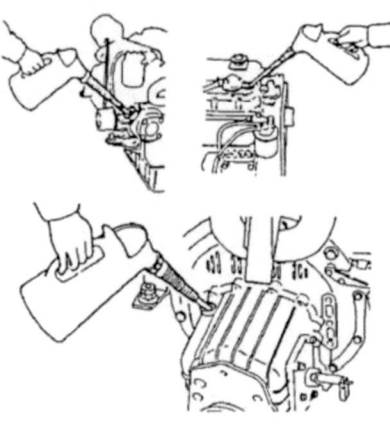

3-2.43 Filling with cooling water

(1) Open the fressh water tank cap and fill with water.

Fresh water tank capacity	6.0

(ℓ)

(2) Fill with water until the level in the sub-tank is between the full and low marks.

(ℓ)

Sub-tank capacity	Full
	0.45

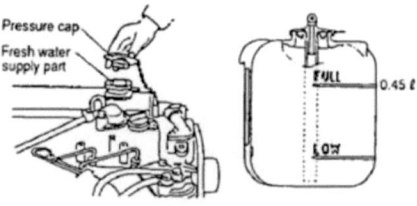

3-2.44 Check fuel injection timing

(1) Open the fuel tank cock and shift the fuel feed pump priming lever for air bleeding.

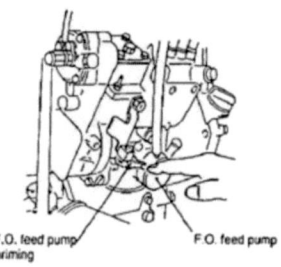

(2) Check injection timing by turning the flywheel and looking through the inspection hole in the flywheel housing.

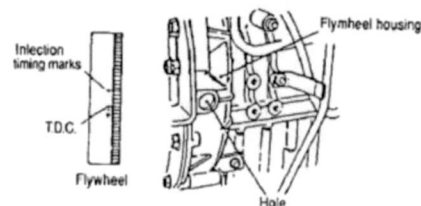

Chapter 10 Disassembly and Reassembly
1. Disassembly and Reassembly Precautions

(3) If injection timing is off, change the mounting position using the long hole in the injection pump mounting flange. Turning the fuel feed pump towards the cylinder block slows timing down, while movement in the other direction makes it faster.

Fuel injection timing (FID)	b.TDC12°±1°

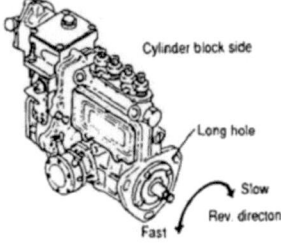

4. Table of Standard Measurements for Maintenance

4-1 Cylinder head

Item		Model	3JH3(B)(C)E	4JH3(B)(C)E	Limit
			Standard		
Distortion of combustion surface			0.05 or less than		0.15
Valve seat angle	Intake		120°		—
	Exhaust		90°		—
Width of valve seat	Intake		1.07~1.24		1.74
	Exhaust		1.24~1.45		1.94
Intake valve	Outer dia. of stem		7.960~7.975		7.9
	Guide inner dia.		8.010~8.025		8.1
	Oil clearance		0.035~0.065		0.2
Exhaust valve	Outer dia. of stem		7.955~7.970		7.9
	Guide inner dia.		8.015~8.030		8.1
	Oil clearance		0.045~0.075		0.2
Amount of valve guide spray			15		—
Amount of intake/ exhaust valve sinking	Intake valve		0.306~0.506		1.0
	Exhaust valve		0.3~0.5		
Thickness of valve umbrella	Intake valve		1.244~1.444		0.5
	Exhaust valve		1.35~1.55		
Intake valve timing	Open	b.T.D.C	6°~20°	10°~20°	—
	Close	a.T.D.C	40°~50°	48°~58°	
Exhaust valve timing	Open	b.B.D.C	51°~60°	51°~61°	
	Close	a.T.D.C	13°~23°	13°~23°	
Valve spring	Free length		44.4		—
	Distortion		—		1.1
	Tensile strength(kg) (1mm under pressure)		2.71(Axonometric pitch) / 3.61		—
Intake/Exhaust valve clearance			0.15~0.25		—

4-2 Cylinder block

(mm)

Item		Model	3JH3(B)(C)E	4JH3(B)(C)E	
			Standard		Limit
Cylinder inner dia			84.000~84.030		84.20
Cylinder inner dia	L mark		84.020~84.030		
	M mark		84.010~84.020		
	S mark		84.000~84.010		
Cylinder circle degree			0.00~0.01		0.03
Cylinder cylindrical degree					0.00~0.01

4-3 Valve equipment

(mm)

Item		Model	3JH3(B)(C)E	4JH3(B)(C)E	
			Standard		Limit
Intake/Exhaust valve arm	Valve arm bearing outer dia.		15.966~15.984		15.95
	Valve arm inner dia.		16.000~16.010		16.09
	Oil clearance		0.016~0.054		0.14
Distortion of push rod			0.03 or lower		—
Tappet	Tappet outer dia.		11.975~11.990		11.93
	Tappet hole inner dia.		12.000~12.018		12.05
	Oil clearance		0.010~0.043		0.12

4-4 Piston

(mm)

Item		Model	3JH3(B)(C)E	4JH3(B)(C)E	Limit
			Standard		
Piston outer dia.			83.945~83.975		
Piston outer dia.	L mark		83.965~83.975		83.90
	ML mark		83.960~83.965		
	MS mark		83.955~83.960		
	S mark		83.945~83.955		
Minimum gap between pistons and cylinders			0.040~0.070		—
Top clearance			0.660~0.780		—
Piston and Piston pin	Piston pin outer dia.		25.987~26.000		25.90
	Piston pin hole inner dia.		26.000~26.009		26.02
	Oil clearance		0.000~0.022		0.12

4-5 Piston ring

(mm)

Item		Model	3JH3(B)(C)E	4JH3(B)(C)E	Limit
			Standard		
Top ring	Ring groove width		2.065~2.080		—
	B measurements		1.970~1.990		—
	Minimum gap between groove and ring		0.075~0.110		—
	Clearance		0.200~0.400		1.5
Second ring	Ring groove width		2.035~2.050		—
	B measurements		1.970~1.990		—
	Minimum gap between groove and ring		0.045~0.080		—
	Clearance		0.200~0.400		1.5
Oil ring	Ring groove width		4.015~4.030		—
	B measurements		3.970~3.990		—
	Minimum gap between groove and ring		0.025~0.060		—
	Clearance		0.200~0.450		1.5

Chapter 10 Disassembly and Reassembly
4. Table of Standard Measurements for Maintenance — 3,4JH3(B)(C)E

4-6 Connecting rod
(mm)

Item		Model	3JH3(B)(C)E	4JH3(B)(C)E	
			Standard		Limit
Large end hole	Large end inner dia.		51.000~51.010		—
	Crank pin metal thickness		1.492~1.500		—
	Crank pin outer dia.		47.952~47.962		47.91
	Oil clearance		0.038~0.074		0.16
Small end hole	Small end hole inner dia.		26.025~26.038		26.10
	Piston pin outer dia.		25.987~26.000		25.90
	Oil clearance		0.025~0.051		0.2
Distortion and parallelism			0.05 or lower for 100 mm		0.08

4-7 Cam shaft
(mm)

Item		Model	3JH3(B)(C)E	4JH3(B)(C)E	
			Standard		Limit
Gear side	Cam shaft outer dia.		44.925~44.950		44.85
	Oil clearance		0.040~0.130		—
Middle	Cam shaft outer dia.		44.910~44.935		44.85
	Oil clearance		0.065~0.115		—
Flywheel side	Cam shaft outer dia.		44.925~44.950		44.85
	Oil clearance		0.050~0.100		—

4-8 Crank shaft
(mm)

Item		Model	3JH3(B)(C)E	4JH3(B)(C)E	
			Standard		Limit
Journal	Crank shaft		49.952~49.962		49.91
	Thickness of metal		1.995~2.010		—
	Oil clearance		0.038~0.068		0.15
Distortion			0.02 or lower		—

Chapter 10 Disassembly and Reassembly
4. Table of Standard Measurements for Maintenance

3,4JH3(B)(C)E

4-9 Side clearance and backlash
(mm)

Item	Model	3JH3(B)(C)E	4JH3(B)(C)E
		Standard	
Side clearance	Crank shaft	0.140~0.220	
	Cam shaft	0.05~0.20	
	Connecting rod	0.2~0.4	
	Idle gear	0.1~0.3	

(mm)

Item	Model	3JH3(B)(C)E	4JH3(B)(C)E
		Standard	
Backlash	Crank gear, Cam gear, Idle gear, Fuel injection pump drive gear	0.07~0.15	
	Lube oil pump gear	0.11~0.19	

4-10 Miscellaneous

Item		Model		3JH3(B)(C)E	4JH3(B)(C)E
				Standard	
Delivery of lube oil pump	High speed		ℓ/min	19.0 (at 3000rpm)	
	Low speed			8.0 (at 800rpm)	
Open valve pressure for oil pressure adjustment valve			kgf/cm²	3.5~4.5	
Operation pressure for oil pressure switch			kgf/cm²	0.1~0.3	
Sea water pump			ℓ/min	60 (at 3800rpm)	
Delivery of fresh water pump			ℓ/min	70 (at 3800rpm)	
Thermostat valve open temp.	Valve open temp		℃	75~78	
	Fully open list		mm	8.0 or more (at 90℃)	
Thermostat switch operation temperature	ON		℃	97~103	
	OFF			87 or more	

5. Tightening torque

5-1 Main Bolt and Nut

(kgf-m)

No.	Name	Torque / Model	3JH3(B)(C)E · 4JH3(B)(C)E
1	Head bolt	Coat with lube oil (Screw dia. × pitch)	9.0~9.6 (M10×1.25)
2	Rod bolt	Coat with lube oil (Screw dia. × pitch)	5.0~5.5 (M9×1.0)
3	Flywheel retainer bolt	Coat with lube oil (Screw dia. × pitch)	8.5~9.0 (M10×1.25)
4	Metal cap retainer bolt	Coat with lube oil (Screw dia. × pitch)	9.8~10.2 (M12×1.5)
5	Crank V-pulley fastening bolt	Coat with lube oil (Screw dia. × pitch)	11.5~12.5 (M14×1.5) ※ 8.5~ 9.5 (M14×1.5) ※※
6	Nozzle fastening nut	No lube oil (Screw dia. × pitch)	0.7~0.9 (M6×1.0)
7	Timer fastening nut	No lube oil (Screw dia. × pitch)	6.0~7.0 (M12×1.75)

※ For 4JH3(B)(C)E and for P·T·O V-pulley (optional) of 3JH3(B)(C)E (Material: steel).
※※ For 3JH3(B)(C)E (Material: casting iron).

5-2 Standard Bolts and Nuts (without lubricant)

(kgf-m)

Name	Screw dia. × pitch	Tightening torque	Remarks
Hexagon bolt t (7T) and nut	M6 × 1	1.0~1.2	1) When bolting the aluminum parts, tighten the bolts with 80% of the tightening torque specified in the Table. 2) 4T bolt and lock nut should be tightened with 60% of the torque shown in the table.
	M8 × 1.25	2.3~2.9	
	M10 × 1.5	4.5~5.5	
	M12 × 1.75	8.0~10.0	
PT plug	1/8	1.0	
	1/4	2.0	
	3/8	3.0	
	1/2	6.0	
Pipe joint bolt	M8	1.3~1.7	
	M12	2.5~3.5	
	M14	4.0~5.0	
	M16	5.0~5.5	

6. Test running

6-1 Preliminary Precautions

Before making a test run, make sure of the following points.
(1) Warm the engine up.
(2) Remove any precipitation from the F.O. filter, water separator, and F.O tank.
(3) Use only lube oil recommended by Yanmar.
(4) Be sure to add Yanmar anti-rust agent to fresh cooling water.
(5) During cold weather, add Yanmar anti-freeze to the cooling water.
(6) Provide good ventilation in the engine room.

5-2 Check Points and Precautions During Running

Step	Item	Instructions	Precautions
1	Checks before operation	1) Make sure that the Kingston Cock is open. 2) Make sure there is enough lube oil and (fresh) cooling water 3) Operate the remote control handle and check if the devices connected to the engine side work property	3) Lamp should go off when engine is running.
2	No load operation : warm up operation	1) When the lube oil temperature is raised to allow the engine to start, the pilot lamp goes off. 2) When the engine is started, check the following: • there is no water and no oil leakage. • gas does not leak when the engine is started. • there are no abnormal indications on the instrument panel. • there is no abnormality in cooling water discharge, engine vibrations, or engine sounds. 3) To warm up the engine, operate at low revolutions for about 5 minutes, then raise the revolutions to the rated rpms and then to max. rpms.	2) • Fit leaks if any. • Check the intake/exhaust valves, FO. injection valve. and cylinder head. 3) Do not raise the engine revolutions abruptly.
3	Cruising (load) operation	1) Do not operate the engine at full load yet, but raise the rpms gradually for about 10 minutes until they reach rated rpms. 2) Make sure that exhaust color and temperature are normal. 3) Check the instrument panel and see if the water temperature and oil pressure are normal.	
4	Stopping the engine	1) Before stopping the engine, operate it at 650-700 rpms for about 5 minutes. 2) Raise engine rpms to 1,800 just before stopping the engine and idle the engine for about 3-4 seconds.	1) Stopping the engine suddenly during high speed operation increases the temperature of engine parts. 2) This procedure prevents carbon from being deposited on the valve seats, etc.
5	Checks after stopping the engine	1) Check again for water and oil leaks. 2) Make sure that no nuts and bolts are loose. 3) Close the Kingston and fuel cocks. 4) When the temperature is expected to fall below freezing, drain the cooling water (sea water). 5) Turn off the battery switch.	1) Check the oil seal area. 2) Especially the engine installation bolts. 4) Drain from the sea water pump.

CHAPTER 11
TROUBLESHOOTING

1. Troubleshooting ·· 11-1

Printed in Japan
HINSHI-H8009

1. Troubleshooting

It is important to thoroughly understand each system and the function of all of the parts of these systems. A careful study of the engine mechanism will make this possible. When problems arise, it is important to carefully observe and analyze the indications of trouble in order to save time in determining their cause. Begin by checking the most easily identifiable causes of difficulty. Where the cause of the difficulty is not readily apparent, make a thorough examination of the system from the very beginning, proceeding until the point of trouble can be determined. While experience is an important factor in pinpointing engine problems, careful study and understanding of the engine mechanism combined with good common sense will help you to rapidly become more expert at troubleshooting.

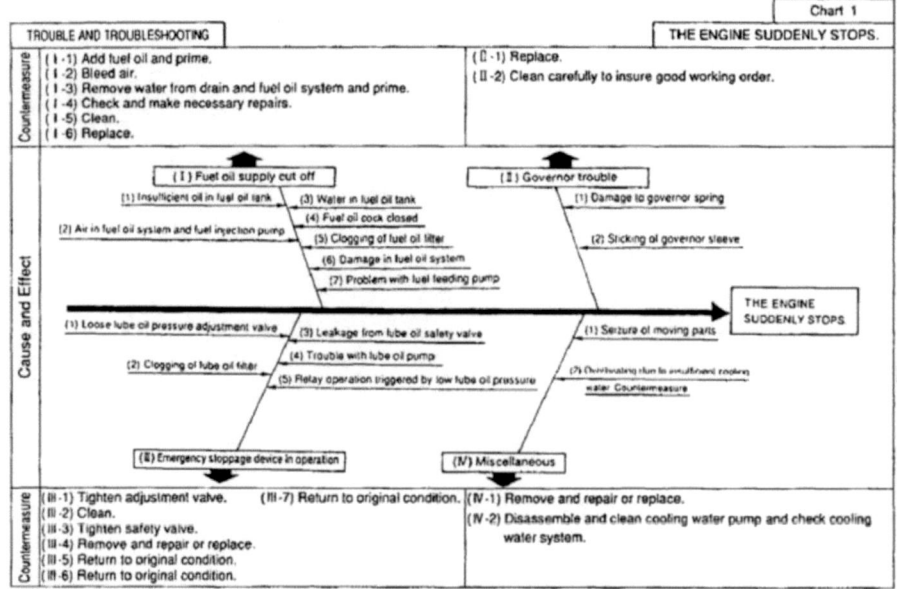

Chart 1 — THE ENGINE SUDDENLY STOPS.

Chapter 11 Troubleshooting
1. Troubleshooting

3,4JH3(B)(C)E

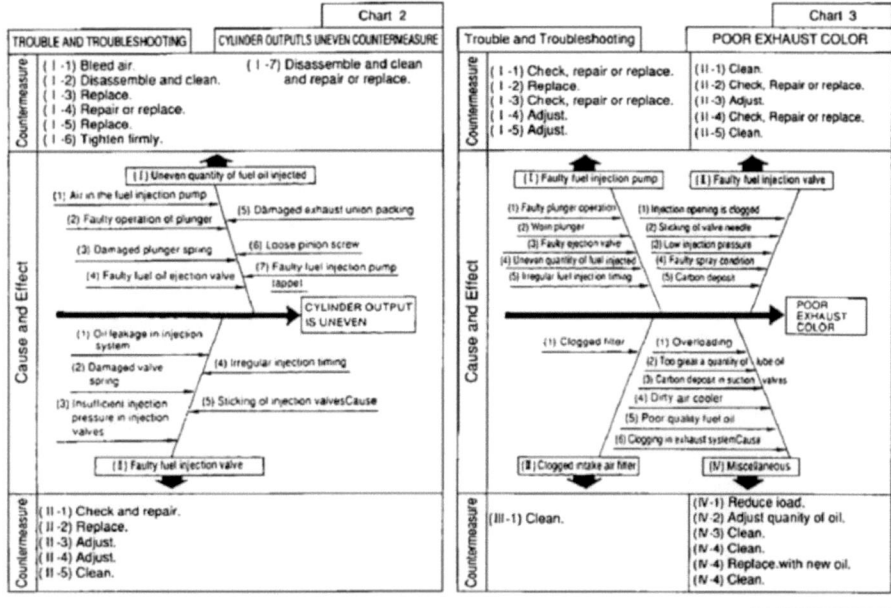

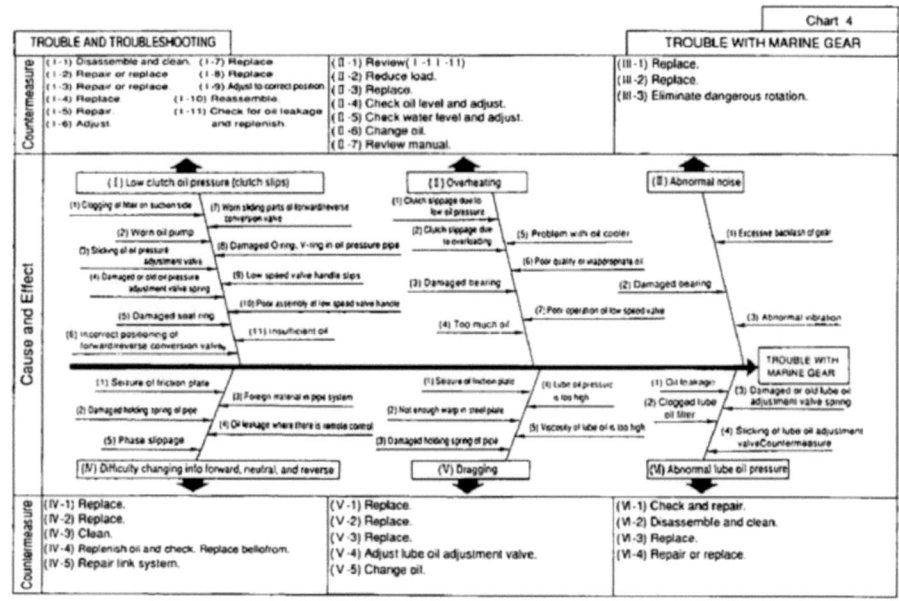

Chapter 11 Troubleshooting
1. Troubleshooting

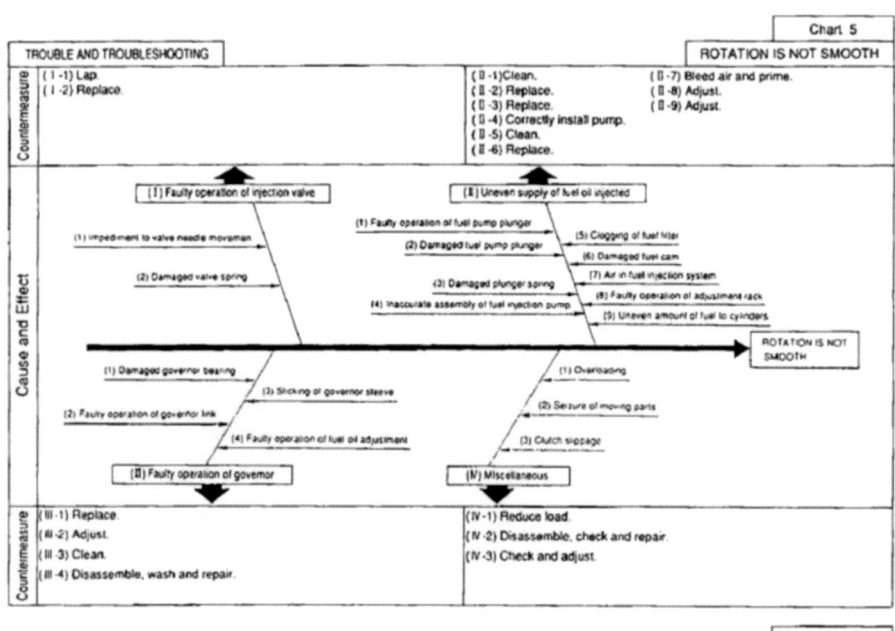

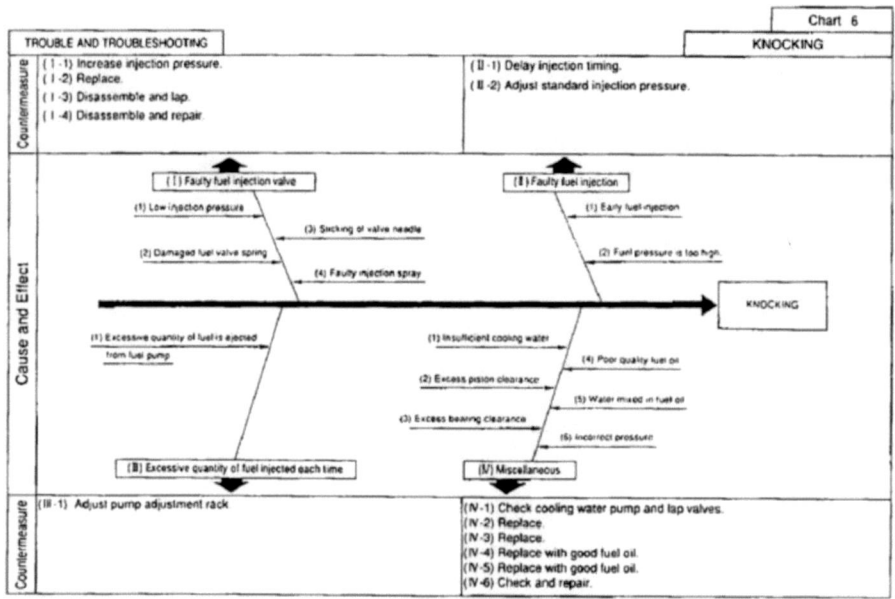

Chapter 11 Troubleshooting
1. Troubleshooting

3,4JH3(B)(C)E

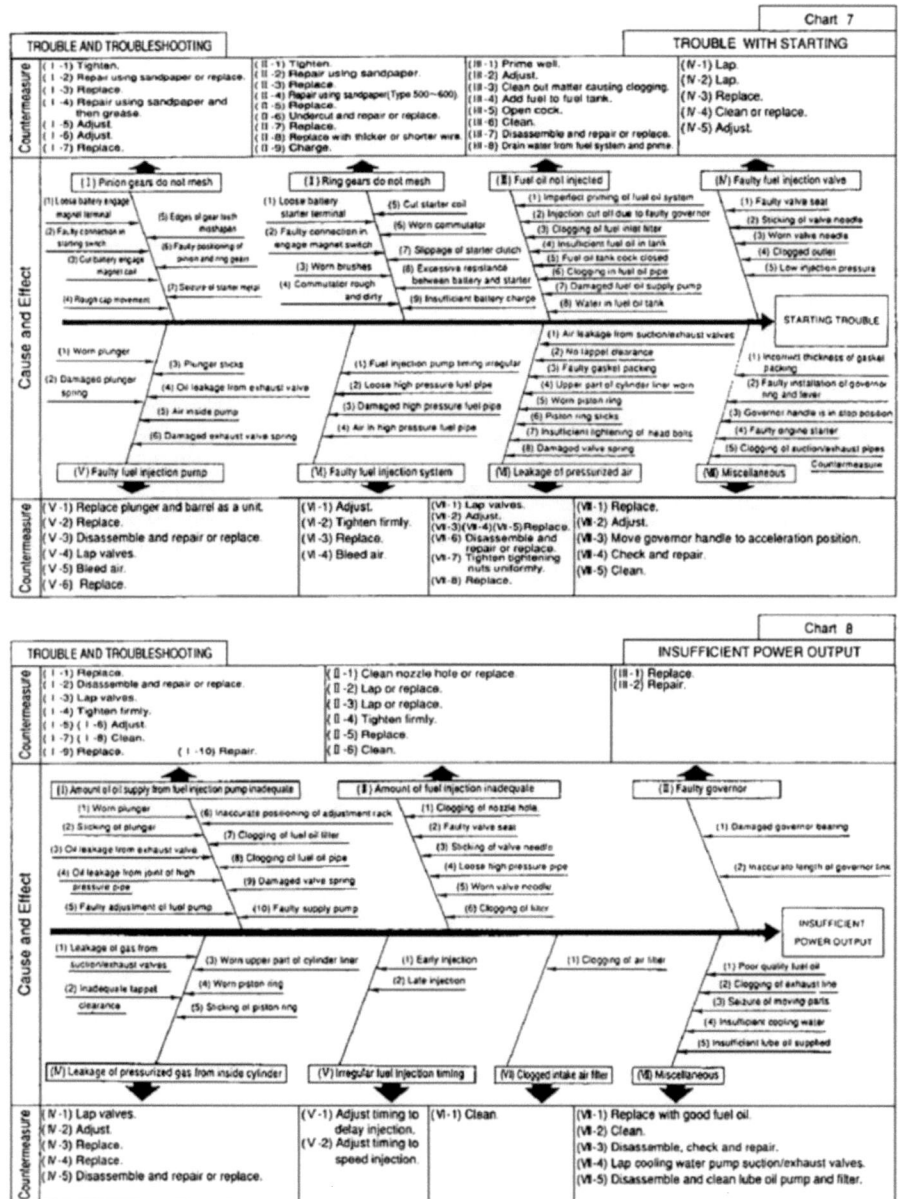

Chapter 11 Troubleshooting
1. Troubleshooting

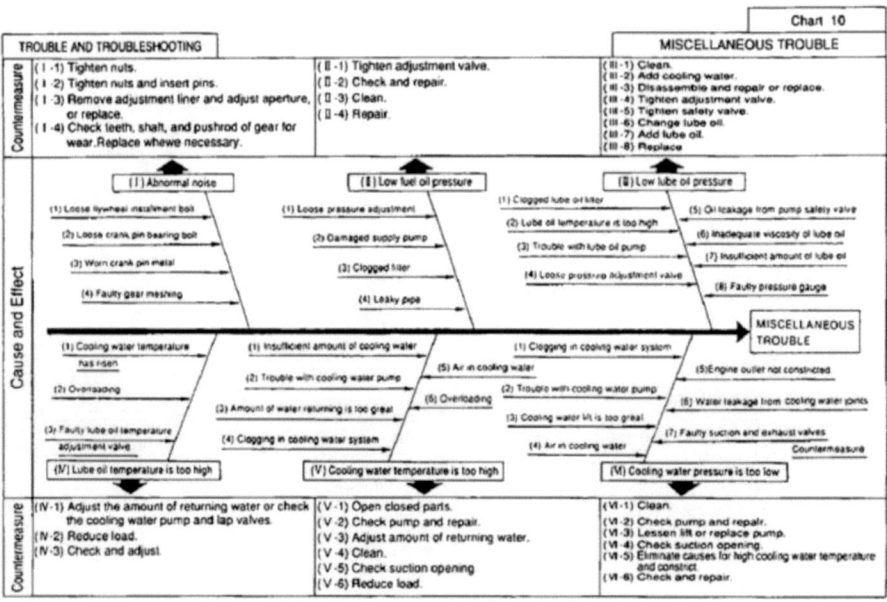

Chart 10